ADDICTION

Addiction: A Behavioral Economic Perspective focuses on the behavioral economics of addiction to explain why someone decides to act against his/her own well-being. It answers the questions of what accounts for self-defeating behavior patterns and how do we best motivate individuals to act according with their long-term goals. A better understanding of decision processes will lead to an improved knowledge of why people engage in self-destructive behaviors and better policy interventions in areas of addiction and obesity. The approach also promises to be valuable as a framework for understanding decisions for an addict's professional and business life. This book will be of particular use to clinicians, students, and researchers in the fields of addiction, public health, and behavior therapy.

Shahram Heshmat, PhD, is a faculty member in the Public Health department at the University of Illinois at Springfield. He specializes in teaching Health Economics of Eating Behavior & Addiction.

ADDICTION

A Behavioral Economic Perspective

Shahram Heshmat

NEW YORK AND LONDON

First published 2015
by Routledge
711 Third Avenue, New York, NY 10017

and by Routledge
27 Church Road, Hove, East Sussex BN3 2FA

Routledge is an imprint of the Taylor & Francis Group, an informa business

© 2015 Taylor & Francis

The right of the editor to be identified as the author of the editorial material, and of the authors for their individual chapters, has been asserted in accordance with sections 77 and 78 of the Copyright, Designs and Patents Act 1988.

All rights reserved. No part of this book may be reprinted or reproduced or utilised in any form or by any electronic, mechanical, or other means, now known or hereafter invented, including photocopying and recording, or in any information storage or retrieval system, without permission in writing from the publishers.

Trademark notice: Product or corporate names may be trademarks or registered trademarks, and are used only for identification and explanation without intent to infringe.

Library of Congress Cataloging-in-Publication Data
A catalog record for this book has been requested.

ISBN: 978-1-138-02616-2 (hbk)
ISBN: 978-1-138-02617-9 (pbk)
ISBN: 978-1-315-77454-1 (ebk)

Typeset in Bembo
by Apex CoVantage, LLC

Printed and bound in the United States of America by Publishers Graphics, LLC on sustainably sourced paper.

CONTENTS

Preface		*vii*
Acknowledgements		*viii*
1	Introduction: Using Behavioral Economics to Understand Addictive Behavior	1
2	Decision Biases: A Primer on Behavioral Economics	23
3	Definition and the Nature of Addiction	46
4	Definition and Functions of Emotions	71
5	The Role of Emotion in Decision Making	93
6	Anxiety and Decision Making	120
7	Choice Over Time	152
8	Addiction and Choice	170
9	Sources of Self-Control Failure in Relation to Sustained Dieting Behavior	193
10	Self-Control: The Ability to Achieve Long-Term Goals	217

11 Using Self-Control Strategies to Motivate Behavior Change	239
12 Conclusion	261
References	265
Index	289

PREFACE

Addicts make a complex decision about the costs and benefits of using drugs. Their evaluations of the costs and benefits may be subject to biases, including feelings associated with the behavior and its outcomes and a priority to the present over the future. That is, addiction is viewed as valuation disease, where the nervous system overvalues cues associated with drugs or drug taking. Thus, addiction can be viewed as a diminished capacity to choose. Addicted individuals assign lower values to delayed rewards than to immediate ones. The preference for immediate gratification leads to self-control problems. For instance, when evaluating outcomes in the distant future, individuals make resolutions to stop smoking, eat less, and exercise. However, as the future gets closer, the individuals engage in overeating and light another (last) cigarette.

This book reviews recent developments from behavioral economics studies to explain addiction and ways to overcome self-destructive behaviors. Conceptualizing addiction as a failure in decision making leads to a number of solutions for reducing addiction, such as teaching economic rationality to emphasize the importance of long-term rewards, strategies to promote self-control behaviors to resist immediate gratification, and changing the context in which individuals make decisions. These interventions help to reduce impulsive urges and encourage individuals to behave in their own best self-interests.

ACKNOWLEDGEMENTS

This book is based on my lecture notes for an introductory course to addiction, which I have been teaching at the University of Illinois Springfield (UIS) since the fall of 2002. The text provides a framework to explain addictive behavior and other self-defeating choices that can be integrated into the formulation of preventive strategies.

I owe many thanks to my students. Having the opportunity to teach this course over so many years to terrific students, I gained a great deal as they kept asking the important questions about addiction. The overwhelming positive responses I got to the lectures energized me while writing this book. I am grateful to George Zimmar, who saw the importance of behavioral economics and encouraged me to get this book off the ground. I owe many thanks to Chris Teja, my editor at Routledge, who helped to shape the final product.

I am now older and wiser than when I began preparing this book. My children are now in college, and I can now discuss the book with them, which they seem to appreciate more. I dedicate this book to my children, Colin and Claire.

1

INTRODUCTION

Using Behavioral Economics to Understand Addictive Behavior

Introduction

Why do people often behave in ways that are known to have dire consequences for their long-term health and well-being? The purpose of this book is to provide an understanding of this question using the framework of behavioral economics. Behavioral economics presents a valuable organizing principle to understand when and how people make decision errors, and how people's decision making can be improved. This chapter provides an overview of the subject.

I have three central objectives in writing this book: first, to inform readers of the behavioral economic aspects of addiction. Second, I want to enhance students' understanding of the decision-making processes behind addictive behavior. Third, I want to explore the practical implications of behavioral economics combined with a public health perspective to overcome addiction. A better understanding of decision processes should lead to an improved knowledge of why people engage in self-destructive behaviors and to better policy interventions in areas of addiction and obesity.

The main focus in this book is on what motivates people to use drugs. Many of the reasons that young people start using drugs have little or nothing to do with being informed about the dangers of using them. For instance, a discussion of the dangers of drug use will have little impact on the chance that a person who is experiencing anxiety, depression, and low self-esteem will self-medicate with drugs and alcohol. Similarly, there are many situations, such as craving or strong feelings, in which people experience a disconnection between what they desire at the moment and what is best for their long-term self-interest. Moreover, it would not be helpful to go into a lower-class neighborhood and point out that their unhealthy behaviors are killing them. While information might help people to increase their awareness of such situations, once one is in the situation, the most accurate information is unlikely to have much if any impact on behavior. For example, if I accurately predict that I will get arrested if I use illegal drugs, that knowledge does me no good unless I can act on it and control my impulses to use the drugs.

This text is part of a broad study concerning the role of emotion in decision making, and to understand how, why, and under what circumstances emotions shape decisions. My goal is to develop a foundation from which to better understand the relative contributions of cognition and emotion to individual behavior in order to explain how individuals make decisions, and how we can influence those decision processes to improve their decision making and enhance their well-being. There is a general tendency in psychology and behavioral economics to focus on cognitive aspects of decision making. This book shows that focusing on emotion is crucial for a deeper understanding of individual motivations for impulsive desires and addictive behavior. This approach complements the cognitive approach and provides implications for interventions.

The book focuses on behavioral applications, such as addiction, overeating, procrastination, and other areas of life. There is a strong similarity between addiction and obesity suggesting that addiction theory provides a useful framework for understanding and treating compulsive eating. That is, the study of addiction helps to understand why people tend to do too much of anything that they like, not just drugs. This book views addiction as a unitary condition and the focus is on similarities, rather than differences, among substances. The psychoactive drugs are not similar, for example, heroine produces a calming effect, while cocaine produces excitation, and alcohol reduces stress activation.

Self-defeating behaviors (McWilliam, 2012),[1] such as addiction or obesity, pose fascinating questions from the perspective of maximizing pleasure and minimizing pain. Why would someone decide to act against his own well-being? What accounts for self-defeating behavior patterns? How do we best motivate individuals to act according with their long-term goals? To promote desirable behavior requires an understanding of human behavior. What motivates people when they initiate a new behavior as opposed to procrastinating, failing to act on their intentions, or getting distracted? In short, the text intends to raise awareness of the general principles underlying human behavior and the nature of decisions that people so often make that bears a mixed relationship to their own happiness. Furthermore, if we can understand how addictive habits are made and changed, we can also better understand how to change other habitual behavior like anxiety and depression.

Self-control plays an important role in addicts' decisions. Addicts show diminished capacity for response inhibition and ability to maintain a goal in the face of distraction. However, this does not mean that they are never in control. The behavioral economic framework guides people in identifying strategies to make healthier choices. To overcome self-control problems such as addiction and obesity, individuals use commitment devices to attempt to protect their long-term goals from short-term consumption decisions.

The behavioral economic approach promises to be a valuable framework for understanding decisions for public health professionals. The possible contributions of behavioral economics have mostly been ignored by the public health field.[2] Behavioral economics could therefore become an essential complement to the traditional public health tools. This approach provides an integrated view of individuals confronted with an array of short-term temptations and long-term prospects, and addresses self-defeating choices in the context of addiction.

The behavioral economic perspective also promises to be valuable as a framework for understanding decisions for our professional life, business life, and the way we look at the world. In the following chapters, you will find in-depth discussions of the role of emotions in decision making that may illuminate something about your personal life, such as how emotions shape our choices and alter your capacity to regulate our behavior. Improving decision making is a starting point for improving your life.

What Is Behavioral Economics?

This book presents a behavioral economic perspective for understanding addiction. Behavioral economics provides a framework to understand when and how people make errors. The field of behavioral economics blends insights of psychology and economics to increase the explanatory and predictive power of economic decision making. Behavioral economics is a subdiscipline of economics (Angner and Loewenstein, 2012). Behavioral economics emerged against the backdrop of the traditional economic approach known as rational choice model. Economics provides conceptual models (e.g., rationality) of how we make decisions, and psychology illuminates the processes of those decisions (e.g., decision biases and emotional influences).

Economics provides a conceptual framework to understand how people decide to allocate their limited resources (e.g., money and time) among available alternatives to maximize total happiness. A key assumption in economics is the notion that individuals are mostly rational and seek to maximize total utility (happiness). Utility is understood as the strength of a decision maker's preference for a particular option, meaning that we assign values to certain things. For example, suppose you are considering buying a new car. You weigh (assign utility) the following features: brand new vs used, comfort, good gas mileage, price, and reliability. Your final choice will require trade-offs within the limits of your budget. In general, the rational person is assumed to correctly weigh costs and benefits and calculate the best choices for herself.

The rational person is expected to know his tastes (both present and future) and to never flip-flop between two contradictory desires. He is supposed to make good decisions that maximize his utility (whatever that is). That is, he will choose the option that will satisfy his long-term preferences. He has perfect self-control and can restrain impulses that may prevent him from achieving his long-term desires. Traditional economics use these assumptions to predict real human behavior. The standard policy advice that stems from this way of thinking is to give people as many choices as possible, and let them choose the one they like best (with minimum government action). Individuals are in the best position to know what is best for them because they know their preferences better than government officials do.

In contrast, behavioral economics attempts to describe actual behavior and shows that actual human beings do not act according to the rational model. People have a great deal of trouble exercising self-control. Human beings have limited cognitive abilities and limited willpower. They are profoundly influenced by context, and often have little idea of what they will like next year or even tomorrow. People tend to discount the future; that is, they let present satisfaction spoil future prosperity. As Daniel Kahneman (2011, p. 5) put this, "it seems that traditional economics and behavioral economics are describing two different species." Behavioral economics shows that we are exceptionally inconsistent and fallible human beings. We choose a goal and then frequently act against it, because a self-control problem causes us to fail to implement our goals.[3] As discussed in the following chapters, behavioral economics traces these errors to the design of the human mind.

Furthermore, the rational model views the mind as more or less unitary. Neuroscientists argue that the mind consists of many different parts (mental processes), each operating by its own logic (Kurzban, 2011). Because these parts are designed to do different things, they don't always work in perfect harmony.[4] A key insight is that the brain is a democracy (Tononi, 2012). That is, there is no dominant decision maker. Although the behavioral goal of an individual can be stated as maximizing utility, reaching that goal requires contributions from several brain regions. Decisions are made in cooperation of many specialists, each providing its unique contribution. This important insight about the human mind explains why we are conflicted and inconsistent. The inconsistencies in the mind give rise to self-control problems.

The field of behavioral economics recognizes that we are driven by forces beyond our conscious control, hence our capacity for irrationality. That is, many decisions are made on the basis of emotional and unconscious processes (Bargh, 2002).[5] For instance, most diets fail because the conscious forces of reason and will are simply not powerful enough to consistently subdue unconscious urges. Yet people might be unaware that their environment is influencing their behavior; they may be unaware of the stimuli that can activate goals and cravings. Because of this, individuals frequently make decisions that depart systematically from the predictions of economists' standard models.

Behavioral economics attempts to understand these departures and, more generally, integrate psychologists' understanding of human behavior into economic analysis. In this respect, behavioral economics parallels cognitive psychology, which studies the interactions of emotion and cognition and nudges individuals toward adaptive decision making. Much like a cognitive therapist, behavioral economists attempt to guide individuals toward more healthy behaviors by correcting cognitive and emotional barriers to the pursuit of genuine self-interest (Loewenstein and Haisley, 2008).

Behavioral economics also provides insight into the working of the mind, the irrationality of human nature, and the nature of the decisions that people so often make that bear a mixed relationship to their own happiness. For example, anxiety and depression may induce negative emotions, often leading to addiction. People with these types of problems having successfully quit their "bad habits" (alcohol abuse and overeating), often find a different "habit" to replace the old one. The behavioral economic approach allows us to focus inward and try to understand how irrational behavior is reflected in the context of addictive behavior. This book makes an attempt to enter the private mind to understand its nature and emotion and to convey that understanding to the reader. Problems are best solved when they are pulled out of darkness. In the words of Nobel laureate Eric Kandel (2012), to discover the truth about behavior, we must look below the surface appearance of things. Most of our mental life (cognitive processes) and behavior are shaped by unconscious forces at any given moment.

An important implication of unconscious motivation is the recognition that we are all at some level strangers to ourselves. Indeed, when we introspect, we routinely deceive ourselves, because we only tap into a small fraction of what is going on in our heads. That is, you know far less about yourself than you feel you do. Social psychologists argue that people are in general quite ignorant of their motivations and that awareness of what motivates them to act is a construction (Kiverstein, 2012). For example, the desire for altruism and volunteerism may mask a desire to be recognized as special, and the altruistic act may be partially an expression of a self-righteous desire to be morally superior to others. In resolving a problem, the cognitive system often fills in information in a rather blind manner without insight or self-awareness. In contrast, the unconscious (intuitive) system has the ability to see the whole picture or see the problem in a new light (Schore, 2012). I will say more on this in later chapters.

This lack of awareness compromises psychological freedom and perpetuates self-defeating behavior.[6] These private thoughts that are mostly inaccessible to experience are called "intuition," "gut feelings," and so on. These private thoughts are also sources of misunderstanding among people. (That is what a lot of marriage counseling is about.) We try to silence our painful emotions, but if we succeed in feeling nothing, we lose the only means we have of knowing what we suffer from, and why (Grosz, 2013). To uncover the essence of a particular behavior (such as addiction and overeating), we need to dig deeper, like archeologists in their excavations, to illuminate the mental processes between a stimulus and the individual response to it. As Panksepp and Biven (2012) note, the deeper we go into our emotional brain, the more we understand our mental origin and the origins of mental illnesses such as addiction. By becoming more aware of our unconscious wishes, we experience ourselves as free rather than as victims.

In sum, behavioral economics presents a valuable organizing principle to conceptualize addiction and other self-control problems. The approach helps us to understand when and how people make errors. Systematic errors or biases recur predictably in particular circumstances. The focus on errors improves the ability to identify and understand decision disorders and suggest interventions to limit the damage from poor decisions. Finally, behavioral economics suggests ways that policy makers might restructure environments to facilitate better choices. The understanding of where people go wrong can help people go right.

Delay Discounting

A key concept in behavioral economics is that of how delayed rewards are discounted by individuals and deviation from the rational-choice paradigm. Delay discounting refers to the reduction in the present value of a reward when its delivery is delayed. A discount rate indicates how much more you value a reward sooner, as opposed to later. A small discount rate means that you don't mind waiting for a reward very much. A high discount rate means that you like to have the reward now. The delay discounting decision-making model focuses on how consumers balance the consumption of a small amount of a commodity now compared to a large amount later. Choices between temporally separated outcomes are known as intertemporal choice. In an intertemporal choice, the subjective value of the future outcome is reduced in proportion to the delay until its delivery.

The attraction of immediate pleasure plays out in addiction and overeating, as we trade our health for a few minutes of pleasant moments. Evidence shows that steep delay discounting (relative inconsideration of future consequences) is a key aspect of addiction, obesity, and a risk factor for relapse (Bickel and Vuchinich, 2000). Addicts display steeper discounting during intertemporal choice compared to normal individuals. The impulsive behavior might facilitate drug use by reducing the weight given to its negative long-term consequences. Research shows that impulsive discounting among youth predicts adult drug use (MacKilop et al., 2013). High discounting also plays an important risk factor for treatment failure. In addition, the use of addictive drugs might also increase the steepness of temporal discounting. This inability to appropriately weigh delayed rewards can be quite harmful to an addicted person who may be willing to sacrifice future gains or incur major losses (imprisonment) in exchange for instant gratification.

It is hardly irrational to value immediate rewards over delayed ones. In the same way that preferences for food items differ across people, so do preferences for time. Some people are much more focused on short-term gains than others: they base their decisions on a higher discount rate than other people. *Young people make different trade-offs from those made by old people.* They think of their future selves in the same way that they think of strangers. So they are less concerned about their future well-being. Thus, caring less about the future than the present can be rational. For example, one decides to go to college and become an engineer and another person decides to settle for immediate gain by attending a trade school. Such a person with a consistently high discount rate does not experience internal conflict (a self-control problem). So, a rational overeater or drug addict may have a problem, but it is not a self-control problem.

In contrast, behavioral economics conceive the individual as a successive agent[7] with conflicting preferences. For example, a person makes resolutions to stop overeating and start physical exercise and then fails to carry them out (preference reversal). Well ahead of the time of choice, the person prefers the option, say, of not overeating. Yet, when an occasion for indulgence comes closer in time, the attractions of palatable foods come to loom larger than those of good health. In these examples, the person's judgment at the time of action diverges from her calm and reflective judgment. Her own future self becomes the obstacle to attain her current preference (resolution), resulting in a state of internal conflict between selves over time.

The preference reversal or present bias (known as hyperbolic discounting) describes conflicts between short- and long-term motives. The hyperbolic discounting model is an expression of a "divided self,"[8] of preferring, for example, indulgence for the immediate self, and prudence for the future one (Ainslie, 2001). Different self can be thought of as having different discount rates (time inconsistency) competing for control, one more present-oriented and the other more future-oriented. For example, large proportions of addicts report being motivated to change their behavior and do indeed seek treatment, but later voluntarily drop out of treatment or relapse despite successfully completing treatment (MacKilop et al., 2013).

In sum, the behavioral economic model of discounting (hyperbolic discounting), or present-biased preference, predicts that individuals act irrationally in that they excessively discount the future. They favor long-run maximization at all times except as smaller rewards become more immediately available. Consequently, they often end up acting against their own best, long-term interest. They do worse in life because they spend too much for what they want now at the expense of desirable outcomes they want in the future.

The Dual Decision Model

This book illustrates the application of decision making with dual processes to addiction. This model illustrates the competition or conflict that arises between the different valuation systems in making a choice. The dual decision framework suggests that choice reflects the interaction of two, distinct decision systems in conflict with each other: a goal-directed, flexible, cognitive, deliberative system and an automatic, habit-based system. These two systems have also been referred to as controlled (System 2) and impulsive (System 1), or conscious (planning-based) and unconscious (habit-based).[9] The deliberative system is conscious, analytical, reason-based, verbal, relatively slow, and easily disrupted. The impulsive system, in contrast, is relatively effortless and spontaneous. Choices favoring the immediate reward are associated with the habit or impulsive system. In contrast, choices favoring the temporally distanced options are associated with the deliberative system. For example, whereas many people prefer high-fat foods, they also prefer to be healthy (avoid obesity); this preference for a healthier lifestyle conflicts urge to eat high-fat foods.[19]

The variability in delay discounting behavior within and between individuals is associated with the functions of impulsive (automatic) and cognitive (self-control) valuation processes. These valuation processes guide the choices we face every day. Cognitive valuations are required for long-term goals, for which automatic valuation processes are inadequate. Automatic processes facilitate choices to achieve immediate gratification. These evaluative systems correspond to different discount rates, with the automatic system exhibiting steep discounting, and the cognitive system placing more equal weight on immediate and future rewards (McClure et al., 2004). People differ substantially in how they discount the value of future reward. For example, people with chronic deficits in impulse control (e.g., addicts, individuals with ADHD, young adults) tend to respond impulsively to tempting rewards that are immediately available.

The triangle space (Figure 1.1) illustrates the relationship between System 1 (S1) (dark shaded area) and System 2 (S2) (light shaded area of cold reasoning).

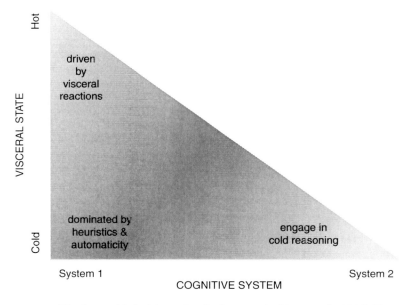

FIGURE 1.1 The hot-cold decision triangle framework (Yang et al., 2012) illustrates the relationship between the S2 and S1 influences (reprinted with permission from INSTEAD).

There is a trade-off between rational thinking (S2 reasoning) and the hot, emotional reaction (Yang et al., 2012) Experiencing hot, emotional, or visceral reactions, such as cravings and hunger or fear inhibit S2 processing. This is because hot, emotional states drive people to please their immediate urges. However, S2 reasoning can help avoid the onset or reduce the power of visceral urges.

The goal of treatment is to help recovering addicts avoid viscerally hot states where temptation will be difficult to resist. At a policy level, interventions can help design "cooler" decision environments in which individuals will be less influenced by S1 (e.g., ban on smoking in public places). Adequate decision making reflects an integration of cognitive and affective systems, and the ability to properly weigh immediate pleasures against the long-term losses of an action (Damasio, 1994).

Decision Making

The main idea in this book is that addiction is a consequence of falling victim to decision failures. Decision failures can lead to incorrect or inappropriate decisions regarding substance use, thereby leading to addiction. The identification of addiction as failures in decision making means that understanding addiction will require an understanding of how we make decisions. This understanding provides insights as to how addictions may develop and be maintained.

Decision making is defined as the ability to select the most advantageous response from an array of immediate, possible choices. Pleasure and pain are the currency to all decisions. Decisions require weighing the potential pleasure and pain. In the best cases, this may lead to good, rational decisions. For example, imagine an 18-year-old who is deciding to choose a major. How can she evaluate different career paths for each major? How can she predict changes in her personal preferences? Or what career will be in demand in four years from now? A reasonable solution to this decision would be to select a path that could be adapted as conditions change (Michel-Kerjan and Slovic, 2010).

The following describes basic steps involved in making a choice. Roughly speaking, there are five steps to every decision:

- The first step involves representing the decision problem. We perceive a situation, and construct a representation of the decision problem, which involves identifying internal states (e.g., hunger level), as well as external states (e.g., threat level).
- The second step requires the identification of the different courses of action under consideration.
- The third step is the selection of one of the options on the basis of their valuations, that is, we calculate which course is in our best interest. This step involves assigning a value (valuation) to each option. The internal and external states (step 1) inform the valuation process. For example, the hunger level influences how much value one assigns to food. Also, the value that is

assigned to a choice might depend on the delay with which those payoffs occur. In all these decisions, there is a time lag between actions and outcome. A person who devalues (discounts) too strongly will overemphasize near-term pleasures and underemphasize far-future costs.
- The fourth step involves implementation of the decision and monitoring the desirability of the resulting outcomes.
- In the final step, the outcome evaluation is used to update the other processes to improve the quality of future decisions (learning). These steps are not rigid, and some steps may be performed simultaneously. For example, the option selection and valuation might be carried out simultaneously.

Most experts agree that step three (valuation) is the most important one. This step involves comparing the different values and the selection of one of the options on the basis of their valuations. In general, there are three types of valuation systems: Pavlovian, habitual, and goal-directed (Rangel et al., 2008).

Pavlovian System

Pavlovian systems assign values to a small set of behaviors that are innate ("hard-wired") responses to specific cues, such as cues that predict the delivery of food. Similarly, cues that predict a punishment or the presence of an aversive stimulus can lead to avoidance behaviors. For example, if you come across a garter snake, you will perceive it a "threat," and will experience the urge to attack or jump. With sufficient training, animals can also learn to behave in response to other stimuli. For example, rats and pigeons learn to approach lights that predict the delivery of food. A wide range of human behaviors might be controlled by Pavlovian systems, such as overeating in the presence of food, behaviors displayed in people with obsessive-compulsive disorders (OCDs), and addiction (choosing immediate, smaller rewards at the expense of delayed, larger rewards).

Habitual System

Much of the time, people proceed by routine, habit, and automatic processes. Habit systems can learn, through repeated training, to assign values to a large number of actions (stimulus–response associations). Examples of habits include a smoker's desire to have a cigarette at particular times of day (e.g., after a meal).

Goal-Directed System

In the goal-directed system, goals are defined as subjectively desirable states of affairs that the individuals intend to attain through action. To attain a desired goal, one needs to deliberate, form intentions, choose the proper means, and reflect on one's progress toward that goal (or state). The goal-directed system assigns values to actions by determining action-outcome associations and then evaluating the benefits associated with the different outcomes. An example of a goal-directed behavior is the decision of what to eat at a new restaurant. In contrast to the habit system, the goal-directed system updates the value of an action as soon as the value of its outcome changes. If you did not enjoy the food, you would update your preference for that food to avoid it in the future.

This mode of decision making is similar to the rational-choice framework, which considers decision making as conscious and under volitional control. That is, behavior is a function of a deliberate intention formed by individuals on the basis of their evaluation of the expected consequences of that behavior. Free will produces goal-directed behavior. People experience some of their actions as freer than others.

We also have the ability to shift our decision modes. With experience, a goal-directed decision is transferred to the habit system. However, chronic stress is shown to affect the ability to shift decision modes. Research in animal studies has shown that chronic stress freezes animals into automatic/habit responses mode. This effect is associated with changes in the brain, where areas linked to habitual responses are enlarged, and the opposite occurs in those areas associated with goal-directed responses. The stressed animals can't shift back to goal-directed behaviors and they keep doing the same things over and over. Why should the stressed brain be prone to habit formation? Perhaps it is to help shift as many deliberative decisions as possible over to automatic pilot, and focus on the crisis at hand (Dias-Ferreira et al., 2009).

Addiction as Failures in Decision Making

Addiction can be viewed as a decision disorder—biased in the reward valuation process (Volkow and Baler, 2013). The main idea is that drugs have an unprecedented ability to induce decision errors about what is best. For instance, the Pavlovian system can assign increased emotional motivation to a drug, and the habit system overvalues the drugs. Alcohol leads to a reduction in anxiety (thus forming a habit), and reduction in the effectiveness of self-control and a reflective system. As the process of decision making fails, addicts progressively make less advantageous decisions for themselves and for those who are close to them. The strong feelings (i.e., cravings or negative affect) lead otherwise rational persons to commit acts they later regret. Decision failures might explain why addicts pursue and consume drugs even in the face of negative consequences or the knowledge of positive outcomes that might come from quitting the drugs.

The errors in decision making may arise from individual predisposition (either due to genetic or social environmental factors) as well as from direct interactions with the drugs themselves. The interactions between genetics and social environment may explain why some people become addicted and some do not. For example, an individual who is very sensitive to reward would receive a stronger dopamine kick with each puff of cigarette and become vulnerable to nicotine addiction.

Alternatively, drug use may interfere with the proper development of the brain decision system, and distort the normal decision-making process. For example, evidence indicates that children with attention-deficit/hyperactivity disorder (ADHD) are at a higher risk to develop serious substance abuse problems as adolescents and adults. The use of stimulant medications (Adderall and Ritalin) can desensitize these children to other mind-altering substances. They tend to be less averse to prescription drugs at an early age, and learn that medication is the way to feel better (Humphreys et al., 2013).

All addictive drugs either trigger pleasure or relieve pain, which is why some people gravitate toward them. The rewarding effects of drugs are related to their ability to increase dopamine (pleasure chemical) in the brain. Dopamine responds to primary rewards (e.g., food, water, and sex) as well as secondary rewards (e.g., money). In those individuals for whom drug use develops into addiction, drug use become compulsive and inflexible, representing a bias in decision making (Volkow and Baler, 2013). The result is compulsive use of the substance at the expense of other rewards such as spending time with friends or family. This overvaluation of drugs and inflexibility is viewed to reflect impaired decision making.

In the context of the dual decision model, addiction can be viewed as a diminished capacity to choose (Rangel et al., 2008). The dual decision model views addiction as a consequence of perturbed balance in favor of impulsive system (a flawed reward valuation) (Volkow and Baler, 2013). The ability to resist the urge to use drugs requires the proper functioning of S2 to oppose the S1 influences that drive the motivation to seek reward.[11] This imbalance can be triggered by the repeated consumption of a drug, and becoming sensitive to rewarding stimuli. Drugs perturb the brain's capacity to assign appropriate value to choice options. In other words, an addict lacks a "healthy mind." The disruption can result in compulsive drug use. In short, compulsive drug use results from a failure in top-down self-control over bad habits. The capacity to inhibit impulsive behavior is a major contributor to an individual's vulnerability to addiction (Heyman, 2009).

Chronic drug use can also lead to a discrepancy between the predicted value of reward from drug use and its actual enjoyment. Chronic drug use and exposure causes neuroadaptations in the brain's reward system leading to increased pathological "wanting" as opposed to "liking" for the drug (Berridge and Robinson, 2003). The two subcomponents, liking (pleasure) and wanting (desire), are partly separated brain pathways. While "liking" corresponds to the experience of reward, "wanting" corresponds to motivation and anticipated reward. Chronic and excessive use of drugs leads to exaggerated wanting for these drugs in the absence of a positive increase in liking. For addicts, intense wanting or craving for addictive substances is not necessarily accompanied by enjoyment of their consumption. That is, even after the drug no longer brings pleasure, an addict can still feel a strong urge to use. He or she is craving the drug even when the drug is no longer pleasurable (Kringelbach and Berridge, 2010).

Furthermore, chronic drug abuse has been recognized to be associated with impaired self-awareness, which manifests as compromised recognition or denial of the severity of addiction and the need for treatment (Naqvi et al., 2007). Research shows that continued drug use is associated with a dysfunction of the insular cortex. The insular cortex plays a key role in subjective emotional feelings (interoception). Interoception is the collection of processes by which physiological signals in the body are transmitted back to brain, giving rise to an awareness of bodily feelings (e.g., pain, touch, temperature). This dysfunction leads to lack of self-awareness and insight. Indeed, the impaired insight about the severity of the addiction problem might derive these individuals' excessive drug use. Individuals with insula damage are impaired at the recognition of emotion and pain in themselves and others. For example, damage to the insular cortex can lead to a disruption in smoking behavior, whereby individuals no longer experience cravings to smoke (Naqvi et al., 2007). As one participant in the study put it, "My body forgot the urge to smoke" (Naqvi et al., 2007, p. 534). In short, this poor metacognition leads to poor choice and decision making (Verdejo-Garcia et al., 2012). In this respect, mindfulness is an important approach shown to improve awareness.

In sum, addiction arises when the automatic system wins the competition against the deliberative system for behavioral control. Both systems are important to forming decisions, and good choices appear most likely to emerge when the two systems work in concert. Eventually, there must be a connection between these two systems to control the impulsive system to treat the addictive behavior. For example, treating alcoholism is more than just stopping drinking alcohol, it requires addressing the forces that compel the need for alcohol. Alcohol numbs the pain and allows one to think that one is doing just fine. Overeating (food high in sugar and fat) is used to deal with fear, doubt, and insecurity. For an addict to get well, it is necessary to bring those forces to conscious-awareness and to connect them to the thinking mind to end the conflict between the two systems (i.e., hypocrisy). Without harmony between two systems, we cannot be whole and integrated. In fact, the goal of therapy is to bring memories from the nonverbal to the verbal areas of the brain, to connect and integrate them (Panksepp and Biven, 2012).

Overcoming Self-Control Problems

As discussed, self-control problems (e.g., addiction and overeating) typically arise in situations involving choice over time. That is when the costs and benefits of a choice are separated across time. For example, for a 17-year-old, the smoking of a cigarette now has an immediate pleasure; while the health damage that may follow is probably at least 30 years away. If the heath damage occurred immediately, smoking would not be that attractive. Valuations of immediate negative value (withdrawal) are likely to be weighed more heavily than valuations of long-term negative value (adverse health impact). Thus, any health investment activity is vulnerable to self-control problems or present bias, because it is hard to see the value from moment to moment. Consequently, people tend to avoid and/or delay investment health behaviors.

However, we are not destined to grab immediate rewards that we will later regret. There are ways that individuals can counteract the shortsighted behavior to avoid addiction and overeating. By making immediate reward seem less compelling or making the later reward attract more attention, one can resist the immediate temptation, and make choices in her best long-term goals. Thus, an important implication of impulsive (present bias) behavior is the need to design interventions that provide individuals with very immediate costs and benefits about their behaviors. This book will discuss several approaches to combat temporal discounting. Strategies have to be developed either that bring some of the costs from these activities back from the future, or that reduce some of the benefits from the activities (i.e., changing the values of the choices).

To counter self-control problems, sophisticated decision makers (agents) employ commitment devices in an attempt to protect long-term goals from short-term consumption decisions. Commitment means to pledge or bind oneself to some particular course of action. These commitment strategies include diminishing the value of the immediate pleasure (e.g., imposing punishment for drug use), decreasing the delay until receipt of the delayed rewards (e.g., permitting oneself to splurge on a movie at the end of a drug-free week), and increasing the salience of the delayed reward (e.g., reflecting on the long-term benefits of abstinence). These devices inhibit existing urges from translating into actual behavior.

In short, a self-control model describes a person in the cold mode to invest in self-control (e.g., plans to foreclose options, or engage in cue management). The investment may reduce the self-control problems. The level of investment varies from person to person. For instance, two individuals can face the same stimulus (temptation) and differ in their self-control response. The person who expects strong vulnerability will be more likely to exercise self-control and adhere to his goals than will the person who does not anticipate such strong vulnerability.[12]

The diagram below illustrates a model of how we control our behavior.

Emotion State:

_____ | **invest**_____ | **stimulus** _____ | **act**_____ | **end**_____ post-state _____

Being in a hot state (e.g., craving, hunger, or anger) can affect decision making so much that we feel a stranger to ourselves while in the other state. When people are under the influence of emotions, they often act in ways that they will regret later. However, self-awareness can avoid this bias. If people can anticipate this tendency, they can take precautions of the kinds chosen by Odysseus (in *The Odyssey*) when he had his men tie him to the mast as they approached the island of the Sirens (Elster, 2000). Able to foresee this temporary change in his preferences, he came up with an effective commitment device to foreclose his options. The story of Odysseus is an example of a precommitment strategy that one can use to limit her choices in advance against the foreseeable temptations (e.g., avoid driving by the liquor store on your way home from work, or the empty-fridge strategy). For an addict, the two selves are in conflict. Thus, from a distance, he makes one choice to prevent himself from making the wrong choice if given an opportunity later. The ability to precommit to one option over another is one of the most powerful self-control strategies (Redish, 2013).

From the dual decisions perspective, addicts' reliance on deliberate intentions ("Never again!") is a main barrier to recovery because decision making choice doesn't rely solely on deliberation. Addicts need to modify their environments and rearrange their opportunities so that temptations are minimized and eventually habits lose their grip. Slors (2013) calls this self-programming: using forethought to change future behaviors by redesigning the day-to-day environment. Similarly, the public authorities may do so on behalf of people.[13] For example, legislating or imposing delays on the purchase of firearms, marriage, and divorce is often justified in these terms (Camerer et al. 2003). That is, we can engineer our environment in such a way that enhances the capacity for self-control. Thus, public policy approaches that augment self-control will promote healthy behavior.

What Can Addiction Teach Us?

This book is about studying extreme behavior. Addictive behaviors are simply extreme variants of normal psychological phenomena and ordinary behaviors (Maddux and Winstead, 2012). So what is the value of studying extreme behavior to understand normal behavior? There is a viewpoint in psychology that we can learn a good deal more from extreme behaviors than ordinary cases (Dumont, 2010). Extreme behaviors are often useful for understanding ordinary problems in life. Extreme behaviors are like a magnifying glass that makes a phenomenon bigger than life. It tells us something about the way we think and behave that we can't learn from ordinary life.

In psychology, normal mental life and mental illness form a continuum. Mental illnesses often represent exaggerated forms of normal mental processes. We can learn about mental processes by studying how they are disrupted by brain disorder; this makes us aware of a capability that an individual is deprived of it. For example, neuroscientists have traditionally relied on the effects of brain lesions to understand how the normal brain works.

Addiction is a good example of an extreme case for behavioral economics to study self-destructive behaviors. Addiction allows us to see the process of motivation at work and provides insights into the underlying structure and processes of decision making. The study of addiction may, therefore, shed light not only on addiction itself, but may help to illuminate other behaviors that are influenced by strong emotions. This kind of analysis might also apply to a wide range of practical examples from public health that seem to exhibit inconsistent and irrational behaviors, such as overeating, compulsive shopping, impulsivity, and other self-control problems. They seem to reflect an excessive influence of strong feelings on behavior.

Addiction is a fascinating example of human behavior. The study of addiction could be a central tool in understanding human nature. Desire for pleasure is part of human nature, and drugs do elicit desire and pleasure. Effective education about addiction should help young people learn how to manage these desires and pleasure. Thus, studying addiction can prevent individuals (e.g., students) from using certain substances. Even though offering such as a course is not meant to convince students that they should not use unhealthy substances. However, increased awareness can be a powerful prevention policy. Along the same line, Layard (2005) argues that people would benefit from courses devoted to "Education for Life" to increase personal happiness. The research summarized in this book can be also seen in the light of this overall goal (building resilience in young adults).

Why This Book?

This book is based on my lecture notes for an introductory course to addiction, which I have been teaching at the University of Illinois Springfield (UIS) since the fall of 2002. The text provides students with a foundation to explain addictive behavior and other self-defeating choices that can be integrated into the formulation of preventive strategies.

The idea for this book was conceived after a fruitless search for a text covering the principles of behavioral economics of addiction. Although there are a few good texts[14] on the behavioral economics of addiction, these books are either too technical, which makes them inaccessible to most students, or provide too much information, which, in most cases, is irrelevant for those seeking some basic knowledge on the subject. Therefore, in the absence of an appropriate text, I have prepared this text drawing from several books and numerous, select readings from published articles in order to provide a primer on the behavioral economics of addiction.

The course is offered to nonmajor students. It is targeted for persons interested in becoming more informed about addiction and prevention policy from an interdisciplinary perspective of economics and psychology. The text is accessible to a broad audience. The primary audiences are students in public health and related health professional programs. The secondary audiences are policymakers to examine the barriers for individuals to make healthy choice. By questioning some of the basic assumptions held by economists and social scientists about rational choice, it should be an important resource for students in psychology, economics, and political science. Students taking this course consistently gain a deeper appreciation of the basic elements of rational choice by studying the errors of judgments that many people make. Furthermore, whether giving talks in conferences or teaching classes, I have found that as I offer the behavioral economic description of addiction, people's faces light up with recognition. They see themselves, or the friends and relatives in their lives, in terms of the behaviors, and they find the behavioral economics approach quite practical and useful.

In developing these chapters, I have gained insights (and continue to do so) as I struggled to explain my understanding of the behavioral economics of addictive behavior. Almost none of the original ideas included in this text are my own. My contribution is an attempt to integrate all these concepts into an introductory format for students. These chapters are accumulated wisdom on addictive behavior. However, they are my own synthesis and reflect my interpretations and conclusions. In keeping with expectations for an introductory text, this text is not intended to provide an exhaustive summary of the vast literature, but rather to provide a framework in which to take a fresh look at the persistent, public health challenge of addictive behavior. I have erred in the direction of oversimplifying rather than confusing the ideas and concepts to reduce anxiety for students taking this introductory course. My aim is to provide some basic understanding of addictive behavior, not to satisfy the concerns of addiction theorists (i.e., my aim is not to resolve any of the conceptual problems).

How to Create an Enduring Learning Experience

This book is about helping individuals to change. We resist change because change is loss, even one that is in our best interest. We resist change because we fear both being denied of the pleasures we know and the consequences associated with that loss. Your understanding of the principles of behavioral economics of addiction will be enhanced if you start applying the concepts described in this book to yourself in your everyday life. Readers/students are encouraged to choose a troublesome pattern or a habit to work with during the semester. You are entirely free to select your own focus. In this project, you make yourself the subject of your own real-world study. As you read through the chapters, try to apply the concepts to your experience of behavior change. Begin to observe your own beliefs, emotions, and behavior, and pay attention to your own preference shifts. By doing so, you will teach yourself to identify your own systematic biases and modify your distorted thinking and choices.

Because the chapters deal with changing well-established habits of mind, you will need to be patient because the fruits of your efforts may not show straight away. Changing a habit is like gardening—we have to prepare the soil, plant the seeds, ensure that they are adequately watered, and then patiently wait. William James, in his book *The Principles of Psychology*, (1890) states: "Sow an action, and you reap a habit; sow a habit, and you reap a character; sow a character, and you reap a destiny" (quoted in Eysenck, 2012, p. 10). The strategies presented in this book will be helpful for any goal you choose (e.g., improving health, overcoming any bad habits, managing stress, procrastination, or improving your career).

Structure of the Book

I will use notes at the end of each chapter for material that is important enough that you might want to read it, but not so important that it needs to go in the main text. I will also use references to others' work, which are listed at the end of the book. In this book, I make a lot of assertions without citing any references. In terms of references, when the authors of cited material are mentioned in the text, I often add a date in parentheses—Elster (2001), for example—to enable readers to go directly to the reference. These sources are rather selective and recent. The book is organized into 12 chapters. The chapters are structured around a series of basic concepts, with ample examples and questions to reinforce learning.

Chapter 1, an overview, describes addictive behavior within the framework of behavioral economics.

Chapter 2 provides a primer to behavioral economics. It describes biases in our cognitive system. It provides some insights from the field of cognitive psychology on understanding how we learn, and how we can perform better. The purpose is to expose common habits of thinking and flawed beliefs that can lead to everyday biased thinking (e.g., my friend didn't respond to my email, she must be avoiding me). The take-home lesson of this chapter is that we should be cautious when guided by our intuitions and common sense.

Chapter 3 provides some explanations on addictive processes to understand addiction. It deals with the questions: What is an addiction? What brain mechanisms are responsible for the development of compulsive use of drugs? What are the neurobiological causes of addiction?

Chapters 4, 5, and 6 are devoted to the role of emotion in decision making. Readers might wonder why, in a course devoted to the idea of addiction, it is necessary to discuss emotions. Addictive behavior is linked to emotions. These chapters show that treating addicts requires changing someone's mind. Their brains need to be helped to rid themselves of this problem. These chapters also help to see our emotions clearly and to learn to use them for the betterment of our lives.

Chapter 4 provides a brief introduction to some basic concepts and mechanisms of emotions to provide an understanding on the nature and function of emotion. Most theories of emotions assume that emotions consist of a set of components, such as facial expressions, physiological changes, cognitive appraisals, subjective affective experience, and action tendencies. The purpose is to discuss such questions as these: What are emotions, and why do we have emotions? What are the rules by which emotion operates? Are emotions beneficial? Are they essential to our rationality?

Chapter 5 explains the importance of emotion in guiding individual behavior. It describes the relationship between emotion and cognition. It shows that emotions tend to shape cognition and distort our thinking about the consequences of behavior. The discussions show that the emotion and cognition distinction is inaccurate and misleading: emotions are forms of judgments. The chapter describes a conceptual framework for understanding the role of emotions in decision making. Our behavior is the outcome of an interaction between the deliberative system and the emotional system that operate according to different principles and often clash with one another. The final decision is determined by the relative strength of emotion and reflective systems. The insight may account for seemingly inconsistent or irrational behaviors, such as impulsivity, overeating, and drug addiction.

Chapter 6 explains how we make decisions under anxiety and uncertainty. Fear and anxiety influence our decisions. Anxious decision making is characterized by a selective information search, limited consideration of alternatives, and rapid evaluation of data.

Chapter 7 describes the discounting, and the ways in which people undervalue the future consequences of their actions. Discounting of delayed rewards refers to the observation that the value of a delayed reward is discounted (reduced in value or considered to be worthless) compared to the value of an immediate reward. Behavioral economics provides a framework for conceptualizing and investigating this central "now vs later" dynamic in the addictive process.

The central goal of this book is to discuss the relevance of a decision-making framework to addiction phases (initiation, maintenance, and relapse). Chapter 8 presents a perspective from the principles of behavioral economics to explain the "myopia" for the future manifested in the behavioral decisions of many individuals with addiction problems. Addictive behavior can be understood as an instance of intertemporal choice in that the user chooses whether to engage in an immediately pleasurable activity (using the substance) that carries a long-term cost (negative consequences for health, job, and so forth). Preference for short-term rather than longer-term rewards is a hallmark of substance abuse and other addictive behaviors. For example, smokers know that smoking may give lung cancer, and yet they still smoke. The key to successful recovery is to reverse this myopic preference by shifting behavior allocation away from the addictive behavior and toward engaging in adaptive behaviors that increase individual future well-being. Moreover, the cognitive concepts that we typically associate with "willpower," such as resisting impulses and an ability to delay gratification, are disrupted in drug addiction. A host of genetic or environmental factors serve to reinforce or mitigate these effects. They underscore the powerful ways in which addiction constrains one's ability to resist.

The previous chapters have mostly focused on showing errors and biases in individuals' decision-making processes. Chapters 9–11 discuss how findings in behavioral economics can be used to help individuals improve their decision making and enhance their well-being. These chapters introduce the principles of self-control to understand when and why it occurs as well as how to prevent it. Self-control is often referred to as the choice of a more delayed outcome that is ultimately of more value over a less-delayed outcome that is ultimately of less value. By ignoring self-control, an individual might limit her freedom of action.

These chapters describe self-control with respect to addictive behavior. Pathways between the prefrontal cortex and the affective system add flexibility and greater intelligence to emotional responses. Part of what is learned is how to shift attention elsewhere and how to dampen the very feeling of temptation. Learning to exercise control is important not only concerning temptations, but also concerning impulses, fear, emotions, and other seductive choices. Eventually, self-control practices lead to habits, so that you don't always have to work at maintaining control. Your brain's willpower gets stronger.

Chapter 11 illustrates self-control strategies people use protect themselves against irrational tendencies that help maintain a high probability of pursuing long-term goals despite the short-term costs. With regard to the addictive behaviors, it seems critical to deliberately increase training our cognitive, executive prefrontal brains to overcome emotional, habitual responses.

Finally, Chapter 12 discusses implications of the behavioral economics as a knowledge base for designing prevention policies that mitigate self-defeating behavior and improve human well-being. Such policies can be seen as a form of libertarian paternalism that guides consumers to be better off without necessarily restricting their choices.

In sum, this book covers the essence of behavioral economics with an emphasis on its relevance to the addictive behavior.

Conclusion

In this book, addiction is presented as a disease impacting specific brain systems that control free will, even though the action taken by addict (e.g., to use a drug) appears voluntary. These changes are long-lasting, persisting even after years of drug discontinuation. Addicted individuals attach excessive importance to the drug and drug-related cues, and at the same time, insufficient importance to nondrug-related rewards and stimuli, such as social relationships. This suggests that efforts should be focused on interventions with the goal of decreasing the rewarding effects of the drug, and enhancing the relative value attributed to nondrug-related rewards. The dual model facilitates designing interventions aimed at breaking the impulsive behaviors with self-control competencies. Thus, addiction recovery includes restoring balance in the motivational forces: interventions must reduce impulse or increase inhibition forces.

It is important to note that a variety of factors (e.g., genetic, environmental, social, and behavioral) lead someone to addiction. The theory of addiction presented as a decision malfunction is not sufficient for understanding drug additions. Fully grasping the human addiction problem with its multiple causes is beyond the reach of any single book. However, the decision-making framework accounts for many of these paths for addiction. This framework is consistent with a growing body of literature that has demonstrated addiction as decision impairment (e.g., Redish et al., 2008).

To fully appreciate the behavioral economics of addiction depends on a clear understanding of basic concepts. Thus, the discussions include a fair amount of detail in the conceptual framework. This detail may challenge the readers' patience in making a possible connection to addiction, which comes later in the book. Of course, readers are the final judges of this strategy. I hope that by reading these chapters, you will have gained some interesting insights about human behavior, and learned ways to improve your own decisions, especially in conditions of intense feelings.

Notes

1 In this text, the term *self-defeating* is defined broadly to refer to decision errors that lead to health problems. That is, people often behave in ways that are known to be detrimental to their long-term well-being. In psychology, the term *self-destructive* (roughly equivalent to *masochistic*) refers to individuals who repeatedly involve themselves in activities painful to them, despite their often conscious efforts to do otherwise (McWilliams, 2011).
2 The public health promotion field has been criticized for its lack of a coherent model of self-defeating behavior (Karoly, 2010). This book presents a perspective from behavioral economics to account for self-defeating behaviors and designs ways to prevent these adverse outcomes.
3 That is why behavioral economics is also called as a study of natural stupidity (Khaneman, 2011).
4 The key word is *modularity*, which is the equivalent of our "division of work" in society. The brain is made up of centers dedicated to certain kinds of processing, such as vision, memory, language, and emotion.
5 Consider the priming effect, which shows that reminding people of their old age makes them walk more slowly (Bargh, 2002). If you are primed to find flaws in your partner, this is exactly what you will find. Priming effect arises from our emotional brain, and we have no conscious access to it.
6 In the words of the novelist Doctorow (2014), the brain's mind is a kind of jail.
7 Agency refers to a person's ability to control her actions and, through them, events in the external world.
8 This does not mean the person is suffering from multiple personality disorder. Pathology reflects the failure to contain or tolerate inner conflicts.
9 From an evolutionary perspective, deep down, we are mammals with unconscious instincts and drives, and on the surface, we have our conscious, rational processes. This top layer does its best to exercise some restraint and self-control.
10 The typical analogy is that of a horse and rider. The horse has a mind of its own and sometimes goes its own way, regardless of the directions of its rider.
11 This is not to suggest that reflective systems necessarily lead to better outcomes than impulsive processes. The content of a reflective system and attitude could be detrimental to one's health (e.g., an anorexic individuals' standard to be thinner).
12 However, people may underestimate their own vulnerability. For example, it may be a while before people notice that they are angry—point of no return (as the saying goes: "you can't unring the bell").

13 For example, the Illinois "self-exclusion program" allows problem gamblers who voluntarily enrolled in the program to ban themselves from receiving prizes over $600. The program provides a tool for individuals to strengthen their resolve (tying their hand). Of course. this doesn't prevent the gamblers from going out of state and gambling all they want.
14 Angner (2012); Bickel and Vuchinich (2000); Diamond and Vartianen (2007); and Wilkinson and Klaes (2011). My aim is not to duplicate these achievements, but to do something different: to view addictive behavior from a behavioral economic perspective.

2
DECISION BIASES
A Primer on Behavioral Economics

Introduction

Decision errors happen on a regular basis in most people's lives, not just addicts. In the normal course of our daily lives, we tend to suffer from common errors in reasoning or thinking. Our mind is wired with biases. The influence of these errors undermines a logical perspective on the world around us. By becoming aware of these biases, we could develop a better pattern of thinking and performance.

This chapter describes biases in our cognitive system. It provides some insights from the field of cognitive psychology on understanding the way we think and learn.[1] The purpose is to expose some common habits of thinking and flawed beliefs that can lead to everyday biased thinking and diminished well-being. The discussions provide an understanding of how we act under conditions of incomplete information, and our vulnerability to errors. The take-home lesson of this chapter is that we should be cautious when guided by our intuitions and common sense.

Two Systems for Learning: Intuitive and Analytic

We learn and respond through two systems: the intuitive system (or automatic) without awareness, and the cognitive system (or reasoning). The two systems are alternative ways to learn and solve problems. In the economics and decision-making literature, a distinction has been made between System 1 (S1) and System 2 (S2) mechanisms (Kahneman, 2003). System 1 corresponds closely to intuitive system or automatic processing, and System 2 corresponds closely to cognitive (analytical) or controlled processes. System 1 quickly proposes answers to problems as they arise, System 2 monitors the quality of answers provided by System 1 and, in some situations, corrects or overrides these judgments. System 2 encompasses all processes that require effort, that is, attention and deliberation.

The analytic system is the domain of formal education. That is, learning takes place within the deliberate system, which requires explicit effort and attention. The intuitive system involves little or no conscious deliberation. The essence of intuition or intuitive responses is that they are reached with little apparent effort, and typically without conscious awareness, such as decision making in fire fighters and paramedics. In *Blink: The Power of Thinking without Thinking*, Malcom Gladwell describes the ability to "thin-slice," a concept closely related to intuitive thinking. It is a skill that experts tend to be better at it, but it's a learned skill.[2] Instinct is not the same as intuition. Instinctive behaviors have an evolutionary advantage (e.g., a "fight or flight" reaction to danger).

System 2 is lazy and people tend to avoid mental effort or to think as little as possible[3] (Kahneman, 2011). It often follows the path of least effort. That is, if there are several ways of achieving the same goal, people will eventually gravitate to the least demanding course of action. For example, when we first encounter problems, our initial reactions are typically intuitive. We implicitly want to see whether we can answer the question without having to use cognitive effort. Using less effort for one task means there is more left over for another task if they both must be completed simultaneously. In other words, we are under pressure to engage in shallow thinking (act foolishly). For an educator or a speaker, this suggests that anything you can do to reduce cognitive effort will make your message more memorable (i.e., using simple language or intuitive explanation).

The laziness of System 2 often leads to the selection of seductive and easier solutions that turn out to be wrong. For an example, compare the two tables (Shepard, 1990). How do size and shape of the two tabletops compare? Our analytic system would show that they are equal lengths, but our intuition misleads us. These tables are the same exact size, though they look different.[4] In the default mode of S1, we cannot rid ourselves of seeing the two tables as being of different lengths. This idea applies to perceptual judgment, in which we take the content of our perceptions at face value.

Furthermore, our mood affects our thinking. Pleasant feelings make us respond more intuitively and reduce cognitive effort. In contrast, negative feelings focus the mind, leading to better concentration. For example, rainy weather makes us more introspective and thoughtful, while fine weather increases our positive mood. When we are in a good mood, we become more intuitive and more

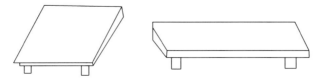

FIGURE 2.1 The illusion is produced by the different arrangement. S2 gets this, but S1 cannot.

creative, but also less vigilant and more prone to cognitive errors. A good mood makes us feel safe and that it is all right to let our guard down. When we are in a bad mood, we lose touch with our intuition and rely on System 2. In cases of an immediate threat, this is good, for it concentrates processing power upon the danger. When creative problem solving is required, this is bad, for it leads to a narrow, tunnel vision.

Our intuitive system favors the first impression, or the so-called *halo effect*. It is the tendency to like (or dislike) everything about a person (including things you have not observed). This bias plays a large role in shaping our view of people and situations. For example, in an interview, you make judgments about the person's management skills based a good presentation, and avoid further information that might contradict your story. Of course, System 2 is capable of revising if new information comes in. But System 1 is insensitive to the quantity of information. So the combination of lazy System 2 and intuitive thinking lead one to jump to conclusions on the basis of limited information.[5]

The analytic brain constitutes a relatively small part of the brain (Hogarth, 2001). However, our intuitive thought is used far more extensively than deliberate or conscious processing. These two systems can be compared to an iceberg, in which much of our mental function is submerged. The analytic system lies above the surface of the water. It can be seen and assessed. The intuitive system lies below the surface, and it cannot be seen and therefore cannot be known. The deeper a mental function lies below the surface, the less accessible it is to consciousness. Much of our learning happens below the level of consciousness. At the conscious level, we just don't know how much we know. We know more than we think we know!

Intuitions are acquired through experience. As you become skilled in a task, its demand for effort diminishes. We learn knowledge consciously, which will eventually sink into the unconscious mind. As an activity becomes more automatic, it fades from consciousness. Through practice, learning becomes automatic, thereby reducing demand on attention. As people acquire more practice in certain activities over time, responsibility for information processing passes from the conscious level to the intuitive processor. Knowledge becomes more and more engrained and automatic. Something already learned is made to be second nature, so as to perform a skill effortlessly and quickly. This frees attention and thought for new discoveries. For example, learning to ride a bicycle initially involves conscious attention to one's body and the bicycle, but eventually, riding becomes an automatic, unconscious motor activity. Indeed, one of the hallmarks of expertise in any fields is the use of automatic processes such as visual imagery and categorization. New physicians faced with a common ailment consciously and carefully think about the checklist of symptoms before making a diagnosis, but experienced physicians "feel" the answer in an instant. The same is true in sports. Over time, such experts convert some of their high-level skills into intuitive processes; as a result, those experts cannot explain how they actually do those things. On the other hand, self-preoccupation can interfere with its execution (choking under pressure) (Leary, 2004). For example, public speakers and job applicants choke under pressure because they are excessively self-focused. As soon as the pressure is gone, they tend do well because the System 2 is no longer trying to control the action.

In some cases, repeated use of particular specialized systems can produce physically recognizable changes. This is known as *neural plasticity*, which enables the adult nervous system to change in a dramatic way. The brain is constantly rewiring itself based on daily life. Studies have found that, for example, violinists who finger violin strings with their left hand show enlarged development of cortical regions corresponding to fingers on the left hand, and the brain regions responsible for navigation and spatial memory (the hippocampus) of London taxi drivers are larger than comparable areas in nontaxi drivers (Schwartz and Begley, 2003). In the end, what we choose to pay attention to defines who we are.

Thus, one way to reduce demand on the deliberative (analytic) system is to develop habits. We reach for habits mindlessly, setting our minds on autopilot and relaxing into the unconscious comfort of familiar routine. Forming a habit is a very efficient way of navigating the world, where your System 2 and System 1 activities are seamlessly integrated (Churchland, 2013). In fact, addictive behavior is similar to highly skilled behaviors (e.g., driving a car), which are under the control of automatic behavior, outside of conscious awareness.

Learning Traps

Much learning occurs simply by observation, without intentional experimentation—namely, learning in which we simply observe that certain actions are followed by certain events. Certainly, children learn by observing. Lower animals also learn by observation, as is acknowledged by the expression, "monkey see, monkey do." Given implicit learning (knowledge gained without awareness), how do we know whether the "knowledge" that we are acquiring is valid? How do we know when our knowledge is correct? Implicit learning underlies habituation and classical conditioning.[6] The implicit learning (automatic processes) are not guided by a scientist, schooled in the principles of scientific method, and who only collects data in a way that allows the drawing of valid conclusions. Instead, automatic learning processes can entice people into learning traps. The remainder of this chapter describes several mental shortcomings that contribute to learning traps and decision biases. These biases are viewed in cognitive terms, but mostly reflect the influence of intuitive (affective) factors (Angner and Loewenstein, 2012).

Working Memory

Working memory is widely thought to be one of the most important mental faculties, critical for the cognitive system. Working memory and attention are closely related concepts (Klingberg, 2013). Working memory is largely synonymous with the ability to control attention, and distraction, such as irrelevant emails or text messages. Working memory keeps information up front just when we need it, such as solving a problem or remembering instructions.

Working memory has limited capacity. That is, we are more likely to forget a longer instruction than a short one. When a task is mentally demanding, the students within the lower working memory find it hard to concentrate. People fail to realize that working memory or attention is a finite resource. Like money, attention is the ultimate scarce cognitive resource that needs to be allocated wisely. The more attention that is devoted to one task, the less is available for other tasks (i.e., opportunity cost of attention), and it is difficult to focus one's attention on more than one thing at a time. Acute stress can undermine working memory capacity. There is an optimal level of stress, and either too much or too little undermines performance. This is usually described as an inverted-U function. Working memory improves at a low level of stress, but deteriorates at times of high stress.

Individuals with greater working memory capacity are generally more intelligent than those with smaller capacity. Working memory is more strongly related to fluid intelligence than to crystallized intelligence. Fluid intelligence involves a rapid understanding of novel relationships.[7] People who have fluid intelligence have superior attention control compared to those with a low capacity, and as a result, they are less susceptible to distractions.

Researchers studying twins have found that working memory capacity is largely (at least 50%) hereditary (Klingberg, 2013). However, there are several strategies to make it easier to overcome a poor working memory or reduce demands on working memory. For example, using a briefer instruction that doesn't overload working memory, or reducing the number of distractions. We can avoid mental overload by dividing our tasks into multiple, easy steps. From an economizing perspective, ignoring useless information can help people increase their capacity to remember what is really important. Thus, we engage in selective processing, giving priority to one at the expense of another. For example, we refuse to try to solve a problem while driving, because it requires mental effort. Research also shows that physical exercise and a better diet are good for improving cognitive skills. The benefits of physical exercise relate to bringing more oxygen-rich blood to the brain. Physical exercise reduces stress levels and improves sleep, which in turn is crucial to the function of working memory, long-term memory, and attention.

James McGaugh (2003) suggests that if you want to learn something, you must rehearse. You must make an effort to make the memory stronger. This means to be able to transfer information from short-term to long-term memory (consolidation of a memory). Most of the information we acquire is forgotten and never makes it into long-term memory. The long-term memory is the memory system that stores learned facts, rules, names, and experience. When we learn a complex problem, the working memory is freed up and the action becomes automatic.

Cramming for finals is a very bad way to learn something that will last. Information from cramming will come in and go out. If you want to retain what you learn, you must spread out the learning process. The most effective strategy seems to be to gradually spread-out periods of rehearsal, so that the first occasion takes place immediately after initial learning with successive relearning at gradually lengthening intervals (Klingberg, 2013). That is, spacing improves later recall, an hour of study tonight, an hour on the weekend, and another session a week from now. The idea is that forgetting is the friend of learning. When you forget something, it allows you to relearn, and do so effectively, the next time you see it. By distributing learning events, students can raise their level of knowledge without extending their time of study.

It also helps to attach emotional significance. Much of learning takes place in the form of emotional learning without any help from cognitive system. McGaugh (2003) cites a story about a memory aid used in medieval times. In medieval times, before writing was used to keep historical records, other means had to be found to maintain records of important events, such as the granting of land to a township, an important wedding, or negotiations between powerful families. To accomplish this, a young child about seven years old was elected, instructed to observe the proceedings carefully, and then was thrown into a river. In this way, it was said that the memory of the event (as the record) would stay for the child's lifetime. Most of the learning in other animals occurs when there are strong feelings involved. In evolutionary terms, it's logical for us to imprint dangerous situations with extra clarity so that we may avoid them in the future. (What were you doing on 9/11 when you heard about the attacks?)

Despite the importance of working memory capacity for analytic problem solving, research suggests that too much focus and persistence can be harmful for creative problem solving (Wilely and Jarosz, 2012). Creative problem solving requires a completely original approach that is less fixated by prior knowledge. Exercising attention control during creative problem solving may limit the possibilities of solutions to be explored. Creative people, and the brain states that underlie creativity, may be characterized by a lack of inhibition.

Context Matters

Our mode of thinking (S2) and our intuitions (S1) depend on the context in which the information is presented. Context plays an important role in the perception of people. Context refers to a set of conditions within which something is perceived, which influences meaning of what is perceived. We react to a piece of information not on its logical merit, but on the basis of how it registers with our mental machinery. For example, people are willing to sit for nine hours in an airplane during a transcontinental flight, but can become annoyed if their baggage is returned 30 minutes late. People might travel a long distance to save $5 on an item that would cost $20 in a nearby grocery store, but it is less likely that they would go out of their way to save $5 on a $200 item. For most people, a $50 savings is significant for a DVD player, costing $100, but small for the $1,000 laptop. That is, we tend to use the background price (context) to determine the "reasonable" price.

Often, the explanation of behavior is found in the situation rather than in the person. People who behave badly in some contexts often behave well in others. For example, a man may be consistently aggressive and make sarcastic remarks to his wife, yet be calm and generous to other people. One person might be highly aggressive with individuals over whom he has power, but exceptionally friendly with those who have power over him. In certain social conditions, a very large and muscular male may be less stressed than a slighter male because other males will fear provoking him. In these social conditions, such individuals are treated with respect and are seldom provoked, so they come to be known as gentle giants. However, in a more macho social context, the same person may be tested by others precisely because of his size. In these "prove yourself" contexts, the man's stress levels may be higher. He is often provoked, so he is regularly alert for provocation and he responds accordingly. So, he may seem more aggressive than gentle in the stressful environment.

In the case of drug use, the availability of drugs (e.g., supply, cost) and social acceptance within the user's primary reference group may contribute. Availability is the crucial variable. For example, the availability of drugs explains why physicians in Germany, the United States, and other countries have historically had narcotic addiction rates up to 100 times that of the general population (Courtwright, 2001). The immediate social environments as well as nationwide cultural trends influence the prevalence of illicit drug use. On a global basis, proximity to the production area and smuggling routes seems to increase risk of drug use. For example, the prevalence of cocaine use is high in South America (including Columbia, the main source of cocaine) and in North America compared with most parts of the world. Similarly, the prevalence[8] of opiate use is particularly high is some Asian countries close to Afghanistan and Myanmar, the main producing countries.[9]

In short, context plays a powerful role in shaping individual preference and behavior. The context in which people behave shapes the options they face and their ability to choose. Our mind is not a central, all-purpose computer that starts with logical rules and applies them equally to all possible situations. Instead, each person's mind contains emotions, cognition, memories and habits, which compete for control. Context matters in determining which of these internal players gets to control behavior at any instant. This explains why we can manage to effortlessly solve a problem in a social situation, but struggle when it is presented in an abstract, logical format. Conversely, some people are better at understanding the textbook problem than its practical application. Thus, it is important that we become cognizant of the context within which we decide.

Anchoring

Anchoring and adjustment highlights the power of first choices (Tversky and Kahneman, 1974). When we are guessing about something (size of the population), we start with some anchor, and adjust in the direction we think is appropriate. In one experiment, college students were asked two questions: (a) How happy are you? (b) How often are you dating? When the two questions were asked in this order the correlation between the two questions was quite low (0.11). But when the question order was reversed, so that the dating question was asked first, the correlation jumped to 0.62. Apparently, when prompted by the dating question, the students might react, "Gee, I can't remember when I last had a date! I must be miserable." This example shows that our attention is often framed by our current circumstances and even by the way the questions are posed.

Anchoring implies that judgments are based not on absolute values but on comparisons with implicit reference points ("anchors"). Consider the price tags in a car dealership. The sticker price is merely an anchor that allows the car salesperson to make the real price of the car seem like a better deal. This shows our brains' inability to dismiss irrelevant information. In classroom settings, students get anchored on certain opinions and react too slowly to information that should change those beliefs. This bias explains why supermarkets can sell more cans of soup with signs that say "limit 12 per customer" rather than "limit 4 per customer."[10] Supermarkets and convenience stores use promotions like "2 for $2" vs "1 for $1" that lead us to buy more than we normally would. People unknowingly anchor or focus on the number they first see and let that bias them.[11]

Anchors play an important role with respect to health behavior changes. For example, consider two scenarios: in the first case, you tell people that 35% of the population is heavier than they themselves are. In the second case, you tell them that 65% of the population is thinner than they are. People would place more importance in weight control in the second scenario. In the second scenario, people compare themselves to thinner people (65% as the anchor). Framing and anchoring the context affects individual behavior (i.e., the otherwise equivalent description). The reference point influences what people perceive as "normal" weight and perceptions of their own acceptable weight and desire for weight loss attempts. Standards of physical appearance are powerful motivators for human behavior.[12]

The Scarcity Mindset

Economics is the study of how we use our limited resources (time, money) to achieve our goals. This definition refers to physical scarcity. Mullainathan and Eldar (2013) broaden the concept of scarcity by asking the following questions: What happens to our minds when we feel we have too little? How does the context of scarcity shape our choices and our behaviors? They show that scarcity is not just a physical constraint. Scarcity affects our thinking and feeling. Scarcity orients the mind automatically and powerfully toward unfulfilled needs. For example, food grabs the focus of the hungry.[13] For the lonely person, it is the poverty of social isolation and a lack of companionship. Scarcity is more than just the displeasure of having very little. It changes how we think.

On the positive side, scarcity prioritizes our choices and it can make us more effective. Scarcity creates a powerful goal dealing with pressing needs and ignoring other goals. For example, the time pressure of a deadline focuses our attention on using what we have most effectively. Distractions are less tempting. When we have little time left, we try to get more out of every moment. For example, we are more frugal with the toothpaste as the tube starts to run empty, and college seniors tend to get the most out of their time before graduation.

Scarcity forces trade-off thinking. We recognize that having one thing means not having something else. If you spend $10 on anything, there is $10 less left for something else. Economists call this the opportunity cost—the alternative use of the money. Thus, low-income consumers are more responsive to an increased cigarette tax than rich consumers and smoke less. The poor is careful to squeeze the most out of every dollar spent. The poor must ask themselves what they must give up to afford the new price. However, slack frees us from making trade-offs. For example, as your budget grows, the purchase of the iPad takes up a smaller fraction of your disposable income. Thus a bigger budget makes decision less consequential and lessens feelings of scarcity.

Focusing on one thing means neglecting other things. Scarcity causes us to focus single-mindedly (tunnel) on managing the scarcity at hand. However, this narrow focus leads us to neglect other, possibly more important things. For example, when you are angry with someone, you focus only on the annoying traits and neglect their good traits. Thus, scarcity distorts the trade-off we make. That is, things outside the narrow focus are harder to see clearly and easier to undervalue, and we are more likely to ignore them.

Scarcity taxes our cognitive capacity (e.g., fluid intelligence and impulse control). The scarcity context can make a person less intelligent and more impulsive. Imagine a financially strapped college student who underperforms in exams. He may look incapable and careless, but he must contend with persistent money concerns. He is lost in thought about how to make rent this month and tuition bills. Similarly, dieters do poorly on cognitive tests. For these dieters, concerns related to diet are at the top of their minds. With limited cognitive capacity, we are more likely to give in to our impulses. Readily available junk food may cause overeating in the poor and busy persons. But, it is less of a threat for the rich and the relaxed person. Dieting creates a scarcity of calories, and that scarcity in turn places the desert at the forefront of the mind.

The context of scarcity makes you myopic (a bias toward here and now). The mind is focused on present scarcity. We overvalue immediate benefits at the expense of future ones (e.g., procrastinate important things, such as medical checkups, or exercising). We only attend to urgent things and fail to make small investments even when the future benefits can be substantial. To attend to the future requires cognitive resources, which scarcity depletes. We need cognitive resources to plan and to resist present temptations. Thus, a key concern in the management of scarcity is to economize on the cognitive resources. Cognitive resource is about allocating our limited information-processing abilities. For example, you can break a big project into progressively smaller chunks that can be completed without the feeling of urgency.

The Concept of Utility

Utility refers to how desirable a task or choice is for an individual. It is a yardstick on which disparate events can be compared. It is a measure (or scoring systems, if you like) of how people feel about experiences. Utility represents motivation. Utility motivates all human choices. Motivation is a starting point for all economic decisions. Motivation is described as an individual having a "utility function." The content of this utility function characterizes what people care about. For example, a person may care about today's consumption and about future consumption. A good decision is to maximize utility. Thus, utility is a placeholder term for whatever people maximize when choosing among options.[14]

The consumption of most goods and services is subject to diminishing marginal utility. Marginal utility refers to the pleasure or pain from an additional unit or "dose" of a good consumed. All pleasures (e.g., a cup of coffee in the morning, an afternoon walk) follow a law of diminishing returns. All pleasurable activities start out very enjoyable, and within a few minutes, we get used to it. That is why people eat chocolate bars in pieces, waiting and savoring, or they space their cigarette through the day.

Utility is not all of one type. There are four types of utility involved in decisions: decision utility, experienced utility, predicted utility, and remembered utility (Kahneman, 2000).

Decision utility is the essence of an actual decision, the valuation of the outcome manifested in choice and pursuit. Traditionally, economists believed that the best way to measure individuals' preference was just look at what they do and infer their preferences from their behaviors. Decision utility is what people reveal by choosing (known as *revealed preference*). Most typically, it is revealed by what we decide to do. For example, the decision by smokers to have a cigarette reflects decision utility. Standard economic theory assumes that all observed behavior is utility-maximizing from the perspective of the person making decision.

Experienced utility is what people actually like when they consume. It is the hedonic impact of the reward that is actually experienced when it is finally gained. For many, experienced utility is the essence of what reward is all about. The term hedonic refers to positive aspects of experiences. For example, many people believe that beer tastes better when it is consumed with friends. So the utility is derived from the experience as well as the consumption of the product itself.

Remembered utility is what people recall liking (retrospective evaluations of an experience). The evaluation of remembered utility requires the individual to remember a stream of experiences, and to aggregate them in some way. Remembered utility is the memory of how good a previous reward was in the past. It is the reconstructed representation of the hedonic impact carried by the remembered reward. Whenever we decide about outcomes (*predicted utility*) we have previously experienced in our past, remembered utility is perhaps the main factor determining predicted enjoyment. That is, we generally expect future rewards to be about as good as they have been in the past. For example, we plan our vacation based on predicted enjoyment consequences.

Miswanting occurs when there is a disconnection between decision utility and experienced utility. Decision utility could deviate from experienced utility if people have not yet learned what they like, or if there is some dissociation between decision utility and experienced utility. Such divergence can lead to bad decisions. Examples include buying exercise equipment, joining health clubs, and shopping compulsively, where there is a possible disconnection between the decision utility (transitory pleasure) from buying these goods and the experienced utility (later pleasure) from consuming them.

The central idea is that at the time of decision, people think that they will obtain a certain amount of utility (satisfaction) from a certain product or activity—but they sometimes err. We might think that a very expensive car would be a joy to own, but we might get used to that car, and after a while, we might not get a lot of pleasure from it. In an extreme case, a young person may underestimate that the use of addictive drugs creates tolerance and possible future withdrawal. Thus, decisions made on the basis of false, predicted utility are likely to turn out to fail to maximize eventual experienced happiness.

As an illustration, consider people's vacation experiences. Wirtz and colleagues (2003) tracked college students before, during, and after their spring break vacations and compared their predicted, experienced, and remembered utility. They found that predicted and remembered experiences were more intense (i.e., more positive and more negative) than was actually the case, as reflected in concurrent reports collected during the vacation. However, the remembered experience best predicted the desire to repeat the vacation, illustrating that we learn from our memories rather than from our actual experiences. In retrospect, our minds play games with us, and we rewrite the past in a favorable light, something that is pretty close to what we expected. This rosy view of the past has a downside, which may explain why people often seem to repeat the mistakes of the past.

Satisficing vs. Maximizing

The fundamental human motive is the desire to seek to obtain pleasure and avoid pain. People and animals are motivated to avoid pain and attain pleasure, and they organize their actions around those twin pursuits. In the same vein, economics assumes that people make decisions based on their own self-interest, maximizing their total utility (satisfaction) wherever they can. Behavioral economists, however, have shown the limits of this maximizing behavior. Herbert Simon (1955) proposed that decision makers (everyone) should be viewed as bounded rational,[15] and offered a model in which utility maximization was replaced by satisficing. Satisficing people are individuals who have a minimum threshold for what is acceptable to them. Maximizing individuals are people who strive to get the very best out of every decision.

Overall, maximizers achieve better outcomes than satisficers, but they tend to be less happy with their achievements. Once maximizers have made a choice (e.g., a job offer), they are likely to second guess themselves, and wonder whether they could have made a better choice (Schwartz, 2004). Why? One reason is that they have more regrets. Second, they are more prone to make social comparisons. For example, consider a choice of college. Maximizers rely heavily on external sources for evaluation. Rather than asking themselves if they enjoy their choice, they are more likely to evaluate their choices based on its reputation, social status, and other external cues. In contrast, a statisficer asks whether his college choice is excellent and meets his needs, not whether it is really "the best."

A key problem with maximizing is when the decider faces an abundance of options. For example, Schwartz (2004) shows that when shoppers had to choose among 20 choices of jams (or six pairs jeans), they experience conflict and are less satisfied with their final selection. But, they are likely to be more satisfied with a smaller selection. Too many attractive options make it difficult to commit to any choice, and after the final selection, one remains anxious about the missed opportunities (maybe the other pair of jeans was a better fit). In short, when we face too many attractive choices, we feel anxious about missing out (Shenhav and Buckner, 2014). Psychologists suggest that to make "best" choices, listen to your gut feelings, don't worry about getting the very best all the time, and evaluate each outcome on its own merits rather than against others (e.g., Kahneman, 2011).

Expectation Effects

People's expectations influence their views of subsequent events, such as the expectation that a certain kind of beer would shape their taste (Ariely, 2008). In other words, previously held impressions cloud our point of view. For example, when people are told that previous participants have found the movie to be very funny, they showed a similar preference (a self-fulfilling prophecy). If you tell people up front that something might be distasteful, it is highly likely that they will end up agreeing with you. In short, what one expects to happen tends to strongly influence what actually happens.

Expectation is essential for building the reputation of a brand or product—providing information that will increase someone's anticipated and real pleasure. For example, putting the word "Perrier" on the water bottle changes our experience. Using brain scanners to monitor the minds of wine drinkers, researchers found that people given two identical red wines got more pleasure from tasting the one that they were told cost more (Plassmann et al., 2008). The author concludes that the pleasantness of consuming a product depends on more than the product's intrinsic properties, such as flavor in the case of wine. The brain also relies on certain beliefs, such as the notion that expensive wines probably will taste better. People have general beliefs that cheaper wines are of lower quality, and that translates into expectations about the wine tastes.

Value expectation (or attribution) describes our tendency to characterize someone or something with certain qualities based on perceived value, rather than objective data (Brafman, 2008). For example, we may turn down a pitch or idea that is presented by a college student or blindly follow the same advice of someone who is highly regarded (e.g., a graduate of an elite college). Expectations also shape stereotypes (e.g., female students are weak in math).

People who become addicted develop expectancies or beliefs that using a substance results in positive, desired effects, such as the ability to avoid or escape negative moods states. These expectancies influence motives (utility) to use drugs (Thombs and Osborn, 2013). Common alcohol expectancies include relaxation, social and physical pleasure, and increased assertiveness. People who state that they expect alcohol to help relieve tension are more likely to turn to alcohol when stressed. These expectancies are acquired through social learning and media messages, and are shaped by repeated experiences of positive and negative reinforcement with a substance.

In sum, the value expectation alters our reality, and can effectively influence the taste and sensory perceptions. When we believe in advance that something will be good, therefore, it generally will be good, and vice versa. This is not to suggest that sensation plays no role in experience. It is rather that sensation is always colored by our beliefs, including our beliefs about essences.[16] In the case of addiction, individuals formulate beliefs about the effective consequences of using a substance (e.g., feeling relaxed after a cocktail).

Endowment Effect (The Emotion of Ownership)

When we own something (car, dog, home, idea), we begin to value it more than other people do. The ownership of something increases its value in the owner's eyes. The endowment effect perhaps has to do with self-enhancement—we feel good about ourselves, and we enhance the value of our choices and devalue the road not taken. In general, people view gains and losses differently. They tend to become extremely attracted to objects in their possession, and averse to giving them up. Why? Three irrational factors about human nature explain this bias.

First, we develop attachment. Examples include the "trial" promotion such as movie channels, or "30-day money back guarantees" for purchasing furniture. The trap is that we become partial owners even before we own anything. Ownership is not limited to material things, it also applies to ideas. Once we take ownership of an ideology (about politics or sports) we prize it more than it is worth. We tend overvalue our ideas. However, we run the risk of dismissing others' ideas that might simply better than ours. Thus, a good strategy to help others adopt a new idea would be to provide opportunities for them to come up with the ideas on their own.

Second, we focus on what we may lose, rather than what we may gain. Our aversion to loss is a strong emotion. This is known as *loss aversion* or negative bias (Khaneman, 2011)[17] (bad is stronger than good). The pain of a loss is approximately twice as potent as the pleasure generated by a gain (Khaneman, 2011). Consistent with this principle, avoiding pain takes precedence over seeking pleasure.[18] For example, while we indulge in buying things (larger home, new car) and think that we can always downsize if we could not afford it, the reality is that downgrading to a smaller home is psychologically painful. Being wealthy doesn't help. Having accumulated wealth implies that we have more to lose than to gain (Taleb, 2012). For rich people, the pain of losing their fortune exceeds the emotional gain of getting additional wealth, so the rich become vulnerable and anxious. The idea of loss aversion is shown in consumer behavior. For example, Daniel Putler (1992) has shown that consumers are more responsive to price increase than to decrease: from July 1981 to July 1983, a 10% increase in the price of eggs led to a 7.8% decrease in demand, whereas a 10% decrease in the price led to a 3.3% increase in demand.

Third, we assume other people see the transaction from the same perspective as we do. It is difficult to imagine that the person on the other side of the transaction, buyer, is not seeing the world as we see it. What is the cure? Being aware of it might help (forewarned is forearmed). Try to view the transaction as if you were nonowner. If you have nothing to lose, then it is all gain, and you are less vulnerable.

Attribution Error

Psychologists use the term attributions (or causes) for people's explanations of the events in their lives. Attribution theory is about how people make causal explanations. It is about how people answer questions beginning with "why?" For example, people may make attributions as to why their lovers left them, or why they are having a problem at school or work. Attributions are fundamental to understanding the way people make sense of their world (Heider, 1958). For example, people who attribute failure to themselves try harder to improve their performance. Those who attribute their failures to external forces are less likely to try harder. In many cases, causal links are more prevalent in our minds than in reality. That is, we manufacture our own reality.

People make attributions that are biased in a self-serving direction. In general, we take credit when we think we performed well than when we think we performed poorly. For example, when students receive grades on a test, those who get good grades feel satisfied about their performance and think the test was fair, whereas those with lower grades tend to see the test as unfair.

Similarly, the concept of *fundamental attribution error* suggests that we inappropriately explain behavior by character traits when it is better explained by context. That is, we tend to attribute our success to our enduring character traits, and our failures to unfortunate circumstances. For example, someone might say, "you failed because you did not try hard enough; I failed because I had a headache from staying up all night with my son." The fundamental attribution error could be motivated. An alcoholic may be happy to tell himself he "just cannot help it" in order to have an excuse for persisting.

The attributions that people make for an event influence their reactions to it. Even though the event is the same, the attribution a person makes can evoke quite different emotional reactions to it.[19] Inaccurate attributions are a major source of inaccurate expectations (e.g., misunderstanding the causes of feelings). For example, by incorrectly attributing responsibility for obesity mostly to individual characteristics rather than to the environment or context, the nonobese can view themselves as morally superior. But the reality is that poverty and neighborhood characteristics may constrain the food and physical activity choices available.

Overcoming this error can be liberating. For example, first-year college students who are told that most freshmen do poorly but that their grades subsequently improve, in fact do somewhat better in later years than those who are not given this information. The latter are more likely to attribute their poor performance to their ability (trait) than to the unfamiliar and distracting college environment. Not believing they can do better, they are less motivated.

Illusion of Causality

Often correlation is confused with causation, and people make theories out of coincidence. An important function of the cognitive system (System 2) is the ability to generate concepts of cause and effect. Our intuitive system (System 1) is not prone to doubt, it seeks causes and believes in a coherent world in which random phenomena do not make sense. System 1 will often see causal and other meaningful links when there are only correlations or where there are no meaningul connections at all. When this happens, thinking results in erroneous conclusion.

We learn by observing connections, and we are motivated to attribute meaning to what we observe. Humans are evolutionarily programmed to try to look for patterns because that is how we navigate the world around us. Moreover, events do not come labeled "random." Instead, this must be inferred. This bias can influence the way we interpret random events. The human mind is built to identify for each event a definite cause and can therefore have a hard time accepting the influence of unrelated or random factors.

Random processes are fundamental in nature and are pervasive in our everyday lives. In practice, randomness is basically incomplete information. A lot of what happens to us (e.g., success in our career) is as much the result of random factors as the result of preparedness and hard work. How, for example, do you know whether your success at a task was due to something you did or to chance? The world is complex and appearance fools us. As the saying goes, "even a broken clock is right twice a day." Sometimes we obtain success through pure luck.

This pattern-seeking bias is shown in the so-called gambler's fallacy. This bias refers to the belief that a long streak increases the chance of a different outcome on the next go. For example, if a coin comes up heads five times in a row, people will have a powerful sense that the next flip is more likely to come up tails than heads. However, any single flip has an equal chance of coming up heads or tails. Statistical thinking suggests that the coin does not have any memory. A flood this year says nothing about whether a flood will happen next year. But the intuitive mind senses that a flood this year means a flood next year is less likely. Our intuition does not grasp the nature of randomness.

One of the aspects of superstition is the idea of magical thinking that you have control over the world. This magical thinking promotes individual confidence that you can affect personal outcomes. For example, knocking on wood to protect yourself against misfortune. Many people endorse the ten-second rule that says you can eat food that has fallen on the ground only if you pick it up immediately. Consider this. Mlodinow (2008) writes about a man who won the Spanish national lottery with a ticket that ended in the number 48. In an interview, proud of his "accomplishment," he revealed the theory that brought him the wealth. He said, "I dreamed of the number 7 for seven straight nights, and 7 times 7 is 48." Ignoring the math error, this example illustrates how people concoct explanations for the occurrence of chance events, making it explainable and predictable. Many gurus make a fortune out of exploiting these so-called causes![20]

The Narrative Bias

This bias is associated with our tendency for pattern detection from raw truths (Taleb, 2007). It takes considerable effort to see facts (and remember them) while withholding judgment and resisting explanations. The urge for explanations is automatic. Human beings have a universal desire to find meanings and patterns everywhere (Elster, 2009). When an unpredicted event occurs, we immediately come up with explanatory stories that are simple and coherent. Our System 1 is the sense-making organ, which sees the world as simple, predictable, and coherent. This coherence makes us feel good.

Why it is hard to avoid narrative bias? There are two problems with information processing and storage. First, information is costly to obtain. Second, it is costly to store. The more orderly, less random, patterned, and narrated, the easier it is to store in our minds. A novel, a story, or a myth, all have the same function: they spare us from the complexity of the world and protect us from its randomness. Consider this: "Bill died and Mary died." Compare it to this: "The husband died, and then the wife died of grief." This example shows the distinction between mere information and a plot. The second sentence is, in a way, much less costly to process and to remember.[21]

There is an upside to storytelling. We can use a narrative for a good purpose. We use stories and metaphors to convey ideas. Stories are more convincing. They are easier to remember and more fun to listen to. Stories have the ability to capture a person's attention. It appeals to our intuitive knowledge. Students poorly learn about human behavior by mere statistics. These facts, no matter how compelling, will not change long-held beliefs rooted in personal experiences. Students learn much better by being surprised by individual cases and stories. Stories are effective tools, because students can find relevance to their own behaviors, which can influence their intuitive system (S1). However, one should be careful not to distort the reality.

Narrative can be therapeutic. It helps us to see past events as more predictable, more expected, and less random than they actually were: "Hey, it was bound to take place and it seems futile to agonize over it." For example, breakups are less of a fuss if you can devalue or vilify the ex, and if you want to disturb yourself, then the person you had doubts about three weeks ago can quickly become the One Who Got Away.

Psychologist James Pennebaker uses writing as a tool for healing. Patients who spend 15 minutes every day writing an account of their daily troubles indeed feel better about what has befallen them. You feel less guilty for not having avoided certain events; you feel less responsible for it. Things appear as if they were bound to happen. An important part of therapy is to help patients with troubled pasts to reframe their memories in more beneficial, affective perspectives. People who dwell endlessly on their problems may only make matters worse.

Cognitive Dissonance

The cognitive dissonance theory suggests that when people do things against their better judgment, they experience internal discomfort, much like hunger or thirst (Festinger, 1957). That is, when a person experiences an internal inconsistency or dissonance among his beliefs and values, we can expect some kind of mental readjustment that will eliminate or reduce the dissonance. Typically, the adjustment will choose the path of least resistance.

Cognitive dissonance results from a tension between a desire and a belief (Elster, 1999a). The tension is resolved by modifying the belief and desire. It is a case of detecting your own hypocrisy, and hypocrisy is a powerful motivator of compensatory behavior. For example, when we lose in a contest, we come to want the prize less because we interpret it as less valuable. This is similar to the fable of a fox who tries hard to get his hands on a tasty vine of grapes, but fails in all of his attempts to acquire the grapes; at which point, the fox convinces himself that he really didn't want those grapes that badly after all.

Often it is our beliefs that get adjusted, rather than our desire. A smoker who reads about how smoking causes cancer experiences cognitive dissonance if she continues to smoke then she is knowingly doing something that will harm her. There are two ways to relieve the discomfort. The first is to quit smoking (reduce desire). But that is difficult, so most smokers convince themselves that the links between smoking and lung cancer are not quite as strong as doctors assert (modify belief). They are rationalizing away the risks.

In general, we strive to ensure that the picture we have of ourselves is coherent (not dissonant), which is a means for maintaining a positive self-evaluation. Dissonance reduction and other motivated belief formations are caused by unconscious mechanisms. We may not understand well how they operate, but they are based on optimization processes. They maximize the pleasure the person derives from his belief about the world. For example, if I have unjustly harmed another person, I may be unable to admit to myself that I am at fault. Instead, I will seek out a fault in the other person that justifies or at least excuses my behavior. An extreme example of this is how often, rapists will say, "she dressed provocatively."

Confirmation Bias

Confirmation bias refers to the tendency to see data that confirms our views (prejudices) more vividly and ignoring disconfirming elements. Once we have formed a view, we embrace information that supports that view while ignoring, or rejecting, information that casts doubt on it. For example, a person who wishes to believe in horoscopes may notice the one time that their reading seems accurate and ignore (or rationalize) the many times when their horoscopes are worded so ambiguously that they could mean anything. Statements, such as "many smokers live a long time," and "smoking is better than excessive eating or drinking," are examples of confirmation bias. Confirmation bias suggests that we don't perceive circumstances objectively. We pick out those bits of data that make us feel good because they confirm our prejudices. Thus, we may become prisoners of our assumptions.

Imagine that you have tried to reach a friend (with whom you have an ambivalent relationship) by telephone (or email), leaving messages, yet have not received a call in return. In situation like this, it is easy to jump to conclusions in an intuitive manner, such as thinking that your friend wants to avoid you. The danger, of course, is that you leave this belief unchecked and start to act as though it were true. Our intuitive thinking (S1) contributes to the confirmation bias, which favors uncritical accceptance of our favorable view. Conscious doubts and uncertainty are the domain of the deliberative system (S2). When S2 is lazy or tired, we become vulnerable to believing a false statement. Seeking to confirm our beliefs comes naturally, while it feels strong and counterintuitive to look for evidence that contradicts our beliefs. This explains why opinions survive and spread.

Contrary to the scientific approach that requires testing hypotheses in order to reject them, people seek information that is likely to support the beliefs they currently hold. Disconfirming instances are far more powerful in establishing truth. Disconfirmation would require looking for evidence to disprove it. The take-home lesson here is that you should set your hypothesis and then look for instances to prove that you are wrong. This is perhaps a true definition of self-confidence: the ability to look at the world without the need to look for instances that please your ego.[22] For group decision making, it is crucial to obtain information from each member in a way that acknowledges that they are independent.[23]

Wishful Thinking

When people would like a certain proposition to be true, they end up believing it to be true. Wishful thinking occurs from the direct influence of desire on beliefs (Elster, 2009). It is a form of motivated belief formation that arises when the individual stops gathering information and when the evidence gathered so far supports the belief one would like to be true. For example, a self-control problem often involves self-deception, such as *just this one, it's not that fattening*, or *I'll stop smoking tomorrow*. Or, when someone is "under the influence," she feels confident thats he can drive safely even after three or more glasses.

Self-deception can be like a drug, numbing you from harsh reality, or turning a blind eye to the tough matter for gathering evidence and thinking (Churchland, 2013).[24] However, in some cases, self-deception is good for us (Lazarus and Lazarus, 2006). For example, for dealing with certain illnesses (such as cancer), having positive thinking may actually be beneficial, but the same would not hold true with diabetes or ulcer. There is limited evidence that believing that you will recover helps reduce the level of stress hormones, giving the immune system and modern medicine a better chance to do their work. However, false optimism is largely wishful thinking if it sends you to the faith healer instead of cancer clinic. As the saying goes, *everyone wants to go heaven, but nobody wants to die*.

Self-Fulfilling Prophecy

The idea refers to a false belief of a situation that evokes a behavior that in turn makes the false belief become true. Consider an allocation decision facing Joe, a waiter working in a busy restaurant, assuming his goal is to maximize his tips. Based on a limited number of observations, he forms a hypothesis (belief) that well-dressed people are good tippers and that badly dressed customers are not.[25] By acting on this belief, he sets in motion a *self-fulfilling prophecy* by providing different level of services based on the customers' appearance. When the restaurant is busy, well-dressed customers do leave above-average tips, and badly dressed customers do not, precisely because of the differential level of services that Joe provides. Had Joe wanted to test his belief, he should have conducted an experiment in which he randomly provided good service to well- and badly dressed customers alike. The resulting data would have told him whether there really was a relation between dress and tipping behavior.

In the context of health behavior change, our learned self-perception becomes a self-fulfilling prophecy. That is, by expecting to fail, we make failure a certainty. We never really try, and the end result is more self-control problems. A related bias is known as self-handicapping. If a person is uncertain about her true ability and afraid to find out what her true ability is, she might refrain from doing the work that might reveal her as having low ability. If she nevertheless does well, she can congratulate herself on her exceptional ability; if she does badly, she can blame it on lack of effort rather than on lack of competence.

Optimism and Overconfidence

People tend to be unrealistically optimistic. Overconfidence fools us because we focus on what we know and fail to think properly about what we don't know. In most situations, what we don't know is more important than what we do know, and as a result, we end up with a poor outcome.

Overconfident individuals think that they are blessed, that they are well liked by others and that they'll come out on top (As the bumper stickers states, "Jesus loves you, but I'm his favorite."). For example, 90% of all drivers think they are above average behind the wheel, 94% of professors at a large university were found to believe that they are better than the average professor. About 50% of marriages end in divorce. But around the time of the ceremony, almost all couples believe that there is approximately a 0% chance that their marriage will end up in divorce. A similar point applies to entrepreneurs starting new businesses, where the failure rate is at least 50%. In short, people have poor insights into their skills and abilities, despite spending more time with themselves than with any other person (Levitt and Dubner, 2013).

Overconfidence leads to self-serving biases (Hogarth, 2001). Self-serving bias is the tendency to overrate oneself—to be overly confident of one's knowledge, abilities, or good fortune. Unrealistic optimism can explain a lot of individual risk-taking behavior, especially in the domains of risks to life and health. As a result, people may fail to take sensible, preventive steps. For example, many people think they are more active than actual measurement reveals. Based on the individual report, 30% believed they met current exercise guideline. However, direct measures indicate that less than 5% of individuals meet the recommended 30 minutes of moderate physical activity five days per week. Smokers are aware of the statistical risks, but most believe that they are less likely to be diagnosed with lung cancer and heart disease than most nonsmokers. Persons who engage in risky sexual activity often deceive themselves in thinking, "it won't happen to me." Nordgren, van Harreveld, and van der Pligt (2009) found that among a group of people trying to quit smoking, the ones who gave especially high ratings to their own willpower were most likely to fail (Nordgren, van Harreveld and van der Pligt, 2009).

The Problem of Silent Evidence

This bias is the difference between what you see and what is there (the appearance-equals-reality rule). The most important fact about learning from experience is that people learn content and rules by what they experience, not by what they do not experience. We learn from *what we see*, but not necessarily from *what we do not see*. We see the obvious and visible consequences, not the invisible and less obvious ones. For example, patients in dialysis centers are often surprisingly reluctant to be on the waiting list for a kidney transplantation. One reason is that all the transplanted patients they ever see are those for whom the operation failed so that they had to go back on dialysis (Elster, 2009).

This bias may explain the so-called nerd effect: why those who "study" and do well in school have a tendency to be clueless about reality, and they think inside the box. As psychologist Abraham Maslow (1966, p. 15) once said, "[i]f all you have is a hammer, everything looks like a nail." This is equivalent to looking for a lost wallet under a street light even though it was lost in a dark alley a block away. Focusing only on what we already know can limit our ability to think more expansively. On the other hand, imagination allows us to learn from what we do not see. Imagination is not limited to what is physically possible. Imagination is a tool for the exploration of all the options.

Conclusion

Human beings are not born as blank mental slates. Early in life, young individuals develop very powerful theories of the world. They do so without the need for formal instruction—we might say that these are natural or "intuitive" theories. More generally, individuals will go to great lengths to square apparently conflicting information with their firmly held beliefs. That is how we cope with "cognitive dissonance"—the apparent inconsistency between what our parents (or our textbooks) tell us and what we believe to be true.

Gardner (1999) argues that the mind is a surprisingly conservative mechanism. As discussed in later chapters, our implicit attitude or schemas are typically slower to form and change because they are based on accumulated learning and stored in memory (e.g., the habit of stereotyping). Indeed, when it comes to the theories that one is expected to master in school, the mind proves remarkably stubborn to change—persisting in its original, unschooled theories even when, on the surface, a person can say the appropriate line. Figuring out how to reduce or escape biases is a formidable educational challenge.

In the context of a two-system model of human behavior, we can conclude that S1 is generally lazy, not totally alert. Our S1 is strongly biased toward causal explanation and does not deal with uncertainty. When our attention is called to an event, our associative memory will activate automatically any cause that is already stored in the memory. Following our intuitions is more natural than acting against it.

Notes

1 Cognitive psychology studies how people think and reason in terms of processes that, although not "observable," could at least be described. Learning processes fit into a larger picture of human information processing.
2 Gladwell notes that more information sometimes obscures what is important. He cites a study by Nalini Ambady about students' snap judgments of teacher effectiveness being the same with those made by students after a full semester of classes.
3 For example, it is known that morning type people tend to perform poorly in the evening, while evening people do poorly in the morning. Why? Thinking is slow in those times.
4 To view this and more, go to: http://www.michaelbach.de/ot/
5 People are also biased by the "health halos" that accompany labels and tend to overeat when foods are labeled as "low fat," or perceived as healthier vs less healthy (e.g., "90% fat-free").
6 For example, in the United States up-down head movement is associated with an attitude of acceptance, and left-right with an attitude of rejection, however, in Albania, the opposite is the case. For some visitors this could be quite amusing and perhaps confusing.
7 Fluid intelligence is the ability to find connections and draw conclusions independent of previous knowledge. Fluid intelligence is the kind of intelligence tested on I.Q. examinations (e.g., pattern recognition and abstract thinking). There is also crystallized intelligence. which depends on knowledge and expertise and can be assessed by a vocabulary test. Crystallized intelligence generally refers to skills that are acquired through experience and education (e.g., verbal ability, inductive reasoning, and judgment) (Eysenck, 2012). It is known that there is a connection between education and cognitive ability as people age. This suggests that college education has long-term benefits (mental fitness) well beyond career opportunities.
8 Prevalence refers to the total number of individuals in a population who have ever used a drug, whereas incidence refers to number of times a drug was used within a given time period.
9 According to novels and movies (e.g., *Apocalypse Now*, 1979), the easily availability of drugs doubled the addiction for opiates among enlistees (Erickson, 2007).
10 This pricing practice of limiting the number of items per person (e.g., two cans of soup per person) can lead to increased sales. However, in this case, anchoring is not the only explanation for increases in sales, the sign implies that the items are in short supply and shoppers should feel some urgency about stocking up (see the following section).
11 The effect explains why people are much more likely to buy meat when it's labeled 85% lean instead of 15% fat.
12 In 1994, the average weight for an American woman was 147 pounds, and the average desired weight was 132 pounds. By 2002, those numbers were 153 and 135, respectively (Heiland and Burke, 2007). The figures suggest a reduction in social pressure to maintain lower weights.

13 Evidence shows that children who grow up in homes with restrictive food rules, where a parent is constantly dieting or desirable foods are forbidden or placed out of reach, often develop stronger reactions to food and want more of it when the opportunity presents itself. This suggests that restriction on desirable food creates scarcity and increases a child's focus on the restricted food. This effect was stronger for children with a genetic predisposition to overeat (Rollins et al., 2014).
14 The concept of happiness is not the same as the concept of utility. There is probably more to life than even life satisfaction. In other words, happiness is considered as one component of utility. That is, utility is a broader concept than happiness. For example, utility goes up as you have children even though it may be stressful at times.
15 Bounded rationality implies biases in acquiring information, biases in processing information, biases in transmitting information, and biases in receiving and storing feedback.
16 The implication is not to underestimate the power of presentation (e.g., when coffee ambience looks upscale, the coffee tastes upscale as well).
17 Tennis player Andre Agassi in his autobiography reveals that "[a] win doesn't feel as good as a loss feels bad, the good feeling doesn't last as long as the bad. Not even close." (Agassi, 2009: 165).
18 This is why, in marital interactions, it generally takes at least five kind comments to offset one critical comment.
19 For example, one of the important explanations of suicide is the "no one left to blame." That is, there is no one left to blame one's unhappiness and thus suicide becomes more likely (Lester, 2013).
20 Historically, sport players have used whatever substances they believed would improve their performance. In 1889, Pud Galvin, the first probaseball player, ingested monkey testosterone as a performance-enhancing drug.
21 The entire notion of biography is grounded in the arbitrary attribution of a causal relation between specified traits and subsequent events.
22 It is known that Abraham Lincoln intentionally filled his cabinet with rival politicians who had extremely different ideologies. When making decisions, Lincoln always encouraged vigorous debate and discussion.
23 For example, as part of police procedure, to derive the most reliable information from multiple witnesses to a crime, witnesses are not allowed to discuss it prior to giving their testimony. The goal is to prevent unbiased witnesses from influencing each other.
24 In 2008, Madoff cheated his clients of $50 billion. Those people taken by the Ponzi scheme were characterized by desperation and hope, not necessarily greed and stupidity. People are prone to believe what they want to believe, and in rising markets, a kind of irrational euphoria takes hold in which we are not inclined to ask difficult questions.
25 Connections are also established in people's minds by what they have been told by others. Imagine that a friend told Joe that well-dressed customers tend to leave good tips.

3
DEFINITION AND THE NATURE OF ADDICTION

Introduction

What is an addiction? What makes addiction a distinctive phenomenon? How does the human brain get addicted? What are the neurobiological causes of addiction? Addiction is characterized by a basic loss of control and by tolerance, craving, withdrawal, and relapse. Addiction begins as voluntary drug use for no clear medical indication, but then becomes involuntary, resulting in substantial impairment of health and social functioning. This chapter reviews some explanations on addictive processes to understand addictive behavior in terms of its initial development, mechanisms, and basic characteristics. The phrase *addictive behavior* here is used in a broader range of compulsive behavior (e.g., psychoactive substances and gambling). The terms *addiction* and *dependence* are used interchangeably.

A Historical Perspective

The use of psychoactive substances dates back to the dawn of recorded history, and may well represent a basic, neurobiological process that has contributed to human evolution. Human beings consumed psychotropic plant substances as food in prehistory for millennia. The neurotransmitters (dopamine and serotonin) extracted from these substances were essential for normal human functioning. During most of our history, due to famines and seasonal food shortages, people experienced neurotransmitter deficits with considerable regularity. These neurotransmitters produced energy, prevented fatigue, increased tolerance for hunger, and stress. Archaeologists note that coca has been grown in the Andes since before Jesus was born. While much of the West associates coca with cocaine, many Bolivians chew it to alleviate altitude sickness, combat hunger pangs, or stay alert, a daily ritual much like drinking coffee in Western countries. The leaves contain nutrients and a necessary supplement to the diet. As history progressed, human beings developed the ability to purify psychoactive plant substances and use routes of administration that were more direct than ingestion. Drugs that can be injected into the bloodstream provide rapid delivery, which greatly increases their potential abuse, dependence, and harm. These developments have contributed to the propensity to overuse and abuse these substances in contemporary times (Davis and Cater, 2009).

Today's illegal drugs were patent medicines in the nineteenth century. Morphine and opium were freely available in both Europe and America; cocaine was the basis of remedies for the common cold; and amphetamines and cocaine have been used during World War II. They were used in other areas by the armed forces to sustain performance. Throughout the eighteenth century, opium was a common treatment for anxiety (Horwitz, 2013). In central Asia, marijuana has been grown for more than 10,000 years. It was used as remedies for such ailments as malaria and arthritis. In recent years, interest in the medical properties of marijuana has been revived all over the world. Studies show that it can help patients with certain medical conditions.

Historians note that drug commerce flourished in a world in which the hungry psyche was replacing the physical hunger (Kagan, 2007).[1] Increasing focus on pleasure and emotional gratification, as opposed to consumers' material needs, and the rise of bureaucratic institutions in Western societies led to increased demand for drugs (Kagan, 2007). Because most workdays are predictable, boredom is common, hence the demand for additional sources of arousal.

Consider the history of opium in China. Although the early history of opium is largely European, addiction appeared first in China. Opium smoking spread rapidly in China (giving rise to opium dens). What explains the emergence of opiate addiction in China? The historians speculate on the possibilities of societal, historical, and genetic factors. A key player was the spread of tobacco. The shift from oral self-administration to smoking played a critical role in the addiction epidemic. The lungs deliver opium's active components to the brain much more rapidly than does the stomach, thereby increasing its concentration at the sites of action. The societal factors include a surplus of wealth and available leisure time. Smoking opium takes up a good deal of time and required disposable income. Finally, many Chinese have a toxic reaction to alcohol. Alcohol makes them sick, and the cause is an inability to rapidly metabolize a poisonous metabolite of alcohol (acetaldehyde). Thus opium may have been more valued by the Chinese than other people because they did not have alcohol as alternative (Dikotter et al., 2004).

In sum, the historical perspective explains why the use of psychoactive drugs for nonmedical reasons is ordinary behavior in many parts of the world, despite the best efforts of governments to prevent, eliminate, or control it. Psychoactive drugs act on the brain pleasure center, which has evolved to respond to reward and punishment. Thus even though the environment has changed markedly, the human brain and its mechanisms are largely unchanged. That is, humans are vulnerable to addiction (Miller, 2013).

What Is Addiction?

Addiction is defined as compulsive drug use despite negative consequences (Koob, 2003). The dictionary definition of addiction identifies it as a "state of being given up to some habit" (Newman, 1965). This definition asserts that an addiction is a habit that has gotten out of hand. Habit is at the core of all addictions and that addictions come in a variety of strengths.

Similarly, economic theory views addiction as a type of habit formation. Becker (1992) defines addiction simply as a strong habit. Habit formation refers to a situation in which consuming a particular substance increases one's preference for it. The higher the "habit stock," or the extent of past consumption, the higher the marginal utility (pleasure) will be of consuming the substance. Within the category of habit formation, a distinction is often made between negative and positive habits. Negative habits, such as harmful addiction, arise when the habit stock has a negative impact on overall health and happiness. Positive habit formation refers to situations in which enhanced liking of certain goods and activities—such as good music, fine wine, reading, and so on—is thought to enhance overall happiness.

The majority of the biomedical community considers addiction as a brain disease similar to other chronic, relapsing conditions, such as heart disease and diabetes, and addictive behaviors are the result of genetic, biological, psychosocial, and environmental interactions (Erickson, 2007). The conceptualization of addiction as a chronic disease implies that addiction doesn't stop with one episode of treatment. It is like the treatment of other chronic diseases, such as asthma, diabetes, or hypertension. A disease model of addiction holds that the development of addiction is not the addict's responsibility. However, this view doesn't absolve addicts from their responsibility for their own recovery. In the same vein, patients diagnosed by heart disease are expected to be responsible for their recovery by following health lifestyles, and so on. The disease model is a compassionate alternative designed to encourage and address addiction as a health problem rather than a moral failure. The disease model also paved the way for third-party reimbursement and increased its accessibility to those in need. The following sections detail important features of addiction:

Rewards

There are two kinds of rewards from addictions (Elster, 1999b). The primary effects are pleasure or euphoria. At first, the drug experience is extremely great. Addicts report that they are swept away by feelings of connectedness, tranquility, and competence. But as drug consumption continues, the ecstasy fades and is replaced by withdrawal symptoms, health problems, career problems, and financial problems. Unfortunately, these negative effects linger much longer after the intensely pleasurable sensations are over.

The secondary reward is the need to escape reality. Avoiding pain is a strong motivation. In these cases, what is craved is not a positive experience of euphoria, but rather an escape from a miserable existence (e.g., self-doubt and feelings of unworthiness, an unhealthy relationship, responsibility, or memories). For instance, addicts have the desire to cover their shame by using the drug that would erase the emotional, deep nagging ache of their inadequacy. When they are high, their fears of inadequacy and unworthiness fade away. Users often report a sudden dissociation from self. For example, alcohol and heroin are often sought for their numbing effect. Cravings for cigarettes amount to a desire for order and control, not for nicotine. It serves as organizing function to achieve a feeling that one is in charge of events.

Tolerance

The term tolerance is a physiological process in which repeated consumption of a drug over time elicits a progressively diminishing effect and the person requires greater amounts of the drug to achieve the same levels of satisfaction. With repeated usage, the body (in particular the liver) develops an increased capacity to destroy the drug (known as metabolic tolerance).

Tolerance makes life difficult, especially for heroin and cocaine addicts, because as their dosage escalates, expenses for the drug become ever more difficult to afford. Ordinary legitimate sources of income soon prove insufficient for all but the wealthiest addicts; then robbery, burglary, theft, embezzlement, other property crimes, and prostitution are seen as practical ways to obtain the necessary drugs. The question, then, becomes if an addict get into trouble because of the dosage escalation, why don't they just stop using the drug and let the tolerance (which is fully reversible) dissipate? This has to do with dependence.

Dependence and Withdrawal

Dependence and withdrawal are two sides of the same coin. Dependence develops during periods of drug intoxication and is revealed by withdrawal symptoms in periods of during abstinence. Withdrawal symptoms reflect organ or mood responses that are opposite to those caused by the drug in question. That is, withdrawal reactions reflect the compensatory biological changes that were induced by extended use. For example, the classic withdrawal symptom with sedative drugs is insomnia. The acute effects of opiate include a sensation of warmth, muscular relaxation, constipation, elation, and sleepiness, whereas the withdrawal symptoms include chills, spasms, diarrhea, and restlessness. Nicotine withdrawal symptoms include depressed mood, poor concentration, restlessness, increased appetite, and irritability. Nicotine, like other drugs that stimulate a serotonin release in the brain, reduces appetite, and in some cases decreases the consumption of sweet tasting foods.[2] Similarly, for alcohol, withdrawal can cause a fatal seizure. The seemingly magical ability of an addictive drug to relieve its own withdrawal syndrome makes it hard for addicts to abstain; they know that drug will bring immediate relief. An early-morning headache is the first sign of caffeine withdrawal, and caffeine addicts know how to cure it with that first morning cup of coffee.

There are two types of withdrawal (Elster, 2001). As aforementioned, primary withdrawal reflects somatic symptoms. Secondary withdrawal reflects the awareness that one is ruining one's life and perhaps that of others; this awareness may be so intensely unpleasant and induce so much guilt or shame that one craves for relief. For example, overwhelmed by shame and panic in reaction to having overeaten, a person with an eating disorder lessens the shameful and panicky feelings by purging or excessive exercising and jogging. However, unlike bingeing, which produces an antidepressive effect, purging relieves shame (Ulman and Paul, 2006).

Craving

Accompanying every withdrawal syndrome is an intense craving for the drug that was withdrawn. Craving is produced by prolonged drug use, and it is an all-consuming sensation.[3] Craving is an overwhelming emotional experience that takes over your body. It consumes you and produces a unique motivator of behavior. When addicts are craving, they are experiencing emotional behavior of wanting and seeking drugs. Craving leads to preference reversal. People who have decided to stop drinking may change their minds when offered a drink. Wise (1988) describes craving as the memory of the positively rewarding effects of drugs. The addicted brain has an excellent memory for the drugs it has learned to love. For every addict, the memory is formed in the first hit. This explains why craving may occur even years after the last drug dose.

Craving is triggered by cues, belief (perceived availability), cost, priming, and stress. Cravings may be produced by exposure to a setting in which drugs have been consumed. Addicts may drink because the sight of a bottle elicits a craving great enough to overcome their other motives.

The perceived opportunity to use drugs is important for craving to occur in response to drug-related cues. For example, presenting smoking-related cues to smokers generally increases their craving for a cigarette. However, this effect is eliminated or at least blunted when smokers believe that they will be unable to smoke in the near future. In one study, smokers experienced greater cigarette craving when they believed that there was either a 50% or a 100% chance that they were about to have the opportunity to take a puff on a cigarette than when they believed that there was no chance that they could do so (Carter and Tiffany, 2001). Similarly, when the smoker is placed in a context in which the substance is not available (during a nine-hour flight) the craving will lessen, but the craving will intensify at the airport where there is an opportunity to smoke. Takuya and colleagues (2013) used imaging technology in a study of smokers to learn how anticipation influences brain activity. The MRI scans showed that areas of the brain involved in arousal and attention were essentially shut down in those who did not expect to smoke. Apparently, when the brain knows that a reward will not be forthcoming, it shifts its attention elsewhere. This suggests that cue-induced craving is mediated by beliefs (cognitive cues) about the availability of substances (Field and Cox, 2008).

Cost can alter craving response. Skog (2003) showed that when the Swedish state-owned monopoly stores for alcoholic beverages switched to self-service, purchases increased substantially. This is equivalent to a reduction in time cost.

Animal and human experiment reveals a "priming effect" of a drug to which a subject was previously addicted. This means that a small dose of the drug, administered to an abstinent ex-addict, can immediately initiate self-administration behavior (as the Lays Potato ad claims: "You Can't Eat Just One!"). This is the very phenomenon that AA warns of, that abstinent alcoholics can't resume occasional drinking without losing control.

Finally, stress can play a pernicious role in triggering cravings. Daily stress can cripple the prefrontal cortex, the brain's executive center, which takes care of functions such as concentration, planning, and judgment.[4] As a result, addicts lose the ability to be reflective (regulate behavior), and impulses take a stronger hold over their behaviors (Marlatt and Donovan, 2005).

One important skill in coping with cravings is the use metacognitive a process (think about thinking) that teaches addicts how to mentally take a step back from their experience and engage in a mindful process that explores their experience (Marlatt and Donovan, 2005). The technique known as SOBER breathing space, which stands for Stop, Observe your feeling, Recognize the feelings, focus on your Breathing, Expand your awareness of the consequences, and Respond mindfully. This metacognitive strategy provides a mental space between the cue and the urge or cravings. Viktor E. Frankl (2006, p. 95) famously captures this agonizing human experience: "Between stimulus and response there is a space. In that space is our power to choose our response. In our response lie our growth and our freedom."

Relapse

Relapse is the single most important issue in addiction (Koob and Le Moal, 2005). Relapse is, of course, always preceded by a decision to use. Even after prolonged abstinence, a former addict may mindlessly revert to drug use. Cue-induced craving is one of the most frequent causes of relapses, even after long periods of abstinence, independent of whether drugs are available (e.g., seeing someone using drugs on TV). Thus, for addicts, the trouble begins once they decide to give up the addiction.

Relapse is frequently due to cue conditioning, and stress. The conditioned responses make the treatment of addictions a challenge. Addicts will frequently relapse after reentering an environment where they have previously taken drugs, even if they have just spent time in a rehabilitation program. The importance of environmental or contextual cues helps explain why reentry to one's community can be so difficult for addicts leaving the controlled environments of treatment or correctional settings and why aftercare is so essential to successful recovery. Recovering addicts have learned the hard way that spending a significant time with one's using buddies invites relapse. In fact, one of the major goals of drug addiction treatment is to teach addicts how to deal with the cravings caused by the inevitable exposure to these conditioned cues.

Most relapse in human addicts happens because of stress or frustrating situations (e.g., illness of a family member, the loss of a job, or simply being insulted by somebody at work) that could trigger a series of negative feelings about themselves. These sort of negative mood states are very frequently associated with a relapse to drugs.

The constant effort required to avoid cues, and to resist craving when it does occur, progressively undermines willpower, which may help to explain the dismal, long-term abstinence rates. Thus, long-term abstinence seems to require not only willpower, but also a successful implementation of strategies that substitute for willpower.

Successful quitting often requires a substantial investment in a change of environment and lifestyle because addiction "poisons" persons, places, and things associated with it in the sense of giving them the ability to induce craving. As Siegel (1982, p. 335) notes, "users will attempt to avoid all contact with cocaine, cocaine paraphernalia and cocaine users when attempting this self-initiated detoxification. Others engage in destruction of paraphernalia, and still others employ physical restraint by taking a vacation or even moving to another house or city." That's why AA talks about "people, places, and things." Avoid the people you used with, avoid the places you used, and avoid the things associated with use, like the pipe. For example, during the Vietnam War, thousands of American soldiers, especially toward the end, were addicted to heroin.[5] Of the 43% of American servicemen that had tried heroin, 20% of them qualified as addicts. However, only one in eight of the addicts continued with his addiction after returning to the United States, and by two and three years after their return, the addiction rates among those who had served were no higher than among those who qualified for the draft, but did not serve in Vietnam (Robins et al., 1980). A plausible explanation is that veterans encountered fewer environmental triggers (familiar circumstances associated with drug use) upon returning to the United States.

Summary

In sum, the essential features of addiction are loss of control over consumption, obsessive thoughts about the drug, and continuation of use despite knowledge of negative health and social consequences. The decision of whether or not initiate treatment can be found in the American Psychological Association's (2013) *Diagnostic and Statistical Manual of Mental Disorders*, known as DSM 5. The DSM 5 advises treatment when three or more symptoms (out of seven) having been present during the last 12 months: 1) tolerance; 2) withdrawal; 3) often consuming more than was intended; 4) persistent desire or unsuccessful efforts to cut down; 5) spending a great deal of time with drug-related activities; 6) giving up important social, occupational, or recreational activities; 7) continuing consumption despite physical or psychological harm that the individual knows is caused by his abuse.

Learning What We Like

Animals and humans can be motivated by what they learn. For example, infants are not born craving money; as they grow up, children absorb the idea that money is valuable. This basic learning process is known as associative learning, or conditioning. It is the foundation on which most forms of learning are based.

Russian physiologist Ivan Petrovich Pavlov (1849–1936) was the first researcher to study the learning procedure called classical conditioning. He famously demonstrated that salivation can occur in anticipation of feeding, and that dogs can be trained to associate many external cues with the imminent appearance of food. The gut and brain are intimately linked and work together in digesting food. The senses convey information about the external environment to the brain. The central nervous system interprets this information within the constraints of experience, and then sends messages to the appropriate organs to begin the physiological processes. The anticipatory responses to cues improve the efficiency with which animals digest food. In fact, Pavlov demonstrated that when he bypassed the mouth and placed the food directly into stomach of dog, it was poorly digested. The physiological responses can be conditioned. This suggests that appetites or hunger can occur in anticipation of food being available. We can be trained to be hungry at certain times.[6]

Classical Conditioning

Pavolov's dogs learned to salivate at the sound of a bell because it was previously associated with food. That is, dogs become conditioned to salivate after the bell is rung. In the terminology of classical conditioning, the food is called an unconditioned stimulus (US) that reflexively elicits an unconditioned response (i.e., salivation). If a neutral stimulus (e.g., the sound of a bell) is repeatedly presented at the same time as the unconditioned stimulus (i.e., the food), the neutral stimulus by itself eventually elicits the same response (i.e., salivation). At that point, the neutral stimulus has become a conditioned stimulus (CS) that elicits a conditioned, or learned, response (Tiffany, 1999). In Pavlovian learning, the unconditioned response shifts in time from the unconditioned stimulus (food) to the conditioned stimulus (the sound of a bell). Thus, classical conditioning in the brain does not require motivation. It simply requires the pairing of two stimuli.

Addictive behaviors do have special characteristics related to the social contexts in which they originate. Environmental cues are paired in time with an individual's initial drug use experiences and, through classical conditioning, take on conditioned stimulus properties (e.g., the pairing of the rewarding effects of alcohol with the sight and smell of vodka). When those cues are present at a later time, they elicit anticipation of a drug experience and thus generate tremendous drug craving. However, if the cue and the drug use are decoupled after a while, "extinction" (or "unlearning") begins and the conditioned response does not occur anymore.

Operant Conditioning

Similar to classical conditioning is operant conditioning, which is closely related with the work of B.F. Skinner (1953), one of the leaders of behaviorism.[7] Operant conditioning starts with a behavioral response. If such behavior is followed by a rewarding experience, an individual learns to adjust her behavior to reproduce the rewarding experience, and as such, the shown response is more likely to occur in the future (e.g., a dog performs a trick to get a dog treat). In human beings, operant conditioning allows them to learn behavior leading to certain rewards (consequences). For example, after an individual learns that drug use is followed by a reduction in distress, that individual will be more likely to use drugs in the future. In the words of Thorndike (1911), reward makes you come back for more. In short, operant conditioning is a form of learning in which behavior is controlled by its consequences (reward or punishment). Those behaviors that produce satisfaction tend to increase in frequency (reinforcement) while those behaviors that result in frustration tend to decrease in frequency.

What Is Reinforcement?

The term reinforcement is a behavior that results in a desirable outcome such as access to food or water for a hungry or thirsty animal, which, in turn, increases the probability for that behavior to be repeated. In this case, the food is a reinforcer (reward) because it strengthens (reinforces) the probability that the behavior will be repeated. For example, you do A, and then you are rewarded. But if you do B, then you are punished. These consequences shape our behaviors. Animals learn patterns of behavior in order to obtain a reward. Reinforcement is simply the association between a stimulus and a response. The more immediate the reward following the behavior, the more successful and frequent that behavior becomes in similar situations. In other words, reinforcement is a behavior in which emotional feelings promote learning (Panksepp and Biven, 2012). It is not surprising to consider that many abused drugs are strong reinforcers as drug addicts will engage in a substantial amount of behavior to gain access to these strong rewards. However, if behavior no longer produces reward, it will eventually be discontinued. The idea of operant conditioning suggests that behavior modification requires the rearrangement of external incentives (LeDoux, 1996). For instance, one can readily reduce undesirable behaviors by paying people to avoid their bad habits, a procedure that is currently commonly used in treating addictive urges. Although there are subtle differences, for simplicity, I use the term reward rather than reinforcement throughout the text.

Extinction

Then how would an ex-addict eliminate conditioned craving? The answer is desensitiziation (extinction of the conditioned cues). That requires being exposed repeatedly to situations that were formerly associated with drug use, but without drugs being available. To desensitize, to break the conditioned association to that cue, means regularly and consistently getting into the car without smoking that particular cigarette. Regulations that establish smoke-free environments are very helpful to nicotine addicts and ex-addicts in reducing their consumption or maintaining their abstinence. According to George Vaillant (1995), one reason abstinence for opiates under parole supervision and abstinence from alcohol under AA supervision are more enduring than abstinence achieved during hospitalization or imprisonment is that the former experiences occur in the community. Thus, abstinence is achieved in the presence of many conditioned cues (community bars, other addicts, and so on).

Addictions as Bad Habits

Bad habits refer to those "habits" that people say they want to stop even while indulging in them (e.g., overeating, obsessive-compulsive disorder, dwelling on negative thoughts, episodic rage, chronic procrastination, destructive relationship, an abnormal desire to pull out one's hair, and "shopaholics"). Ainslie (2001) argues that bad habits and addiction do share similar characteristics, namely behaviors caused by pursuing immediate pleasure. When we do one of these things repeatedly, it has the feel of an addiction, whether or not it gets us into enough trouble to warrant being clinically diagnosed. We look forward with worry to the possibility that it will happen again, but once it's happened, we pursue the behavior vigorously and later on feel regret or guilt and wonder how to prevent it from happening again.

Strong habits produce addiction-like reactions and it forces the brain into autopilot, even in the face of strong negative consequences. Having been conditioned to do anything from an early age makes it extremely difficult to change. So unless we deliberately change a habit, the pattern will unfold automatically.

What Is a Habit?

The term habit refers to any behavior that involves a significant element of automaticity through associative learning. Habits are repeated responses that come to be cued by recurring features of contexts without any specific goal. For example, in a sample of college students, about 45% of the behaviors participants listed in their diaries tended to be repeated in the same physical location almost every day (Wood and Neal, 2007). Substantial amounts of repetition in stable contexts also have been documented with other naturalistic studies (e.g., everyday behaviors such as watching TV, purchasing fast food, driving a car, and recycling). These behaviors are performed without any explicit goal.

Habits can inform our goals. Given that habit formation typically originates in goal pursuit, we can infer our goals from our habitual behavior. Habits may blindly carry out the work of the goal that initially prompted people to develop the habit. For example, purchase of a particular newspaper each morning with coffee initially is guided by a goal (e.g., acquiring information). However, the goal becomes progressively less necessary as the newspaper purchase is repeated and becomes integrated with the morning coffee. Consider the role of habit in avoidant behavior. Someone with an avoidant behavior has developed internal working models early in childhood to hide feelings of any vulnerability (i.e., "stay away; don't connect"). Such a behavior is a defensive strategy to avoid the pain of a caregiver's rejection to satisfy attachment needs as much as possible. However, once the behavior is established, the pattern continues habitually. That is, the avoidant individual may avoid intimacy because of the anxiety it elicits.

How Are New Habits Formed?

Human behavior can be considered along a continuum. At one end of that continuum are behaviors that require effort and deliberation. These deliberate actions can become habitual if done repeatedly. At the opposite are those behaviors that can be done automatically without effort and awareness. This automaticity can allow our bad habits to gradually come back. You see a plate of cookies, and you automatically reach for it without thinking. Many people know well the feeling of having worked hard to change their bad diet habit only to have it come back again.

Habits emerge because the brain is constantly looking for ways to save effort. This allows us to stop thinking constantly about basic behavior, such as choosing what to eat or wear. Habit formation is essentially an outsourcing of decision making to environmental cues and context that can activate automatically the response. For example, buckling a seatbelt is activated by a context of getting into a car. When habits emerge, the brain stops fully participating in decision making.

The process by which the brain converts a sequence of actions into an automatic routine is called "chunking"[8] or packaged movements (Duhigg, 2012). We rely on several of these behavioral chunks every day, such as getting dressed or making breakfast in the morning. The process involves three steps. First, there is a cue that tells the brain to go into automatic mode. Second, there is the routine, which can be physical or emotional. Third, there is a reward, which helps our brain figure out if this routine is worth remembering. Reward can range from food or drugs that provide pleasure. As we associate cues with certain rewards, a subconscious motivation (craving) emerges which pushes us toward the cue (e.g., the smell of Cinnabon).

How Do We Create a New Habit?

A golden rule for habit change is to keep the old cue and the reward, but to insert a new routine. For example, if you want to establish a habit of daily exercise, then you need to place your exercise outfits (visual cues) the night before in a visible place, and reward yourself after the workout. By doing this regularly each day, the brain develops a chunking pattern.

An alcoholic usually can't quit unless he finds some activity to replace drinking when his craving for a drink is triggered. Alcoholics crave a drink because it offers rewards, such as escape, relaxation, and companionship. The Alcoholic Anonymous (AA), for example, provides a system of meeting and companionship for the attendees who need escape and distraction instead of drinking. And once they incorporate the new routine for coping with stress and anxiety into their lives, the behavior will become automatic. Furthermore, alcoholics need to believe that they can cope with the stress without alcohol. Belief is an important ingredient that makes a new habit permanent. The AA community can help an alcoholic believe that she can stay sober.

In sum, anyone struggling with bad habits can benefit by understanding habits' mechanisms, the cues, cravings, and rewards that drive the behavior, and then find ways to replace their self-destructive routines with healthier alternatives. However, to modify a habit, you must decide to change it and to exert willpower to overcome temptations.[9] These topics will be discussed in a later chapter.

The Biology of Addiction

It has been observed that drug addiction results from the interactions of the drug with the regions of the brain that are evolutionarily quite old. These regions, such as the limbic system, regulate an organism's response to rewards such as food, drink, sex, and social interaction. The consequence is virtually uncontrollable compulsive drug craving, seeking, and use. It is as if drugs have hijacked the brain's natural motivational systems, resulting in drug use becoming the top, motivational priority for the individual. These individuals may neglect nutrition and gainful employment while they devote excessive amounts of time to drug-seeking behavior and associated criminal activities (Nestler and Malenka, 2004; Hyman, 2005).

Neuroscientists commonly divide the brain into crude regions: the reptilian brain, the limbic brain, and the neocortex. The "reptilian brain" plays a central role in the regulation of basic survival behaviors (sustenance, shelter, safety, and sex). The limbic brain plays an essential role in the regulation of other emotions and in learning, also known as the visceral brain. The neocortex is the outer portion of our brain. The neocortex makes language, including speech and writing, possible. It renders logical and formal operational thinking possible and allows us to see ahead and plan for the future. The human cortex rides on lower brain functions like a man riding a horse (MacLean, 1990).

As shown below, if you picture the human brain as an onion, composed of layer upon layers of cells, then the outside layers are generally the most recent addition from the evolutionary perspective. Deeper inside the brain and closer to the brainstem are older, more primitive structures. In other words, the deeper you go, the farther back in time you travel.

The primitive structures of the brain are shared with countless species, but the size and scope of the human neocortex is unique. The human cortex is simply a lot bigger than that of other creatures.[10] For example, whereas human cocaine users experience cycles of bingeing and abstention (Gawin, 1991), rats allowed to self-administer cocaine, ignore hunger, reproductive urges, and all other drives, consuming the drug until they die.

Neural Plasticity

A neuron is one of the smallest, but most significant, parts of the brain. Neuron connections create the neural networks that form the biological basis of brain activity. The three-pound brain has about one hundred billion neurons, each one can make contact with thousands, even tens of thousands, of other neurons, resulting in about 10^{14} (15 zeros) different connections. These contacts, or synapses, are the means by which neurons communicate with one another. The ability of nerve cells to change the strength and even the number of synapses is the mechanism underlying learning and long-term memory.

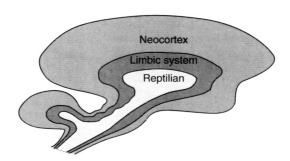

FIGURE 3.1 The Triune Brain.

Neural plasticity refers to the change in brain development due to environmental stimuli. Our brain has the ability to grow new synaptic connections as a result of experience. Research suggests that as you create new habits of thought, you fundamentally rewire your brain (LeDoux, 2002). The more you repeat something (action or thought) the more brain space is dedicated to it. For example, in musicians, the part of the brain that controls fingers used to play an instrument is up to 130% larger than that section in the rest of us. That is, just as biology shapes behavior, so behavior can shape biology. Thus, if you remember anything from this book, it will be because your brain is slightly different after you have finished the reading.

The idea of plasticity suggests that the brain is not marble, rather it is clay, and our clay never hardens. Even identical twins with identical genes have different brains because of their different life experiences. In short, the concept of neural plasticity ensures that we are never done with our changes, each day start with a new brain. We are not imprisoned by genetics. Each of us is free, for the most part, to live as we choose to, blessed and burdened by our elastic nature.

Reward System

The brain reward system (pleasure center) is the home of preferences. It is a motivational system in our brain causing us to seek pleasure and avoid pain. Seeking pleasure and avoiding pain is important for survival. The rewarding system helps energize our cognitive system and motivate us to do things, such as reading this book and learning from it. At its best, the system promotes growth-enhancing engagements with the world.

Dopamine is the main neurotransmitter used in the brain reward system, the neurotransmitter that promotes reward-seeking behavior and drug abuse. Neurotransmitters are chemicals that carry information from one neuron to another across synapses. Neurons that use dopamine as a neurotransmitter to communicate information are called dopaminergic neurons. Normal levels of dopamine are important for normal motivation (Wise, 2004). The lack of dopamine in the brain prevents individuals from being responsive to external stimuli. Dopamine is responsible for making us feel satisfied after a filling meal, happy when our favorite sport team wins. Individuals with a sweet tooth will be amused to learn that chocolate causes the greatest dopamine surges! The same goes for sex, fatty foods, and monetary reward. The feeling of pleasure and satisfaction leads to self-initiated repetition of the stimulation. The sensory cues and actions that precede and occur with those pleasurable experiences will be remembered.

Drugs of abuse (e.g., cocaine or amphetamines) are addictive because they directly enhance the effects of dopamine providing pleasurable experience. Drugs that block the action of dopamine also decrease drug self-administration. Depressive feelings emerge when the dopamine system is underactive, for instance, during withdrawal from addiction. In fact, the dysphoria experience during the withdrawal of addictive drugs is a state similar to depression. In short, the reward center is where all drugs of abuse, directly or indirectly, have their effect. So, this rewarding system needs to be trained well in order to reduce human tragedies.

The reward system did not evolve to facilitate the effects of drugs, but to provide stimuli essential for survival (e.g., foods, water, sex, and safety) with psychological reward properties (Koob and Le Moal, 2005). However, drugs activate the pathways artificially, and after repeated consumption of drugs, the system loses sensitivity to more natural rewards. So, over time, drugs disrupt the reward system and trick the brain into acting as if the drugs were necessary for survival. The physical changes (neural plasticity) in the brain could explain why, for example, some smokers will still crave a cigarette 30 years after quitting.

With most substances of abuse, rapid delivery of the drug to the brain is critical. The faster the absorption, the more intense is the high. The same amount of stimulants can have very different effects depending on which method is used. The fastest and most effective method is through injection in the blood stream, where the maximal effect is obtained after a few minutes. Once a dose crosses the blood-brain barrier, it interacts predominantly with the pleasure center. For example, nicotine, when administered through cigarettes or smokeless tobacco, is highly addicting. Yet, nicotine patches and gum are so unappealing that many State programs give them away. Coca leaf chewing (a traditional practice in the Andes Mountains of Peru and Bolivia) is not the same as crack smoking. Similarly, drinking on an empty stomach produces more immediate effects than drinking immediately after a large meal, as the meal will delay the absorption of alcohol.

The study of reward systems was first undertaken in the 1950s by Olds and Milner at McGill University in Canada. These two scientists did a very crucial and famous experiment. They wanted to know whether there were areas of the brain that would respond positively to electrical stimulation and would feel good when stimulated. So they put electrodes in the brains of rats. There were levers for the rats to press that would let them stimulate themselves. These scientists demonstrated that rats learn to return to locations where they have received direct electrical stimulation to the midbrain. When provided with opportunities to self-administer by pressing a lever, the rats rapidly became addicted, giving themselves approximately 5,000–10,000 "hits" during each one hour daily session, ignoring food, water, and opportunities to mate. These rats were willing to endure painful electric shocks to reach the lever (Gardner and David, 1999). These rats represented a replica of the ruined lives of human drug addicts. This led to the postulation by Olds (1956) of "pleasure centers."

In sum, addictive drugs hijack the brain's reward systems normally involved in pleasure and learning (Wise, 1980, 1989). The "hijacked" view of addiction implies that the brain is the innocent victim of certain substances that come from outside and take control over the brain's normal responses. The neurochemicals produced by the substances such as alcohol, nicotine, or certain foods overpower and take control of (hijack) it.

Can people learn to release dopamine? The number of things people do to increase their dopamine firing rates is unlimited. Imagine that you've just finished a great term paper and received a good grade. And you feel a certain amount of pride and reward and you get a certain amount of dopamine for that. The pleasure one gets when a business person has released a new product and it just catches on like wildfire and his stock just soars. In short, novelty, money, cocaine, a delicious meal, and a beautiful face all activate the dopamine system to varying degrees. Exactly how much dopamine an individual generates in response to a particular reward is determined by past experience and by one's own biological makeup.

Can pain be the source of satisfaction (as the saying goes "It hurts so good")? Relief or the removal of pain is pleasure. Our brains produce endorphins, a kind of internal morphine, that suppress pain. Stressful pain in humans can activate our endogenous opioid system. In the "runner's high," running elicits a flood of endorphins (the body's home-brewed opiates) in the brain. The endorphins are associated with mood changes, and the more endorphins a runner's body pumps out, the greater the effect. It could also occur with most intense endurance exercise.

Why can the anticipation of drug use be more pleasant than the actual use? Before humans (and animals) are able to consume rewards, they must anticipate the rewards. Animal studies find that dopamine is released during presentations of cues predictive of drug, food, and alcohol use (Goldstein, 2001). The dopamine system can anticipate, in a sense, the actual drug delivery (a priming effect). This anticipatory release of dopamine is not seen without a history of drug use. Conditioned stimuli or cues (e.g., the process of opening a pack of cigarettes) that have been associated with a particular drug, when presented in the absence of the drug, elicit compensatory reactions (the release of dopamine). Thus, the anticipatory release of dopamine explains why addict feels "high" on the way to buy drugs. The anticipation may be more pleasant than the actual consumption.

Conditioned salivation in anticipation can be helpful in digesting the substance/food. When a cue predicts food, we will start generating an appetite at the moment that it will maximize the reward for eating. Therefore, gastric activity might be considered to reflect a preparation response for food. Thus, the interaction between brain and gut begins before food is ingested. The sight, smell, or even just anticipation of food triggers physiological cascades that prepare the gut to receive and digest food and other organs to metabolize the absorbed nutrients. For addiction, physiological reactions serve as a compensatory role for diminishing the effect of the drug intake (Siegel, 1989). The anticipatory release of dopamine may actually be something that's associated with vulnerability to relapse. In other words, a cue in the environment could, particularly if one is in a negative mood, produce a craving that might lead to relapse.

Adaptive Brain

There are two major sources of motivation with drug addiction (Koob and Le Moal, 2005). There is the pleasure that the person becomes hooked in the first place, but after a while, the brain system has become so compromised (the neuroplasticity) that one is taking the drug to return to a normal state. The biological imbalance of the brain, as a single dose wears off, could produce just enough discomfort to motivate the user to repeat the dose. In this view, the essence of drug addiction is that an addict has created an artificial, but negative, state. In effect, an addict is not trying to get some extra pleasure, but just trying to feel normal or avoid feeling worse (Goldstein, 2001).

According to the concept of *opponent process*, the brain system contains mutually opponent processes (e.g., processes that limit the reward value of drugs) (McGilchrist, 2009). That is, one process tends to directly dampen the effects of another process that precedes and triggers it for stabilization of emotional states. In the case of addiction, this concept is defined by two processes (Solomon, 1980): arbitrarily termed as the *a-process* and the *b-process* (reward and anti-reward system). The *a-process* includes euphoria or positive reinforcement. The *b-process* appears after the a-process to neutralize the drug's effects. In other words, initially drug use disturbs individual's natural balance (i.e., homeostasis[11]) in a positive direction (*a-process*), and eventually the *b-process*, the opponent process, is enacted to restore homeostasis. For instance, the positive affect of certain addictive drugs is internally counteracted by the build-up of negative affective feelings inside the brain, which leads to the distress of drug withdrawal. The difference in magnitude between *a-* and *b-processes* determines whether the user experiences a pleasurable state or a dysphoric state.

The initial use is normally pleasant, which reinforces further use. However, with repeated use and growing tolerance, the *b-process* begins to dominate the *a-process*. Eventually, abstinence is the only means by which *a-* and *b-processes* can be restored to baseline levels. However, chronic drug use moves the homeostasis reward set point from its natural position. That is, eventually, the opponent process fails to bring the user back to a normal homeostatic range. This normal homeostatic process eventually fails as individuals move to the compulsive drug use or addiction. The resulting adaptation is metaphorically termed as the "dark side of addiction" (Koob and Le Moal, 2005).[12] Furthermore, excessive drug taking activates the brain's stress system and this activation is manifested during abstinence, producing anxiety and irritation (Koob and Kreek, 2007). This negative emotional state makes ex-addicts vulnerable to stress and drug cues.

Thus, addictions are sustained not only by positive feelings, but also by the potential for strong negative feelings that build up internally. The positive reinforcement may be more important in the earlier stages of addiction, and negative reinforcement could become important for maintaining drug-seeking behavior in longstanding addicts who claim that they no longer feel any euphoric response to their drugs. That is, excessive drug use leads to the deficit in the reward system, which becomes the main motivation to seek more drugs. To obtain a psychoactive effect again, the dose has to be raised to override the adaptation.

For example, in "cold turkey" (the process of suddenly stopping any use of drug), if all the drugs were suddenly removed faster than the brain can adapt, the abrupt unmasking of the adaptation is manifested as a withdrawal syndrome.

Withdrawal from a stimulant like cocaine and amphetamines causes depression or anhedonia (absence of pleasure) because of dopamine depletion due to repeated overstimulation (Kassel et al., 2009). The loss of dopamine has negative consequences on one's ability to experience pleasure, which motivates one to use the drug to replenish dopamine.

Sensitization

Sensitization is the opposite of tolerance (or habituation).[13] Sensitization refers to an increase in responsiveness after repeated stimulation, whereas habituation refers to a decrease in responsiveness after repeated stimulation. The dopamine system reacts more strongly than normal if the drug is taken again.[14] Sensitization occurs when drug effects become enhanced. That is, the brain system can be triggered into abnormally high levels of activation by drugs or related stimuli. As a result, addicts actually become more sensitive to the drug and they have a bigger response to a smaller dose than they did at first.

Sensitization appears to involve structural changes in the brain, both in the neurotransmitter systems, and in the neurons themselves. Consequently, dopamine levels are raised, and certain cues have a far greater impact than they would otherwise. Neural sensitization can last for years. The long-lasting nature of neural sensitization may help explain why recovered addicts, who have been drug free for months or years, are still sometimes likely to relapse back into addiction. Addicts who relapse and take even a small dose of drugs after a period of abstinence will get a pleasure rush that is much stronger than that felt by a first-time user because of the drug sensitization.

Animals sensitized to one substance often show cross-sensitization to a different drug or substance. Animals sensitized to one drug may show increased intake of a different drug. In other words, one drug acts as a "gateway" to another. In the addiction literature, a "gateway effect" occurs when the use of one drug leads to taking another. For example, nicotine acts as a gateway to cocaine. Animals sensitized to nicotine consume more alcohol compared with nonsensitized animals. Sensitization is the reason why many clinicians require complete drug abstention as a condition of treatment for addicts[15] (Wise, 1988).

In sum, repeated use of stimulants sensitizes certain aspects of the reward system so that a small amount of the drug or even an environmental cue previously associated with the drug can precipitate renewed drug use. As explained below, sensitization explains why addicts often report that they "want" the drug, which is beyond "liking" the drug.

The Pleasure Gap: "Wanting" vs. "Liking"

Desire is rational as long as people choose what they expect to like. A truly irrational choice would be to choose what you expect not to like. Usually, for pleasant incentives, liking and wanting do go together, virtually as two sides of the same coin. This suggests that in everyday life, if activities you pursue do not, on reflection, bring you pleasure, it is time to reconsider your desire. The human brain appears to contain a separate hedonic system that is responsible for producing sensations of "well-being." The two subcomponents, liking (pleasure) and wanting (desire), are partly separate brain pathways. The experience of pleasure "liking" is separable from "wanting," mediated by separate brain systems. Addiction can be characterized by strong desire or wanting over liking. Addicts often express that they continue to use substances even when they no longer derive any pleasure. For example, some cigarette smokers express a deep hatred of smoking, but they continue to smoke regularly. Research shows that after long periods of drug use, wanting dominates motivation for drug use, and addicts no longer derive much pleasure from their drug of choice (Berridge, 2004).

The neuroscience literature pioneered by Berridge and Robinson (2003) draws a distinction between the "liking" system responsible for the feeling of pleasure and pain, and the "wanting" system responsible for the motivation or incentive to seek pleasure and avoid pain. Wanting and liking are mediated by two, distinct brain systems. Liking, under control of opioids, deals with the immediate appraisal of food items and has been shown to be active when subjects (rats) are more or less sated. Wanting is mediated by brain dopamine systems, which do not need to be consciously experienced in order to control behavior. Transient, irrational wanting comes and goes with the cues. For example, the sight of food may create a powerful impulse to eat, while an odor may create a powerful impulse to seek food.

The liking reflects consumption gratification and wanting represents appetitive behavior. The liking effects include feelings of pleasure and affective facial reactions during the pleasurable state. For example, mice constantly lick their lips when given sweet-tasting foods. Just like infants, bad-tasting food will lead them to shake their head, and frantically wipe their mouths. The wanting effects include the desire and urge to obtain the drug, such as the feeling of craving (related to the action of seeking, obtaining, and consuming the drug). The wanting system is triggered when stimuli in the environment are attention grabbing, and we have an urge to reach out and grab it.

This distinction is critical to understanding why repeated exposure to drugs leads to mistaken usage. If a person's brain dopamine systems were highly activated, and the person encountered a reward cue, it seems possible that the person might irrationally want the cued reward even if the person cognitively would not like it very much. An irrational, cue-triggered want may even surprise the person who has it by its power, suddenness, and autonomy.

Cues could trigger irrational wanting in an addict whose brain was sensitized even longer after withdrawal was over (because sensitization last longer). This explains why addictive relapse is so often precipitated by encounters with drug cues, or even the mere contemplation, which triggers wanting drugs. The wanting system not only creates a strong (and misleading) impulse to seek and use the substance, but also undermines the potential for cognitive override. Cognitive override still occurs, but in a limited range of circumstances. For example, recovering addicts may pay too much attention to drugs, activate and maintain thoughts about the drug too easily, and retain particularly vivid memories of the high.

In sum, the pleasure gap leads to joyless addiction (like a dog chasing a car).[16] Intense wanting for addictive substances is not necessarily accompanied by enjoyment of their consumption. Goldstein (2001, p. 249) captures this phenomenon: "the addict had been suddenly overwhelmed by an irresistible craving, and he had rushed out of his house to find some heroin . . . it was as though he were driven by some external force he was powerless to resist, even though he knew while it was happening that it was a disastrous course of action for him." This example illustrates that, for addicts, the choice of drug use is driven by wanting, rendering addiction as irrational choice. Thus, even after the drug no longer brings pleasure, an addict can still feel a strong urge to use. An effective treatment requires uniting the wanting and liking mechanisms (Kringelbach and Berridge, 2010).

Reward Prediction Error

There is now consensus among scientists that the dopamine system is constantly making predictions about what to expect in terms of rewards. The dopamine neurons are more concerned with predicting rewards than actually receiving them. Thus, under normal conditions, dopamine is only involved in the process of pursuing a reward, not in the enjoyment of it. But this process can be distorted by the use of drugs such as heroin, cocaine, and amphetamine. When dopamine continues to be released beyond the normal period, the brain is thrown into a perpetual state of "wanting," which is the essence of addiction.

Animal studies show that the release of dopamine signals the brain to expect a reward. Wolfram Schultz (2006) tracked dopamine production in a monkey's midbrain using squirts of apple juice that the animal liked. He found that when the monkey got more juice than it expected, dopamine neurons fired vigorously. When the monkey got an amount of juice that it expected to get, based on previous squirts, dopamine neurons did nothing. And when the monkey expected to get juice but got none, the dopamine neurons decreased their firing rate, as if to signal a lack of reward. The monkey felt upset because the prediction of juice was wrong. In other words, if the monkey's expectation was not met, the dopamine cells instantly sent out a signal announcing their mistake and stopped releasing dopamine.

In humans, the dopamine signal is also sent to a higher brain region (the frontal cortex) for more elaborate processing. When a person gets an unexpected reward, the equivalent of a huge shot of delicious apple juice, more dopamine reaches the frontal cortex. When a person expects a reward and does not get it, less dopamine reaches the region. And when a person expects a reward and gets it, the brain is silent. That is, the prediction error is the difference between what is expected to happen and what actually happens (dopamine neuron response = reward occurred − reward prediction).

Suppose you're at a vending machine and you put in a dollar. But instead of one candy, as you would expect, you receive two candies. You think, "this is better than I expected." As a result, your dopamine response goes up. If you put a dollar into the machine but don't receive any, your dopamine goes down ("worse than I expected"). On the other hand, if you put a dollar into the machine and receive one candy, as expected, there is no change in the dopamine. In fact, if you do not receive an expected reward, the experience feels more like a punishment. In short, an increase in the level of dopamine signifies "better than expected" and a decrease signifies "less than expected." Unpredictable rewards produce much larger reward signals than anticipated ones.[17] Your reaction to situations that are either better or worse than expected is generally stronger to those you can predict. For example, part of the appeal of live sporting events is their inherent unpredictability. Watching a surprise win in a game, thousands of spectators simultaneously experience a huge surge of dopamine. People keep coming back, as if addicted to the euphoria of experiencing unexpected rewards.

Learning From Mistakes

Learning takes place only when something unexpected happens. Nothing focuses the mind like surprise. When nothing unexpected happens, as when the same amount of delicious apple juice keeps coming, the dopamine system is quiet. When the learned rule is violated, the dopamine neuron responds, signaling a reward prediction error. The reward system gets the message that old rules don't apply anymore and it may be time to learn a new association. Every time a learning event occurs, the value that humans or animals attach to different actions is updated (the belief formation). People learn from their mistakes, and the lesson is committed to the memory. In general, how much we learn in life depends on how big the difference is between what we expected and what actually happened. We only learn by making mistakes!

People with a genetic mutation that reduces the number of dopamine receptors involved in the detection of errors are less likely to learn from negative reinforcement. For example, these people are significantly more likely to become addicted to drugs and alcohol. Because they have difficulty learning from their mistakes, they make the same mistakes over and over. They can't adjust their behavior when it proves self-destructive. In short, when the dopamine system breaks down completely and neurons are unable to revise their expectation in light of reality (like the monkey), mental illness can result. For addicts, their emotions are uncoupled from the events of real world.

Novelty-Seeking Behavior

The need for novelty is innate to human beings.[18] A novel event can be almost anything—seeing a painting for the first time, learning a new word, having a pleasant, or unpleasant, experience. The key factor is surprise. For example, although one may thoroughly enjoy a particular conversation, the same conversation a second time around would be dull. New activities are exciting at first, but then become boring; watching TV is fun, but then gets tiring; after a few hours of reading, our eyes get tired, and so on. This is the curse of everything being new. For the new is inherently unapproachable. Individuals make choices based on the values of the outcomes, and, in turn, the choices alter the values of the outcomes.

There is a link between curiosity, or novelty seeking, and the reward system. Novelty seeking implies dissatisfaction with the status quo. Great achievements are also facilitated with dissatisfaction with status quo. Goldberg (2009) writes that the great globe-trotting Christopher Columbus would have never embarked on his great voyage had he not been temperamentally dysphoric and had Prozac been available in those days. The need for novelty has made us who we are—intelligent, curious, and constantly seeking for next thing. Curiosity increases with one's expertise in a particular domain. It derives from the "information gap"—the difference between what you know and what you want to know. Indeed, the value of information can be measured by the extent to which a piece of information reduces our uncertainty about the world. That is, information could be measured by the degree to which something was surprising. This implies the addictive quality of curiosity.

Balancing Novelty Seeking With Persistence

The brain regions in charge of processing a task when it is still novel are not the same as those in charge of processing the same task once it becomes familiar. Goldberg (2009) has shown the roles of the two hemispheres with respect to the novelty and routinization. The right hemisphere, associated with emotion, is dominant at early learning stages while the task is novel. The left hemisphere (analytical brain) is dominant at task routinization.[19] In the right combination with other traits, novelty-seeking behavior is a crucial predictor of well-being. Novelty-seeking is one of the traits that keeps people healthy and happy and fosters personality growth as we age (Cloninger, 2012). The combination of this adventurousness and curiosity with persistence provide the kind of creativity that benefits society as a whole. Persistence may sound like the opposite of novelty seeking, but the two traits can coexist and balance each other. People with persistence tend to be achievers because they'll keep working at something even when there's no immediate reward.

The Journey Is the Reward

In sum, the basic idea is that neurons release dopamine in proportion to the difference between the anticipated and realized rewards of a particular event. The purpose of the dopamine surge is to make the brain pay attention to new and potentially important stimuli.

The dopamine neurons are activated by new stimuli, however, if the presentation is repeated, they quiet down and discharge less and less frequently. Thus, it is not so much the absolute value of a reward that brain cells are concerned with, but its relative value. When the stimulus ceases to be novel, we become accustomed to it (habituation). The true reward is the journey itself. When our goal is achieved, we feel satisfaction, fulfillment, and pleasure—and those feelings then help us to learn and remember. The world is dull again until we find another subject to be excited about. Seeking out more novel experiences keeps dopamine pumping.

Conclusion

Addictive substances interfere with the normal operation of the reward system by acting directly on the process that leads the reward system to generate the anticipatory response. With the repeated use of a drug, cues associated with past consumption cause the reward system to forecast grossly exaggerated pleasure responses, creating a powerful (and disproportionate) impulse to use. The result is decision malfunction, which leads to mistakes in decision making. Subjectively, this effect manifests itself through intense wanting, or cravings. Loosely, drugs fool a subconscious, hard-wired brain process into anticipating an exaggerated level of pleasure. An addict can try to compensate for this effect by exercising cognitive control, but he can't consciously correct it. From the perspective of society as a whole, they have lost control over their drug use because, in effect, their lives have become completely centered on the drug experience. In other words, they don't do anything else—the whole focus of their lives is on getting and using drugs.

The release of dopamine contributes to the laying down of long-term memories and associations that remodel the connections in the brain and can last forever. This means that the brain has created a rewards system for something that is harmful to the body. We often think of treatment as quitting and staying quit. Most addicts would agree that the quitting part is easier than the staying quit. Thus, a heroin addict craving a fix years after kicking the habit is not simply weak-willed, but may be tormented by enduring changes in the brain caused by the drug itself. This means that addiction may be a form of "pathological learning." For example, evidence shows that tobacco smokers who suffered a stroke that damaged the insula (a region of the brain involved in emotional, gut-instinct perceptions) no longer felt a desire for nicotine (Naqvi et al., 2007).

Notes

1 The CEO of Starbucks is quoted saying that "our mission is not to fill gut, but to fill the soul."
2 Hunger is a symptom of nicotine withdrawal and people may gain an average of 7.7 pounds from stopping smoking.
3 Buddhists consider craving to be one of the primary toxins of the mind. Unlike psychologists, who restrict the idea of craving to states produced by substance abuse, Buddhists use the term more generically to encompass the desire for attachment to objects and situations for oneself (Goleman, 2004).
4 As discussed in a later chapter, PFC is often called the brain "executive" because of its role in executive functions such as emotion regulation and impulse control.
5 As Robins et al. (1980) discuss, it is not very difficult to imagine why American soldiers found heroin attractive: their life was, like that of most soldiers during the war, a mix of boredom and terror. The supply found its market soon enough. (It was even said that the Vietnamese communists spread addiction deliberately to weaken the resolve and capacity of American soldiers.)
6 In 1904, Pavlov received the Nobel Prize in Physiology for his work on digestive responses. Interestingly, the prize was not for the learning studies that he is known for. He showed that the gut and the brain work in coordination to prepare organisms to digest food in anticipation of its being ingested. The consensus among physiologists at that time was that the central nervous system was not involved in the digestive system.
7 Throughout much of the first half of the twentieth century, behaviorists believed that the subjective inner states of mind (such as, feelings, thoughts, plans, desires, motivations, and values) were inaccessible to experimental science and unnecessary for a science of behavior.
8 For example, it is quite helpful to remember a phone number as "888–1616" instead of "8-8-8-1-6-1-6." Chunking helps to combine a sequence of information or actions into a single memory unit, such as driving a familiar route or brushing your teeth before going to bed.
9 Habitual consumption and excessive use of specific products are also encouraged by modern economics of concentration and social norms. We have become more rigid in our ability to switch to another product. The more we become dependent on a certain good, the more vulnerable we are.
10 In humans, for example, the neocortex accounts for about 33% of brain mass, compared with 17% of chimpanzees, and 3% for rats. These differences in brain structure are correlated with behavioral differences.
11 The term homeostasis refers to internal stability despite environmental change.
12 A similar phenomenon in obesity is the impairments in physiologic mechanisms regulating food intake and shifting the set point towards gaining weight and obesity.
13 The increasing irritation produced by exposure to a disliked roommate is a familiar example of sensitization. Similarly, multitaskers are sensitive to incoming information. For these individuals, the chime of incoming e-mail can override the goal of writing a term paper or having a conversation with their spouse.
14 For some foods, repeated exposure not only reduces initial subjective unpleasantness (adaptation), but later continues to increase subjective pleasantness (sensitization). For example, dry meat by military air crewmen.
15 Panksepp (2001) cautioned about children with attention-deficit/hyperactivity disorder who are routinely treated with dopamine-promoting psychostimulants. These

drugs may sensitize the brain chronically and make these kids vulnerable to addictive tendencies.
16 Dogs love to chase large game (e.g., deer, moose, elk). They do this because that was how they got their food—that was their evolutionary niche. Domestic dogs chase cars. It is pretty clear that if a dog ever caught a car, it would not be able to eat it. But they chase cars for the sake of the chase.
17 Gambling is designed to produce surprising rewards. The gambler is buying the prospect of a positive surprise. Evidence shows that in the financial market, when the Federal Reserve unexpectedly lowers interest rates, the market reacts more sharply than on those occasions when investors expect the action (Coates, 2012).
18 In the same vein, people use drugs because they are means of satisfying an inner desire to alter consciousness and awareness. This desire for altered consciousness explains the universality of drug use by human beings (Inciardi and McElrath, 2014).
19 Left-handedness tends to preferentially engage the right hemisphere, and vice versa. This reasoning supports the old claims that left-handed people tend to be creative, restless, and novelty-seeking individuals. They may also be incapable of implementing their own ideas, because task routinization is the domain of left brain.

4
DEFINITION AND FUNCTIONS OF EMOTIONS

Introduction

In the previous chapter, addiction was characterized as a complete absence of control when confronted with an object of desire. This characterization of addiction makes it important for studying the struggle between appetite (reason and desire) and emotion. The question is how emotions matter and how they influence individual actions.

Traditionally, emotion is considered harmful to decision making. When we act under the influence of emotions and strong feelings (anger, fear, craving), they may cause us to deviate from plans laid in a cooler moment and act impulsively against our own best judgment. However, many thinkers now suggest that emotions can be very helpful in making decision with little or no conscious deliberation.

This chapter provides a brief introduction to some basic concepts and mechanisms of emotions to provide an understanding on the nature and function of emotion. The purpose is to discuss such questions as, what are emotions, and why do we have emotions? What are the rules by which emotion operates? Are emotions beneficial, as essential to our rationality? The focus is on the role of emotions in information processing and decision making.

The Importance of Emotion

We organize our lives to maximize the experience of positive emotions and minimize the experience of negative emotions. Emotions determine the quality of our lives and are of interest to everyone. They set our priorities, make our lives meaningful, and communicate our intentions (Ben-Ze'ev, 2000). Emotions are motives that direct our attention by selecting what attracts and holds our attention. Without that sense, decision making and actions are derailed. A thorough understanding and exploration of any subject matter requires persistent motivation and curiosity. Without fascination and obsession, much of learning is unlikely to be above and beyond the ordinary.[1]

Emotions are also powerful forces influencing our behavior, such as alcoholism, drug addiction, suicide, and violence. Emotional emptiness is frequently mentioned as one of the reasons for depersonalization and suicide. Emotional disorders are the sources of psychosomatic diseases, such as hypertension.

World events continue to be shaped by inflamed passions that are directed toward destructive ends and often are not channeled where they are in fact necessary (e.g., global warming). Berthoz (2006) notes that we live in a century that discovered many technological inventions, such as powerful computers and informatics; this is evidence of the victory of reason over emotion. Yet, the influence of emotions is increasing rather than decreasing. Passion trumps reason, because reason has forgotten to make room for passion. Lobel and Loewenstein (2005) argue that our emotions systems evolved long before the Internet offered the possibility of instant shopping, gambling, etc. People are manipulated through increasingly sophisticated emotional triggers ("hot-button issues"), and emotion-inducing marketing techniques at the expense of rational deliberation. Thus, our understanding of our emotions contributes to our self-knowledge, our relationships with others, and the world around us.

Schore (2012) emphasizes the primacy of emotion. The highest human functions, such as stress regulation, humor, empathy, compassion, morality, insight, intuition, and creativity, are all produced by emotion. What would the world look like if the cognition (left brain) were to become so far dominant that it managed, more or less, to suppress the emotion (right brain)? This would result in a world characterized by increased bureaucratization, inability to see the big picture, valuing technology over human interaction, and a lack of respect for judgment and skill acquired through experience.

Nevertheless, we do not understand our emotions. We are prone to self-deception, suppression, and even denying our emotions. Solomon (2007) notes that we have to learn how to recognize our emotions, how to deal with them, how to use them, and this is a set of skills that most of us have picked up only casually, and thoughtlessly.

Our understanding and appreciation of our emotions is essential to our well-being. Spinoza once remarked that "[e]motion which is suffering, ceases to be suffering as soon as we form a clear and precise picture of it" (Damasio, 2003, p. 74). As a social being, we urgently need to understand other people and their motives. This means, to some extent, understanding their emotions (e.g., to answer the question: "Why did she do that?"). Thus, better understanding of emotions will improve our daily lives by showing how emotions influence the way we choose, and help us avoid or minimize conflict.

A Historical Perspective

Historically, emotions or "passions" have been viewed as a destructive force in human behavior[2] (Nussbaum, 2004). A traditional view, going back to Plato at least, sees a dichotomy between thought and feeling. Greeks believed emotions are far too heated and unpredictable to be much use to rational thought. It was advised that one should suppress or disregard emotions. That is, emotions are an obstacle to intelligent and rational judgment. Our angers, fears, and envies interfere with proper reasoning and lead to irrational behaviors. Plato remarked that passions and desires and fears make it impossible for us to think. For him, emotions were like wild horses that have to be reined in by the intellect. Emotion was also strongly associated with women, and therefore representative of the weak, inferior aspects of humanity.[3] The stereotype of women as the more "emotional" sex is one that persists today.

Emotions were essentially linked with desires, particularly self-interested, self-absorbed desire (Elster, 1999a). So the early Christian preoccupation with sin led to designate certain passions and desires as sin. Since they did not trust the power of reason to control emotions, they made a handful of problematic emotions central to the deadly sins (the commitment of which did make death something to fear): Pride, Envy, Anger, Sloth, Greed, Gluttony, and Lust. Although today, most people would consider pride to be a positive emotion. Some argue that it was the emotional state of hubris[4] to which ancient religious scriptures generally refer when condemning pride as a character flaw (Hart and Matsuba, 2007).

More recently, in the *Theory of Moral Sentiments*, Adam Smith viewed human behavior as a struggle between the "passions" and the "impartial spectator." The passions refer to immediate motivational forces and feeling states, such as hunger, thirst, anger, and sexual lust. The impartial spectator refers to the human ability to take a dispassionate view of one's own conduct. That is, to evaluate one's own behavior as if through the eyes of another person who is unaffected by the passions. Smith viewed the ability to assume the perspective of an impartial spectator as an important aspect of human behavior (Ashraf et al., 2005). The notion of the impartial spectator is quite similar to the mindful awareness (metacognition) practiced through meditation by Buddhist monks. It is the ability to stand outside of yourself and watch yourself in action.

These contrasting aspects of the mind (reason and emotion) reflect an outmoded adherence to a fundamentally moralistic worldview (reason as angelic, passion as beastly). This and the following chapters show that emotion corresponds to an aspect of human information processing. The thinking and emotional brains process information in their own unique fashion and represent conscious and unconscious systems. The cognitive brain is conscious, analytic, and the emotional brain is nonverbal and unconscious. Moreover, as discussed in the following chapter, there is a new consensus that emotions are necessary for proper reasoning and decision making (Damasio, 1994). For example, fear narrows and focuses our attention on what is important, rather than analyzing many irrelevant pieces of information.

What Is an Emotion?

At some level, we know what emotions are since we feel them, and don't need experts to tell us about them. We've all felt love and anger and fear. Descartes once said, "everyone has experience of the passions within himself, and there is no necessity to borrow one's observations from elsewhere in order to discover their nature" (Damasio, 2003, p. 67). But an emotion is a complex phenomenon to describe as discussed above.

Emotion is movement. The word *emotion* comes from a Latin word that means "to move" or "to stir up." Emotional behavior indicates an urge to act. One who is feeling lonely is motivated to seek company. The definition of "emotion" in the *Oxford American Dictionary and Language Guide* is: "any agitation or disturbance of mind, feeling or passion; any vehement or excited mental state." Likewise, the definition in *Webster New Collegiate Dictionary* is: "a psychic and physical reaction subjectively experienced as strong feeling and physiologically involving changes that prepare the body for immediate vigorous action." Thus, emotion can mean feelings of pain or pleasure. It is also described as "a physiological" departure from homeostasis that it is subjectively experienced as a strong feeling (such as love, hate, fear) and manifests itself in bodily changes that prepare us to an act that may or may not be performed.

Ancient Greek called it passion or mental events involving passivity. That is, the person feels the behaviors passively rather than making efforts to initiate her action. A passionate person is emotionally driven and she is insensitive to rewards. A passionate person feels that emotion automatically guides his behavior and thought without his initiative (Frijda, 2007). For example, an addict or one in love tends to do certain things even though the negative consequences make it advisable to stop.

An emotion has public aspects, expressed in our behavior, as well as private or unique aspects, for example, certain feelings. The public aspects of emotions are actions or movements, many of them visible to others as they occur in the face, in the voice, or in specific behaviors. Feelings, on the other hand, are always hidden, unseen to anyone other than their rightful owner (Damasio, 2003). Feelings are more psychological, defined as the subjective experience of emotion (Plutchik, 2003).

Emotions can be described on different levels, for example, physiological, psychological, and sociological. The physiological level, for instance, consists of neurotransmitters and autonomic and somatic activities of the nervous system associated with increased heart rate, respiration, and muscular tension. On the psychological level, an emotion consists of feeling, cognition, and motivation. For example, fear is associated with the feeling of dread, and the desire to avoid the peril. At the sociological level, emotions can result in mass mobilization for desirable ends, such as defeating Nazism, sending a man to the moon, or helping victims of natural disasters, such as the 2004 tsunami in the Indian Ocean. The discussion here focuses mostly on the psychological levels.

Features of Emotions

Most theories of emotions assume that emotional states consist of a set of components, such as facial expressions, physiological changes, cognitive appraisals, subjective affective experience, and action tendencies (e.g., Elster, 1999a; Scherer, 2005). This section defines emotions in terms of eight features.

Sudden Onset

Emotions are things that happen to us rather than things we voluntarily choose. We have little control over our emotional reactions. Like forces of nature, such as gusts of wind or the currents of the sea, they move, and move the person. In the face of physical aggression or danger, the emotion of anger and fear can arise in a split second. We feel suddenly happy when, at the airport, we greet a family member whom we've not seen for some time. Or we may feel anger at a slight. Such an emotion fills our consciousness. Paul Ekman (2003) notes that quick onset is fundamental to the adaptive (survival) value of emotions, mobilizing us to respond to important events with little time required for consideration or preparation.

Brief Duration

Typical emotions are essentially transient. What comes up often comes down. The mobilization of all resources to focus on one event cannot last forever. Emotions have varied time durations. They tend to run their course until they have "spent themselves." A typical emotional response involves a quick rise lasting for a few minutes and then followed by a relatively slow decay. Some emotions tend to have a very short duration. They go through a fairly rapid onset, a peak of intensity, and rapid decay (e.g., fear and surprise). For example, anger usually lasts for more than a few minutes, but rarely more than a few hours. Eventually the emotion burns itself out through exhaustion. Sometimes one emotion is replaced by a different emotion.[5]

However, people tend to mispredict the short duration of an emotional response. For example, a romantic breakup indicates an unstable state in which the existing context has changed, but no new context has yet established. But, the heartbroken people are unable to anticipate the decay of their emotions. One of the reasons for adolescents' high risk for suicide is because when they feel pain, they lack the life experience to know it is transitory. After a while, the change becomes a normal and stable situation. If emotions provoke an immediate action (knee-jerk reaction), then it may sometimes be difficult to later undo the decision of the past. For example, when young people join a terrorist group in a moment of passion and later want to leave it, they may find themselves trapped (the option to leave is no longer available to them). Had they been able to anticipate the decay of their enthusiasm, they might have abstained from joining the group.

Physiological Expression

Emotions have characteristic, observable expressions. These include bodily posture, voice pitch, blushing, smiling, showing one's teeth in anger, laughing, frowning, and crying. This aspect of emotion serves as a form of communication. For example, monkeys may communicate their emotional state to others by making an open-mouth threat to indicate the extent to which they are willing to compete for resources, and this may influence the behavior of other animals. Consider the expressive behavior of a cat when confronted by an attacking dog. The cat opens its mouth to show its long teeth, pulls back its ears, erects the hair of its body, arches its back, and hisses. This pattern of emotional expression associated with mixed fear and anger has definite signal value to the attacker. It makes the cat look larger and more ferocious and decreases the chances of a direct confrontation. This, in turn, increases survival possibilities for the cat.

This aspect of emotion was emphasized by Darwin, and has been studied more recently by Ekman (2004).[6] Ekman has investigated the degree of cross-cultural universality of facial expressions. He reviews evidence that facial expressions in humans can be classified into the categories happy, sad, fearful, angry, surprised, and disgusted. This categorization may operate similarly in different cultures. He has also described how the facial muscles produce different expressions (there are 10,000 facial muscles). Our face is a window into our emotional states. Even without language, our faces say something about what type of person we are and how we feel. For example, a closed mouth often accompanies decision making. Decision making requires withdrawal and concentration. Darwin associated a sealed mouth with a strong character. Having a half-opened mouth was for him a sign of a weak character (Ekman, 2003). When people lie, they tend to be careful (not waving arms or jabbing finger) and unconsciously inhibit their motions. People concocting a story prepare a script that is tight and lacking in detail. By contrast, people telling the truth have no script, and tend to recall more irrelevant details and may even make mistakes. They are sloppier.

The fact that emotions have physiological expressions makes it possible for the emotion felt by one person to shape the behavior of other agents. Consider, for example, the emotion of embarrassment. Psychologists have found that reddening cheeks soften others' judgments of bad or clumsy behavior, and help to strengthen social bonds rather that strain them. A blush comes out in two or three seconds and says, "I care; I know I violated the social contract" (Keltner, 2009). Darwin proposed that the blush mainly reflected the human capacity for imagining others' perceptions.

The inability to judge emotional expressions can result in miscommunication. Individuals who have difficulties in producing facial expression (e.g., patients with Parkinson's diseases) say that their social interactions are made difficult (Ekman, 2003). Evidence shows that delinquent youths who get into trouble with the law may find it hard to interpret facial expressions of disgust or anger more often than their peers. Misrecognizing an expression may lead them to see a situation as more hostile than it is. Similarly, heavy drinking can affect the ability to recognize other people's facial emotions. Thus, not all facial expressions are necessarily perceived the same by everyone, and delinquents and alcoholics may be at a special disadvantage in detecting emotional facial expression, which we all naturally use to convey information, such as warnings, love, and anger, among others, and assume that the intended message is accurately perceived (Marinkovic et al., 2009).

Intentional Object

Emotions are about something, such as a person, object, or event. One is always angry about something, one is always in love with someone or something, one is always fearful of something (even if one doesn't know what it is). The object may be an action committed by a person or it may be that person's character. Anger, guilt, admiration, and pride are directed toward actions; hatred, contempt, shame, and liking are directed toward the person's character. In short, every emotion is necessarily about something, however vague, and this something is determined by the cognitive state (the evaluative judgment).

Triggered by a Cognitive State

Emotions are triggered when one evaluates (interprets) an event or outcome as relevant for one's concerns or preferences. Emotions are appraisals of the environment with respect to the person's important goals, concerns, and aspirations (Lazarus, 1991). Appraisal refers to the process of judging the significance of an event for personal well-being. One doesn't become emotional over something trivial. It is also worth noting that emotions can be produced just as much by the recall of past events as well as current, external stimuli. Thus, emotions differ from physical sensations in that emotions typically require cognitive appraisals or being initiated. In contrast, pleasure depends heavily on bodily stimulation (e.g., eating or otherwise stimulating the body).

Action Tendencies (Temporary Preference)

Emotions have action tendencies or motivational forces, which may also be seen as a temporary preference.[7] Action tendencies are impulses or inclinations to respond with a particular action. These are urges and impulses to execute a given kind of action. We might feel an urge to hug someone or to stomp out of the room. The action tendency of love is to approach and touch the other, for envy, it is to destroy the envied object of its possessor, and for guilt, it is to make repairs, to confess, or to punish oneself. The action tendency of shame is to disappear or to hide oneself, and in extreme cases, to commit suicide. It is important to emphasize that these are action tendencies. Even though we may feel a brief destructive urge at the sight of another person, most people learn to shrug it off without further action.[8] For emotion to result in action, one needs to deliberate and choose.

The Valence of the Emotions

Emotions are accompanied by pleasure or pain (valence). Psychologists use the term *valence* to refer to the fact that emotions are experienced as pleasant or painful, desirable or undesirable, with a neutral zero point of emotional indifference. The pain and pleasure that accompany emotions offers an obvious bridge to rational-choice theory. One might indeed think that the pain and pleasure of emotions are simply negative and positive utilities (or satisfaction, well-being, value) that may contribute to the overall utility of a given choice. Positive affect creates utility and negative affect creates disutility. For example, drinking a glass of cold water on a warm summer day is judged as pleasant.

Each Emotion Has a Unique Qualitative Feel

This component refers to the subjective emotional experience. The subjective emotional feelings determine what it is to be a human being. Each emotion has a certain feel. An angry person feels a kind of warmth and agitation; it is directed usually at another person or is the result of a slight or offense. A person who is disgusted feels a kind of nausea; it is directed at the object that provokes the disgust. Fear is identified with a chilled and queasy feeling. The feeling of a "warm glow" accompanies donations to charity.

Summary

This section outlines several components of emotion. Together, these components comprise the experiential content of the emotion. The experiential content of an emotion reflects how emotions are felt and what emotions mean to the person experiencing them. Thus, for a full understanding of emotions, we should not look at changes in a single emotion component, but rather at patterns of changes across several components. The knowledge about the experiential content of an emotion helps to understand the motivations that arise during this experience, and allows us to make specific behavioral predictions. For example, the experience of anger in individuals goes with feelings like exploding, thoughts of unfairness, and tendencies to behave aggressively, and with a motivation to retaliate. Guilt is seen as one of the moral emotions that are linked to the interests of other people and that motivate prosocial behavior.

Types of Emotions

Emotions can be classified as primary and complex. There are at least eight primary or basic emotions—interest, joy, distress, anger, fear, anxiety, surprise, disgust—associated with a single facial expression (Plutchik, 2003). Primary emotions are universal and innate. We all tend to think this as we express "people everywhere are essentially the same." We inherit the capacity to have these basic emotions. A smile is recognized in all cultures as a signal of happiness and social welcome, and weeping is a signal of sadness. The basic emotions can be characterized by a number of features that are immediately observable. For example, tightening the lips is one of the most reliable signs of anger because it is physically hard to do, and often takes place before people are aware that they're doing it.

The primary emotions are not necessarily dependent on cognition. They act as cognitive shortcuts, as opposed to ordinary, deliberative cognition, with which people react to stimuli. The transition from appraisal to the emotion is always unconscious. We cannot choose to feel anger or fear. Introspection can tell us why we are angry (because someone insulted us), but it cannot reveal the transition from the appraisal to the emotion.

In complex or social emotions, the social world is a principal theater of emotions since other people are very important for our well-being. These emotions act as a very important glue that links us to others, and the links to others are important determinants for the generation of emotions. The social emotions include jealousy, guilt, shame, sympathy, embarrassment, pride, indignation, admiration, gratitude, and contempt. For example, the emotion of envy is triggered by the thought of the possessions of others. Shame is a painful emotion responding to a sense of failure to attain some ideal state. Social emotions have cognitive content, have less distinct physiological manifestations, are less uniform across cultures, and have fewer obvious correlates in animals. Social emotions begin to appear later in human development, probably only after the self begins to mature—shame and guilt are examples of this later develoment; newborns have no shame and no guilt, but two-year-olds do.

In mixed emotions, a person can feel sad and guilty or happy and proud at the same time. Many young women who had just eaten a chocolate bar report a blend of joy and guilt. The sadness that follows a mother's death is often combined with guilt over a past failure to be sufficiently affectionate to the parent when she was alive. Nostalgia consists of the mixture of pleasure coming from the recollection of something lived, and the pain caused by that event being irrevocably gone. Students graduating from college tend to feel both happy and sad. The question is what happens in these situations. Which emotions will influence behavior? It could be the case that the strongest emotion cancels out the action tendencies and motivations of any other emotion. That is, the strongest emotion simply gets action priority (Frijda, 1986).

For many generations, philosophers have assumed that complex emotions are derived from primary emotions. Plutchik (2003) explains this idea by drawing an analogy between the perception of color and emotions. The primary pigment colors are red, blue, and yellow. The secondary colors, purple, orange, and green, are obtained by mixing two primary colors. Combining these few colors at different intensities produces millions of colors. Niether colors nor emotions are clear-cut cateogries with sharp boundaries. By mixing two or more emotions at different intensity levels, it is possible to create hundreds of terms representing the language of emotions. For example, the mixture of joy and acceptance produces the mixed emotions of love. The blending of disgust and anger produces the mixed emotional state of contempt or hatred (hostility). Fear and trust give rise to submission. Jealously stems from our suspicions that a third person might displace us in a relationship with someone we love. The basic emotion may be fear or anger. The complex emption of hatred is a mix of anger and fear with an aggressive tendency. Unlike anger, hatred is not healed by time. The combination of fear and anger produce the feeling of urgency for closure (e.g., the preference for early action after the attacks of September 11, 2001).

The conception of graduation (dimensionality) implies that an emotion is a continuum, not a discrete category. Some people believe they should have only one feeling toward someone (e.g., either like or dislike). But very few people are so simple to have either positive or negative feelings. These feelings tend to be contradictory. Accepting conflicting feelings is very important because it indicates that you are using more information. For example, if you breakup and have conflicting feelings, it means that you are using more information about how complicated two people can be together or apart. Mixed emotions (or emotional ambivalence) reflect how mature and intelligent we are and how we are able to recognize conflicting aspects of being human.

Affect and Mood

How can emotions, as defined above, be distinguished from other affective phenomena such as moods or attitudes? Generally, the term *affect* describes an internal feeling state. The term *affect* is an umbrella term that encompasses emotion, moods, attitudes, evaluations, and preferences. Some writers use affect as a general category that includes various kinds of states: stress response, emotion, mood, and impulse (e.g., hunger, thirst, sex, and pain).

Moods are usually thought of as low intensity and are diffused throughout affective states that generally lack source identification, and often last longer than emotions (e.g., being cheerful, gloomy, or depressed). Moods are objectless and free-floating (Plutchik, 2003). Moods may exist without an obvious stimulus or object that brings them about, and they are often experienced without an awareness of their cause. In contrast, emotions are reactions to specific, significant events. The difference between emotion and mood is apparent in everyday conversation when we say that we are angry "about" something, but that we are "in" a bad mood. Rarely do we know why we are in a mood. It just seems to happen to us, which could lead to misattribution. It can be argued that the object of mood is the world as a whole (Solomon, 2007). Being in positive mood, one may feel totally at peace with the world.

In contrast to emotions, moods bias cognition more than they bias action tendency (Gross, 2014). Our moods influence the contents of our thoughts and judgments. For example, on sunnier days, we tend to tip more at restaurants and express higher levels of overall happiness. According to the mood maintenance hypothesis, people in a good mood would like to maintain their pleasant state and thus try to avoid hard decisions.

A mood activates specific emotions. When we are irritable, we are seeking an opportunity to become angry. A mood turns into an emotion as its object becomes more focused, for instance, when an angry man fixes his rage on one unfortunate victim. An emotion turns into a mood as its object becomes more generalized; for example, when a specific set-back, say getting fired from one's job or divorced, gets generalized from being depressed about getting fired/divorced to being depressed about one's whole life and everything about it.

Psychologists (e.g., Leander et al., 2009) also talk about mystery (incidental) moods. Mystery moods emerge without awareness, or for reasons beyond our knowledge, and they can influence (color) our attitudes, goals, and judgment. The major sources of mystery moods include the success or failure at unconscious goals (achievement puts us in a good mood), the automatic evaluation system may generate mood states (imagine a phobic person surrounded with images of snakes), and interpersonal interactions, such that we might unconsciously "catch" the moods of others. We spontaneously mimic the behaviors of those around us, often without conscious awareness (mirror neurons).[9] Once an individual is in a mystery mood, she may misattribute mystery moods to irrelevant sources in the environment. People also engage in mood-regulating behavior, such as behaving aggressively toward other individuals or engaging in overeating if near the refrigerator. So if you find your partner in a negative mood, remember that his mood may have nothing to do with you. The best way to avoid such errors is to recognize the influence of incidental emotion (emotional "hangovers") on our preferences. Being aware of this possibility can help to defuse the influence of incidental emotions (being in a terrible mood) in our subsequent judgments and choices.

Damasio (1999) writes that mood is background emotions that color conscious experience and have potential influence on behavior. We experience some people as nice and others as mean, some foods as delicious but others as distasteful. People have limited ability to track the causal connections. Instead, a person makes attributions and interpretations of background emotion. For example, the person mistakenly attributes the happy feelings to the object and therefore perceives the object to be more pleasant than it would otherwise seem.

In contrast to mood, preferences are defined as relatively stable evaluative judgments in the sense of liking or disliking a stimulus, or preferring it or not over other objects or stimuli. Psychologists equate preference with emotion (e.g.,

Zajonc, 1980, Zajonc and Markus, 1982). Thus, preference is another term in the emotion family—a silent emotion waiting for an opportunity to express itself in a choice we make. Robert Zajonc regards a simple preference for one event over another (choosing vanilla over chocolate ice cream) as an emotion, even if the person did not experience any change in feeling as a choice was made. Similarly, Joesph LeDoux (1996) defines an emotion as a brain process that computes the *value* of an experience. This refers to events that are either good or bad. The perceived pleasantness or unpleasantness is linked to reward values that guide behavioral priorities. This type of hedonic evaluation was named "utility" by the English philosopher Jeremy Bentham.

Furthermore, people tend to misattribute the cause of their bad mood to people or circumstances that surround them. They tend to make this attribution even when the actual source of the feelings is totally unrelated to the object of attention. For example, consider the emotionally complex situation of divorce. Experts note that husbands' reactions are often dominated by anger, an emotion that allows them to maintain a confident and dominant position. A therapeutic goal in these situations is sometimes to help them recognize that some of their negative affect may come from sadness, hurt feelings, and fear, emotions that are more painful and scary and that husbands may be especially motivated to avoid. Misattributions usually disappear when people are made aware of the true source of their affective states.

A common goal in therapy is to turn moods into emotions. Because of their unfocused nature, moods can be misread as a response to a wide range of different causes. But once we attribute the mood to a specific cause, its impact on unrelated judgments vanishes. For example, when an individual reports a general mood of depression, a therapist might attempt to learn what the depression is in response to. By identifying the object of the depression, the diffuse mood changes into a specific emotion. As a result, the client can begin to engage in problem-focused coping, rather than simply trying to suppress the feelings. As the depressive mood becomes constrained by specific objects, their spillover to other aspects of one's life become more limited, and it is less likely for the mood to cause general distress. The goal is thus to have the individual focus directly on the pain and to describe both where and how it hurts in great detail.

Mood and Cognitive Performance

Moods influence the manner in which people process information. In general, in a task situation, a happy mood leads to a global focus, or a big picture view, whereas a sad mood leads to a local focus, or a more detailed view processing. Sad persons may pay more attention to details than the happy person; happy people perceive the world as less dangerous. Thus, different conclusions may be drawn from the same information. A sad person would do better on those tasks requiring more analysis, and less on creative works. A positive mood (mood-as-a-resource) may promote a sense of self-competency. People in a positive mood can handle negative feedback much better than those in a sad mood. Happy people solve nearly 20% more word puzzles than unhappy people (Subramaniam et al., 2009). The cognitive scientist Mark Jung-Beeman speculates that in a positive mood, the brain areas associated with cognition are not as occupied with managing emotional life. The end result is that the cognitive brain is freed up to focus on the problem.

The *Broaden-and-Build* theory developed by the psychologist Barbara Fredrickson suggests that when people feel positive emotion, they are jolted into a different way of thinking and acting, their thinking becomes creative and their action becomes adventurous and exploratory, and this in return will further broaden and build thinking (Fredrickson and Joiner, 2002; Fredrickson, 2009). For example, joy sparks the urge to play and be creative. Interest sparks the urge to explore and learn. In one study, medical internists placed in a positive mood did best while considering medical diagnosis compared with the control group.[10] Here are the take-home lessons. If you are taking tests or preparing income tax, carry them out on a rainy day. For creative thinking, such as pondering a new career field or whether to marry someone, carry these tasks out in a setting that will enhance your mood (comfortable chair, with suitable music), or surround yourself with people you trust to be unselfish and good willed. Positive moods open up certain kinds of possibility and close down others (e.g., "love is blind").

Emotion and Memory

Emotionally charged events are remembered better than those of neutral events (McGaugh, 2003). You will never forget some events, such as the joy of the birth of your first child, or the horror of the 9/11 terrorist attack. It has been known for a while that adrenaline, the hormone released during stress and anxiety, enhances memory and consolidates memory contents. Since emotions narrow attention to a few stimuli, the recall of these stimuli is facilitated by greater emotional intensity. Focusing upon fewer objects increases the resources available for each and hence increases emotional intensity. It is like a laser beam that focuses upon a very narrow area and consequently achieves high intensity at that point. However, emotional intensity is no guarantee of memory accuracy. Biases due to changes in cognitive appraisals of the events, as well as a desire to see things differently, may contaminate our memory.

Memories of painful emotional experiences linger far longer than those involving physical pain. There is an old saying that "sticks and stones can break your bones, but words can never hurt you." To the contrary, evidence shows that hurt feelings could be worse than physical pain. The memories allow humans to relive, re-experience, and suffer from social pain. It is harder to "re-live" physical pain. With physical pain, you can see the bruise, but in emotional abuse, there is often fear and anxiety which remains.

According to mood-congruent recall, your current emotional state facilitates recall of experiences that had the same emotional state (or at least a similar affective tone). When we are in a happy mood, we tend to recall pleasant events and vice versa. This is because moods bring different associations to mind. For example, recalling positive childhood experiences while in a good mood. Being in a bad mood primes a person to think about negative things.

Appraisal Theory

Appraisal refers to cognitive processes by which the person determines the personal significance of the stimulus and what it means for her goals (Lazarus, 1994). Appraisal theory states that emotions result from the meanings people attribute to life events and depend fundamentally on what is important to each person. Cognitive evaluations come between the stimulus and the emotional reactions, and the brain appraises the significance of the stimulus. It is this computed significance that gives rise to emotions, and emotions affect perception, attention, memory, and judgment. Appraisals then lead to action tendencies. If there is no appraisal of harm or benefit, no emotion will result. The concept of appraisal implies nothing about rationality, deliberateness, or consciousness. Appraisals can be either conscious or unconscious. For example, grief about someone's death represents a judgment about that person's importance to the person. Depression (not the clinical kind) involves a global attitude about the world, the belief that one is unable to control one's environment. The sign that that states "smoking is dangerous for your health" can cause fear of cancer. These examples suggest emotional reactions as a function of a private interpretation of an event (Nussbaum, 2001).

Stimulus (Events) → Appraisal (Thought) → Emotion (Feeling) → Action Tendency

In addition to cognition, social norms intervene between emotion and action. For example, when people are getting divorced, it is supposed be a very sad event, but yet people can be joyful that they are ending a bad relationship. But social norm says that we are supposed to feel sad. In Zimbabwe, the failure of a woman to give birth to a male child is a source of serious depressive reactions in Zimbabwean women. The appraisal of such failure includes a serious decline in social status, undesirability as a marriage partner, and potential divorce (Horwitz and Wakefield, 2007). Emotions are culturally scripted as to when and how to feel and display our feelings.[11] Through socialization processes, individuals learn when and how to feel and express their emotions. In other words, individuals are like actors acting on a stage configured by social norms in front of others. They use strategies to present themselves to others, manipulate their forms of talks, role cues, and bodies to achieve their goals (e.g., gain favor, power, or status) (Mesquita, 2007). Indeed, guilt and shame follow the violation of social norms (Elster,

1999a). Social norms inspire fear. For example, if I drink too much in public and act drunk, I will be socially ostracized if my network values modesty and discretion. Social norms in the strictest sense do not benefit, or harm, anyone. Rather, they define the boundaries of the community. My drinking behavior may leave me socially ostracized, but no one can take my house away for verbal indiscretion. Thus, social norms, or culture, are an integral part of the emotion, and anticipated guilt or shame exerts powerful control on our behavior. Such emotions are absent in psychopaths.[12]

In sum, appraisal theory implies that emotions are forms of judgment. They involve evaluative judgments about the importance of things for our well-being. Generally speaking, if I am furious at X for doing Y, my anger reveals an implicit judgment that X could have acted differently, and that action Y has negative consequences for my well-being (or otherwise violates my values). The concept of appraisal provides insights into the individual differences in emotion reactions. Since goals and values differ, so will the meaning attached to a given event. Thus, an emotion is a special kind of thinking about what we make of an event. The appraisal is like discovering the black box of a plane crash that recorded flight data just before the aircraft went down. Without a "psychological autopsy" into someone's appraisal process, we are in the dark.

Adaptation: Change and Habituation

As discussed, all emotions involve a perceived change whose significance is determined by us. Like burglar alarms going off when an intruder appears, emotions signal that something needs attention. This phenomenon of being sensitive to changes in rewards is adaptive. For survival purposes, it is crucial that the organism pay special attention to significant changes that may increase or decrease the chance of survival. Responding primarily to changes is a highly economical and efficient way of using limited resources. Repetition reduces excitement and may have a relaxing function. People have more emotions when performing new activities than habitual or familiar ones, and that fact suggests that emotion is more relevant for learning new things than for performing familiar acts.

People are very excited when facing changes in their lives: the birth of a child, marriage, entering school for the first time. Hence, while continued pleasure wears off, continued hardships also lose their negative impact. This may explain boredom in marriage, why rich people who seem to have everything are not necessarily happy—after a while they get used to having everything, and only changes make them happy. This may be a regrettable fact, but nevertheless, it expresses the structure of our emotional system. From this perspective, changes are essential to an exciting and meaningful life. The change, rather than the general level, is of emotional significance.

For instance, in United States, average incomes have more than tripled in the last 50 years, while average life satisfaction has held steady (Frank, 1999).[13] The evidence suggests that if income affects happiness, it is relative, not absolute, income that matters (Frank, 1999). Also, you get used to earning more money, so after a while, it doesn't cheer you up as much as it did at first. Some experts have likened the pursuit of happiness to a hedonic adaptation.[14] Hedonic adaptation is the tendency to feel less hedonically sensitive to an ongoing stimulus with the passage of time. The process of hedonic adaptation eventually returns people to a set point determined by their personality. For example, a person who purchases a new car may feel happy at first, but as time goes by, he adapts to the new and no longer feels particularly happy while driving his car. Hedonic adaptation applies to a wide range of experiences, including both positive events such as marriage or winning a lottery, as well as negative events such as the loss of a family member or becoming disabled.

Why does hedonic adaptation occur? The two biggest culprits are increasing aspirations and social comparisons. It is not the absolute level of income that matters most, but rather one's position relative to other individuals.[15] People look upward, not downward, when making comparisons. Aspirations thus tend to be higher than the level already reached. In other words, wealthier people impose a negative external effect on poorer people, but not vice versa.[16] The upward adjustment of aspiration motivates human beings to accomplish more and more. They are never satisfied. Once they have achieved something, they want to achieve even more. The fact that enjoyment of good things wears off is probably a major cause of human progress, because it offers an incentive for continued innovation and striving. The ability to adapt quickly to changing circumstances is also extremely useful when bad things happen. We have a unique ability to recover much our happiness after a debilitating illness or accidents.

Another factor is the idea of the focusing illusion. The focusing illusion occurs when people focus on a distinct feature of a possible choice. We focus too heavily on a single good or bad event when considering how that event will make us feel about our lives (how happy you will be if bough a brand new car?). In another words, we exaggerate the effect a life change will have upon our happiness because we cannot foresee that we won't always be thinking about it. The mismatch in the allocation of attention between thinking about a life condition and actually living it is the cause of the focusing illusion. For example, the new lottery winner, or the newlywed, is almost continuously aware of her state. But as the new state loses its novelty, it ceases to be the single focus of attention, and other aspects of life again occupy her attention.[17] For example, Schwartz et al. (2002) explored how the quality of the car driven (as indexed by the car's Bluebook value) affects the driver's emotional experience. They found that drivers feel better driving luxury cars than economy cars—but only during episodes that are car-focused; that is, in the 2% of episodes that the drivers categorized as "driving for fun." In the other 98% of driving episodes, like commuting to work or shopping, the type of car driven was unrelated to drivers' emotional experiences. In short, the car only made a difference when the car was on the driver's mind.

Marketers exploit the focusing illusion causing people to exaggerate the importance of a good. When people are induced to believe that they "must have" a good, they greatly exaggerate the difference that the good will make to the quality of their lives. Similarly, those who suffer from the belief that they have committed a social blunder are better off to imagine how miniscule the event will seem 12 months later. Having made a fool of yourself in public, you may feel anguish that certainly matters to you at present. But in time, it will diminish and probably disappear. Even if you do not forget the experience, others will: it will be drowned by all the subsequent happenings that eventually push it into oblivion.

Something similar can be said about most of our failures. If we see them from the remote corner of the universe, we are likely to free ourselves from acute remorse ("this too will pass"). The take-home lesson is to look beyond the initial excitement and novelty to the time when the choice will be a routine part of everyday living. Widening our view beyond the transition period helps us to make better decision.

Our capacity to adapt varies considerable across domains. There are some stimuli, such as environmental noise, to which we do not adapt. Indeed, there are even stimuli to which we not only do not adapt over time, but to which we actually become sensitized. For example, after several months' exposure, the office bully who initially took two weeks to annoy you can accomplish the same act in only seconds. Available evidence clearly shows that, even after long periods of adjustment, most people experience the task of navigating through heavy commuter traffic as stressful (Koslowsky et al., 1996). For example, consider urban bus drivers, whose exposure to the stresses of heavy traffic is higher than most commuters, but who have also had greater opportunity to adapt to those stresses. Compared to workers in other occupations, a disproportionate share of the absenteeism experienced by urban bus drivers stems from stress-related illnesses such as gastrointestinal problems, headaches, and anxiety. More than half of all urban bus drivers retire prematurely with some form of medical disability (Evans, 1994).

In summary, we humans are unhappy in large part because we are insatiable. After working hard to get what we want, we routinely lose interest in the object of our desire. Rather than feeling satisfied, we feel a bit bored and begin forming a new desire (Irvine, 2009). You meet the woman of your dreams and succeed in marrying her. But thanks to hedonic adaptation,[18] before long, you find yourself noticing her flaws and begin fantasizing about a relationship with someone new. As a result of the adaptation, people find themselves on a satisfaction treadmill. In short, we take our life and what we have for granted rather than delighting in them.

For instance consider the modern *fear of missing out (FOMO) anxiety*. The *Oxford English Dictionary* online defines FOMO as "fear of missing out: anxiety that an exciting or interesting event may be happening elsewhere, often aroused by posts seen on a social media website." This term was added in 2013. Social media, through its increased social awareness, can heighten distress and insecurities among highly connected people. They can feel negative emotions (e.g., envy and jealous) from seeing how much more fun everyone else is having. This awareness triggers the feeling that we are not good enough and consequently experience lower life satisfaction (Przybylski et al., 2013). They compare and evaluate their lives based on how they see others portraying their own. This is a sure way to never be satisfied with what they have or are doing. Those who are vulnerable to fear FOMO tend to constantly scan their social media or emails. In other words, they don't want to miss out. The FOMO is a modern version of "the grass being greener on the other side."

How to prevent the adaptation process? One key to happiness, then, is to forestall the adaptation process. We need to take steps to prevent ourselves from taking for granted the things we worked so hard to get. To gain happiness is to learn how to desire things we already have. Buddha once said the secret to happiness is to learn to want what you have and not want what you don't have (Irvine, 2009). For instance, let's consider the wisdom of stoicism, a school of philosophy practiced in ancient Greece and Rome. They advocated negative visualization (Irvine, 2009). The Stoics recommended that we spend time imagining that we have lost the things we value (e.g., we lost our job). Doing so will make us value what we already have. When you say goodbye to your child, we silently should remind ourselves that this might be our final parting. In other words, we should live each day as if it were our last. The goal is to change our attitude as we carry out our daily affairs. Thus, negative visualization is a wonderful strategy to embrace whatever life we happen to be living and to extract every bit of joy we can from it.[19]

At the societal level, one may wonder if there are alternative ways of spending the additional resources that could have produced lasting gains in human well-being. There is evidence that having more wealth would be a good thing, provided it was spent in certain ways. There are specific categories in which our capacity to adapt is more limited. Additional spending in these categories appears to have the greatest capacity to produce significant improvement in well-being. Thus the less we spend on conspicuous consumption goods, the better we can afford to alleviate congestion, the more time we can devote to family and friends, to exercise, sleep, travel, and other restorative activities, and the better we can afford to maintain a clean and safe environment. Evidence shows that reallocating our time and money in these ways would result in healthier, longer, and more satisfying lives.

The question is, then, why we have not used our resources more wisely? If we could all live healthier, longer, and more satisfying lives by simply changing our spending patterns, why haven't we done that? Frank (2005) argues that the answer has to with the interdependencies among us—individual's well-being depends on the actions taken by others. That many purchases become more attractive to us when others make them. This means that consumption spending becomes like a military arms race. Furthermore, Rayo and Becker (2007) state that we did not evolve to be happy; we evolved to survive and reproduce, and affective systems are designed to serve that purpose.

Pacing Reward

What makes things interesting? Interest is a distinct emotion. It is a part of positive affect (Silvia, 2006). Novelty, complexity, uncertainty, and conflict have been found to arouse feelings of interest. People tend to find complex things interesting and simple things enjoyable (e.g., a soufflé is pretty and pleasing, but it is mostly air and apt to collapse). Familiar things tend to be enjoyable, whereas new things tend to be interesting. Interest motivates trying a new dish at a favorite restaurant.

Novelty is the most stimulating and the most pleasant when it provides surprise, conflict, cognitive dissonance, deviation, or divergence between expectation and experience. Not knowing exactly what's going to happen next can create a sense of suspense that keeps us glued to our seats watching a thriller and quickly turning the pages in a mystery novel. The element of surprise is what ignites curiosity, the direct result of the "violation of expectations." Why does interest sometimes fades and die? When the person no longer experiences cognitive conflict, the area will cease to be interesting. Rewards and novelty decay very rapidly. We become habituated. However, the practice of self-control helps to pace reward and provide a source of surprise and novelty, which protects from habituation and keeps up arousal levels.

Pacing reward means to scale back stimulation deliberately, and maintain it permanently at the lower level of increasing return. At that level, every additional increment of stimulation provides increasing satisfaction. This means to not maximize consumption, but to keep them under control, to pace it. Doing less, conserving, doesn't come naturally. Humans are natural-born adders, hard-wired to push, collect, hoard, store, and consume. In a book titled *In pursuit of Elegance*, Mathew May (2009) writes that perfection is achieved not when there is nothing more to add, but when there is nothing left to take away. We tend to be looking at what to *do*, rather than what *not to do*. The great companies routinely eliminate activities and pursuits that don't significantly contribute to profit (value), passion (sense of noble and purpose), and perfection (executing flawlessly). In short, we need to know how to make room for more of what matters by eliminating what doesn't. From this perspective, an interesting or happy life might also be regarded as a creative "work of art."

Conclusion

So what have we learned? This chapter focused on addressing the question of "what is an emotion?" Emotions are typically directed at human beings—ourselves or other people. Emotions have a purpose in the lives of individuals. Emotions are concerned with adaptation to the environment and the maintenance of homeostasis, and are involved in survival (love drives sexual reproduction, intimacy for child care, fear motivates prudence, and revenge discourages others from acting selfishly). Emotions are readouts or interpretations of one's own inner signals from body, face, and brain (Johnson-Laird and Oatley, 1992).

However, our emotions can also get us into trouble. When fear becomes anxiety, desire gives way to greed, or annoyance turns to anger or hatred, friendship to envy, or pleasure to addiction, our emotions start working against us. People generally seek behavioral options that maximize pleasure and minimize displeasure (e.g., from morning coffee to the evening brandy). For example, a high proportion of emotional eaters' meals and snacks are based on the motivation to eat in order to cope with negative emotions. Disturbance in emotions, such as depression, obsessive-compulsive disorder, post-traumatic stress disorder, and social anxiety, might also predispose people to health-related problems. Mental health is maintained by emotional hygiene, and mental problems, to a large extent, reflect a breakdown of emotional order. Our understanding and appreciation of our emotions contributes to our self-knowledge and well-being.

Psychotherapy is interpreted as a process through which our neocortex learns to exercise control over evolutionary, old emotional systems. Solomon (2007) argues that most of our emotions, most of the time, are not entirely beyond our control. They do not just happen to us, but we are responsible for them. If we look into our emotional lives with the idea that our emotions are forces beyond our control that happen to us, we are prone to make excuses for ourselves and resign ourselves to bad and destructive behavior that otherwise might be controlled. In other words, we cannot just use our emotions as excuses for our bad behavior. ("I couldn't help it, I was angry.") From his experience in Aushwitz, Victor Frankl (2006) concluded that in the last resort, "everything can be taken from a man but one thing, the last of human freedoms—to choose one's attitude in any given set of circumstances." An essential skill, therefore, is to acquire the ability to regulate emotion. This is the subject of a later chapter.

Notes

1 Similarly, an excitement in one's field can be quite useful in maintaining students' interest in the subject. Emotion is contagious. Students are unlikely to be interested in a subject unless the teacher displays enthusiasm in the importance of the subject.
2 Aristotle considered that the heart was the seat of the soul and emotions, something we still see in our everyday language and symbols (e.g., the universal sign of love is a heart).
3 The idea that women are morally weaker has a long history in the West. Lewis (1987) cites the Genesis creation story about the curiosity of Adam and Eve to sample the fruit of the tree of knowledge. This knowledge in turn leads to their sense of shame. However the important point is the portrayal of the sexes in that Eve, a woman, first breaks God's commandment and then convinces Adam to do likewise. Adam sins, but it was Eve's fault.
4 Hubris refers to excessive pride; individuals who see themselves as god-like may feel boundless pride that is not tempered by the awareness of shortcomings and failures in some of the self's pursuits.
5 For example, envy turns into resentment. An envious person sees himself in an inferior position, not having what he really wants and unable to get it. So the envious rationalizes this inferiority into another mental state and action (unjust oppression).

Definition and Functions of Emotions **91**

6. In 1872, Darwin in his book *The Expression of the Emotions in Man and Animals* showed that some basic expressions of emotion are similar in animals and humans. His focus was on the continuity between animals and humans of how emotion is expressed.
7. For instance, sexual arousal dramatically changes people's risk-taking preference and moral behavior (Ariely, 2008). For example, in the heat of the moment, sexually aroused college students were willing to engage in unsafe sex.
8. Social norms can inhibit spontaneous action tendencies (Elster, 2001). Thus, the urge for revenge is regularly suppressed in societies that teach the principle of turning the other cheek. A fear-induced tendency to flee may be kept in check by norms against cowardice. Social norms can also amplify action tendencies, as in the case of revenge.
9. *Mirror neurons* connect us to each other through a brain mechanism designed to facilitate imitation and mimicry (Iacoboni, 2008). Psychologists have found that immediate social bonding between strangers is highly dependent on mimicry, a synchronized and usually unconscious give and take of words and gestures that creates good will between two people. This is consistent with the old adage that imitation is the sincerest form of flattery.
10. Positive feelings alter your connections with others. Your connections go from classifying people as separate "me" and "you" to "we" and "us." In her book *Positivity*, Barbara Fredrickson (2009) writes that positive feelings even alter our view of the people we don't know. When we feel good, we are more likely to be kind and offer help to strangers.
11. The display rule may explain the double standard for the same job. For example, male lawyers are expected to be aggressive, but aggressive female lawyers are considered unfeminine and domineering.
12. In early America, parents engaged in the pervasive use of shame in dealing with their children. However, as community cohesion declined, parents resorted to guilt as a disciplinary tool (Elster, 1999a).
13. GDP (national income) is viewed as partial measures of society's well-being for a number of reasons. For example, GDP doesn't account for unpaid activities (e.g., cleaning, cooking, and child care) which produce services that could be purchased on the market. GDP doesn't value social activities, such as interactions between friends or husbands and wives, which have an important effect on happiness. Activities are measure by prices, not by the extent of consumer valuation. Diamonds are counted as more valuable than water, yet one could question whether diamonds contribute more to society's well-being.
14. Both the lottery winners and the accident victims had experienced a sudden change in fortune, yet they both adapted to their circumstances, finding themselves surprisingly close to where they had begun in terms of happiness. The constant adaptation condemns all of us to live on a *hedonic treadmill*. The trick is to keep habituation in check so that you can continue to savor the pleasure of the activities you really enjoy.
15. This may explain why it is psychologically preferable to be unemployed in an area where there are many other jobless people.
16. It is found that individuals' aspirations are systematically affected by the average income in the community in which they live. The richer one's fellow residents are, the higher the level of individual aspiration. Thus, happiness = attainment/aspiration or what we have/what we want. Individual variation in material desires or aspirations explains why some poor people (e.g., Amish people) are happy and some wealthy people are not. When aspiration is high or constantly rises, happiness will suffer. No matter the income level, there is always a more expensive car or vacation for which a person can aspire.

17 In a classic experiment (Solley and Haigh, 1957), children had to draw Santa Claus in September, November, and December, including just before Christmas and right after it. Santa Claus was initially quite small, but then he grew, and, in particular, his bag of gifts became larger and larger. But on the day after Christmas, the Santa Clauses were very small again. Objectively, Santa Claus takes a larger and larger place in the children's lives as Christmas approaches.
18 Evidence shows that average happiness increases significantly in the period leading up to marriage, but over the course of a marriage, the happiness level declines to only slightly above the premarriage level.
19 The daily practice of saying grace before meal serves the same purpose—to pause for a moment to reflect on the fact that this food might not have been available.

5
THE ROLE OF EMOTION IN DECISION MAKING

Introduction

This chapter describes the relevance of emotion to understanding individual decision making. The discussions show that individual decision behavior is the outcome of an interaction between a reflective system and affective system, both operating according to different principles and often clashing with one another. The final decision is determined by the relative strength of affective and reflective forces. The relative contribution of affective and reflective processes depends on a number of factors.

This chapter describes a framework for understanding the role of emotion in motivation and behavior. These two mental processes are relatively independent and have different evolutionary origins in the brain. Understanding the role of emotion in decision making provides an insight that may account for seemingly inconsistent or irrational behaviors, such as impulsivity, drug addiction, and overeating. The framework is also valuable for understanding decisions for our professional life, business life, and the way we look at the world. If you really want to understand yourself and others, and the meanings we attach to the everyday events of our lives, you need to understand the influence of emotions in your judgment and decisions.

The Dual Mind

One of the most important ideas in psychology is to understand how the mind is divided into parts that sometimes conflict. At the basic level, the brain can be divided into the neocortex (the outer surface of the brain) and deeper, evolutionarily older subcortical structures (below the cortex) that include the striatum (near the brain's core) and the brainstem (at its base). The old brain was built on simple stimulus-response principles: if an apple smelled good and you were hungry, you ate it. The primitive, emotional parts of our brains interact with our modern cortexes to influence on the choices we make.[1]

The idea of a division between affective and reflective systems appears as early as the discussions of Greek philosophers under the labels of passion and reason. They argued that people act against their better judgment when they are overpowered by their passions. The idea is that reason is generally connected to impartiality, such as the desire to promote the public good rather than private ends, or a focus on long-term interests rather than immediate concerns.

Freud also imagined the mind as divided into three conflicting parts: the ego (governed by the "reality principle"); the superego (the conscience, a sometimes too rigid commitment to the rules of society); and the id (the desire for pleasure, sooner rather than later). The id (pleasure center) contains the reservoir of energy and is commonly referred to as the libido (a sexualized character). The ego strives for a compromise between the often conflicting interests of id and superego. For Freud, the goal of psychoanalysis was to fortify the ego, and to give it more control over the id and more independence from the superego. He believed that most mental disorders (e.g., anxiety) were due to the effect of unrestrained feelings.

Dual-process routes to behavior are pervasive in contemporary psychology and neuroscience, such as cognition and emotion, reason and intuition, consciousness and unconsciousness, or System 1 and System 2 mechanism (e.g., Evans, 2008; Kahneman, 2003). System 1 corresponds closely to automatic processing, and System 2 corresponds closely to controlled processes. Emotion is explicitly linked to System 1, whereas reflective decision making seems much more like a System 2 process. These dual-system models show that in making decisions, we seem to have two minds in one brain or a brain at war with itself (Stanovich, 2010). Examples of where we may become of aware of a System 1 and 2 conflict include compulsive behaviors like overeating, gambling, or smoking. We may judge these behaviors to be irrational because we compulsively behave in ways that are at odds with our explicitly stated (System 2) goals.

Neuroscientists also have proposed a similar distinction. For example, Bernheim and Rangel (2004) have hypothesized that the brain can operate in one of two modes, a "cold mode" or a "hot mode." In the cold mode, the person makes deliberative decisions with a broad, long-term perspective. In the hot mode, the person's decision making is influenced by emotions and motivational drives. Which mode is triggered depends on environmental cues, which in turn might depend on past behavior (e.g., the experience of craving for chocolate cake at a birthday party).

The neocortex (the CEO of the brain) plays the leading role in identifying the options available and their consequences, whereas the emotional brain evaluates these options. The emotional brain is the home of preferences, while the neocortex improves the quality of decision making. The neocortex, which philosophers refer to as a "self-reflective consciousness," has liberated humans from strict genetic programs. With its help, we can make plans, we can postpone actions, we can regulate our emotions, and we can imagine things that do not exist.

Thus, individual decisions are best understood as the interactions between cognition and emotion, and these two systems coexist as independent entities (Loewenstein and O'Donoghue, 2004). The reflective system allows people to think about long-term goals and thereby avoid the sight of tempting objects. The reflective system can weigh long-term health risks against present pleasures, even though the emotion system has a hard time imagining the future. For example, our emotion system wants to order dessert and smoke a cigarette, and our reflective brain knows we should resist the temptation and quit smoking. The final decision is determined by the relative strengths of these two systems. The final decision also depends on the compatibility of the two systems. If the two systems cooperate, the behavior is facilitated. However, the two systems may also compete, which is accompanied by a feeling of conflict and temptation. For example, a person who is on a diet may be tempted to eat a second dessert, while, at the same time, the reflective system generates a behavioral decision to refrain from eating.

Many of our sufferings have to do with the mismatch between our old brain and the modern world in which we live. Obesity is a simple example. For most human history, food was hard to get. In a world in which food is scarce, it is smart to eat when you can and store up the fat. But many human now live in environments in which food is cheap, plentiful, and tasteful. The result is craving for fat and sugar and impulsive overeating.

Table 5.1, adapted from Epstein, compares these modes of thought. In general, the "intuitive system" involves the unconscious and relies on past experiences in making decisions. In contrast, the "analytic system" uses conscious and deliberate

TABLE 5.1 Two Ways of Thinking

Intuitive System (S1)	Analytic System (S2)
Uncontrolled	Controlled
Generalized: conducive to stereotypes types	Analytic—discourages overgeneralization
Emotional: attuned to what feels good	Logical: based on what is sensible
Intuitive	Explicit
Impulsive	Reflective
Low effort	High effort
Associative—Mediated by vibes from past experience	Deductive—Mediated by conscious appraisal of events
Rapid	Slow
Holistic	Analytic
High capacity	Low capacity
Skilled	Rule-following
Self-evident: "seeing is believing"	Requires justification via logic and evidence
Default process	Inhibitory
Unconscious	Conscious

Source: Adapted from Epstein (1994).

cognitive processes to make decisions. The intuitive system processes many things simultaneously and often unconsciously (e.g., speaking in your native language and craving for chocolate). The reflective system has limited capacity, but offers more systematic analysis (e.g., learning a new language, counting calories).

The Reflective and Affective Systems

This section describes a dual-system model in which a person's decision is the outcome of an interaction between reflective and affective systems. The model illustrates the mechanisms through which these systems exert their joint influence on the individual decisions. The two systems use different operations. The affective system is primarily driven by motivational mechanisms and the reflective system takes into account broader goals (Loewenstein and O'Donoghue, 2004).

The term *affect* is an umbrella term that encompasses emotions, mood, and drive states (e.g., hunger, thirst, sex, and pain). The affective processes are those that motivate approach or avoidance behavior. All affects carry "action tendencies," such as anger motivating us to take action, pain to take steps to ease the pain, and fear to escape or freeze. Affective processing is effortless, impulsive, or automatic, and initiated by events or objects present here and now. The resulting actions are automatic because they are overlearned. For example, a person who, as a child, was repeatedly been bitten by a dog may come automatically fear the sight of a dog. This automatic processing is the default mode of information processing. Response from this mode can be adjusted by reflective processing that enables the person to overcome the fear of dogs. The reflective (or deliberative) system tends to be invoked deliberately, and is often associated with a subjective feeling of effort.

Because reflective processing is conscious, people often have reasonably good introspective access to it. If students are asked how they solved a math problem or choose a new car, they can often provide a fairly accurate account of their choice process. By contrast, when it comes to emotional reactions, a person may not be able to give a more satisfying explanation of an action except that "he felt like it."

There is a bidirectional link between reflective and affective processes to indicate the mutual influence that they have on each other. The dual model is a simplistic and intuitive framework to explain the organization of the brain. Neurobiologists argue that the two-system model is inadequate, and they note that decisions are determined by the interactions of various brain systems. The brain region that supports emotion and the brain region that supports cognition are completely intertwined processes. Every region in the brain that has been identified with some aspect of emotion has also been identified with aspects of cognitive processes (e.g., Davidson and Irwin, 1999). However, the intention here is to convey the idea that behavior is the outcome of an interaction between distinct affective and reflective systems.

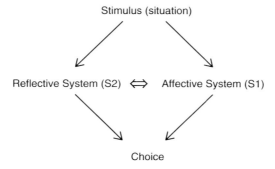

Factors Influencing S1 and S2

The following describes the factors that enhance the activation of the affective system and reflective system that ultimately influence decisions.

Stimuli

An environmental stimulus might activate the affective system, as when the sight of a delicious food motivates you to eat, or it might activate the reflective system to remind you that you are on a diet. Stimuli are assumed to trigger the affective system through conditioning. Chronic exposure to highly palatable foods or drug use changes our brains, conditioning us to seek continued stimulation. Environmental cues are paired in time with an individual's consumption and, through classical conditioning, take on conditioned stimulus properties. When those cues are present at a later time, they elicit anticipation of a reward and thus generate craving. The learned cues capture our attention and motivate us to act. Cues can gain power even if we are not consciously aware of them. Over time, the repeated responses to a relevant cue followed by an immediate reward strengthen the association between the cue and its reward. Most importantly, affective processes of behavior determination operate in an effortless manner.

The Role of Proximity

The proximity of a stimulus exerts a powerful influence on the affective system. Proximity can be defined in many dimensions, such as geographic, temporal, visual, social, and so forth. For example, a tasty food is more likely to evoke hunger to the extent that it is nearby, easily available, visible, or being consumed by someone else (in close proximity). In short, emotions are highly tuned to temporal proximity. The affective systems kick in when rewards and punishments are immediate, but not when they are remote. For example, if seated next to an annoying individual in a classroom, one could simply get up and move to a seat further away. Thus, physical distance from an emotional stimulus can influence one's emotional response to stimuli. Deliberation is, in contrast, much less sensitive to immediacy.[2] One can weaken the emotional response by imagining a greater distance between self and an emotionally charged stimulus; this sentiment is found in common advice, "some distance will help you feel better."

The Vividness Effect

The affective system is highly attuned to visual imagery, whereas the reflective system is much more keyed in to the logic of costs and benefits. Abstract information generally has a weak impact compared with the impact of pictures and of events actually seen. For example, to teach the hardship of parenting, a school program provides teenagers with dolls that require constant attention. The rationale is that, absent such a vivid experience, teenagers may have an overly romantic view of parenting, even if they are provided with more detailed information about the demands of parenting. Research also shows that imagining our emotional reactions, or anticipated emotions increase the urge to act (Mellers and McGraw, 2001). For example, imagining one's satisfaction from eating chocolate cake may undermine the deliberative system by making the taste and smell of the cake more vivid in one's imagination. Activation of these vivid attributes may become so striking that they outweigh other factors (e.g., weight gain, calories or fat content). Thus, individuals faced with a desirable stimulus may overweigh the impact of the joy from satisfying the impulse compared to the guilt associated with the failure to control the impulse.

Thus, news media coverage can maintain our emotional interest by describing global situations (e.g., global warming or an earthquake) in terms of particular stories about individual people or families. When we hear of the war casualties of thousands of people in a war taking place in a remote region of the world, our emotional response comes nowhere near the intensity of our sadness at the death of a single victim of the same war we see on TV. We establish some emotional connection with that particular victim. However, this emotional partiality impairs our ability to see the big picture. In other words, our emotional processing prevents us from acting rationally to see the overall benefit (utilitarian calculation).

Time Pressure

Because deliberation is slow (time is energy), deliberative processing takes time. Hence, any factor that imposes time pressure on a judgment or decision will tend to undermine deliberative processing. Under time pressure, people fall back on old habits (e.g., snacking on chips) even when they are not the desired response. With sufficient time to think, people are able to correct their gut-level response.[3]

The Interplay of Affect and Cognition

An emotional reaction to a stimulus is not necessarily, or even usually, a reflective action, but it often involves an appraisal of surrounding conditions. According to the appraisal theory, an emotional reaction is a function of a private interpretation of an event. Appraisals can be either conscious or unconscious. For example, a person who is unaware of his lack of affection to his wife may find that he is fascinated to read about divorce advice stories in popular magazines. Thus, the concept of appraisal provides insights into the individual differences in emotional reactions.

The affective system can influence the reflective system, and often distorts our thinking about the consequences of a behavior. For example, under the influence of aggression, one could categorize a baseball bat and a golf club as ways to hurt or kill someone rather than as, say, objects used in athletic games. Emotions change how we see the world and how we interpret the actions of others. We behave differently when we are in a good mood than when we are in a bad mood (satiated or hungry). Our emotional state determines the value of options we face in decision making (such as food to a hungry person). Such input from the affective system may be required for sound, deliberative thinking. The input from the affective system may help focus the reflective system on relevant bodily needs. For example, when the affective system transmits hunger up to the reflective system, it helps focus the reflective system on the decision whether to eat. Affect can also distort and disrupt reflective processing in various ways. Under the influence of powerful emotions, people are ready to believe almost anything. For example, people who are desperately ill are often ready to embrace quack remedies, contrary to all scientific evidence. That is why placebos are so effective. In fact, a placebo is an effective pain therapy without any side effects. Medical studies have shown that placebos can be fairly effective against a wide variety of diseases such as heart problems, depression, and ulcers. The placebos are effective because people believe in them (Ariely, 2008).

In the case of collaboration, the two systems positively influence each other. For example, when a person is hungry, there is a greater appetite for food. Furthermore, if someone who is hungry and thinks of food, the "thought" of food exacerbates the state of hunger. Therefore, the final decision of how much food to buy in order to avoid hunger is altered by the hunger state itself and the cognition, so that the person is likely to overestimate the amount of food needed.

Under many circumstances, the behavioral choice activated by the affective and the reflective systems, may conflict with each other. Which process wins out over the other in these cases will depend on the relative strength of affect and cognition. For instance, when a person is passing by the chocolate at the supermarket checkout line, the sight of the chocolate bar may activate the affective system to purchase it. Meanwhile, the reflective system may generate a behavioral decision to stop the purchase due to weight concerns. Such a struggle between incompatible behaviors by the affective and the reflective system is often accompanied by a feeling of internal conflict or temptation that characterizes many impulsive decisions.

The extent of collaboration and competition between cognitive and affective systems, and the outcome of conflict when it occurs, depends critically on the intensity of affect. At low levels of intensity, affect appears to play a largely "information" role (e.g., affect-as-information theory[4]). At intermediate levels of intensity, people begin to become conscious of conflicts between cognitive and affective inputs. Finally, at even greater levels of intensity, people often report themselves as being "out of control" or "acting against their own self-interest." This is a moment when we are the least motivated to use the reflective system (Kirby et al., 1999). Extreme fear produces panic and immobilization rather than effective escape. Uncontrolled anger toward another person can lead to behaviors, such as crimes of passion, that often end up doing the most damage to one's self. Thus, hyperactivity of the affective system can overwhelm or "hijack" the influence of the reflective system.

The Primacy of Affect

Although interactions run in both directions, affect seems to hold a kind of primacy over reflection. That is, affect is "first on the scene" and plays a dominant role in behavior. Anyone who has ever been put in front of freshly baked cookies and who has found herself eating without having made any deliberation can appreciate this notion.

There are many more neural connections going from the emotional systems to the reflective systems than the other way. According to LeDoux (1996), while conscious control over emotions is weak, emotions can flood consciousness. This is so because the connections from the emotional systems to the cognitive systems are stronger than connections from the cognitive systems to the emotional systems. Some individuals (e.g., aggressive people) tend to have a less active prefrontal lobe in general.

Automatic priming is a good example of the primacy of affect. Priming exerts an automatic effect on individuals' behavior. Exposure to hot affective cues triggers automatic action initiation. For example, a study (North et al., 1999) exposed customers in a supermarket drinks section to either French music or German music. The results showed that French wine outsold German wine when French music was played, whereas German wine outsold French wine when German music was played. However, the majority of customers denied that type of music playing influenced their choice of wine. Similarly, the portion size primes food consumption, presumably because larger amounts highlight the tempting features of food and reduce people's capacity to consciously monitor the amount they have eaten.

Willpower

An important aspect of being human is the ability to engage in reflective, controlled behavior (Higgins, 1997). Although the emotion system seems to hold a kind of primacy, the deliberative system can often override affective responses (at least partially). The existence of neural connections from the prefrontal cortex to the affective system suggests that the reflective system can influence the affective system. The reflective system allows individuals to have a fairly large degree of control over choices and action. Rollo May (1981) defines freedom as the pause between stimulus and response. When we pause, we become free; we are no longer a part of the automatic reaction. Thus, reflective processing allows freedom of choice and free will.

The efforts by the reflective system to override affective motivations require an inner exertion of effort, often referred to as willpower (Baumeister et al., 2007). In general, willpower refers to effortful control that is exerted with the purpose of controlling our behavior. Willpower operates within the broader domain of self-regulation, defined as the process of controlling thoughts, behavior, attention, and emotions to achieve a personally desirable goal. When people exercise willpower or self-regulation, they inhibit their normal, typical, or automatic behavior. For example, if someone typically drinks sodas with meals, then it requires the exertion of willpower to alter this habit.

Willpower strength (or self-regulatory resources) fuels the reflective system. The low, self-regulatory resource levels disable reflective activation and hence the impulsive system will have a greater influence on behavior. However, willpower strength is a limited resource. Like any other limited resources, it is subject to the law of diminishing returns. Once the strength is used up, the reflective system becomes vulnerable to temptation. For instance, after resisting the temptation to eat freshly baked cookies, participants in one study quit sooner on a subsequent task requiring effortful persistence, compared with participants who did not have to resist eating the cookies. Resisting the temptation to eat the cookies presumably depleted an energy resource that could otherwise have been used to persist on the subsequent task (Baumeister, 2002).

Similarly, making many decisions leaves the person in a depleted state and less likely to exert willpower. When resources are depleted, people tend to make poor choices and are more likely to be swayed by desires, urges, and cravings, although they may regret it in the long run. Depleted persons succumb to various flawed decision strategies, by taking short cuts instead of reasoning out the problem.

The good news, however, is that practice increases willpower capacity. Like a muscle, willpower seems to become stronger with use. The self-control theorists have suggested that willpower strength can be cultivated—just as muscular strength can be developed—so that repeated exercises of self-control in one domain (such as dieting) may make future displays of self-control easier, both in the domain of dieting and in other domains (Baumeister, 2002). The idea of exercising willpower is seen in military boot camp, where recruits are trained to overcome one challenge after another. Positive emotional experience may also help replace expended self-control energy. Positive emotions can recharge a depleted self-regulatory system (Tice et al., 2007).

Free Will

The concept of free will is closely linked to the reflective system (System 2) processing. People tend to associate free will with conscious deliberation, and with acting against one's selfish impulses, and with resisting external pressure. The definition or nature of free will is ultimately a philosophical question;[5] whether people believe they have free will is a psychological one. Psychologically speaking, free will is the perception of choice, agency, or self-determination. In most domains of life, people experience themselves as the origins of their actions. Moreover, they believe that what they do is the result of their free will. Particularly in the domain of economic behavior, the freedom to choose seems to be a basic assumption.

Free will is conceptualized as exercising self-control (i.e., overriding momentary impulses to attain long-term goals) and making rational choices (i.e., carefully weighted decisions) (Baumeister et al., 2008). Self-regulation enables the person to resist the impulse that arises in a given situation. By exerting free will, the person expands his options and freedom. So self-regulation provides freedom of action, that is, the capacity to do what we wish to do. The capacity for free will hinges on self-regulatory resources that can get temporarily depleted by prior acts of choice or self-control. For example, when people struggle to quit smoking, they eat more, become crabby (failing to regulate emotion), and show other signs of poor self-control.

Some scientists argue that free will is an illusion. In a series of famous experiments in the 1970s and 1980s, Benjamin Libet measured people's brain activity while telling them to move their fingers whenever they felt like it. Libet detected brain activity suggesting a readiness to move the finger half a second before the actual movement and about 400 milliseconds before people became aware of their conscious intention to move their finger. Libet argued that this leaves 100 milliseconds for the conscious self to veto the brain's unconscious decision.

Even though free will is an illusion, it is a necessary one (Baer et al., 2008). Without believing in free will, we cannot hold people accountable for their actions and the foundations of society would be in jeopardy. People have a deep-seated need for autonomy and self-determination (Deci and Ryan, 2002). People benefit from experiencing freedom and viewing themselves as free creatures. When feeling free and self-determined, we generally flourish. Believing that things are beyond your control is a recipe for helplessness.[6] Viewing ourselves as free and responsible agents is the groundwork for self-discipline and self-initiatives. People with a strong sense of personal control smoke less, wear seat belts more, make more money, more often practice birth control, resist conformity, and delay gratification.

Erroneous Sense-Making

We have far more introspective access to cognitive rather than to emotional processes. Consequently, we tend to interpret our own behavior as a result of deliberate decision making even when this is not the case (Wilson, 2002). We tend to quickly come up with explanations for things we don't really have an explanation for. The reasons that people give when asked to explain their own behavior are rarely insightful. What they offer for their behavior are generally rationalizations. We feel pressed to understand and to justify our emotions, and we retrospectively justify our action (Wilson, 2002). For example, the person who has consumed the tempting good, but feels guilty about it may try to alleviate her guilt. She would do so by coming up with additional reasons that justify her behavior. In general, people know little about their motivations.

It is a fundamental feature of human beings that they have an image of themselves as acting for a reason. Ramachandran (2004) remarks that our conscious life is nothing but an elaborate post hoc rationalization of things that we really do for other reasons. Post hoc fallacy is a logical error that occurs when one concludes that event A caused event B simply because event A happened before event B. Michael Gazzaniga (2008) argues that the pressure to justify one's actions reflects the operation of "an interpreter system" housed in the left-hemisphere brain (analytical thinker).[7] The interpreter (the "I") is driven to generate explanations and hypotheses regardless of circumstances. The left hemisphere may generate a feeling in all of us that we are integrated and unified. Gazzaniga claims that the interpreter is behind the human's adoration of reason. People engage in confabulation. That is, people readily fabricate reasons to explain their own behavior. In short, the brain does not necessarily seek to obtain "objective" truth about the world. It assigns itself a goal and assesses reality with respect to the goal. In other words, the brain only perceives what it wishes to. In short, making sense is a deep human motivation, but making sense is not the same as being correct. We rationalize many of the decisions we take by filling in our reasons from a logical perspective.

Robert Wright (1994) points out that the brain is like a good lawyer, and like a lawyer, the human brain wants victory, not truth. Lawyers begin with a conclusion they want to convince others and then seek evidence that support it. Similarly, it appears that the causation in our thought processes tend to go from belief to evidence. The psychologist Jonathan Haidt argues that the human mind is designed to be both a scientist (seeking objective truth) and a lawyer (seeking evidence to justify what we desire to be truth). Because motivated reasoning is unconscious, people's claim that they are unaffected by bias or vested interests can be sincere (Mlodinow, 2012). For example, an interviewer motivated to support an applicant tends to assign high importance to areas in which the applicant excels and ignoring areas in which the applicant falls short. That is, the interviewer uses his preferred conclusion to shape his analysis. However, motivated reasoning has an advantage. For example, being optimistic about our ability (e.g., writing a book or starting a new project) gives us strength to overcome the many obstacles in life that might otherwise overwhelm us. It is a gift that we can adopt a theory about ourselves that motivates us in the direction of success and happiness. This hopefulness tends to drive exploration (e.g., "the grass is always greener on the other side of the hill").

Do words reflect feelings? Kagan (2007) notes that humans invented language to communicate required behaviors, to persuade others of the desirability of a course of action, to teach skills, and to indicate the location and the nature of resources and dangers in the world. The accurate description of private feelings was not intended as a primary function of speech for two reasons. First, it is not adaptive to reveal the anger, jealousy, envy, sexual feelings, or intimidation felt with respect to others. Second, the brain sites that are primary foundations for feelings are less fully connected with sites that represent language.

A major implication of the mind's tendency for erroneous sense-making is that one needs to be suspicious to view one's own behavior as the outcome of deliberations. Donald Hebb once noted that outside observers are far more accurate at judging a person's true emotional state than the person herself. Introspective understanding of the causes of emotion states can be limited, especially when people are asked to reflect back on an episode after it is over. Emotions are difficult to verbalize and that is why we need the field of psychology. We focus too much on things that are verbal and conscious and are oblivious about emotion affective processes. Our emotion often drives our decisions, with conscious cognition trying to come up with rationalizations for the decision. Some economists argue that free market does not automatically produce what people really want. Rather, it produces what they *think* they want and are willing to pay for. If consumers are willing to pay for snake oil, the market will produce snake oil (Akerlof and Shiller, 2009).

Reward and Motivation

How appetites that give mainly pleasure, delight, joy, or harmless entertainment can sometimes become so excessive that they threaten to spoil our lives. This book widens the framework for our understanding of addiction by studying emotion and motivation that govern human nature. What motivates people? What do people really want? The psychological literature describes the motivation to move toward desired end-states and to move away from undesired end-states (i.e., to maximize pleasure and minimize pain).

As discussed before, emotions are closely related to motivation, because they drive us to select courses of actions. Motivation is to approach pleasure and avoid pain. For economists, motivation is a starting point for all economic choices, and preferences revealed in choices. To be motivated is to have preferences directing choices. In economics, motivation is described by an individual having a "utility function," and what goes into them characterizes what people care about.

For example, a person may care about today's consumption and about future consumption. A good decision is to maximize utility (that option with the best benefits-to-costs ratio of outcomes).

It is also important to know where the preferences that direct choices come from. Our preferences are derived from those that served adaptive and functional ends in the past. Our preferences have roots in human evolution. Evolutionary psychology views our goals not as ends in themselves, but rather as means in our struggle to acquire the resources needed to survive and reproduce.

What Is Reward?

Reward has been a foundation topic for economists and psychologists. Rewards are experienced as "making things better" and are thus liked, desired (wanted), and pursued (Berridge and Robinson, 2003). The survival and continuation of species requires that organisms learn the circumstances under which they can obtain food and other resources for bodily needs and find opportunities for mating. Such goals function as rewards. This suggests that for any incentive system to be effective, its reward must be things that people find desirable. A key feature of all rewards is that consumption of certain goods leads to their satiation for a certain period of time, during which excessive consumption would even lead to unpleasant sensory experiences. A prominent example is food, where after having eaten a certain amount, hunger is satiated, and "overconsumption" makes the individual feel worse off.

In contrast to natural rewards, drug rewards tend to become overvalued at the expense of other rewards, contributing to compulsion and to a marked narrowing of life goals to obtaining and using drugs. Drug addiction is considered as the "hijacking" of motivational systems that evolved to support biologically critical functions, such as feeding. Addictive drugs do not serve any beneficial homeostatic or reproductive purpose, but instead often prove detrimental to health and functioning.

What motivates people? Motivation is considered as a relation between an internal need and an objective in the external world that satisfies that particular need. It is a mechanism by which people direct their lives and select their environment. We tend to select friends, hobbies, careers, and spouses that are in accordance with our interests, goals, values, and needs. People who report that their goals are congruent with their inherent needs report higher well-being.[8] Such motivational tendencies include characteristics that developed during evolution to improve the fit between individuals and their environments.

Evolution has designed us to enjoy things that are good for us. Rolls (2000) presents a behavioral model as follows: genes defines goals for action → goals/desires (hunger, sexual, social acceptance, status, social cooperation, curiosity, etc.) → emotions (rewarding) → behavioral motivations to seek the goals. According to this view, genes build our brains in such a way that our genes can specify the goals of our actions, and thus what we do. The idea is that emotion, the evolution's ancient tool, motivates us to pursue certain goals that maximize our reproductive success. The model, using a Darwinian approach, explains why we, and other animals, are built to have emotions. The attainment of a particular feeling is an important motive. For example, we are designed to have taste for sweets. Individuals with a taste for sugar would be more likely to have acquired the nutrients required for survival and reproduction. Loneliness prompts a desire to affiliate. Like hunger, it is a warning to do something to alter an uncomfortable and possibly dangerous condition. The anticipation of guilt normally discourages cheating.[9] Depressed persons fail to work toward their goals. For example, if a raise in salary or status did not produce a pleasant feeling, people would stop working so hard.

Why do we form the desires we have? We have two types of desire: instrumental and terminal. We have a desire to do Y (instrumental) → to obtain X (terminal desire). Terminal desires are desired for their own sake.[10] For example, the desire to end my hunger pangs is a terminal desire. Pleasure of eating is inherently desirable. Instrumental desires are desired for the sake of something else (e.g., my desire for transportation to obtain food). Sometimes we want something not for its own sake, but in order to fulfill some other desire (e.g., attending this class). People say that they want money, dominance, status, fame, or friendships, but they strive for these events in order to experience the feelings that achieving those goals allows. As an instrumental desire, power can increase one's opportunities for belonging, and reduce the risk of being abandoned. Most of our desires are instrumental, such as, I want to wear this pair of shoes to avoid humiliation; or I want to avoid humiliation because it feels bad. Power and wealth are usually associated with being able to convince other people to work toward our goals. The means-end chain could go on forever if there were not some terminal goal. A person's desire at the end of the mapping process will almost certainly be different.

The incentive power of chemical substances, such as alcohol and nicotine, does not depend on their ability to produce other goods and services. Instead, they produce a distinct physiological state by direct action on some part of the brain. Problem gamblers don't appear to value money for its own sake, they are seeking for reward. As soon as a drug stops producing any physiological satisfaction, its uses will stop.

Often, what actually satisfies a terminal desire does not direct choices. Consider the common concern that people often don't appreciate (or value) something until they don't have it anymore ("sometimes you don't know what you have until you've lost it."). The general point is that because some needs are generally being satisfied, when suddenly the need is not being satisfied, then people experience their attraction to it. Only then do they value it highly and make choices on that basis. For example, you are with someone and you are not happy with the relationship, but he provides a sense of security. Then you broke off and he becomes so valuable and you regret why you took him for granted. The point is that you are missing the security that he provided, not him. Our desires generally don't exist in isolation, they come into existence because we want something else—they are instrumental desires.

The Sources of Desire Consist of Emotion and Reason

We have two sources of desire within us, our emotion and our intellect. Emotions form terminal, hedonic desires, and the intellect forms instrumental desires, fulfillment of which will enable the emotions to get what they want. Generally, the objects of terminal desires formed by the emotions are inherently desirable, and the objects of instrumental desires formed by the intellect are not (Irvine, 2006). Emotions specialize in the formation of desires, and the intellect specializes in the formation of instrumental desires. The instrumental desires in many cases are doing the bidding of the emotions—helping them fulfill some hedonic, terminal desire.

The relationship between the intellect and the emotions can best be viewed as an uneasy alliance: when emotions and intellect work in tandem vs when they compete (frustration). Emotion has the veto power. Emotion wears down the intellect. It begs, whines, and bullies like a five-year-old child. When you are dieting, emotions will scream: "I don't care about any damn diet. I want chocolate!" If our willpower is sufficiently strong, our intellect can override desires formed by our emotions. Intellect has the power of persuasion in dealing with emotions. The fact that we make resolutions shows that we are not in control of our desires. In making them, we are, in effect, announcing to the various sources of desire within our brains that we, not them, are in charge.

Many desires arise out of our unconscious mind. That is, the desire formation process is much less rational than one might think. Desires simply pop into our heads, uninvited and unannounced, and take control of our lives. We don't choose our desires, but they choose us. This explains why sometimes we don't really know why we want what we want. Advertisers, of course, realize this. They design ads that will trigger the unconscious desire formation process within us and then help us rationalize the desire the ad has created.

Where do one's goals come from in a given moment? The relation between goals and the individuals holding them is strikingly similar to that between genes and their host organisms (Bargh and Huang, 2009). Evolutionary biologists view motivations as the crucial link between genetic influence and adaptive behavior. That is, genes provide us with general and specific motivations, which are translated into our nervous systems as "goal programs," and it is these goal programs that guide our behavior in the everyday life. For example, a predator stalking its prey, the prey fleeing from the pursuing predator, or a male displaying to a female are acting purposefully, yet unconsciously.

Genes are the primary policy makers and brains are the executives. In his classic work *The Selfish Gene,* Dawkins (1976) described how our genes have designed us (through the blind process of natural selection) to be their "survival machines" on which they depend for their propagation into future generations. The core of his argument was that genes, not individual organisms, are the basic unit of natural selection. Moreover, genes were said to be essentially "selfish" in that their own propagation is their only concern, not the welfare of the host organism: "each gene is seen as pursuing its own self-interested agenda against the background of the other genes in the gene pool" (p. ix).

Social scientists argue that we can view our "selfish goals" as operating in direct service to a unconscious agenda. Being selfish means putting one's own welfare and needs above those of others. Selfish goals do not imply selfishness at the level of individual person, because the individual or "self" comprises of many, often-conflicting goals (self-interested, but also prosocial and morally principled ones as well). For instance, a threat to one's self-esteem (e.g., failure at a task) can trigger a self-protecting goal to restore positive self-regard. On the other hand, priming individuals with a strongly held goal of fairness activates treating other people (minority) fairly. In short, the idea is that goals can be selfish without making their "owners" selfish.[11] The active goal is the unit of autonomous behavior control, not the individual human (or "self"). The selfish goal pursues its agenda regardless of whether this fits the agenda of its individual host. That explains why it is so hard to "know thyself."

The Importance of Emotion to Thinking

Is it best to reason with a cool head, or should we follow our feelings? Do we need emotion for thinking? Accumulated evidence shows that emotion is part of the mechanism of reasoning.[12] The lack of it is very detrimental to decision making. It is not enough "to know" what should be done; it is also necessary "to feel it." People rely to some extent on their feelings and hunches in order to make successful decisions. Experience matters. If you have seen something before, you are more likely to anticipate it the next time.

In a series of seminal papers with titles such as "Feeling and Thinking: Preferences Need No Inferences" (1980), and "On the Primacy of Affect" (1984), Zajonc presented the results of studies that showed that people can often identify their affective reaction to something—whether they like it or not—more rapidly than they can even say what it is, and that their memory for affective reactions can be dissociated from their memory of the details of a situation, with the former often being better. We remember whether we liked or disliked a particular person, book, or movie, without being able to remember any details other than our affective reaction (Bargh, 2002). The human brain affectively tags virtually all objects and concepts, and these affective tags are brought to mind effortlessly and automatically when we encounter objects and concepts.

Wilson (2002) reports a number of carefully structured experimental situations in which people were required to do things and then say why they did what they did. For example, in one study, an investigator had students in a photography class at Harvard choose two favorite pictures from among those they had just taken and then relinquish one to the teacher. Some students were told their choices were permanent; others were told they could exchange their prints after several days. As it turned out, those who had time to change their minds were less pleased with their decisions than those whose choices were irrevocable. Why do introspections mess up our reactions? Wilson argues that "thinking too much" about the picture causes us to focus on all sorts of variables that don't actually matter.[13] Instead of just listening to our affective preferences, our rational brains search for reasons to prefer one picture for another. When we overanalyze, we ignore the wisdom of our emotions, which are much better in assessing our preferences.[14] This is like when a joke is explained, the humor is lost.

The Somatic Marker Theory

The main idea of the somatic marker theory is that decision-makers process the consequences of alternative choices affectively (Damasio, 1994). That is, emotional experiences leave affective residues in the body (somatic markers). The term *somatic* refers to the collection of body-related responses produced by affective and emotional responses (gut feelings). These gut feelings are stored, evaluative information stemming from past experiences, and are potentially helpful for guiding future behavior. In other words, anticipatory emotional feelings ("somatic markers") come to be connected to predicted outcomes and act as a warning signal. If a person makes a costly mistake, the next time he approaches that experience, the somatic marker will be activated, creating a bad feeling that in effect warns the person not to make similar choice. These emotional signals or somatic markers are often unconscious, although they can become conscious and experienced as a "hunch" or a "gut feeling" that a given choice may be good or bad. For example, when deciding to speed on a highway because you are late for an interview, the "thought" of being stopped by a police, or the "thought" of getting into an accident will trigger somatic states (e.g., some form of a fear response). These somatic states are indeed beneficial, because they consciously or unconsciously bias the decision in an advantageous manner.

The somatic marker theory was developed to address the problems of decision making encountered in patients with certain kinds of prefrontal damage and with impaired emotion processing, in spite of maintaining a normal intellect. These patients have difficulty planning their workdays and in expressing emotions and feelings in appropriate situations, and they are unable to learn from previous mistakes. However, these patients show few obvious deficits (as revealed by psychological tests) in functions like perception, attention, memory, and language. The somatic marker theory attributes these patients' inability to make advantageous decisions in real life to a defect in an emotional mechanism that rapidly signals the possible consequences of an action, and assists in the choice of an advantageous response option. Deprived of this emotional signal, these patients rely on an extensive, reasoned cost-benefit analysis of numerous and often conflicting options. The impairment degrades the quality of making decisions. For these patients, Damasio argues that their reasoning has become dissociated from the emotional responsiveness that is critical for making decisions.

Evidence shows the presence of decision-making impairments in addicts as measured by the abnormal generation of anticipatory emotional responses (somatic markers) (Bechara and Damasio, 2005). This indicates that at least some of the decision-making alterations observed in addicts may have actually preceded the drug abuse stage, and in fact, served as a predisposing factor that contributed to the switch from a casual drug use to a compulsive and uncontrolled substance dependence problem. Decision-making deficits have also been reported in adolescent binge drinkers, individuals with Antisocial Personality Disorder, and pathological gambling. These individuals tend to act in such a way that brings about immediate reward, even when that comes at the risk of incurring extremely negative future consequences, which may include loss of job, home, important life relationships, and reputation, and often troubles with the law. Such individuals act seemingly in ignorance of this risk.

The Iowa Gambling Task (IGT) was developed as a behavioral measure to detect decision-making impairment (Bechara and Damasio, 2005). In the Iowa Gambling Task, subjects are given four decks of cards and $2,000 in play money with which to play a game, and are instructed that their goal in the game is to win as much money as possible. Each card tells the player whether she wins or loses money. The subject is instructed to turn over a card from one of the four decks. The cards are distributed at random. Decks A and B offer short-term rewards but long-term punishments, leading to a net loss. These decks have bigger payouts ($100 per card), but the losses are large ($1,250). The other two decks, decks C and D are advantageous, drawing lower rewards per card ($50), but with smaller penalties such that playing mostly from these decks leads to an overall gain. If the gambler drew only from C and D decks, she would come out ahead. In the experiment, a number of substance-abusing populations made more impulsive choices. They selected cards from these disadvantageous decks (higher immediate payoff) significantly more than the nonaddict groups. They often went bankrupt and had to take out "loans" from the experimenter. Selecting from A and B decks may reflect hypersensitivity to large gain and/or insensitivity to large losses (two characteristics of addicts).

While each subject plays the game, measures are taken of skin conductance responses (SCRs) to test their unconscious responses to making card choices. The laboratory experiments have shown that after a player has drawn only ten cards, his body usually tenses up and his hand gets "nervous" when it reaches for the risky decks. Although, the subjects have little clue which decks are the most advantageous, their emotions have developed an accurate sense of fear. The emotions know which decks are dangerous. These wise, yet inexplicable feelings are an essential part of the decision-making process. In other words, all normal subjects express a "hunch" that A and B are riskier.

Overall, the findings demonstrate that the generation of somatic states can guide us toward beneficial behaviors without any input from our conscious deliberations. In contrast to normal subjects, addicts and subjects with bilateral prefrontal damage do not generate this response. Their reflective systems are not generating somatic states that help bias the response away from disadvantageous decisions. Thus, they do not choose advantageously, despite the fact that, when asked, they describe with accuracy what strategy will win the game. For addicts, the absence of a somatic response is an example of a dysfunction in the decision-making control mechanisms. This phenomenon demonstrates that it is more than an intellectual understanding of consequences that guides a person's actual behavior in the real world. Similarly, for addicts, they know the consequences of their drug-seeking behavior[15] (Bechara and Damasio, 2005).

In sum, the somatic marker provides a neurological framework of the impact of emotions on decision making. Evidence supports that not only cognitive, but also affective, mechanisms are crucial for decision making. Patients with brain injuries on the frontal lobes engage in decisions that lead to negative consequences without learning. Their decisions often lead to a variety of losses, including financial, social, and family and friends.

Vulnerability to Depression

How and why do we become depressed? This section provides an overview (not an exhaustive review) of various vulnerability factors to depression that involves the interaction of affect and cognition. The focus on depression provides insights into how emotional dysfunction can interact with cognitive processing. For example, a sad mood may result from an undesired outcome (stimulus), but a sad mood can also lead to increased emphasis on the negative aspects of alternatives in decision making (e.g., the decision to relocate).

Depression is among the most prevalent of all psychiatric illnesses. The World Health Organization (WHO) has ranked depression as the single most burdensome disease in the world. Around 12% of men and 20% of women will suffer major depression at some time in their lives. The risk for women to experience depression is considerably higher than for men (average ratio is close to 2:1).[16] The economic cost of depression in terms of lost productivity in the United States is estimated to be $36 billion (Kessler et al., 2006).

How Depression Works

Depression can be thought of as the presence of a depressed mood, a loss of interest or pleasure in nearly all activities, a feeling of worthlessness or excessive guilt, and a diminished ability to think and concentrate (Ingram et al., 2011). The inability to take pleasure removes the motivation to do much of what we do on a daily basis. A diagnosis of depression is given only when a number of these elements are present at the same time for at least two weeks, and are shown to interfere with a person's ability to perform her daily activities. Depression is frequently comorbid with anxiety. For example, the chances of a person with depression suffering from panic anxiety are 19 times greater than the odds of someone without depression experiencing panic. Once a person has been depressed, it tends to return, even if he has been feeling better for months. At least 50% of those experiencing depression find it comes back, despite the fact that they appeared to have made a full recovery.

Freud defined depression as a response to a loss in childhood, often involving repressed anger turned inward (Greenberg, 2010), and with help of therapy, a depressed person learns to release the anger and stop accusing the herself. Andrew Solomon (2001) described depression as a "flaw in love:" flaws in self-love (guilt, shame, suicidal thoughts), love for others (blame, aggression, accusation), and even the extinction of a desire for love (lethargy, withdrawal, dullness). Depression is an emotional pain without context or any obvious cause.

Melancholy is a subtype of major depression, which strikes mostly older adults, in which people are unable to eat or sleep or smile. It is more common among people who also suffer from anxiety. Melancholia appears suddenly in response to great loss (e.g., loss of work, or loss of a romantic partner through death or divorce). These men and women have lost a work-focused life, and to be old or retired is for them is to feel unwanted (Kahn, 2013). The highest rate of completed suicide is among men in their 60s. Elderly people with little perceived purpose in life are nearly twice as likely to die as their peers who see an important role for themselves. The core cognition of melancholia includes guilt (burden), loss of pleasure, and hopelessness. Treatment includes regaining purpose, role, and hopefulness, instead of thinking of oneself socially useless or feeling the guilt of burden.

Similarly, in a midlife crisis, people feel a sense of emptiness even though they may have satisfied their own personal ambitions and lived up to the demands of their society. In the context of adaptation, pleasures fade and pursuing and attaining happiness might appear to be hard to recapture. Having succeeded in a profession, and possibly in the raising of a family, they begin to wonder obsessively about the choices they have made. They are perturbed by the possibility that their lives may really be "meaningless." This preoccupation often becomes a painful midlife crisis.

What Makes People Psychologically Vulnerable to Depression?

The biological model of depression suggests that depression is a result of a "chemical imbalance" of neurotransmitters in the brain. Imbalance in the production and transmission of neurotransmitters such as serotonin and dopamine are commonly observed in the central nervous system in major depression. For instance, the serotonin hypothesis states that serotonin is central to the theory of depression and the functioning of mood. Antidepressant drugs such as Prozac act on serotonin. A central theory is that antidepressants work by raising serotonin levels in the brain. Depleting serotonin in depressed patients often causes relapses. Also, depression is commonly associated with low levels of physical activity. Sedentary behaviors such as watching television or using the computer are associated with an increased risk of depression.[17]

What is the role of cognitive biases in depression and sustained negative affect? It is also common not to recognize our own roles in contributing to the troublesome patterns that we repeat in our lives. Psychologist Aaron Beck believes depression is the consequence of false logic, and that by correcting negative reasoning, one may achieve better mental health. Individual differences in cognitive control can influence a person's ability to reappraise events and disengage from negative situational cues. That is, cognitive appraisals determine the emotional experience and emotion regulation.

Negative and depressed individuals tend to suffer from cognitive distortions, which negatively bias the individual's evaluation of self-worth, adequacy, social acceptability, or achievements (Beck and Alford, 2009). The typical cognitions show a variety of deviations from logical thinking, including self-doubt, overgeneralization, low self-evaluation, and rejection expectations. Their anticipations of the future are generally an extension of what they view as their present state. They seem to be unable to consider the possibility of any improvement. These depressive thoughts tend to be automatic, even when the person is resolved not to have them. As the depression progresses, patients lose control over their thinking processes. That is, even when they try to focus on other subjects, the depressive cognitions continue to intrude and occupy a central position. Thus, cognitive biases have important implications for treatment policy (Gotlib and Joormann, 2010). The aim of the therapy is to reorient the patient to more rational ways of thinking.

Similar to cognitive processing, the concept of self-schema is crucial for understanding depression. Self-schema is cognitive structures that shape information processing (worthlessness or inadequacy). These automatic thoughts are triggered by internal and external stimuli and they are target for intervention by cognitive therapy. For example, the experience of repeated failures or criticism during early childhood experiences is likely to lead to a biased association between the self and schema (themes of low worth). Later on, potential job loss may automatically bring to mind thoughts of failure, leading to depressive moods. To remedy this cognitive vulnerability, the patient is required to engage in reflective processing to correct biased thinking in the presence of negative mood states.

Similarly, according to the stress generation hypothesis (Hammen, 2006), depressed people often make themselves sick by persistently overestimating just how bad things are. This model indicates that depression occurs at least in part to dysfunctional attitude, maladaptive behaviors, circumstances (e.g., mate selection and marital quality), social problem-solving skills, personality styles (e.g., neuroticism), and deficits in impulse control. For example, the depressed-prone person tends to act rashly when experiencing negative affect (Liu and Klieman, 2012). The person with social skills deficits who is inappropriately critical of others may cause disturbances with relationships that result in the generation of stress. Thus, depressive individuals are not simply passive respondents to stressful events[18] in their lives, but are actively contributing to stressful environments by their negative interpretations of themselves and their worlds. These individuals may benefit from increased awareness and emotion regulation strategies.

Another cognitive style is the hopelessness theory (Seligman, 2011). This model explains depression as an aspect of learned helplessness, in which individuals come to believe that they have no power over events in their own lives. These individuals are passive and believe that they cannot do anything to relieve their suffering. Hopelessness develops in the presence of a negative life event in an important area of the individual's life. Treatment requires that patients regain their belief that they can control events important to them.

There is also a possibility that affect, in turn, influences the thinking and furthers the depressive thoughts. Depression makes you believe certain things such as you are worthless and unlovable. In making any self-appraisals, the depressed person is prone to magnify any failure or defects and minimize or ignore any favorable attributes. Andrew Solomon (2001) notes that depression interacts with personality. That is, some people can tolerate symptoms that would destroy others. It takes a certain survivor impulse to keep going through the depression, not to cave in to it.

Hasler (2012) argues that depression reflects a shift in cost-benefit analysis, and consequently in impaired decision making. Dopamine deficiency in a depressed person may specifically increase the valuation costs (e.g., time, effort, enduring pain, and tolerating risk) along with decrease the satisfaction from their normal daily activities and interactions. A continuous interaction between thinking and feeling may lead to a typical downward spiral of negative feelings. However, Beck argues that faulty interpretation comes before affective changes, so reducing negative thought content leads to the greatest reduction of negative affect.

According to the mood-congruent bias, mood can bring to mind certain types of thoughts, memories, and beliefs (Williams et al., 2007). Depressed patients attend selectively to mood congruent cues (sad faces) and look longer at scenes having themes related to a sad mood (Mathews and MacLeod, 2005). Dysphoric moods automatically bring to mind themes of loss and worthlessness. Depression forges a connection in the brain between sad mood and negative thoughts, so that even normal sadness can rekindle major negative thoughts (Segal et al., 2012). After repeated episodes of depression, strong connections are formed between the moods and the negative thinking patterns. This means that when a person feels sad again (for any reason), a relatively small amount of this mood can reactivate the old thinking (e.g., feeling lonely and unwanted) that is connected with the sad mood. This happens quite automatically. The memories of past failures and the images of feared future scenarios further worsen the mood.

Depressed individuals are prone to ruminate on negative thinking. They have the tendency to get stuck in the negative mood. Rumination is a form of repetitive thought. It is defined as turning one's attention towards symptoms of depression and the causes and consequences of those symptoms (Nolen-Hoeksema, 1991). People want to find answers to their depression. Rumination is automatic. Unfortunately, rumination tends to maintain or amplify negative thinking. The ruminative tendency is a dangerous mental habit, because it leads people to fixate on their flaws and problems. Rumination results in more prolonged depression. Rumination is like trying to dig yourself out of a hole; the hole gets bigger the more you dig, because rumination can take you deeper into negative feeling. Rumination hijacks the prefrontal activity (consciousness), and we become deeply attentive to our pain. For example, the rumination for a depression triggered by a bitter divorce might take the form of regret ("I should have been a better spouse"), and anxiety about the future ("How will the kids deal with it?"). The end result is poor performance on tests for memory and executive function, especially when the task involves lots of information.

From a dual mind perspective, reflective processing can correct this automatic, negative, and biased thinking (Beevers, 2005). However, if cognitive resources are depleted due to a life stress, distraction, or time pressure, intuitive processing is the default mode of information processing. Thus, depression vulnerability may be observed when reflective processing is impaired by life stress. For instance, stressful life events can deplete attention capacity to suppress negative cognitions effectively (Ingram et al., 2011). This reduced ability of inhibitory control system makes it difficult for depressed individuals to redirect their attention away from negative thoughts (forgetting) and rumination, which hinders recovery from negative affect (Gotlib and Joormann, 2010). As Andrew Solomon (2001) writes, the opposite of depression is not happiness, but vitality and resilience. Good control over one's attention could thus protect against depression.

Many people who suffer with undiagnosed depression self-medicate to relieve their emotional pain. Overeating and addictions can often mask depression. That is, addiction and eating disorders may be the tip of an emotional iceberg that will cause trouble in the future if ignored. The decision to use drugs to cope with depression is a version of the strategy of seeking immediate gratification. In fact, one can argue that addiction is mostly survival. People who are depressed abuse substances in a bid to free themselves of their depression. For example, depression may be found in as many as 33% of people with bulimia (Ingram et al., 2011). Depressed persons often try to lose weight in the hope of feeling better, but the negative feeling returns. So it is when depression is the primary motive for abusing substances.[19] Although it is not clear which disorder came first, abuse may begin as self-medication against a depressive tendency.

According to the food addiction theory of obesity, an excessive intake of highly palatable food resembles addictive behavior. The idea is that palatable foods may be addictive in a way that is seen with drugs of abuse (Avena et al., 2012). Food reward, not hunger, is the main driving force for eating in the modern society. The most commonly craved foods are chocolate, pizza, and chips (Alsio et al., 2012). These foods are craved for their palatability rather than nutritional value. While initial drug use is motivated by the rewarding value (e.g., a euphoric high) of the drug, continued use is assumed to be motivated to relieve a negative emotional state that arises from withdrawal (Parylak et al., 2011). Binge eaters have greater rates of depression and anxiety compared to the general population. This suggests that negative emotional states can trigger overeating and relapse to binge eating. In sum, overeating may be an attempt to self-medicate with "comfort food." However, repeated consumption of such palatable foods may produce addictive behavior that ultimately promotes depressive and anxiety responses when those foods are no longer available or consumed.[20] Thus, adding cognitive therapy to help manage general mood and coping, as well as dysfunctional beliefs concerning their body and eating control, can reduce relapses to overeating (Werrij et al., 2009).

In summary, depression is characterized by a specific pattern of biased processing of information that includes rumination of negative experiences, difficulties disengaging from negative information, and a deficit in cognitive control when processing negative material. Later on, experiences of negative mood states and negative life events can trigger mood-congruent thinking. To avoid this negative affect, the person engages in escapist behavior such as binge eating and alcohol abuse. Furthermore, depressive symptoms may decrease an individual's motivation to engage in healthy dietary habits (Anton and Miller, 2005). If we are convinced we are useless or unworthy, how likely are we to pursue the things that we value in life?

While the antidepressant drugs make people feel better, no real progress is ever made. For example, patients treated with medication were approximately twice as likely to relapse as patients treated with cognitive behavior therapy. The high relapse rate suggests that the drugs aren't really solving anything. In fact, they seem to be interfering with the solution, so that patients are discouraged from dealing with their problems (Beck, 2008). As Solomon (2001) wrote about his own experience with depression, the antidepressant drug will not reinvent a person, or the everyday choices. From a dual model perspective, treatment can influence associative processing and reflective processing. Interventions focused on directly modifying cognitive biases and on increasing cognitive control can improve the effectiveness of the treatment of depression.

Conclusion

This chapter has demonstrated that individual behavior is best understood as the outcome of a struggle between an emotion system and a reflective system. These two systems use different modes of operations that lead to different behavior. The final choice will depend on the relative strength of the competing systems.

For example, under conditions of sufficiently available self-control resources, the deliberative system will have the upper hand. However, under conditions of cognitive overload, the reflective system may fail to activate inhibitory action. Consequently, impulses should better predict choices. The key insight here is that, rather than thinking about our decision as being governed by a unitary preference, it can often be better described in terms of the interaction between different subsystems that might favor different alternatives for a given decision. Maintaining a healthy balance between the affective system and the reflective system remains one of the fundamental challenges of human life.

Many decision-making disorders may originate in an improper division of labor between the systems. The choice of an impulsive individual is highly influenced by external stimuli, pressures, and demands. By contrast, an obsessive-compulsive person will subject even the most trivial decisions to extensive deliberation and cost-benefit calculation. In situations in which it is entirely appropriate to make a quick decision (e.g., a choice of video rental), the obsessive-compulsive person will get stuck. Under certain circumstances, the affective system prevails, and people succumb to things like drug addiction and overeating. When the deliberative system is damaged, then the affective system loses its restraint (Bechara, 2005). Thus, our desire and emotions are immune to the power of reason.

The understanding of the role of emotion in decision making helps to recognize that people's choices involve both automatic and reflective processes. This approach integrates each of two systems as well as environmental conditions in behavior determination. The intervention strategies to promote healthy behavior that rely primarily on health messages (reflective process) will have limited impact on behavior change. A more effective approach will address both automatic processes and reflective determinants of healthy behavior. For example, impulse-oriented interventions may target tempting stimuli triggered by situational cues that lead to excessive consumption. Thus, paying attention to the affective determinants of healthy behavior complements the traditional approach intended to improve the reflective system, such as changing attitudes and beliefs.

Notes

1 Psychologist John Haidt (2006) describes the dual model by the metaphor of the elephant and the rider. The affective system is like a great, big, and determined elephant. The reflective system is the rider sitting on the top with rather limited control. The elephant (affective system) is not as easy to control as we may want it to be.
2 The ability to stand back from the immediacy of experience enables us to plan and think flexibly rather than simply react to it passively.
3 Psychologist Alison Lenton and economist Marco Francesconi (2011) illustrated the role of time pressure in speed dating. They analyzed records from 84 different speed dating events held in bars and clubs across the United Kingdom. Speed dating involves lots of choices within a limited time (three to five minutes). The result showed that when people have too many romantic choices, they tend to choose partners based on

superficial physical characteristics, and ignore attributes such as education, smoking habits, and occupation.
4. Central to the affect-as-information logic is the assumption that people draw on their affective experiences as a source of information. To make decisions, people may consciously inspect their feelings to see "how they feel" about the options. For example, when selecting a video, one considers various choices until one of them feels right (e.g., "would I have fun watching this movie?").
5. One of the twentieth century's most passionate advocate of free will was Jean-Paul Sartre, who famously argued that humans were "condemned to freedom" and who asserted that all human acts are free (existentialist philosophy). He noted that freedom of action is tied to conscious deliberation and intentional decision.
6. In addition to social environment, people live in a psychic environment largely of their own making. The self-management of inner life is also part of the belief in free will through which people improve the quality of their emotional well-being by exercising control over their thoughts and emotions by a variety of cognitive and behavioral strategies.
7. Another version of the dual model is the left- and right-brain model (McGilchrist, 2009). The left hemisphere takes a focused short-term view, whereas the right hemisphere sees the bigger picture. The right brain gives emotional value to what is seen.
8. Individuals vary in the weights that they attach to the satisfaction of different desires. This accounts for the differences that are experienced in experiments about what is motivating for the individual (e.g., for some people, grades or status are more motivating than money, for others not).
9. If you take a pill that blocked any guilty feeling, you would more likely cheat on your exam.
10. Aristotle called the final end the good life, or happiness. Like Aristotle, many people believe that happiness is the ultimate goal underlying all human action. Of all the goals we may pursue in life, happiness is the only one to have worth in itself. All the others—health, power, money, beauty, success—make sense only as means of achieving it. To many people, life would be unbearable without the belief that they can be happy.
11. Spencer et al. (1998) found that stereotype activation was increased in participants whose self-esteem had been threatened. When a person receives a self-esteem threat, the goal to attain a positive sense of self is triggered. The individual has learned over the course of her life that belittling others makes one feel good about oneself. This is especially effective if the others are easy targets for degrading, such as members of disliked groups or minorities that are associated with clear, negative stereotypes.
12. For instance, children with Autism lack emotional capacity to grasp other human beings' feelings or motivations. They identify with others out of an egocentric stance and fail to share their world (Hobson, 2005).
13. In one experiment, a white rat in a maze repeatedly beat groups of Yale undergraduates in understanding the optimal way to get food dropped in the maze. The students overanalyzed and saw patterns that didn't exist, so they were beaten by the rodent.
14. This experiment also challenges our common assumption that we would be happier with the option to change our minds, when in fact, we're happier with closure.
15. Pignatti et al. (2006) test the ability to make favorable, long-term decisions in 20 obese and 20 nonobese adults. They report that the obese subjects made more poor choices and seemed less able to learn how to make good, long-term choices in their experiment. They note that such impaired learning and judgment is consistent with brain defects impairing executive decision making.

16 Relationships can be a major factor. For instance, women place greater value than men on friendships and relationships as a source of self-worth. But, relationships can be fragile, which makes women and their sense of self-worth susceptible to the uncontrollable changes in relationships.
17 Research shows that lifestyle choices, such as diet quality (Mediterranean diets such as fish, fruits, vegetables, nuts, and olive oil), sleep, and exercise play an important role in the production of serotonin or dopamine and the treatment of depression (Lopresti et al., 2013).
18 Stress can be viewed as the life events (major or minor) that cause interruptions of the person's routine or habitual functioning (i.e., physiology, emotion, and cognition). They are the life events that challenge the person's coping resources.
19 In Nepal, when an elephant has a splinter in his foot, his drivers put chili in one of his eyes, and the elephant becomes so distracted with the pain of the chili that he stops paying attention to the pain in his foot, and people can treat the foot without being trampled to death (and chili washes out of his eye in a fairly short time). For many depressed individuals, eating is the chili that distracts from the more intolerable depression (Solomon, 2001).
20 Furthermore, attempts to control body weight via dietary restriction are associated with increased weight gain. For example, anticipation of a social stressor (a public speaking task) increased food intakes in restrained eaters. Such negative affect-driven food intake can disrupt weight maintenance.

6
ANXIETY AND DECISION MAKING

Introduction

This chapter describes how we make decisions under anxiety and fear, the principles that govern anxiety and fear, and the manner in which they play out in decision-making and addictive behavior. To overcome an anxiety problem, one needs to know about its causal mechanisms and its deeper, underlying roots. Why does it occur? Why are some people more at risk? This chapter concludes by reviewing several treatment strategies, such as cognitive therapy, exposure, and mindfulness. This chapter can benefit a broad audience, including those who are currently coping with anxiety. The chapter draws from the fields of psychology, sociology, behavioral economics, and neurobiology.

An important goal of studying mental disorder is to increase our understanding of human behavior and to inform treatment (Weeks, 2014). The focus on anxiety provides insight into how emotional dysfunction can interfere with decision making and addiction. The body of literature has shown that when anxiety is involved, individuals' thought processes are often flawed. Anxious decision making is characterized by a selective information search, limited consideration of alternatives, rapid evaluation of data, and a "jumping-to-conclusions" style of decision making (Bensi and Giusberti, 2007). Fear and anxiety not only bias our decisions, but also limit our well-being. Anxiety is associated with intense subjective distress and social impairment, and other medical and psychological comorbidity. Anxiety can restrict our relationships, performance, and possibilities.

Understanding the effect of anxiety on decisions has important implications for public health. Anxiety is thought to increase the risk for cardiovascular, psychiatric, and psychosomatic diseases, and it also encourages unhealthy lifestyle behaviors, such as substance abuse and eating disorders. Indeed, anxiety disorders and impulse control frequently precede drug abuse and represent a specific risk factor for addiction (the need for self-medication). The escalation of addiction, in turn, worsens anxiety and impulse control disorders (Pani et al., 2010). Thus, anxiety may have indirect effects on health, and these effects may be mediated by the individual's poor decisions, which offer immediate reward at the cost of long-term, negative consequences. From a preventive perspective, attempts to improve decision making can strengthen an individual's capacity to cope with anxiety and promote resistance and resilience.

Fear and Anxiety

Fear and anxiety are closely related. Both contain the idea of a danger or possibility of injury. Anxiety is defined as a future-oriented emotion, self-focused, and characterized by perceptions of uncontrollability and unpredictability in potentially aversive events and/or severity of threat (Clark and Beck, 2009, 2012; Barlow, 2002). In general, fear is seen as a reaction to a specific, observable danger, while anxiety (or dread) is seen as a diffuse, objectless apprehension (Barlow, 2002). Thus, fear is anxiety that is attached to a specific thing or circumstance (Horwitz, 2013).

Anxiety is also referred to emotional states such as doubt, boredom, mental conflict, disappointment, and bashfulness. Other related terms include agony, terror, dread, phobia, fright, panic, consternation, alarm, and apprehensiveness. Anxiety is a basic emotion that is experienced by every single person. However, the level of anxiety varies across the normal population.

Anxiety involves a nameless dread that is perceived as being potentially threatening in the future. This perception often results in an apprehensive mood accompanied by increased arousal and vigilance, which, when taken to an extreme, persists for a long time. For instance, worries about dying are more likely to take the form of nagging anxiety than specific fear. The ambiguous nature of anxiety makes it difficult to overcome. If we don't know the source of our anxiety, it is difficult to deal with the problem.

The behavioral tendency of fear is the "fight or flight" options to potentially life-threatening dangers. When an individual feels threatened, fear revs up the metabolism in anticipation of an imminent need to defend oneself or flee (this flowing of blood away from the skin is what makes a frightened person appear pale), the pupils dilate and hearing becomes more acute so that the fearing person or animal can better appraise the situation.[1] In contrast, a panic attack involves the interaction of the fear system with inappropriate and maladaptive learning (i.e. false alarm). Panic is marked by sudden feelings of dread and imminent doom, as well as a number of uncomfortable and distressing physical sensations such as racing heart, difficulty breathing, shaking, stomach and muscle tension, and so forth.

Fear is contagious. If someone becomes afraid of something, this fear has a tendency to spread to others, who in turn spread it further. This may occur even though there was initially no rational basis for the fear. For example, consider the case of a stampede where a crowd of people collectively begins running with no clear direction or purpose. Consequently, the victims are trampled as they rush down a narrow path to escape.

Many fears are rational. The capacity to orient and respond quickly to the gravest threats improves the chance of survival.[2] Imagine yourself driving a car that unexpectedly skids on an icy road. You will find that you have responded to the threat before you became fully aware of it. Security consultants insist that it is our first line of defense ("Trust your fear"). Long before there was probability theory, risk assessment, and decision analysis, there were intuition and a gut feeling to tell us whether an animal was safe to approach or the water was safe to drink. As life became more complex and humans gained more control over their environment, analytical tools were invented to "boost" the rationality of our intuitive thinking.

The neurological evidence indicates that the emotion of fear and rationality are not opposed, but are complementary and intertwined. Neurologist Antonio Damasio (1994) writes that some of his patients with damage to the amygdala not only have lost the capacity to feel fear, but the capacity to make rational decisions as well. They have no sense of what is important and what is not, what is a risk and what is not. Take, for example, a young woman who suffered a brain lesion and lost all fear of strangers, she trusted everyone, and failed to see how others are deceiving or manipulating her. Moreover, she did not learn from her repeated bad experiences, and suffered a predictable series of betrayals and cheats. People with limited capacity to be anxious rarely display psychological problems, but are often found in jails or hospitals because of their reckless behaviors.

In sum, fear is a constructive emotion. When we worry about a risk, we pay more attention to it and take action where warranted. Fear keeps us alive and thriving. An optimal stress response rises high enough to respond appropriately to danger, but not so high as to cause incapacitating anxiety. Thus, fear is not bad, in and of itself, and in many cases, it is a productive emotion. Similar to fear, it is important to note that anxiety is seldom pathological, even when intense, until it becomes chronic and consistently interferes with performance and enjoyment of life (Horwitz, 2013).[3]

Anxiety can be a source of strength. Anxious temperament can lead to better job performance. Rollo May (1953) writes: "The problem of the management of anxiety is that of reducing anxiety to normal levels, and then to use this normal anxiety as stimulation to increased one's awareness, vigilance, zest for living." Worriers are more likely to be more goal oriented, more organized, and self-disciplined (Stossel, 2013). They plan effectively for unforeseen events and consequences that others may ignore. They are better at taking care of their health. In short, anxiety is productive when it is not excessive.

In fact, the goal of therapy is to reduce anxiety, not eliminate it. When anxiety is excessive and disconnected from reality, it no longer provides an accurate and reliable signal of danger. Thus, you might feel anxious thinking about an important exam, going to a dinner party where you don't know people, or traveling to an unfamiliar place. These anxious thoughts are driven by "what if?" thinking (e.g., "what if I don't do all my studies?" or "What if I don't know anyone?"). This anxious emotional state is the focus of this chapter.

Thinking and Feeling

From a dual-model perspective, threat is processed through two neural pathways (Loewenstein et al., 2001): affective system and deliberative system. They are also known as System 1 and System 2 (Kahneman, 2011). The deliberative (cognitive) system (S2) works slowly. It calculates and considers evidence. When S2 makes a decision, it's easy to put into words and explain. The affective system (S1) is intuitive, fast, mostly automatic, and not very accessible to conscious awareness.

Fear response is largely traceable to the amygdala (fear network), which constantly scans incoming stimuli for indications of potential threat. The reflective system (S2) can moderate or even override the amygdala's automatic response. Consciously identifying automatic anxious thinking can slow down anxious thoughts. Joseph LeDoux (1996) framed this process as *the low and high road*. That is, the fear network (amygdala) responds automatically to cues and bypasses higher cognitive processing. Our initial fear response is often not something that we deliberate. We feel it before we are fully aware of what that danger is or even whether there is a danger there.

For example, our reaction to suddenly seeing a deer on the road while driving happens so fast that we do not have time to think (hit a deer). The time it takes for a nerve impulse to travel from the senses (stimuli) to the amygdale responsible for fear responses is a small fraction of a second. By contrast, the time it takes for a nerve impulse to travel from the senses to the reflective system is much longer. One might compare this to an executive decision in an emergency that must be made quickly as opposed to sending a memo. In short, the connection from reflective system (cognitive appraisal) to amygdala is far weaker than the opposite direction. This explains why it is easier for emotional information to invade our conscious thought than for us to gain conscious control over our emotions.

The discrepancy between emotional reaction to, and cognitive evaluations of, risk is a common source of the anxiety feeling (Figure 6.1). For instance, phobias illustrate the separation of emotional responses and cognitive evaluations that so many people suffer from (Barlow, 2002). The very hallmark of a phobia is to be unable to face a risk that one recognizes, objectively, to be harmless. Individuals suffering from agoraphobia avoid being away from home alone because they are afraid that they will have a panic attack with no one to help them, and over time, some of them become housebound. The anxiety leads to avoidance and procrastination, and the avoidance causes more anxiety. The person with a severe phobia is constantly on guard and cannot rationally choose his own destiny. Even people who are not suffering from full-blown phobias commonly experience powerful fears about outcomes that they recognize as highly unlikely (such as airplane crashes) or public speaking.

124 Anxiety and Decision Making

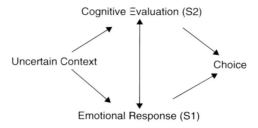

FIGURE 6.1 Emotion and cognitive evaluation of risk.

Cognitive evaluations of risk are sensitive to probabilities and outcome valence (affective experience). In contrast, emotional reactions are sensitive to the vividness[4] of associated imagery, proximity in time, and a variety of other variables that play a minimal role in cognitive evaluations. For instance, as the prospect of an uncertain aversive event approaches in time, fear tends to increase even when cognitive assessments of the probability or likely severity of the event remain constant. People have a tendency to "chicken out" at the last minute.[5] As a result of these differences, people often experience a discrepancy between the fear they experience in connection with a particular risk and their cognitive evaluation of the threat posed by that risk (Loewenstein et al., 2001).

Emotions can also arise with minimal cognitive processing (Zajonc, 1980), and people can experience fear reactions without even knowing what they are afraid of. Social psychologist Zajonc (1980) has demonstrated that increased exposure to an individual can lead to a greater liking for that person without any cognitive awareness. When exposure to an object is repeated, subjects tend to increase their preference for the object. We can love without being aware of it. One explanation is that increasing familiarity reduces uncertainty. For example, Phelps (2004) found that the Caucasian participants displayed more amygdala activation to the African Americans faces than the Caucasians ones. However, familiarity calmed the amygdala via the mere exposure effect.

The dual model implies that reason is no match for emotion. Our reasons become enslaved to our anxious emotions. During intensely anxious moments, the primitive outflows of the amygdala overpower the more rational thinking of the brain. Our brain is designed in such a way that it is easier for our anxious emotions to influence our thoughts than it is for our thoughts to gain control over these emotions.

So, how do we manage our unruly amygdala? Reductions in anxiety are associated with diminished activity in the amygdala and with heightened activity in the frontal cortex. As discussed later on, executive attention holds the key to regulate emotion. The prefrontal executive system "cools the hot" by suppressing the impulse to respond and reappraising the situation. The aim is to eliminate (or reduce) conflict between the fear and appraisal systems. For example, Sam's decision to bungee jump reflects her belief and conviction that there is no real danger in doing so.

Attention Control

Poor attention control is a risk factor for those who worry habitually. Attention control refers to processes underlying the ability to intentionally ignore distracting information (e.g., external noises when trying to read) or shift attention from threatening stimulus (Hartley and Phelps, 2012). People with better attention control can disengage attention from threatening stimuli, whereas people with poor attention control may demonstrate difficulties disengaging from threatening stimuli. Highly anxious people have reduced ability to disengage from frightening stimuli (Clark and Beck, 2012).

Similar to any forms of mental work, worrying requires cognitive efforts because a high level of worry reduces working memory capacity and inability to redirect thoughts. Worried people constantly monitor cues for possible negative future consequences (e.g., "my boyfriend will break up with me"). Excessive worrying disrupts cognitive performance by loading short-term memory with pointless, anxious thoughts.[6] The result is known as ego depletion,[7] which leads to lazy thinking and the failure of rationality, which makes us vulnerable to cognitive errors. For example, in the context of the military, a soldier referred to this compromised rational decision making as "the fog of war," or a loss of clarity. People who are cognitively busy are also more likely to be under the influence of the impulsive system and thus to make more shortsighted choices (e.g., reacting aggressively to provocation and saying the first thing that comes into one's mind). For instance, individuals who are high in social anxiety may experience chronic depletion of self-control due to excessive efforts to manage negative affect and make a positive, social impression (Kashdan et al., 2011). When self-control is depleted, people with higher social anxiety may act in an impulsive or self-destructive manner (i.e., binge drinking).

Anxiety further weakens inhibitory control. This effect may manifest in the difficulty in disengaging attention from distracting, threat stimuli. Anxious individuals recruit less effortful attention control resources to inhibit competing distractors than nonanxious people. Moreover, chronic stress can damage the PFC and the hippocampus. Damage to either of these brain areas can make it more difficult to shut off the fear response and leave the person feeling anxious and afraid much of the time (Arnsten, 2009).

In sum, poor attention control is a risk factor for pathological worry and if worry further depletes the attention control resources, the combination will make it especially difficult to terminate worry episodes for those who worry habitually. In other words, the development and maintenance of anxiety is jointly determined by the relative strength of impulsive system (S1) and cognitive capacity (S2) to control unwanted responses. Evidence shows that individuals with a relatively strong impulsive system and a weak inhibitory control are vulnerable for the development and maintenance of excessive worry (Hirsch and Mathews, 2012). Thus, sufficient levels of inhibitory control might have a protective function in reducing the risk for developing anxiety. Studies have also shown that training attention away from threat can actually reduce symptoms of social phobia and general anxiety disorder (Cisler and Koster, 2010).

Self-Medication

Anxiety can ignite all kinds of maladaptive behaviors, such as drinking, obsessions with work, and so on. The feeling of anxiety is so adverse that we will do most anything to calm ourselves from the anxious feeling. We seek pleasure from praise, food, relationships, entertainment, and all forms of mood-altering substances and pastimes. We are seduced by the short-term "high" without recognizing the inevitable aftermath of increased misery.

The self-medication behavior (or tension-reduction theory) refers to substance use for the purpose of reducing psychiatric symptoms. For example, those with anxiety disorders are more likely to use alcohol to relieve distressing symptoms.[8] There is a strong relationship between substance abuse, particularly alcohol abuse, and anxiety (Kushner et al., 2000). In the national survey of the US adult population, 15% of those with anxiety disorders had comorbid substance use and 17.7% of those with substance use had comorbid anxiety disorders. In contrast, the pure rates for anxiety disorders and substance use, respectively, are 11.1% and 9.4% (Robinson et al., 2011). The pharmacological effects of ethanol (similar to benzodiazepines and opiates) can temporarily reduce anxiety. It is also more likely that the belief that alcohol will reduce anxiety interacts with the depressant effect of alcohol. This belief may be maintained by the popular belief that alcohol will "take the edge off." Alcohol also diverts attention away from anxiety-inducing stimuli. In short, self-medication is a mechanism to help an anxious person endure the feared situations rather than avoid it.

Alcohol, however, does not necessarily reduce anxiety and fear in the long term, and may in fact worsen it, which then motivates further drinking. Thus, anxiety and alcohol use are risk factors for each other. They exacerbate each other. For instance, whereas both social and specific phobias are risk factors for the onset of alcohol use disorders, panic and generalized anxiety disorders tend to follow them.

The anthropologist Ernest Becker in his 1973 book, *The Denial of Death*, proposes that addictive craving is a defense against helplessness and loss-of-control anxiety. Anxiety is inseparable from human existence. We are all aware, on some level, that we are living a tragedy, in that sooner or later we will have to leave everything that gives meaning to our lives. We fear that we will grow old and die and we will lose people we love. Thus, a great deal of human social behavior is designed to conceal the fact of death from oneself (hence his book's title).[9] The Theologian Paul Tillich (1944) suggests that anxiety is a natural reaction to fear of death, guilt, and despair in our daily life. In this way, drugs and food may be used to avoid/ease painful states of mind. However, in reality, addiction is the ultimate loss of control over the drug/food. The novelist Walker Percy noted that worse than despair is to be in despair and not to realize it. That is, to structure your life with distractions to block the experience anxiety. To medicate away your guilt and shame is to medicate away your soul (Stossel, 2013).

Not all anxious individuals engage in self-medication behavior. Individuals who self-medicate tend to have a low tolerance for negative affect and have poor coping skills. They fail to appropriately process the root causes of their anxiety. As discussed below, the experience of anxiety rather than numbing or avoiding it through drug use is the best way to overcome anxiety. Cognitive therapy helps patients to challenge the belief that they must immediately reduce anxiety in order to avoid serious negative consequences.

Anxiety Disorders

The adverse effects of anxiety on health are well documented (Kessler, 2005). Anxiety disorders are among the most common mental health conditions, with estimated annual economic costs over $42 billion in the United States (Olatunji et al., 2011). This accounts for 31% of the expenditures on mental health care in the United States. According to the National Institute of Mental Health, some 40 million Americans, or 18% of the population (nearly 1 in 7), are suffering from an anxiety disorder at any given time. Nearly one-third of women report a lifetime history of one of the major anxiety disorders. Worldwide, a World Health Organization (WHO) survey of 18 countries concluded that anxiety disorders are now the most common mental illness (Kessler, 2005).

Research has consistently shown that the prevalence rates for most anxiety disorder are higher among women compared to men at 2:1. One reason given is that women tend to internalize negative affect rather than externalize distress (Robichaud et al., 2003). Adherence to female gender (e.g., submissiveness and self-restraint) is significantly associated with anxiety across a wide age range. Across the subtypes of anxiety, evidence indicates that only about one-third to one-fifth of affected individuals ever obtain services (Merikangas et al., 2010). From this perspective, this chapter provides an opportunity to increase awareness and education about anxiety.

Anxiety increases the risk of coronary heart disease. Men with the higher levels of phobic anxiety had a level of risk for fatal coronary heart disease three times than that of men with lower levels of anxiety (Kawachi et al., 1994). Anxiety or worry and a neurotic personality (a tendency to dwell on the negative feelings, such as worry, guilt, and depression) are shown to be associated with gastrointestinal distress. Evidence shows that as many as 12% of all patient visits to primary care physicians in the United States are for irritable bowel syndrome (or IBS), a condition characterized by stomach pain and alternating bouts of constipation and diarrhea. Thus, an anxious person has a tendency to convert emotional distress into physical symptoms (Stossel, 2013). Moreover, feeling physical discomfort heightens anxiety, as the anxious person tends to be afraid of losing control over his body.

The following briefly describes the main types of anxiety disorder, including symptoms and causes.

Generalized Anxiety Disorder

Approximately 6% of the US general population will qualify for a diagnosis of generalized anxiety disorder (GAD) at some point in their lifetime. GAD is defined as excessive, uncontrollable worry across a variety of domain, lasting at least six months with significant functional impairments (Barlow, 2002). Excessive worrying is the core feature of GAD (e.g., "what if something terrible happens?"). It is also called the "what-if disease" (Leahy, 2006). People with this type of excessive worry are generally anxious so they often feel more tired, frustrated, tense, distracted, restless, and sleep deprived. The worries of individuals with GAD often focus on issues such as health and illness. These worries may serve as protective factors, decreasing the risk for addiction (Buckner and Schmidt, 2008).

Numerous commentators from St. Augustine through Kierkegaard had described anxiety conditions similar to GAD as being pervasive aspects of the human condition. As they noted, such existential anxiety about the inevitability of death and the threat of meaninglessness was not pathological but an intrinsic and universal aspect of the human condition (Horwitz, 2013).

Social Anxiety Disorder (SAD)

SAD is the most common psychiatric disorder after major depression and alcohol abuse, with an estimated lifetime prevalence rate of 12% (Kessler et al., 2005; Brook and Schmidt, 2008). Extreme shyness is one way to think of SAD. Social anxiety exists along a continuum, ranging from normal shyness to high degrees of social anxiety, and ultimately to SAD. Social anxiety is characterized by fear of negative evaluation, heightened self-focus, and avoidance or escaping social situations. When they are among strangers at a cocktail party, business meeting, or dinner dates, people with this disorder will feel a sudden panicky need to flee for home. Other feared situations include fear of being observed while eating in public, writing, or urinating in public in a crowded men's room.

Socially anxious people are unusually attentive to other people's feelings, but they misread them. That is, they tend to overinterpret anything that could be taken as a negative reaction. They are oversensitive to criticism or negative comments. They use impression management strategy in an attempt to hide the self. This strategy includes attempting to tightly monitor and control one's behavior, overpreparation (rehearsing what to say before and during social interaction), and faked friendliness. The purpose is to present themselves favorably to avoid rejection. Consequently, they appear inauthentic, which actually elicits negative reactions from others. This negative response serves to confirm their fears.

Social anxiety builds during the anticipation of social events. This anticipatory anxiety sets the stage for feeling intense anxiety (such as racing heart, difficulty speaking, and shortness of breath) even before they encounter the social situation. They get more anxious by the worry that their interpersonal awkwardness or blushing will somehow reveal them to be incompetent ("if they notice I am sweating, they will reject me"). After the encounter, they engage in rehashing and overanalyzing a social encounter (How did I perform?) and they overestimate the probability and severity of negative evaluation. These distorted behaviors prevent socially anxious persons the opportunity to learn that what they fear is not necessarily true. These beliefs also influence how past social events are remembered ("My presentation was terrible").

In a nutshell, SAD can be viewed as distorted information processing, and this attitude is reflected visibly in the body movements and behaviors. They keep greater interpersonal space, avoid eye contact, and show anxious behaviors, such as trembling, sweating, blushing, fidgeting, laughing nervously, or speaking fast. SAD can cause loneliness (having fewer friends or romantic relationships) and professional impairment, including being less assertive and more conflict avoidant and interpersonally dependent (Weeks, 2014).

SAD is associated with a significant increase in the risk of substance abuse and dependence[10] (Robinson et al., 2011). For example, rates of smoking are doubled among individuals with SAD. A significant number of adult smokers (81.3%) indicated the onset of their anxiety disorder prior to the initiation of smoking. SAD is predictive of increased risk of cannabis dependence (approximately 60%). Reliance on drugs to cope with social anxiety increases the likelihood that these individuals will be vulnerable to addiction problems (Buckner et al., 2008).

SAD is also a risk factor for eating disorders. Approximately 20% of individuals with an eating disorder also met criteria for SAD, whereas the lifetime prevalence rate of SAD in the general public has been reported at 12.1% (Levinson and Rodebaugh, 2012). Evidence suggests that anxiety tends to precede the development of eating disorders. Fear of negative evaluation is a risk factor to dietary restriction, negative affect, and overall eating disorders over time. As a result of conditioning (e.g., frequent bingeing during negative mood states), negative moods may become a cue that triggers cravings for binge eating.

Thus, the knowledge of why SAD serves as a risk factor for addiction could have important implications for the development of prevention and treatment programs for at-risk individuals.

Panic Disorder (PD)

PD is characterized by sudden, or unexpected, eruptions of intense fear. One of the hallmark criteria of panic disorder is the presence of panic attacks "out of the blue," accompanied by various, intense, physical symptoms. These symptoms may include palpitation or heart racing, sweating, trembling and shaking, feeling of choking, chest pain or discomfort, nausea or abdominal distress, feeling dizzy, light-headed or faint, fear of dying, numbness or tingling sensation, and chills or hot flushes. By definition, the panic symptoms intensify within ten min, and they often subside in 20–30 minutes, although they can last significantly longer.

Estimates of the life prevalence of panic disorder range between 2–5%. Women are over two times more likely to develop PD than men. The disorder is often chronic in the absence of treatment, following a fluctuating course of exacerbation (often in the context of stressful life events) and remission. Comorbidity with other anxiety, mood, and substance disorders is common. In approximately 25% of patients with PD, there is also the development of agoraphobia, which is fear or distress about situations in which escape might be difficult or embarrassing should a panic attack develop. Typically, agoraphobic fears and the resulting avoidant behavior center on being outside the home alone; being in crowds, in a line, on a bridge; or traveling within a vehicle (e.g., Fava and Morton, 2009).

This irrational fear is a major impediment to success and productivity. For example, marriage is less common among those with panic anxiety. The more anxiety a partner experiences, the lower the level of emotional closeness in the relationship. A stable relationship is reassuring, but stability without closeness is disturbing. Many people with panic anxiety end up feeling trapped in this kind of claustrophobic relationship (Zaider et al., 2010).

Adult separation anxiety disorder (ASAD) is comorbid[11] with panic disorder or agoraphobia. The lifetime prevalence of ASAD is 6.6%. Bowlby (1973) suggested that abnormal parent-child attachment leads to enduring separation anxiety, which in turn leads to agoraphobia when the individual is confronted with personally threatening situations as an adult. The sudden arousal of the social separation can lead to panic attacks. Those who suffer from panic attacks often have a history of childhood separation anxiety. The panic attacks and separation anxiety make one feel as if the center of one's comfort or stability has been abruptly removed. The panic attack is accompanied by feelings of weakness and shortness of breath and often a choked-up feeling as if one had a lump in one's throat.

Adults with the ASAD are typically overconcerned about their offspring and spouses and experience marked discomfort when separated from them (Bögels, Knappe, and Clark, 2013) Patients with ASAD may develop panic attacks in the face of separation from loved ones, but the primary fear is the separation, not a panic attack. In addition, fear of losing a primary attachment figure, especially one's partner, may take the form of morbid jealousy in ASAD. They suffer from an excessive and unrealistic fear that the partner may commit adultery and eventually leave them. Patients with ASAD score high on need for approval and preoccupation with relationships.[12] There is a strong association between ASAD and grief, such as the loss of a loved one through death or divorce.

Anxiety sensitivity (AS) plays a key role in PD (McNally, 2002). Individuals with high anxiety sensitivity are prone to panic disorders. Anxiety sensitivity refers to fear of anxiety-related sensations and is measured by the Anxiety Sensitivity Index (ASI).[13] PD patients score high on the ASI. That is, knowing that a person has a specific tendency to fear bodily sensations is a risk factor for PD. Anxiety sensitivity is usually seen as having a genetic contribution, possibly in combination with early, adverse experiences or trauma.

Fears of anxiety-related sensations are similar to the dread of public speaking or flying in an airplane. Anxiety symptoms are interpreted as threatening and harmful to their physical and psychological well-being. Panic attacks arise from, or are worsened by, the catastrophic misinterpretation of bodily sensations (misinterpreting palpitation as a signal of heart attack, dizziness as evidence of impending loss of control). Panic attacks also increase anxiety sensitivity. Panic disorder develops because exposure to panic attacks causes the conditioning of anxiety to internal or external cues.

A specific brain region, the insular cortex activation, is associated with some bodily awareness (interoception) (Craig, 2002). The role of the insular cortex is to monitor the value of sensations (internal and external) on the body state. Individuals suffering from anxiety disorders have dysfunctional insular cortexes. The result is excessive worry and avoidance behavior.

Obsessive-Compulsive Disorder

Obsessive-compulsive disorder (OCD) is defined by the presence of repetitive and distressing obsession and compulsion, which tend to increase in severity during the natural course of the disorder (American Psychiatric Association, 1994). Patients suffering from OCD describe feeling as if a hijacker has taken over their brain's controls. As a result, OCD patients who feel compelled to wash their hands know full well that their hands are not dirty. The main feature of OCD is the occurrence of obsessions (intrusive thoughts) and compulsions (repetitive behaviors in response to obsessions). Obsessions are intrusive thoughts that occur against the individual's will. These intrusive thoughts cannot be ignored and compel the patient to engage in irrational behaviors to relieve temporarily the resulting anxiety. The symptoms of OCD cluster around four factors: 1) cleaning habits and contamination concerns; 2) ordering, counting and symmetry; 3) hoarding behavior; and 4) checking rituals. Modern technology and culture contribute to these behaviors (e.g., dishwasher, soaps, cleaners, forms of saving, and more.). The lifetime rate of OCD is about 2.3% of the population, with many more having a milder form (Kahn, 2013).

One of the main symptoms in OCD is persistent doubt. People with OCD tendencies have lost "the experience of conviction" (Shapiro, 1965). This means that OCD is related to a disturbance in the "feeling of knowing," defined as a subjective conviction functionally separate from the knowledge of objective reality. People with OCD distrust their memory, such as repeated checking. They also doubt their perception, feelings, preferences, comprehension, and other internal states. For example, a patient with OCD may feel uncertain that she feels attracted to her partner or doubt that she fully understands the meaning of a simple word even if she cannot find any objective reason for these doubts. Such pervasive doubts may lead to a variety of pathological behaviors typical of OCD, including excessive self-monitoring, checking, incessant questions, and requests for external validation or reassurance. These ritual behaviors become habitual and automatic.

Theories of Anxiety

Although what causes anxiety is still poorly understood, there are several explanations for the development and maintenance of anxiety, such as genetics, negative childhood events, classical conditioning, cognitive theory, psychoanalysis perspective, and evolutionary perspective (e.g., Antony and Stein, 2009). This section provides a brief account of these theories on the onset and maintenance of anxiety. Collectively, these theories provide various views on why people are not equally afraid.

Hereditary

Anxiety disorder seems to run in families. Like any psychological illness, anxiety disorders are genetically influenced. We inherit a significant proportion (about 40%) of our anxiety (e.g., heritability of social phobia is about 51%). Meta-analyses of genetic studies conclude that having a close relative with generalized anxiety disorder increases your chance of having it from 1 in 25 to 1 in 5 (Kendler et al., 2001). Psychologist Kagan (2008) has shown that genes determine the reactivity of our amygdala, which in turn, helps determine how we will react to stress. That is, the anxious temperament is innate and genetically determined. Research shows that the amygdala of individuals diagnosed with social anxiety disorder tend to be more reactive to the human gaze than healthy populations. They become easily uncomfortable if they notice that someone is starring at them (Stossel, 2013). Children with inhibited and high-reactive temperament have a lower threshold for arousal and novel events. Those children with inhibited traits are more likely to become shy and nervous adults and exhibit fearful reactions to novel situations. Thus, being anxious is not a failure of character or will.

Evidence shows that individuals with less vulnerability to anxiety have significantly higher levels of a brain chemical called neuropeptide Y (NPY). NPY is the most abundant peptide in the brain, involved in regulating diet and the stress response. For example, those in the Special Forces (Navy SEALs and Green Berets) have high NPY levels, which seem to make them immune to developing posttraumatic stress disorder (Stossel, 2013). It is also possible that those in the Special Forces who thrive under pressure have learned to be resilient. That is, their high NPY levels are the product of their training or their upbringing. However, a person's endowment of NPY is relatively fixed from birth, more a function of hereditary than learning. Psychologists have also demonstrated that smart training, building resilient attitudes, and developing a better working relationship with fear can help us achieve true grace under pressure (Ericsson et al., 1993).

In sum, vulnerability to anxiety is largely genetic. Some individuals are naturally less resilient and lose the ability to cope when the stress of life becomes too unbearable. According to the stress-diathesis model of mental illness, clinical disorders like anxiety and depression often erupt when a person genetically vulnerable to mental illness become overwhelmed with life stressors (Dugas et al., 2009).

Learned Behavior

Classical conditioning suggest that fear and phobia develop as a result of a neutral stimulus (e.g., dog) and aversive experience (e.g., being bitten by a dog) being paired. For example, animals learn to fear cues (the light or tone) that predict painful events. Negative dental experiences among children cause greater dental fear at later ages. Panic anxiety develops as a result of conditioning. That is, the panic attacks arise from excessive fear of bodily sensations. Conditioning to body sensation cues can result in seemingly out-of-the-blue panic attacks. Conditioning to external stimuli can result in agoraphobic behaviors. The panic attacks serve to motivate the person to avoid or escape these external situations (e.g., crowded trains or supermarkets). When we have been frightened badly enough or for long enough, the fear system becomes oversensitized (LeDoux, 2002). We learn to fear various specific objects and situations. Our memories of traumatic events may prompt us to suffer from chronic anxiety, commonly accompanied by obsessive ruminations.

Adverse Childhood Experience

Negative childhood events are most likely to lead to learned helplessness when a person makes internal, global, and stable attributions regarding negative events. This pessimistic explanatory style may lead initially to anxiety, followed by depression. That is, the environment may help to foster a schema (thinking pattern), with early experience contributing to the formation of vulnerability. Thus, similar to genetic vulnerability, early life trauma or maltreatment is an important risk factor (e.g., Fava and Morton, 2009).

A schema (or habitual responses) is a cognitive structure for screening, coding, and evaluating stimuli. The schema provides the conceptual framework for interpreting experiences in a meaningful way (Dozois and Beck, 2008; Beck 2008). They are stable and rigid beliefs about oneself and one's relationship with others. For example, a person who has the notion that everybody hates him will tend to interpret other people's reactions on the basis of this attitude. This mental habit, if left unchecked, can reactivate automatic, negative thinking (e.g., feeling inadequate, worthless, and blameworthy). In anxiety or depression, specific schemas assume a dominant role in shaping the thought processes. They can block mental exploration and realistic self-observation.

Where do these schemas or automatic thoughts come from? Schemas come from our conditioning and our learning habits. Once the learning habit has been formed, stimuli similar to original may evoke the conditioned response (Beck, 2008). They shape how we meet later obstacles (e.g., by giving up quickly). For example, according to attachment theory, children form schemas based on previous interactions with caregivers (Bowlby, 1973). Children with insecure attachments with their caregivers perceive the world as unsupportive and view themselves as isolated, vulnerable, or unworthy. Children have no cognitive capacity to temper the impact of the early trauma, so hopelessness and helplessness can be imprinted in the memory.

The task of changing schema is to unlearn the self-defeating old habit and replace it with a new, healthier one. That change is very different from merely intellectual understanding. The change involves the emotional brain. It takes much persistent practice, cultivation of the ability to bring awareness to what had been an unconscious behavior, and sustained effort to try out the new way of thinking and acting. The whole process of changing deep schema patterns can take years.

Cognitive Factor

According to cognitive theory, emotions are largely determined by distorted thoughts, beliefs, and attitudes. For example, a person with a social phobia may believe that he will be ridiculed and rejected by others and consequently begins to experience anxiety and fear. In turn, these beliefs lead to avoidant behaviors, which serve to maintain fear by preventing the individual from learning how to successfully cope with an anxiety-provoking situation. Thus, the anxiety sufferers reduce distress and suffering in the short run by avoiding the stimulus, and they ultimately perpetuate anxiety. People have a panic at home, but what a price to pay.

The central role in all anxiety disorder is the sense of vulnerability. For patients suffering from panic disorder, cognitive factors, such as expectations that an attack will be imminent and harmful and that coping will be ineffective, play a significant role by influencing and maintaining avoidance behavior. Thus, self-efficacy (or self-confidence) becomes the target of therapy.

Parenting Model

Psychologists believe that many phobias are to a great extent acquired. The fear behavior of mothers or fathers, for example, could be passed on to their children (via modeling behavior). For example, a child might observe the parent's fearful responses to a stimulus (e.g., spider), and thus respond in a similar way when faced with the same type of situation. Parenting styles of controlling and overprotection tend to increase a child's overall vulnerability to anxiety disorders by decreasing self-confidence (self-efficacy) and autonomy. For instance, restrictive parenting diminishes a child's ability to explore and learn new skills independently, thereby promoting anxiety in situations of perceived fear. Thus, anxious parents may directly or indirectly communicate and reinforce avoidant behaviors in their children as a result of their own fears.

By being overprotective, parents repress children's natural appreciation of life and the living world. These parents try to eliminate the trial error, adventures, uncertainty, and self-discovery from children's lives. These are elements that make life worth living, compared to the structured and fake life. The ironic result of making life safe is more anxiety (Taleb, 2012). Evidence shows that socially anxious children exhibit quiet restraint and overly cautious styles of responding to novel social situations (Miskovic and Schmidt, 2012). However, not all behaviorally inhibited children become socially anxious adults. It is also possible that an anxious temperament in a child might be shaping a parent's behavior to be protective (Brook and Schmidt, 2008).

Evolutionary Perspective

If anxiety about the future is so often unnecessary, if not maladaptive, then why are people so prone to experiencing anxiety? Humans and other animals seem to be preprogrammed to experience certain types of fears (Gigerenzer, 2007). Cage-reared rats that have never been exposed to a cat show signs of fear if exposed to the smell of cat fur. Stranger fear has been observed in humans in a wide range of cultures and usually develops between four and nine months of age, peaking around 12.5 months, and does not require conditioning experiences with strangers to develop. From the evolutionary perspective, the purpose of panic anxiety is to keep us close enough to home and group that we could find our way back. It would be dangerous if you couldn't find your way home. In primeval human society, panic (separation anxiety[14]) served as an alarm mechanism. It warned people not to wander too far from their mother or from the tribe. From the evolutionary perspective, social anxiety and submissive behavior may reflect the biology of low social rank in the hierarchy. The inner fear in social anxiety is telling us painfully that we are rising above our rank. People with SAD are more followers than leaders, and are not adventurous. For example, many people become anxious about going alone to a social event despite the lack of any objective danger involved

(Kahn, 2013). Individuals with SAD avoid attire or social behavior that may draw attention toward them.

We tend to easily be conditioned to fear objects that posed threats in prehistoric times than to dangers we face in modern times (e.g., height fears). It is also considerably more difficult to extinguish evolutionarily based fears (e.g., spiders, snake, heights, and darkness). On the other hand, people are likely to react with little fear to certain types of objectively dangerous stimuli that evolution has not prepared them for, such as guns, junk foods, automobiles, smoking, sun tanning, and unsafe sex, even when they recognize the threat at a cognitive level. The kinds of dangers that were common in prehistory (e.g., snakes, strangers, deep water, and darkness) pose less threat now than they did back then. However, these old fears continue to be common sources of anxiety in the modern world. This suggests that people typically fear objects or situations without considering the objective likelihood of suffering harm from them. For example, three-quarters of American parents express fears that a stranger might kidnap their children. However, only about 200 to 300 children a year in the United States are reported being kidnapped by nonfamily members (Horwitz and Wakefield, 2012). There is a mismatch between the emotional responses designed in the ancestral world and the one in which we dwell now. That is, our ancient, emotional system might be working appropriately, but in environments where it was not designed to function.[15] This suggests that mistakenly considering this mismatch as a disorder will lead to treatment of natural anxiety. Thus, much of fear and anxiety are normal and natural aspects of human nature (e.g., fear of heights as an evolutionary survival response). Knowing that much of our anxiety is normal can itself relieve some of the anxiety.

Attachment Anxiety as a Vulnerability Factor to Addiction

Attachment anxiety (anxiety over possible abandonment) may develop when attachment figures are inconsistent or unpredictable. Children with insecure attachments are significantly more likely to develop separation anxiety. They suffer frequently from persistent fears, stemming from childhood experiences of neglect or abuse (Panksepp and Biven, 2012). Insecurely attached people are susceptible to rejection, criticism, and disapproval. The effect works through dysfunctional attitudes about the self, such as "I am nothing if a person I love does not love me." These distorted thinking patterns leave insecure people vulnerable to distress and a risk factor for self-destructive behaviors (e.g., addiction and eating disorders).

Those who suffer from panic attacks often have a history of childhood separation anxiety. The sudden arousal of the social separation can lead to panic attacks. Physical pain from separation anxiety is readily alleviated by opiates. This explains why lonely people are more vulnerable to abuse addictive drugs (Mate, 2010).

These individuals may be self-medicating because they have chronic feelings of psychic pain.

Attachment is an inborn system that motivates an infant to seek proximity to a caregiver, especially in dangerous and uncertain situations (Mikulincer and Shaver, 2007). Early attachment difficulty and the experience of child neglect and abuse interfere with the maturation of the cognitive system. A sense of vulnerability keeps a person's mind preoccupied with threats and the need for protection, and interferes with emotion regulation (Ainsworth, 1982).

Over time, interactions with one's caregivers are thought to shape people's attachment styles (Bowlby, 1973): anxious (e.g., excessive demands for attention and care) or avoidant (e.g., denial of attachment needs and self-reliance). Anxious persons are attentive with respect to signs of both the availability or unavailability of the attachment figure. In contrast, the avoidant style involves denying attachment needs and suppressing attachment-related thoughts and emotions. Avoidant individuals rely on distancing (emotional detachment) as a strategy for emotion regulation. These behaviors are natural reactions to the loss or unavailability of an attachment figure, but once established as habitual coping strategies, they contribute to psychological and social difficulties.

Furthermore, the mental habits acquired in childhood are later played out in adult relations. They tend to treat new partners the way they related to past attachment figures. In other words, through the power of projective identification, individuals' interpersonal interactions begin to conform to their internal expectations and experiences (Bowlby, 1969).

Research shows that, to the extent that individuals experience rejection during their formative years, they develop the anxious expectation that others will reject them (Romero-Canyas et al., 2010). This reaction is known as rejection sensitivity (RS): a tendency to perceive even ambiguous events in interpersonal situations (e.g., partner momentarily seems inattentive) as indicators of rejection that quickly trigger automatic defensive reactions (e.g., anger, withdrawal). The negative reactions to rejection often produce the very rejection they most want to avoid (an unfortunate version of the self-fulfilling prophesy).

Since insecurely attached individuals doubt the availability and supports of others, they use other tactics to mitigate and control negative affect (Norris et al., 2002). One compensatory strategy is attachment to nonhuman targets (e.g., objects, blankets in the case of children, intense religiosity, and materialism). In other words, they substitute relationships with objects for relationships with people. For example, teenagers who highly value materialism report having less nurturing mothers. They adopt materialistic values in order to cope with loneliness. Materialists highly value the acquisition and possession of material goods. Hoarding behavior has been linked to anxious attachment, in which people acquire a great deal of material possessions that overcrowd their lives and cause significant distress. However, such pursuit of extrinsic goals may further amplify their loneliness.

Anxious attachment is related to substance abuse (Flores, 2004). For example, insecure attachment among college students was associated both with alcohol consumption in order to cope with stress (Kassel et al., 2009). Avoidant individuals who attempt to detach themselves from psychological distress can use alcohol and drugs as a means of avoiding painful emotions and self-awareness (e.g., Hull et al., 1986). Attachment anxiety also contributes to eating disorders and impulsive food intake (Tasca et al., 2009). Eating and weight-related concerns are defensive methods of directing attention to external problems and goals and to compensate for feelings of helplessness, insignificance, and vulnerability (Wedig and Nock, 2010).

The anxiously attached person chooses the chemical shortcut to avoid pain and frustration, and becomes trapped there (Mate, 2008). The behavior becomes habitual because it can only relieve feelings of inadequacy temporarily because the deficit in the self remains and so the addict returns to feelings of emptiness. The addict does not have the internal resources to sustain feelings of self-approval and self-esteem.

In contrast, secure attachment liberates. According to the "broaden-and-build" theory, attachment security expands a person's resilience resources for maintaining emotional stability in times of stress (Fredrickson, 2009). Attachment security frees up cognitive resources, enabling people to focus on explorations and other important goals. This secure attachment makes it easier to commit to a chosen task (e.g., academic or career) and practice self-control, rather than being impulsive, jumping from one goal to another and never completing a course of action (Panksepp and Biven, 2012).

People who possess a stable sense of attachment security generally feel safe and worthy, hold an optimistic and hopeful outlook on life, and have an increased capacity for emotion regulation. Attachment security is associated with more health-promoting behaviors, such as maintaining a healthy diet or engaging in exercise and avoiding risky behaviors, such as smoking, drinking, and drug abuse (Huntsinger and Luecken, 2004). Whereas secure people's health-promoting behaviors result from growth and self-expansion motives, insecure people's health behaviors may include defensive efforts to overcome mundane frustrations and anxiety about being accepted.

In sum, we are driven innately from birth for close, human contact. To the degree that we are deprived of this and do not possess the ability to accomplish this task, we are emotionally deficient and vulnerable to addiction. Anxiously attached individuals harbor doubts about the availability and responsiveness of others and they are particularly sensitive to the social pain of rejection. In contrast, secure attachment provides psychological resources for dealing with problems and adversity.

Attachment theory suggests that addicted and eating-disorders individuals with attachment anxiety may benefit from a treatment approach that focuses on managing impulse regulation and increasing reflective thinking capacity and interpersonal connectedness.

A Perspective From Psychoanalysis

Motivational accounts provide a primary way of understanding behavior. In everyday life, when behavior in the form of an action seems to be irrational and incomprehensible, we look for "hidden" motives as a means of making sense of it. The unconscious mind is inaccessible to rational thought, but nevertheless influences our behavior. Our unconscious desires (or wishful thinking) guide our facts and our fact-finding and how it is interpreted. These unconscious desires are translated into conscious decisions. For example, if you are worried that someone is annoyed with you, you are biased toward all the negative information about how that person acts toward you. You interpret neutral behavior as indicative of something really negative.

What is psychoanalysis? Psychoanalysis is considered as a theory, a treatment, and a way of thinking about the human motivation or drive (Gabbard et al., 2012). A psychoanalytic perspective includes conscious and repressed unconscious motives and desires. Psychoanalysis is traditionally conceived as an opportunity for a motivated person to reflect deeply about everything she is feeling and thinking without editing or censoring.

Freud developed the first systematic approach of how unconscious mental life exerts its influence on our view of the world. The so-called structural theory organizes the functions of the mind into three conflicting parts: 1) the ego (governed by the "reality principle"); 2) the superego (the conscience, a sometimes too rigid commitment to the rules of society); and 3) the id (the desire for pleasure, sooner rather than later).

The id seeks only immediate gratification and is totally "selfish," operating according to the pleasure principle (the so-called animal spirits) (Akerlof and Shiller, 2009). Contemporary neuroscientists might locate the id in the amygdala, the ancient part of the brain involved in primitive, emotional functioning. The concept of the ego (i.e., one's sense of "I") is relatively compatible with contemporary knowledge of the prefrontal cortex (self-control). The ego responds to id and superego impulses by modifying them as a way of managing conflict and danger. The superego emerges through the internalization of social values and norms. Roughly synonymous with "conscience," the superego is the part of the self that congratulates us for doing our best and criticizes us when we fall short of our own standard. On the other hand, an overly harsh and demanding superego can lead to guilt and a punitive and rejecting stance toward one's own wishes. Thus, one can experience anxiety about the approval of the superego.

Increased awareness through psychoanalysis can help the individual to become less self-punitive and be able to tolerate his emotional experiences. Psychological growth requires self-acceptance, which is a state of mind that marks the end of the life-consuming effort to transform oneself (and others) into the person one wishes one were (or wishes they were) (Ogden, 2010). Becoming aware of the unconscious motives helps the individual to increase the ability to manage and integrate unconscious wishes, and ultimately leads to self-acceptance (Bromberg, 2001).

Freud argued that whenever desires (wishes) from the id threaten to emerge in thought or action, anxiety is generated (Safran, 2012). The anxiety acts as a signal, causing the ego to mobilize repression, along with a broad spectrum of other defenses, in order to block or disguise the anxiety-provoking wish. Thus, anxiety is a motive to avoid an unbearable degree of irrational fear.

The intensity of anxiety differs according to the gap between external demands (dangerous situations) and the person's self-protective resources to handle them. Inability to deal with external events (traumas) could lead to feelings of helplessness and powerlessness. Lacking the capability to cope with negative states, patients will erect powerful, sometimes intransigent, defenses in a desperate effort to avoid feeling them. The person using a defense is generally trying to accomplish the management of anxiety and the maintenance of self-esteem (McWilliams, 2011).

Defense mechanisms are forms of emotional regulation strategies for avoiding, minimizing, or converting affects that are too difficult to tolerate (Schore, 2012). People use several defense strategies, such as withdrawal, projection, regression, and denial to retreat from stress. Projection may be defined as attributing one's own unacceptable thoughts, feelings, or intentions to others, so as to avoid the anxiety associated with harboring them. This attribution of responsibility becomes defensive when it is used to protect the individual from feelings of shame or guilt (self-hating). In regression, people feeling overwhelmed by the challenges of life will begin to whine and feel helpless, like children. In denial, people say to themselves: "this is not happening." For instance, alcoholics insist they have no drinking problem. These defenses are unconscious desires to repress the bad news and, by doing so, people create a false sense of security for themselves.

Dissociation (or estrangement) is another defensive mechanism (Stern, 2011). The unconscious motive for dissociation is to escape from the overwhelming emotions associated with the traumatic memory. Dissociation is the inability to articulate certain aspects of one's experience in verbal language. Such a state of being is *not-me* (alien self), which has never had access to consciousness, and it has never been symbolized. The response is projection (or enactment): "I'm not x; you're x"; "You are the selfish, angry, or the inadequate one, not me." Keeping the unacceptable feelings out of awareness result in the development of a "false self" (Cramer, 2006). The price for this protection is inability to develop resilience.

Dissociated experience does not simply disappear quietly into some hidden corner of the mind. It is enacted. It will "play out" the state of self that one cannot tolerate experiencing directly. Enactments are the only means of encountering dissociated aspects of the patients. Enactment is a kind of unconscious communication that can be brought onto the surface. For example, slips of the tongue, in which a word suddenly breaks into speech, seemingly coming from nowhere. In our slips, our real insecurities are exposed. The success of therapy and lasting change requires that the patient come into contact with previously inaccessible aspects of her inner feelings. The way out of trauma is by going through it (Epstein, 2013).

Dissociation plays a crucial role in addictive behavior. Addiction is described as a defensive strategy to avoid feelings of helplessness or powerlessness (Ulman and Paul, 2006). Addiction has been described as a futile attempt to compensate for inner emptiness without success. The addict tries to compensate via addictive behavior for painful, subjective states of low self-esteem, doubts, and anxiety. The use of drugs supplies a feeling of acceptance and a feeling of temporary self-confidence. An addict substitutes an imaginary world, where he is in complete control, for the real world, where he feels useless and out of control. Repeated use of drugs to gain relief becomes a way of life. The addiction problem prevents the user from understanding his distress, and also prevents the development of the emotional capacity to self-soothe.

In summary, the ego defense or defensive behavior plays a useful and necessary role in everyday life. People use these mental mechanisms to deal with disappointment, anxiety, anger, and other stressful emotions. Defense mechanisms work by changing our internal psychological state (i.e., the way we feel or interpret a situation), but they do not change external reality. However, they often result in a distorted perception of reality. It is the meaning of the event, rather than the event itself, that is changed in such a way as to avoid psychological pain. The effort that goes into protecting ourselves from uncomfortable feeling inevitably shuts down all other feelings too. That is, we close ourselves off from love, joy, and empathy.

How Do Anxious Minds Work?

This section explains how anxiety influences thinking and impairs decision making. Although anxiety disorders are often differentiated by the specific content of their fears and symptoms, they share similar thinking errors. Becoming aware of these errors is an important step in overcoming anxiety (Miu et al., 2008; Ouitmet et al., 2009).

Worrying About the Future

Worry is a common characteristic of persistent anxiety (Barlow, 1988). Worry is a form of problem solving and presumably helps a person plan and prepare for future (potentially) negative events. We feel anxiety when we anticipate that something bad will happen, and we plan to prevent potential harm to ourselves. The problem with worry is that it is always about future events, and no one can know the future, so the desire for safety and certainty is useless. Moreover, the harder people try to not worry, the more they worry (known as the *ironic effects of mental control*) (Wegner, 2002). Thus, sometimes the most demanding way to control our mind is not necessarily the most effective one. Negative moods (including tiredness and pain) fuel worrying (Meeten and Davey, 2011). For example, individuals suffering from OCD have shown to experience a negative mood prior to the onset of a checking bout. Experts suggest if you find yourself worrying in a negative mood, immediately try to do something to lift your mood.

Intolerance of Uncertainty

Worriers are allergic to the word "uncertainty." Worriers believe that they must continue to worry until uncertainty has been resolved. Some individuals will stop worrying about a particular problem not because they have accepted the prospect of the threat, but because they have shifted from one worry to another (Miu et al., 2008).

Exaggeration of Uncertainty

When we are anxious, we tend to overestimate both the likelihood and the intensity of the threat and danger. Indeed, the rationality of a worry can be judged on the basis of the accuracy of an individual's perception of threat. Anxious persons will exaggerate the likelihood and severity of dangers in everyday situations, such as overestimating the probability that heart palpitations reflect an underlying heart problem. The process of blowing things out of proportion leads the worrier to ask automatic questions of the "what if?" kind, and by doing so, the individual sees the worst-case scenario (Davey and Levy, 1998). Therefore, catching our distorted thinking is an important strategy for reducing anxiety.

Jumping to Conclusions

Given that anxious individuals experience uncertainty more stressfully, they are motivated to reduce uncertainty and eliminate the discomfort. For example, in solving problems, they tend to provide the first acceptable conclusion rather than solving the task correctly. There is also a search for relief, often by trying to obtain reassurance from others that everything will be all right. Highly anxious individuals are more likely to endorse superstitious beliefs (crossing their fingers, throwing salt over their shoulders and so on).

Choking Under Pressure

Too much attention and excessive arousal worsen cognitive performance (Stossel, 2013). That is, when levels of arousal are too low (boredom) and when levels of arousal are too high (anxiety or fear), performance is likely to suffer. Worrying about how you will perform on a test may actually contribute to a lower test score. Under situations of low arousal, the mind is unfocused. In contrast, under situations of high stimulation, the focus of attention is too narrow, and important information may be lost. The optimal situation is moderate arousal. Someone who is distracted and unfocused on a conversation is uninteresting. The anxious person also does badly exactly because she cannot think about anything besides managing her anxiety. Instead of listening to her partner and making small talk, she is too focused on "does he like me?" or "am I boring?"

Interpretation

Highly anxious individuals tend to interpret ambiguous events as negative or threatening (Beck, 1995). For example, socially anxious individuals will interpret an ambiguous comment, such as "that is an interesting shirt you have on," emotionally negative. A person with low self-esteem is highly sensitive to being ignored by other people, and they constantly monitor for signs that people might not like them. Distorted internal belief systems that provide incorrect views of the world produce anxiety disorders. The major task of any therapy is to train anxious patients to think accurately and logically about the world.

Defensive Behavior

Highly anxious people see problems as largely "out there," with little coming from their own inner world. They use a defensive strategy, such as projection, to attach their own unacceptable thoughts, feelings, or intentions onto others. This act of projection is a distraction that allows them to ignore the real culprit, the problem within. This realization is an opportunity to take responsibility and develop tolerance for the aversive feelings.

Avoiding Behavior

Avoidance is another well-known form of coping with anxiety (e.g., playing it safe, procrastination, and distraction) (Hasler, 2012). For example, people with social anxiety problems can easily cope with anxiety by avoiding social situations at the expense of professional and personal life. But often, worriers find that the more they try to escape anxiety and its triggers, the worse it gets and the smaller their world becomes.

Self-Efficacy—Beliefs in Your Own Abilities to Cope with Challenges

When we feel anxious, we tend to see ourselves as weak and unable to cope (Beck, 2008). The greater one's doubts concerning one's level of competence, the more one will worry about adverse outcomes taking place. For example, a student who thinks he is quite competent would be less worried about failing an exam. When a confident attitude is adopted, the individual focuses on the positives in a situation, and may even assume a greater sense of personal control. In short, **Anxious Mind = Overestimate Danger + Underestimate Self-Confidence**

What Is the Take-Home Lesson?

Anxiety is a disorder of choice. Similar to alcohol, fear and anxiety impairs judgment (Berns, 2008). Thus, you should avoid making any decisions while under its influence until you are in a calm state of mind and can clearly deliberate on the ultimate goal.

Taming the Anxiety

So what can we do to control our anxiety levels? A person can take a number of actions to help calm anxiety. These actions can help the anxious person become emotionally stronger and counteract the damaging impact of anxiety. Similar to physical fitness, it takes commitment to maintain mental and emotional fitness.

Exposure Therapy

Most of the success in treating anxiety-related disorders comes from behavioral therapies that typically involve some form of extinction-based methods. This method is based on the principle that fear develops from past learning experiences in which a stimulus becomes associated with a dangerous or horrific outcome. The past associations shape behavior. Anxiety is viewed as a problem of maladaptive learning and it could be unlearned.

Exposure therapy is an important component of behavioral therapy, which involves exposing the subject to the stimulus (e.g., snakes or heights) that triggers pathological fear in the absence of the negative outcome (Barlow, 2002). Exposure can be thought of as a form of "desensitization" to increase tolerance for anxiety. Anxiety simply can't last forever. After a period of time, the physical symptoms, such as the dizziness and butterflies in your stomach, will subside. For example, a person who avoids crowded public places can practice exposure by attending a sold-out movie theater and sit in the middle of the row. The exposure experience provides the anxious person with the evidence that her exaggerated thoughts about the probability and severity of threat and helplessness are not supported by real life experiences. It will take courage and determination to face one's fears and persist with the exposure tasks.

Tolerance

Facing our worst fear is a powerful measure in overcoming anxiety. When you confront your worst fear, it goes away and becomes less intimidating (Stutz and

Michels, 2012). When you move away from it, pain grows.[16] When you become confident that you can do this every time, you have mastered your fear of pain. Those who move forward in the face of adversity increase their inner strength. Like muscle development, adversity is a weight against which we develop our inner strength. The purpose is not to stop the pain, but to increase our tolerance for it. The more pain we can tolerate, the more we can learn.

Problem-Solving Skills

Worry may also be reduced with the implementation of more effective problem-solving/coping techniques. Worrying is normally a very inefficient attempt to problem-solve. So when you worry, try to turn this into useful problem solving by considering what you need to do now to deal with the problem. That is, you can turn "what if . . . ?" worries into "How can I . . . ? worries, which is more likely to lead you on to practical solutions. For example, you could turn a "What if I forget what to say in my interview?" worry into "How can I prepare myself to remember what I need to say in my interview?"

Cognitive Behavioral Therapy (CBT)

The eighteenth-century Scottish philosopher David Hume observed that it is not what happens to us that determines our reactions but, rather, how we appraise what happens to us (Beck, 1995). The link between thoughts and feelings is a basic premise of the cognitive model of emotional regulation. Thus, your emotional reactions and your behavioral reactions to adversity largely follow from your beliefs about the adversity, and not from adversity itself.

The core assumption of the CBT is that false beliefs and mistaken patterns of interpretation of events lead to fear and anxiety. Distorted internal belief systems that provide incorrect views of the world produce anxiety disorders. The major task of this therapy is to train anxious patients to think accurately and logically about the world.

Sustained recovery will occur when the underlying thoughts (or beliefs) are corrected. This is the basis of the ABC model of emotional distress. So often we find ourselves in a situation (A) and end up with a feeling (C). Often, we are not aware of a thought (B) that links them. By bringing them to awareness, we have greater ability not to be carried away by the cascade of our emotions. By becoming aware of our thoughts, we cultivate a way of freeing ourselves from the grip of the old mental habit that occurs from time to time.[17]

To identify automatic thoughts on the spot, one needs to ask the simple question: "what just went through my mind?" Behind any automatic thought exists an unarticulated core belief. Often unlike automatic thoughts, a core belief that we "know" to be true about ourselves is not fully articulated until you peel back the layers by continuing to ask for the meaning of your thoughts. For example, the thought that "if people look down on me, it means I'm inferior." The core belief is "I'm inferior." Borkovec et al. (2004) has argued that we worry to avoid some dreaded future threat or danger. For example, an individual might worry about whether he has offended a close friend rather than think about losing that friendship.

The idea behind cognitive theory is that when you change the way you think, you can change the way you feel. The purpose of cognitive therapy is to modify schemas (chronic attitudes). Patients are encouraged to reflect critically on the evidence (or lack of evidence) that confirms or disconfirms flawed thinking patterns. The approach involves teaching skills of empirical hypothesis testing so that the patient learns to distance herself from thoughts, and to correct the dysfunctional beliefs. For example, by recognizing in advance a typical schema (e.g., seeking constant approval to maintain his sense of worthiness), the patient is less likely to overreact. In essence, the purpose of the therapy is to transfer patient's awareness from stimulus → affect to stimulus → cognition → affect. The patients learn to view their automatic thoughts from a distance (metacognitive) and question their validity.

Using cognitive therapy, Clark and Beck (2012) recommend a very useful framework for reducing anxiety: 1) identify your deepest fear (the worst-case scenario) that is the source of your anxiety (e.g., being rejected and living alone); 2) Describe how this scenario might affect you physically and emotionally; 3) Imagine what it would be like to live out this worst-case scenario. After several days imagining the worst outcome, the catastrophic image becomes much less anxiety provoking; 4) Develop a problem-solving plan if the worst-case scenario ever occurred. How would you cope effectively with the adversity? And finally, continue with this exercise until you truly can imagine yourself dealing with your deepest fear with a normal level of anxiety (e.g., one-third of the original level). In short, facing your ultimate fear and working through it with a reasonable and effective coping plan will help calm your anxious mind.

Mindfulness

The alternative approach, mindfulness, focuses not on the content of the thought, but the patients' relationship to their negative thoughts and feelings (Segal et al., 2012). Patients are taught, rather than regarding thoughts as necessarily true or as an aspect of the self, to see negative thoughts and feelings as passing events in the mind that were neither a necessarily valid reflection of reality nor central aspects of the self. As Beck noted, it was not experience itself that made us unhappy, but our relationship to experience or our interpretation of experience. Thus, learning to relate to thoughts as mental events rather the truth, individuals could free themselves from the effects of disturbing thought patterns that might otherwise control their behaviors.

Psychologist Wells (2009) suggests that rather than fight worry, you accept the worry. If your mind decides to worry, let it. Allow the worry thought to float through your mind as if you were a bystander watching a parade (separate your sense of self from the thought). Apply detached mindfulness to the intrusive thoughts and allow thoughts to ebb and flow like tides without trying to understand them. Suppression of thoughts and memories increases the salience of this material. The intrusive thoughts are a normal part of adaptation (psychological healing) to traumatic experiences, and eventually they will subside. Engaging in rumination/worry/analysis or drinking alcohol to numb the pain blocks the adaptation process. This immediate relief is likely to be short-lived.

In short, anxious thoughts are associated with some pattern of physical arousal. We do not process these thoughts dispassionately. We react to them physically. Being able to step back from anxious thoughts may allow us to realize that these thoughts are not necessarily accurate reflections of reality but transient events. It also helps us to appreciate the present instead of continually worrying about the past or planning for the future.

Summary

In sum, cognitive behavioral therapy and medications together create the most enduring treatment effects. Evidence shows that the combined treatment of antidepressant and psychotherapy (mostly CBT) was more effective than any treatment alone. The medications, the selective serotonin reuptake inhibitors (SSRIs), suppress some of the symptoms without affecting the underlying causes. However, the SSRI consumptions over time create changes in the brain, making patients more nervous and unhappy. The side effects of these drugs include dependency and withdrawal problems. Furthermore, suppressing a person's anxiety symptoms may prevent the person from learning that the symptoms are harmless. The CBT, on the other hand, deals with aspects of the underlying causes of anxiety. Anxiety can be a signal that we need to change our lives, not to avoid dealing with the issues causing our anxiety. The CBT may have its effect by enhancing the inhibitory influence on the amygdala, and enhancing our inner strength and resources. Finally, it is important to note that anxiety tends to return. So, one needs be prepared for the possibility of relapsing to old habits of avoiding, becoming less tolerant of anxious feeling, and engaging in safety-seeking behaviors.

Posttraumatic Growth

Posttraumatic growth is a phenomenon by which people harmed by past events surpass themselves. The aftermath of major life struggles, where fundamental assumptions (schemas) are severely challenged, can lead to positive, psychological change or posttraumatic growth (Terdeschi and Calhoun, 2004). However, the change is not simply a return to baseline. But, it is an experience of deeply profound improvement.

The general understanding that suffering can be possible sources of positive change is very old. For example, Nietzsche (1997/1889), cited in Haidt (2006, p. 135), stated that, "[w]hat doesn't kill you makes you stronger." Psychologists note that despair is a prerequisite to the birth of joy. Despair is a necessary preparation for freedom. It is well known that AA states that the alcoholic cannot be cured until she is in complete despair. It is only then that the alcoholic can give up the need for alcohol as a relief for her hopelessness. When a person has "hit bottom," she then can begin to rebuild herself.

Posttraumatic growth[18] occurs with the attempt to adapt to highly negative sets of circumstances that can produce high levels of psychological distress. The growth normally requires a significant change in the fundamental schemas. The growth implies that the established schemas are changed in the wake of trauma. The experience has a quality of transformation in functioning (a paradigm shift). Examples of positive psychological change are an increased appreciation of life, a significantly changed sense of priority, a greater sense of personal strength, and recognition of new possibilities. Things that used to be big deals are not big deals anymore. The experience changes the persons' self-concept and gives them confidence to face new challenges (e.g., if I can survive this, I can survive anything).[19] For example, in the situation where people are more limited in what choices they have, such as becoming unemployed and having a limited budget, they may be willing to explore opportunities never before considered.

People experiencing growth disengage or give up unattainable goals and basic assumptions that cannot accommodate the reality of the trauma, and at the same time persist in an attempt at building new schemas, goals, and meanings. The experience of growth is facilitated by certain personal qualities such as openness to experience and optimism. These qualities may help individuals to focus attention and resources on the most important matters and disengage from unsolvable problems.

In his book, *Antifragile*, Nassim Taleb (2012) writes, "Wind extinguishes a candle and energizes fire" (p.12). This is equivalent to the excess energy released from overreaction to setbacks. The human body can benefit from stressors (to get stronger), but only to a point. For instance, our bones will become denser when episodic stress is applied to them. We increase our willpower capacity the more we practice in dealing with setbacks. This explains why overprotective parents trying to help their children are often hurting them the most.[20] Experiences of stressors and risks make them adapt and change continuously by learning from the environment. Further, making many small mistakes provides valuable information. Failure is information. Failure is a fantastic learning opportunity. The ability to reframe failure as part of a larger process is instrumental in being able to cope with it.

Thus, we can view any emotional pain life inflicts on us as an opportunity that will strengthen our ability to better deal with any future pain. So bearing the pain will seem like an achievement. No pain, no gain (Salsberg and Thurman, 2013).

Conclusion

Anxiety becomes self-defeating or pathological when it is noticeable, intense, disruptive, and triggers self-defeating defensive behavior. The irrational fears can be notoriously difficult to eradicate, even in the presence of the relevant knowledge. Cognitive psychologists argue that the intuitions/gut feelings underlying irrational fear are based on irrational beliefs or appraisals (schemas). Although, some schemas are difficult to change by just adding further information, however, they can be changed by repeated exposure to the disturbing stimulus in question. For instance, lack of self-efficacy is related to anxious responding. Giving people the confidence that they can make such changes is far more effective in reducing anxiety levels.

While it is part of human nature to seek pleasure and avoid pain, culture plays a key role in how we deal with suffering (Ben-Shahar, 2009). In the West, we reject suffering. So we repress, medicate, or search for quick-fix solutions. In some cultures, such as in the East, suffering is acknowledged for its important role. Buddhism discusses the benefit of suffering as wisdom, resilience, inner strength, compassion, and a deep respect for reality. We don't learn as much from success as we learn from our failures. Suffering can make us more resilient and better able to endure hardship. Just like a muscle, in order to build up, it must endure some pain, so our emotion muscle endures pain in order to strengthen. Suffering helps us to respect reality, and accept our potential, limitation, and humanity. Therefore, as we learn to accept suffering, suffering becomes a tool for growth. As Hans Selye (1976) wrote, "the secret of health and happiness lies in successful adjustment to the ever-changing conditions on this globe; the penalties for failure in this great process of adaptation are disease and unhappiness." Similarly, Bertrand Russell pointed out, a "secure life is not necessarily a happy life; it may be rendered dismal by boredom and monotony." There is no life without stress and, at least until we die, the search for stability is a fruitless effort (Jackson, 2013).

Notes

1. The automatic nervous system is composed of two parts: the sympathetic nervous system, which mobilizes the body under conditions of stress, and the parasympathetic nervous system, which conserves resources and maintains functioning under normal nonstressful conditions.
2. Darwin came to believe that emotional expressions have an evolutionary history as well as a survival function in the life of animals. Those who did not carry traits of jumping rapidly back from a striking snake were more likely to be killed by such snakes. They did not survive to reproduce and so were not our ancestors. The snake-escape reactions therefore come to be programmed by our ancestors' gene into our nervous systems.
3. The idea that people can fear anxiety symptoms is not new (McNally, 2002). In 1933, President Roosevelt famously proclaimed in his first inaugural address during the Great Depression: "So first of all let me assert my firm belief that the only thing we have to fear is fear itself—nameless, unreasoning, unjustified terror which paralyzes

150 Anxiety and Decision Making

needed efforts to convert retreat into advances." He was commenting on the economic future of the United States and that unreasonable and overgeneralized fear can have dramatic effects on all aspects of one's life.

4   This has obvious implications for influencing decision making. For example, a media campaign can provoke feelings of vulnerability; people believe that some sorts of risk are more frequent because the media presents examples of real cases with fatal outcomes (e.g., cancer deaths caused by smoking).
5   For example, people get "cold feet" when they fear the commitment of marriage before a wedding ceremony, and back out of a planned marriage. This is because we place greater weight on practical considerations (e.g., do I really want do this?) relative to more abstract desirability (the idea of marriage) as the moment of taking an action draws near.
6   We have all had the experience of forgetting to answer the test questions (our "mind went blank"). In reality, our mind was filled with test anxiety that interferes with our ability to think about the test itself. Anxious individuals tend attend to more limited cues or a more limited data set in making choices.
7   Ego depletion is when we are engaged in making a series of choices that involve conflict, trying to impress others, or responding kindly to a partner's bad behavior.
8   The famed eleventh-century Persian physician Avicenna encouraged melancholics "not to drink only, but now and then to be drunk" (Horwitz, 2013).
9   Military training tries to ensure that the individual soldier will come to value the survival of his group of genetically unrelated comrades over the natural instinct of self-preservation. This is why societies reward this ultimate triumph of self-regulation with medals and citations praising the individual's "complete disregard for personal safety."
10 Socially anxious individuals tend to have a lower level of dopamine. For example, one study showed that half of patients with Parkinson scored high on social anxiety (Weeks, 2014). Thus, a chronic dopamine deficit may help account for drug abuse to elevate dopamine levels, as well to reduce tension.
11 In a mental disorder, comorbidity is the rule rather than the exception, commonly as high as 50–60%.
12 ASAD is correlated with less differentiation of self, and is more common in cultures that place a greater importance in interdependence.
13 The ASI is a questionnaire comprising 16 items that tap concerns about anxiety-related sensations, such as "When I notice that my heart is beating rapidly, I worry that I might have a heart attack."
14 Even now, the ultimate punishment is often solitary confinement ("now go to your room").
15 This is similar to the human taste for fats, sugar, and salt for maximizing calorie intake. We are hardwired through evolution to keep our body weight up. This strategy was adaptive in the past, but is currently maladaptive. In the modern world, where calories are all too readily available, these ancestral tastes can lead to obesity and associated increased risk for many diseases.
16 That is why people feel more comfortable instant messaging each other than a face-to-face conversation.
17 Feelings, such as incidental affects, also give rise to thinking. If we are in a negative frame of mind, we are in danger of getting trapped in the irrational belief that further deteriorates our moods.

18 The term *posttraumatic growth* is not the same as resilience. Resilience is usually considered to be an ability to go on with life after hardship and adversity.
19 As the saying goes: "The drowning man is not troubled by rain."
20 Taleb (2012): "He that wrestles with us strengthens our nerves and sharpens our skills. Our antagonist is our helper" (p. 39). It is said that the best horses lose when they compete with slower ones.

7
CHOICE OVER TIME

Introduction

An important concept in behavioral economics is examining how people make decisions over time. When confronted with a choice of whether, for example, to exercise or overeat, individuals can opt for one of two outcomes: an immediate benefit of pleasure, or a delayed benefit or uncertain benefit, such as health. Such choices pervade our lives, from daily decisions to ones that can have life-long consequences (e.g., savings, education, and marriage). In the trade jargon, these are known as intertemporal decisions. These decisions have a time dimension, meaning that they involve tradeoffs between costs and benefits occurring at different times. We often want instant gratification, such as eating highly caloric foods, while planning to diet starting tomorrow. This implies that people have present-biased preferences.

This chapter provides an understanding of people's decisions in circumstances in which some of the rewards or costs of a choice accrue in the future. The main goal is to introduce the concept of time preference and its determinants, and preferences for immediate gratification. The concept of choice over time provides a conceptual framework in explaining the human taste for instant gratification (e.g., addictions, procrastination, and willpower), as well as promoting healthy behaviors.

Time Preference

Time preference (or discount rate) is an economic concept that refers to the rate at which people discount the future relative to the present. It represents the individual's willingness to give up current consumption in exchange for future consumption. Time preference is a measure of an individual's overall tendency to prefer smaller, sooner rewards to larger, later ones.

The term *positive time preference* refers to the consumer inclination toward consumption now rather than later. A person with positive time preference requires more than one unit of future consumption to compensate him for the loss of a unit of current consumption. Positive time preference motivates a person to act myopically (present oriented). In general, individuals with high rates of time preference will tend to invest less in future-oriented activities, such as health and education.

A given level of time preference can correspond to a higher or lower discount rate. In economics, a discount rate, or rate of return, captures one's preference for consuming earlier rather than later. The discounting of delayed rewards refers to the observation that the value of a delayed reward is reduced in value, or considered to be less worthy, compared to the value of an immediate reward. An individual's discount rate refers to the weight the individual places on future outcomes relative to current outcomes. Higher discount rates give greater weight to benefits and costs accruing early in the life cycle than do lower discount rates. For example, farmers with high discount rates are more likely to plant crops with a short harvesting time and a low yield than crops with a longer harvesting time but a higher yield. The effort required to learn a musical instrument may deter the person with high discount rate from sustained practice. Similarly, a high discount rate may reduce the willingness to give up current caloric intake for the future benefit of lower weight.

In general, the preference for an immediate or a distanced outcome (discount rate) is a function of the value of the respective outcomes and their delays, i.e., the time until they can be realized. Overall, the delay until the arrival of the future benefits is seen as a cost and is weighed against the distant benefits. That is, delay alone can make a good decision into a bad one, or vice versa. For example, a given reward, delivered after a long delay, is less attractive than the same reward delivered after a short delay. So, getting $500 tomorrow is preferred to $1,000 two years from now. Similarly, losing a $500 tomorrow is more painful than losing $1,000 two years from now. This explains why people have an easier time spending money on credit cards as opposed to spending real money. This explains why individuals are willing to buy a cheaper car with less fuel efficiency instead of more expensive one that has lower fuel costs over its lifetime.

Delay discounting is a major contributing factor for drug abuse. Preference for short-term rather than longer-term rewards is a hallmark of substance abuse and other addictive behaviors. Addicts consistently show a greater preference for small, immediate rewards over larger, delayed rewards (e.g., money). This relationship is found in individuals who are nicotine dependent, opiate dependent, or who use alcohol at high (problematic) levels. For addicts, delayed outcomes appear to have little value. For example, smokers know that smoking may give lung cancer, and yet still smoke. Thus, steep discounting may provide a risk factor for drug use and addiction. They are more likely to initiate drug use and subsequently be unable to quit. For instance, Yoon et al. (2007) found that in women who had quit smoking during pregnancy, those with a higher degree of discounting were more likely to have relapsed to smoking by six months postpartum. Deep discounting (impulsivity) is an obstacle in the treatment of obese children (Guerrieri et al., 2008).

A body of research shows that obese individuals (especially women) have higher rates of discounting (i.e., more impulsiveness). Obese individuals make more impulsive food-related decisions compared to those with a normal weight (Weller et al., 2008). The increased prevalence of obesity is linked to ready access to inexpensive, high-calorie foods. These food alternatives may compete with delayed, possibly healthier meals made at home.

However, Bickel et al. (2012) showed that ex-smokers of cigarettes discounted money no differently than nonsmokers. Their findings suggest that either the degree of discounting decreases after abstinence is achieved, or people who are more likely to achieve abstinence discount less steeply.

How Can Delay Reduce Value?

Choice over time has an uncontroversial normative principle. (A normative statement expresses a judgment and addresses what should be rather than what is. In contrast, positive economics deals with description and explanations of economic relationships.) A long time ago, philosophers viewed equal treatment of present and future as a norm of behavior. They considered time discounting undesirable. That is, one time is as good as another and it is immoral to discount (Frank, 2002). To attach less weight to future benefit merely because it is future is as irrational as preferring benefit on Mondays over benefit on Tuesdays. They noted that impatience for future rewards usually made people poorer in the long run. A person who discounts the future very heavily will ruin her health, her family life, and her finances for the sake of short-term pleasures. For example, John Platt (1973) defined *social traps* as situations in which behavior leading to a short-term or individual gain contributes to a long-term or collective loss. In short, these philosophers recognized that the discounting of delayed outcomes is an important barrier to humans' ability to maximize their resources. Thus, a person who ignores the long-term impact of smoking and high-fat food will have a shorter life expectancy.

These philosophers, however, recognized that the tendency to discount future rewards is due to our "defective telescopic faculty." Just as distant objects appear to be smaller than those close up, so do temporally remote rewards appear to be smaller than present ones. In other words, discounting behavior is more similar to an optical illusion than to a motivational bias (Elster, 2006). Although the sun is about 400 times larger than the moon, from here on earth, they both appear the same size in the sky. The similarity of their appearances is an illustration of an objective illusion that it would take equal time periods to go around them respectively. As the picture below demonstrates, the more distanced tracks appear to be shorter than the one close by. In the same way a large sum of money in the future may appear to be smaller than it actually is.

In sum, we are limited in our capacity to contemplate about the future, and consequently place less value on future benefit and cost. We often focus on immediate events with effects close in time and space, and are unable to pay attention to the long-term consequences. For example, when we consume very rich dessert, we don't get an immediate feedback of adverse health effects. The health consequences (shorter life) will come over a long time horizon that we are unable to realize now.

Factors Affecting Time Preference

What determines the level of time preference? Why do humans differ in the extent to which they discount delayed rewards? The following briefly discuss the determinants of time preference. These factors explain why people care less about a future consequence.

Cost of Delay

In the context of economics, two factors explain discounting. The first is the opportunity costs of delay. The interest lost from delaying the receipt of money or paying it out too soon is one example of an opportunity cost. For example, if the interest rate is 5%, waiting one year for $105 instead of taking $100 immediately would cost the decision maker $5 in interest. The second basis is pure time preference (impatience) or the desire to avoid delay of consumption, meaning that a given amount of utility (happiness) is preferred the earlier it arrives. This is the psychological discomfort associated with self-denial. Thus, individuals are willing to accept a small sum of money today rather than wait for a larger sum in the future.[1]

Uncertainty

People tend to equate temporal distance with uncertainty. That is, the distant future is riskier than the near future. In the same way that we prefer a likely reward over an unlikely one, we prefer the proximal reward over the distant reward. For instance, the individuals growing up in an untrusted environment will have the tendency to grab whatever is immediately available. A lifetime of learning not

to trust others to deliver what they promise in the future may play a role in delay-discounting rates. Similarly, the short duration and uncertainty of life (e.g., poor health) influences time preference.[2] Poor health is an indicator of mortality, and will therefore increase one's uncertainty about whether the future reward will be received.

Evolutionary Perspective

An evolutionary perspective provides another explanation for the link between uncertainty and discounting. Throughout evolutionary history, future rewards have been uncertain (Logue, 1988). Our instinct is to seize the reward at hand, and resisting this instinct is hard. In prehistoric human environments, the availability of food was uncertain because of the variability of the environment. Like other animals, humans would survive and reproduce if they had the strong tendency to grab the smaller immediate reward and forgo the larger but delayed reward. If you were out hunting for turkeys to eat, a bird in the hand would be worth two (or more than two) in the bush. It was unlikely that a man would become unhealthy if he gorged himself when food was available. Rather, gorging would serve to effectively bridge the frequent periods when food was scarce. In short, evolution has given people and other animals a strong desire for immediate rewards.[3]

Age

Why do youths sometimes behave as if there is no tomorrow? Young people are more likely than older ones to seek new experiences and discount future consequences. A study by Green et al., (1999) compared the discounting of hypothetical monetary rewards among children (mean age of 12.1 years), young adults (mean age of 20.3 years), and older adults (mean age of 67.9 years). The results showed that children discounted the most, older adults discounted the least, and the young adults' discounting was intermediate between them. The finding shows a U-shape between age and discounting. That is discounting decreases through young adulthood and middle age, and then increases again beyond retirement age.

Childhood and adolescence are points of the life cycle that may be associated with greater uncertainty and perhaps this is an important factor contributing to the widely held view that the young live today as if tomorrow will never come. As we age, we tend to experience more certainty and therefore may consider the future more. Experience of life events that bear lessons about time can change one's time preferences (Liu and Aaker, 2007). For instance, the experience with the death of someone close induces young adults to reflect upon their long-term futures, and become more long-term focused. Thus, as a person gets older and wiser, his apparent discount rate gets smaller.

Resisting short-term reward in favor of longer term requires a capacity to envision the distant future. Having a vivid view of the future ahead is a sign of social maturity for young adults. For youths, this ability is sort of under construction. In adolescents, the emotional (motivational) brain areas are particularly active, while the part of the brain that is supposed to inhibit impulses is not fully developed. Thus, impulsive decision making in adolescents may be related to a relatively underdeveloped cognitive brain (orbitofrontal cortex) combined with overactive emotional brain (limbic reward system).[4] The developmental course may explain why many of the future consequences of drug abuse will be more heavily discounted by youths than by adults. There is now widespread agreement that impulsivity plays a key role in the initiation and development of drug use problems.

In short, time preferences are linked to the ability to imagine future states. Becker and Mulligan (1997) suggest that imagining the future more vividly can decrease our discount rate for that future. They argue that the discount rate is a function of the resources invested in imagining the future (e.g., education). Hence, people will expend resources to make their image of the future vivid and clear. For example, we might spend time with our parents to remind ourselves of what our needs will be when we are their age.

Impulsiveness Trait

Many psychologists believe that impulsivity is a trait, a persistent tendency to behave in an impulsive manner. The trait of impulsivity refers to a chronic and general tendency to act on impulses.[5] People with an impulsive personality are simply more prone to be in an impulsive mood and they tend to show intolerance to delay of gratification or delay aversion (Madden and Bickel, 2010). Impulsivity makes it more difficult for some individuals to resist the psychological discomfort associated with self-denial. For example, the decision of a college student to buy an electronic item (iPod) impulsively without thinking about the long-term consequences. So, individuals with impulsive traits will be at greater risk for numerous problems, such as substance abuse.

A helpful strategy to reduce impulsivity is to think about the future in a more concrete manner. Peters and Büchel (2011) have shown that rewards promised at future times linked to specific events (e.g., $100 payment during the holiday or on September 1) help regulate decision making over time. That is, people are more patient when future dates are linked to specific events. A similar strategy is to focus one's attention on the future consequences of a choice (Magen et al., 2008). For example, consider a choice presented between $20 now and $40 in a month. This choice can be reframed as either $20 available immediately and nothing in a month, or nothing now but $40 in a month. Expressing future consequences of immediate reward help to reduce impulsivity.

Cognitive Capacity

It is well established that cognitive ability is a powerful predictor of success in life. Cognitive development is essential for information processing, learning, and decision making. Higher intelligence is associated with lower discounting.

Discounting involves the executive brain, which is linked to intelligence through the function of the prefrontal cortex. Children with higher intelligence tend to be better at shifting attention away from the affective properties of the rewards. They are also more adept at transforming reward representations to make them more abstract, and, consequently, lower discounting.

There is strong evidence that the process of deciding whether to choose an immediate reward or a delayed but higher reward is strongly associated with success in life. Consider, for example, the classic research conducted by Walter Mischel and his colleagues at the Bing Nursery School at Stanford University. Preschoolers were given a choice between receiving a large reward (e.g., two marshmallows) on the return of the experimenter or, at any time during the delay, forgoing the larger reward by accepting a smaller but immediately available reward (e.g., one marshmallow). The study demonstrates the children's ability to transform the "hot" thoughts associated with immediate gratification into "cool" ones. In a longitudinal follow-up, preschoolers' duration of waiting before selecting the smaller-sooner reward was predictive of academic and social competence in adolescence (Mischel and Ayduk, 2004). Preschoolers who waited longer were more likely than their more impulsive peers to become adolescents who more successfully coped with stress and frustration, demonstrated better abilities to concentrate and maintain attention, better responded to reason, and scored higher on the SAT.

In short, discounting represents a critical factor through which intelligence influences economic outcomes (Heckman, 2006). This explains why individuals with lower intelligence may be more prone to financial hardships, and they tend to have lower levels of financial asset accumulation. The linkage between cognitive abilities and self-control suggests that educational interventions and parenting can affect adult economic performance (Heckman, 2006). Professor Nisbett (2009) in is his book *Intelligence and How to Get It*, provides suggestions for improving I.Q. that include praising efforts more than achievement, and also teaching youth delayed gratification.

Cognitive Deficit

Life is full of distractions. At a cognitive level, the ability to stay on a course depends on the functional integrity of the frontal lobes. Being at the mercy of incidental distraction and displaying an inability to follow plans are common features of frontal lobe disease. When neurological illness affects the frontal lobes, the ability to stay on track becomes lost, and the patient is completely at the mercy of incidental distractions. This syndrome is different than the proverbial "absent-minded professor," where cognitive overloading increases distractions in normal subjects. Patients with orbitofrontal syndrome (due to head injury, brain disease, or dementia) are emotionally disinhibited. Their ability to inhibit the urge for instant gratification is severely impaired. They do what they feel like doing, without any concern for social taboos or legal prohibition (e.g., shoplifting, sexually aggressive behavior, or reckless driving). There is also disparity between knowledge and the ability to guide behavior with this knowledge. These patients will say the right things but make the wrong choices at the same time (Goldberg, 2009).

Scientists first began to gain an understanding of the role of the prefrontal cortex in 1848 with the case of Phineas Gage. Gage, a hardworking and conscientious railroad employee, was the victim of a freak accident in which an explosion drove a steel rod through his skull. Gage survived the accident, but seemed to undergo an abrupt personality change. He retained his intelligence, but he was no longer sober and reliable. He could no longer conform his behavior to specific goals. Scientists now believe that the rod destroyed Gage's orbital prefrontal cortex, the part of the brain in charge of encoding goals and assigning relative value to them. The syndrome is also known as ventromedial syndrome. Damasio (1999) demonstrates that patients with damage to the ventromedial prefrontal cortex (VMPF) lack social maturity for working within a social group. Within a social group, members have different goals and needs and are never in perfect agreement, and the capacity for compromise is a critical mechanism for social harmony. This capacity depends on our ability to control the negative emotions arising from an inability to find immediate gratification. Impulsive or opportunistic choices (e.g., taking advantage of one's friends) provide immediate positive outcomes, whereas their negative consequences (e.g., jail, loss of friends) are discounted.[6]

In short, people with frontal lobe damage tend to be more impulsive, less disciplined, lacking in short-term memory, and easily distracted, especially from tasks requiring sustained attention. They often have a disturbed experience of time and have problem forming goals and making plans. They may also be unable to foresee the consequences of their own actions.

The Socioeconomic Characteristics

Wealthier individuals are more productive at producing future-oriented capital (education, saving, and health prevention). Poverty and the pressure of present needs blind a person to the needs of the future, thereby increasing time preference. For example, if your heat is about to shut off and there is no food in the house, you have more immediate concerns than the possible future poor health consequences of consuming French fries. In this case, poverty focuses individuals' attention on the present and decreases the value that they place on the future.

Environments characterized by economic deterioration and destabilization, in which the future outcomes of one's behavior are typically characterized by risk and uncertainty, may encourage shortsighted behavior (Bickel and Johnson, 2003). The prevalence of substance abuse, overeating, criminal behavior and many other types of risky behavior is higher in urban and low socioeconomic-status (SES) residential environments. In many inner-city environments, where community instability and decay (e.g., poverty and violence) are endemic, considering one's future may seem a fruitless endeavor for individuals who may not expect to experience the future. In such a situation, the most adaptive strategy may be to consider exclusively the immediate consequences of a behavior.

Delay discounting is also related to educational level. Better educated people will have lower discount rates. Education may enlighten the person with regard to the value of deferred versus current consumption. People with more education tend to have a longer time horizon, and they are more likely to look at the long-term consequences of their health behavior. One possible explanation is that the affluent, well-educated population finds the future, especially the prospect of retirement, far more attractive than the lower-income population for whom the future means only continuing economic worries. Another explanation is that education raises cognitive capacity, which in turn improves behavior. For example, better educated people are better at quitting bad habits, or at controlling their consumption. In general, they tend to be more successful in translating intentions into actions.[7] Thus, education seems to influence cognitive ability, and cognitive ability in turn leads to healthier behaviors. The impact of cognitive ability is not so much about the level of information, but the way one processes information. People are generally informed about the negative consequences of poor nutrition and obesity, but the better educated may understand it better (Cutler and Lleras-Muney, 2010).

Emotion Regulation

Delay discounting is associated with the affective environment in early childhood development (Gross, 2007). Children of disengaged and unresponsive parents tend to have poor delay gratification ability. Warm and responsive parents raise children with high positive affect and low negative affect, and who are armed with a host of self-control strategies. Children with more chronic negative affect may be regularly diverting resources from delay gratification goals toward the regulation of their negative affect. Negative affect states are incredibly distressing and relief from them may take priority over long-term goals. In the case of negative affect, energy or resources initially directed toward delaying gratification may be diverted and used toward emotion regulation. In other words, negative affect may change the subjective values of immediate reward, because it has the potential to ameliorate negative affect. On the other hand, positive affect increases one's attentional focus, which may help transcend the immediate gratification.

Anticipation

In contrast to discounting, the desire to reduce dread implies people may prefer to consume bad experiences (like a trip to the dentist) earlier rather than later. For example, people tend to prefer to pay parking tickets immediately rather than defer payment. The usual explanation for such behavior is that waiting for unpleasant outcomes induces anxiety that can be avoided by getting the outcomes over with quickly. On the other hand, pleasant experiences like vacations or dates may be deliberately postponed or planned well ahead of time so they can be "savored." Similarly, lottery ticket purchases may be viewed as a pleasurable anticipation. In general, people tend to derive pleasure from anticipating good things and discomfort from anticipating bad things.

Summary

People are not equally patient. They differ in their degree of discounting. For example, those who are younger, have a low income, or are less intelligent may have higher discount rates. Discounting is a useful diagnostic tool and a key factor to design treatment strategies that will reduce addictions and manage impulsive behavior. Also, if people are taught to value delayed consequences in treatment, the learning could potentially generalize to other aspects of their lives.

Consistent Behavior Over Time

The exponential discounting model predicts consistency of preference over time. This is a standard assumption used in economics that a person's preferences cannot change over time. If an individual prefers one apple today to two apples tomorrow, then she will prefer one apple in one year to two apples in a year and a day. In general, a person's preference between two alternatives does not vary no matter when he evaluates. Individuals who exhibit exponential discounting behavior when faced with a choice between a smaller/sooner (SS) reward and larger/later (LL) reward do not change their preference as the SS reward becomes present. Rather, such individuals continually choose options that maximize their total happiness with allowances for the reduced value of the delayed rewards.

In the context of health behavior, exponential discounting implies a stability of preference over time. That is, resolutions once made are never broken (e.g., resolutions to quit smoking or stick to a diet are always carried out.) This pattern is seen in Figure 7.1, the relative value of two future rewards remains the same as one moves closer toward them in time. The curves represent the present values of two rewards as evaluated at various earlier times.

Myopia and Rationality

Exponential discounting can be highly myopic without being inconsistent. It is important to note that for an economist, rational behavior means acting in a manner that is consistent with one's preference. A person who discounted future rewards extremely, who preferred $10 today to $100 tomorrow, would be deemed myopic (shortsighted) by an economist. But if preference were consistent (if the

162 Choice Over Time

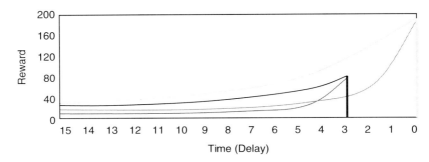

FIGURE 7.1 Exponential discount function.

person preferred $10 tomorrow to $100 the day after tomorrow, $10 in ten days to $100 in eleven days; in general, $10 in x days to $100 in $x+1$ days), the economist would consider that person's preference to be perfectly rational. In other words, exponential discounting can be highly myopic without being inconsistent.

Economists argue that there are no such things as irrational preferences. In the same way that preferences for food items differ across people, so do preferences for time. Some like vanilla ice cream, others like chocolate flavor. Similarly, some like the present, others like the future. One decides to go college and become a lawyer and another student decides to settle for immediate gain by attending trade school. Thus, caring less about the future than the present can be rational. Many people like to smoke and to drink, and they also care about their health, but their health is hardly their priority. Thus, if a person discounts the future very heavily, consuming an addictive substance may, for her, be a form of rational behavior. Such a person with a consistently high discount rate does not experience internal conflict (self-control problem). So, a rational overeater or drug addict may have a problem, but it is not a self-control problem.[8]

Hyperbolic Discounting (Time Inconsistent Behavior)

Imagine you set your alarm clock at midnight to wake up at 6:00 AM the next morning to exercise or work on an assignment. But when the alarm goes off the next morning, the choice that you made last night now "seems absurd." The warmth and comfort of the bed makes you change your mind. What was chosen the night before is now rejected. On the day before, your preference was to get up at 6:00 AM, while when the time comes to get out of bed, your preference is to stay in bed longer. This inconsistency rests on an illusion that we all experience every day. When we can hold all alternatives at a distance, our evaluations of them remain true to their values in our lives. But our subjective evaluation of a reward (our appetite for it) grows when we are closer to the reward than when we are far away, and unless we somehow commit ourselves to our previous preferences, we succumb. This tendency is often referred to as "hyperbolic discounting," present bias, or time inconsistent behavior (Laibson, 2001; Ainslie, 2001). This change in preference is often the source of self-control problems. We often want instant gratification right now, and want to be patient in the future, such as eating highly caloric foods, while planning to diet starting tomorrow (Redish, 2013). This inconsistency is embodied in the wonderful line from Augustine's *Confessions*: "Make me chaste, O Lord, but not today" (Redish, 2013).

Summary

Standard economic theory suggests that each individual has a constant rate of time preference, and the rate is not context dependent. Alternatively, time preference is characterized by a hyperbolic functional form, rendering short-term impulses supreme over long-term goals (Laibson, 2001). In contrast, behavioral economics research has shown that rates of time preference are not constant rates that result in exponential discounting but, instead, vary by the time horizon faced. According to the model, individuals underestimate their future impulsivity, resulting in preference reversal as time passes.

The hyperbolic discounting model, or present-biased preference, predicts that individuals act irrationally in that they excessively discount the future. They favor long-run maximization at all times except as smaller rewards become more immediately available. Consequently, they often end up acting against their own best interest. They do worse in life because they spend too much for what they want now at the expense of things they want in the future. People buy things they can't afford on a credit card, and as a result, they get to buy less over the course of their lifetimes. This model explains several socially important human behaviors such as drug addiction, obesity, and unsafe sex. As discussed in a later chapter, to counter these self-control problems, sophisticated agents employ commitment devices to attempt to protect long-term goals from short-term consumption decisions. The remaining portion of this chapter will review several implications of the hyperbolic discounting.

Local vs. Global Approach to Decision Making

Decision making can be described from two frames of mind: local and global (Heyman, 2009). A local choice perspective refers to choosing between the available items one at a time. In global choice perspective, we organize the items into sequences and then choose between different sequences. For example, deciding each night which meal is better is the local approach. However, deciding between sequences of meals for a week is the global approach. In local choice, choosing the better option means choosing the item that currently has the highest value. In the global perspective, the best choice is the collection or sequence of items that has higher value.

The hyperbolic model is consistent with a local approach to decision making that leads to excessive consumption. The global choice is consistent with the rational economic model. For instance, when planning for the long term, most people intend to eat healthy foods, exercise regularly, watch less television, and quit smoking. They take the global perspective. But such plans require gratification to be delayed. Since on any given day the value of the current indulgence is always higher than the value of any distant health benefit, people tend to put off doing anything about their long-term goals. However, when they regret their past behaviors, they are taking a global perspective.

By the logic of hyperbolic discounting, this example illustrates that if the decision of whether or not to go to gym is made each morning at 6 AM (local perspective), this person will probably prefer an extra hour of sleep. He will plan to sleep just one more time and then start going to gym. Tomorrow, the same reasoning will apply. However, the global perspective will motive one to focus on a pattern of lifestyle choices. Similarly, someone who has a second helping of dessert every night ends up 20 pounds heavier than she had planned. Health behavior choices that create an undesirable way of life are made one day at a time. They are not made at the level of a lifestyle.

Hyperbolic discounting also explains why it is hard to quit. This is because the rewards associated with the global perspective accrue rather slowly, and at the beginning of abstinence, the value of a nondrug day is less than the pleasure of the most recent drug days. That is, on a daily basis, the cost (pain) of abstinence exceeds its benefits. From a local choice, quitting can only occur if there is a change in conditions that markedly reduces the value (pleasure) of the drug relative to the nondrug alternative. This means that quitting requires a steadfast commitment to the global approach to choice and a plan of action that erases reminders of the day-to-day pleasures of drug use.

Why is relapse so often preceded by the statement that this is a "special occasion"? And why is a "special occasion" a good excuse to have another drink? The excuse reflects an underlying dilemma. From a local perspective, the drug is the best choice; but from a global perspective, abstinence is the best choice. The ideal solution is to somehow do both. This is impossible, except in one situation. If the situation can be framed as the "last time," then the dilemma disappears, since the person can say to himself that a new and better life will begin tomorrow.

On any occasion, overeating or using drugs produces limited harm. The damage occurs after repeated indulgences. Thus, the focus of treatment should be less on the individual occasion of impulse control. The better solution arises from reframing the problem such that failure in any occasion is a predictor of failure in all occasions. If I give in today, I shall fail tomorrow as well. By connecting these single occasions into a sequence and thus raising the stakes, the individual can gain a motivation to control her impulses that would be lacking if she just considers one day at the time. By bundling future decisions together, one sees both the immediate and long-term consequences. For example, going to the bar and getting drunk and then regretting it. There is no such a thing as one drink for an alcoholic.

Procrastination as a Special Case of Self-Control Problems

Why do people procrastinate? Consider this. At the beginning of every semester, students make heroic promises to themselves to do their assignments on time. Then they find themselves giving in to temptation while the workload falls farther behind. In the end, they come up with creative stories, excuses, and family tragedies to explain their lateness. This explains why all family tragedies generally occur during the last two weeks of the semester. When students procrastinate in doing their homework, it is not because there is something else they are motivated to do. Often, they are just taking the path of least resistance.

Procrastination is a particular type of self-control problem. In 1978, only 5% of the American public thought of themselves as chronic procrastinators. In 2002, it was 26%[9] (Steele, 2007). About 80 to 95% of college students consider themselves to be a (habitual) procrastinator (Steele, 2007). Part of the problem is that college students are given a fairly high degree of autonomy when it comes to choosing a plan of work for themselves, yet they are deprived of all the structures such as direct parental supervision or social self-control mechanisms.

The costs of procrastination are often considerable. Evidence suggests that the strategy of leaving things until last minute is not a good idea. It generally results in reduced well-being and low quality work performance (Tice and Baumeister, 1997). Studies show that students who routinely procrastinate consistently get lower grades. The procrastinators also received less frequent medical and dental checkups and had more household accidents, a result of putting off dull jobs such as changing smoke detector batteries. Procrastinators tend to postpone getting appropriate medical treatments and diagnostic tests (Sirois et al., 2003). For these people, wanting to do well in their health is apparently not sufficient motivation to sustain the behavior. Why, when so little good comes of procrastinating, do we persist in doing it so much?

Procrastination is a tendency of postponing an unpleasant (annoying) task until later, even with the knowledge that doing so will be against one's better judgment (Andreou and White, 2010). It is hard to imagine students being impulsive when writing a paper. Some procrastinators claim that they tend to work best under pressure, perhaps needing the rush of a last-minute deadline to get started. They may also use this as an excuse to justify dragging their feet. It could be a mere wishful thinking that they tend to underestimate the time it will take to complete a given aversive task.

Irrational procrastination occurs when an individual intends, at time 1, to carry out an unpleasant task at time 2 but, when time 2 arrives, postpones execution to time 3. By doing so, the person passes the buck to one's future selves. In short, procrastination is the voluntary postponement of an intended course of action despite having the opportunity to act and expecting to be worse off as a result of the delay. Thus, procrastination involves harming one's future selves. A simple example of procrastination would be leaving the dishes to stack up in the sink, even though it is easier to clean them right away. A more serious example would be someone who puts off having a colonoscopy and therefore may miss having colon cancer diagnosed at an early stage.

A necessary condition for procrastination is that people perceive the immediate present costs of action more vividly than the future benefits (Akerlof, 1991). Investment goods, like healthy dieting and exercise, require effort at present and deliver benefits in the future. Leisure goods, such as consumption of tempting foods or watching TV, provide an immediate reward and a delayed future cost. We tend to have present-bias toward leisure goods, and to procrastinate investment goods. It always feels better to defer costs. If effort is perceived to be aversive, then procrastination expresses temporary preference for smaller, immediate rewards over later, larger ones. Thus, we may delay getting the car fixed, or going to the doctor for yearly check-ups.

Procrastination is similar to impulsive behavior, as manifested in addiction and impulsive overeating (Ainslie, 2001). Impulses defined as temporary preferences for smaller, sooner rewards over larger, later rewards. For example, we promise to exercise and watch our diet, and then we find a reason to give up our long-term goals for immediate gratification. We say to ourselves "I'll take that slice of chocolate cake and begin the diet seriously tomorrow." The addicts and overeaters want to discontinue their behaviors at some point, but not today. They fail to quit because they continuously procrastinate, and the difficulty of overcoming such procrastination is the main problem with addiction and obesity. The cost of having yet another piece of cake or smoking yet another cigarette may be so small that it is reasonable to see it as insignificant.

Procrastination is also not the same as impulse control in that the person does not suffer from any loss of intentional control. The procrastinating person who fails to do the dishes promptly is not the same as someone who gets drunk or angry, in which situations self-control ability is impaired, and does something that he later on regrets.

In general, there are several causes and correlations of procrastination (Steele, 2007). The most important predictor of procrastination is the task characteristics being unpleasant, boring, and uninteresting (e.g., Christmas shopping or exercise). The more people dislike a task, the more they consider it effortful or anxiety producing, and the more they procrastinate. A person might value being physically fit, but still put off starting regular physical exercise because she simply does not like exercising.

Another important factor is the timing of the reward and punishment. Procrastination occurs when present costs are highly salient in comparison with future costs, leading individuals to postpone tasks until tomorrow without anticipating that when tomorrow comes, the required action will be delayed yet again (Ainslie, 2001). That is, the procrastinator chooses the larger, later evil over the smaller, sooner evil.

Procrastination can also stem from anxiety, an offshoot of neuroticism. Procrastinators postpone getting started because of a fear of failure (and perhaps even expecting failure). As the saying goes, *perfect is the enemy of good*; insisting on perfection often results in no improvement at all. Interestingly, lack of emotion is also deemed as a cause for procrastination. Damasio argues that in certain brain-damaged patients, the incapacity to experience emotion causes people to needlessly spend time over trivial matters.

Lack of self-confidence or self-efficacy (or fear of failures) may discourage people from working as effectively as they might. Fear of a low self-efficacy is a strong predictor of procrastination. So, it is important to ensure that people set realistic goals (not too easy or too hard). For example, many students would likely finish their assignments sooner if they were more confident about completing the task successfully. People must demonstrate to themselves that they are capable of such success.

What can a person do to overcome procrastination? People must demonstrate to themselves that they are capable of success. They surround themselves with cues that confirm their goals and banish any sign that reminds them of temptation. For example, a study showed that procrastination decreased for students who studied in the same location (Andreou and White, 2010). The repeated use of strict time schedules fosters the formation of behavioral habits, and removing temptation cues reduces sensitivity to distractions.

How can you complete those unpleasant tasks in time? By changing the value of the task (e.g., piggybacking distant goals onto more immediate goals) to reduce the distance between effort and reward. Another strategy would be to focus on the intermediate tasks. By shifting one's focus from the ultimate goal to specific intermediate steps, one not only turns an intimidating mountain into a series of doable molehills, but one also reduces the delay between effort and reward. So, while the reward of having written a book may be so far off as to have little motivational pull, the satisfaction associated with having written chapters or, better yet, having met one's target of three pages per day is likely to be much more effective.

To help students overcome procrastination in my own classes, I use weekly quizzes and assignments, rather than giving final exams.[10] Their final grade is based on the cumulative quiz scores. I have noticed that this strategy increases both attendance and overall learning experience. At first, most students do not appreciate it, because they cannot afford to miss the class or procrastinate preparing for the test. Overall, this improves their self-control by forcing them to stay current in the reading and pay attention in class.

Conclusion

Health behavior choices, such as overeating and substance use, involve a tension between a desire for immediate gratification and delayed gratification. Addictive behavior can be understood as an instance of choice over time in that the user chooses whether to engage in an immediately pleasurable activity (using drugs) that carries a long-term cost (sustained addiction with negative consequences for health, job, etc.). When under the sway of craving, the smoker may become indifferent to the information about the harms of smoking. Individuals with such problems overindulge in immediate rewards that later lead to long-term costs. They attach lower value to health-promoting activities, such as prevention and treatment, that would lead to long-term benefits.

This chapter showed that the combination of individual and environmental forces influence the host of vulnerability for temporal discounting. In the language of public health, a genetic predisposition for extreme temporal discounting could be considered as a risk factor. Thus, promoting consideration of the future consequences of behavior may be an important policy tool to improve human well-being.

Notes

1. Opportunity cost refers to the losses that come from doing something (e.g., the loss of opportunities by choosing option A over option B). The presence of cues in modern societies signals the presence of rewards, which implies that there are more rewards around to obtain and motivates individuals to get the job done quicker so that they can get back to those other rewards.
2. This may explain why, for example, there is an inverse relationship between saving rates (a proxy for time perspective) in different countries and fear of nuclear war.
3. For example, consider the choice of a mate. Widow birds prefer males with long tails (a sign of male quality). So a female confronted with a short-tailed male faces a dilemma: settle for the short-tailed male or keep looking. Viewed from the lens of evolutionary approach, the appropriate behavior is a fit between decision mechanisms and the environment in which animal operates. When living in a competitive environment (high uncertainty), waiting imposes opportunity costs for birds with short life spans. Thus, uncertainty motivates the bird to settle for a less-than-ideal mate.
4. Children with attention-deficit/hyperactivity disorder experience the greatest delays in brain maturation in those areas of the cortex most involved in attention and motor control. Many youth eventually seem to grow out of the disorder.
5. Impulsivity is defined: (1) the inclination to choose small, immediately available rewards over larger, delayed rewards, and/or (2) the inclination to respond rapidly without forethought and/or attention to consequences.
6. Attention-deficit/hyperactivity disorder (ADHD), with its extreme distractibility, is usually linked to frontal lobe dysfunction. The person's attention drifts on any task devoid of instant reward (a computer game or sporting event), such as listening to a lecture or reading a textbook.
7. Alternatively, there may be some third factor that influences both education and health behaviors. Research suggests that education affects health because both are determined by individual differences in time preferences and the value people place in future (Fuchs, 1982). Individuals with a low rate of time discounting tend to value education. It is also plausible that higher education may shape time preference in that direction.
8. Elster (2010) notes that rationality differs from wisdom. He defines wisdom as the ability to make choices toward improving one's well-being.

9 The absence of structure and imposed direction in the workplace might contribute to the increase in procrastination. The more complex and individualized societies become, the more individuals will need self-disciple to avoid procrastination and stay competitive.
10 Similarly, while a small weight gain may not be visually noticeable, the weekly Weight Watchers weigh-in forces an individual to confront the implications of his consumption on a weekly basis.

8
ADDICTION AND CHOICE

Introduction

The challenge of addiction is to understand how and why addicts are so insensitive to the future consequences of their drug-seeking behavior. Even more challenging is the understanding of why this same choice is repeatedly made with the negative consequences. An understanding of what drives these decisions is a critical part of the prevention and treatment of addiction. Impulsivity and poor decision making is widely cited to be associated with drug use and relapse. When faced with a choice that brings immediate pleasure, even at the risk of incurring future negative outcomes, addicts appear oblivious to the consequences of their actions. Furthermore, the basic mechanism of addiction impairs the individual's ability to behave in ways that would enable the individual to control the habit. The impairments lead to impulsive behaviors, in which addicts overestimate the immediate value of drug-related stimuli and underestimate the long-term consequences. This description is consistent with a growing consensus in neuroscience regarding the neural basis of addiction as a malfunction of the brain's decision-making circuitry (e.g., Naqvi et al., 2007; Redish et al., 2008).

This chapter presents a perspective from the principles of behavioral economics to explain the lack of long-term perspective manifested in the behavioral decisions of many individuals with addiction problems. Behavioral economics views addiction as a malfunction of decision processes, and helps to identify systematic patterns in errors that people make. The central idea of this approach is that drugs have an unprecedented ability to induce decision errors. As the process of decision-making fails, addicts progressively make less advantageous decisions for themselves and for those who are close to them. The chapter is organized around three questions about the stages of addiction: initial use, compulsive use, and relapse. Consideration of the separate phases is necessary because interventions that are effective in one phase may be ineffective in another phase.

Models of Addictive Behavior

Different explanations from economics, psychology, and neurobiology can be used to describe addictive behavior. The following sections briefly describe various models of addiction. The crucial difference between these models lies in their explanations for why people get addicted, why they persist, and why they relapse. The discussions examine the relationship between addiction and rationality.

The Disease Theory

Genes have a strong influence on our behavior (Raine, 2013). Genetic factors contribute strongly to psychological makeup, such as personality, responses to stress, rational thinking, decision making, and other patterns of behavior. Neurotransmitters are brain chemicals essential to brain functioning. There are more than a hundred of them and they help to transmit signals from one brain cell to another to communicate information. Genes that influence the level of these chemicals can therefore change cognition, emotion, and behavior. For example, the 5HTT gene and the DRD2 gene regulate two important neurotransmitters in the brain: serotonin and dopamine. Serotonin is a mood stabilizer, which has an inhibitory function in the brain. A low-level of serotonin results in violence and impulsive behavior. Without serotonin, people get upset easily when annoyed. Dopamine helps produce drive and motivation. It is like the accelerator in the car that helps move us forward to things that we want. When dopamine is experimentally increased in animals, it fuels appetitive behaviors. It also increases aggressive behavior, since aggressive behavior can be rewarding.

Research shows that cocaine addicts actually have lower levels of dopamine D_2 receptors than control subjects (Volkow et al., 2006). This means that addicts are actually less sensitive to the effects of dopamine. In other words, the sensitivity of the reward system in the brain is in fact decreased. Thus, addicts seek out drugs because of the very potency with which they can increase dopamine in the brain, often at the expense of other pleasurable natural stimulants that do not increase dopamine so dramatically. Reductions in dopamine D_2 receptors are not limited to cocaine users, as similar decreases have been observed in methamphetamine abusers and alcoholics. This appears to be a common finding across a wide variety of addictions. Volkow et al., 2006) found that the amount of dopamine released in alcoholics was 70% lower than in controls. Addictive genetic factors are estimated to contribute 50–60% (Goldman et al., 2005), meaning that approximately half of the statistical probability of developing an addictive disorder is attributable to genetic influences.

Genetic factors may be protective against problematic alcohol use. Research shows that the genes that code for the liver enzyme aldehyde dehydrogenase (ALDH) play an important role in the metabolization of alcohol.[1] Those who have this deficiency experience a range of aversive physiological consequences when they drink, due to a buildup of acetaldehyde. People of Asian descent are more likely to lack the enzyme that aids in the metabolism of alcohol in the liver, and they have a flushing reaction to alcohol. On the other hand, the children of an alcoholic parent are less sensitive to the negative consequences of alcohol, resulting in increased alcohol consumption. For example, due to genetic vulnerability, children of alcoholics are at higher risk for future alcohol problems, and many of these children show high levels of impulsivity. Thus, you may have two glasses of wine and want no more, and yet the vulnerable person cannot stop with six. The take-home lesson is that children of alcoholics should be advised never to touch alcohol. Avoiding the drug at the outset is a sure way to avoid becoming addicted!

Other studies show that addicts' brains make normal amounts of the neurotransmitter, but just can't regulate it properly[2] (Zald et al., 2008). Risky human behaviors such as skydiving and any self-harm actions have been attributed to a desire to overcome emotional numbness, possibly due to a dysfunction in the dopamine system (Leknes and Tracey, 2008). These findings provide a biological explanation for why certain people tend to live life on the edge. The abnormality in their brains predisposes them to keep taking risks and chasing the next high (e.g., drinking too much, taking drugs, or overspending). These individuals have fewer dopamine-regulating receptors, and they get an unusually big hit of dopamine each time they have a novel experience. That blast makes them feel good, so they keep returning for the rush from similarly risky or new behaviors.

Interestingly, the simultaneous presence (comorbidity) of a mental illness (often major depression) is seen in about half of all who are dependent on an addictive drug. Thus, some addicts with a defective reward system might try to compensate by using drugs that stimulate the reward system (Goldstein, 2001). These individuals might display emotional flatness, have difficulty in social relationships, or lack enthusiasm for anything—a classic picture of depression. Even though these individuals are hardwired to become addicted, but the capacity will remain dormant unless the individual actually indulges.

In sum, evidence supports the idea that addicts suffer from a natural deficit of dopamine, and so they self-medicate with drugs. Others have found that addicts' brains make normal amounts of dopamine, but just can't regulate it properly. These studies support viewing addiction as a disease, rather than poor choices or immoral behavior. However, Volkow (the Director of the National Institute on Drug Abuse) argues that this is not a biomarker of addiction. You are not addicted because you have low levels of dopamine D_2 receptors. The reductions may make some people at greater risk for taking drugs. It is not making them addicted. However, given the right environment, biological and genetic predispositions may increase the risk of addiction. Thus, a therapeutic intervention that would increase dopamine D_2 receptors could help patients stop taking drugs, because it would make them more sensitive to other rewards. In short, genes do not determine human destiny, but they do shape parameters of vulnerability and protection. Rose and Dick (2007) argue that people seek specific risk and protective conditions and experiences to match their proclivities and appetites, thereby actively creating conditions that lead to addiction.

Self-Medication

What purpose might drugs be serving in the lives of addicts? The short answer is this: they are painkillers for treating psychological pain, at least in the short-term. Addiction is both a solution and consequence of the psychological pains.

Theories of addiction help us better understand the motivations for drug use. The self-medication theory of addiction suggests that individuals with deficits in emotion-regulation skills (i.e., skills relevant for modifying emotional reactions and to tolerate negative emotions) use drugs in an attempt to manage negative or distressing affective states (e.g., Khantzian, 2003; Khantzian and Albanese, 2008; Berking et al., 2011). For instance, individuals with histories of exposure to adverse childhood environments (e.g., physical and sexual abuse) tend to have diminished capacity to regulate negative emotions and cope effectively with stress.

This view of addiction emphasizes that psychological pain is at the heart of addictive behavior and that vulnerable individuals resort to their addiction because they discover that the addictive substance or behavior gives short-term relief and comfort from their distress. Drugs are more appealing for those who have suffered major traumatic experiences. In other words, addiction problems are less about pleasure-seeking behavior than they are about human psychological pain and deficits in internal sources of self-soothing.

In the initial stage of addiction, drug use can successfully lead to reductions in the negative affect. In low to moderate doses, depressants (alcohol) can relieve states of anxiety or tension associated with depression. But, in the longer period, chronic use contributes to neurobiological changes in the brain. These changes may underlie the transition from the use motivated primarily for achieving a high or relief to the use that is motivated for regaining a sense of normalcy. The end result of such a process is that the individual begins to engage in compulsive drug use. She is no longer in volitional control of her drug use.

For those with a penchant to suffer a range of psychiatric disorders (depression or anxiety), repeated uses of drugs become a way of life. Relief is momentary, but in the long-term, drug use becomes an end in itself. The addiction problem prevents the user from understanding about his distress, as well as the development of emotional capacity to self-soothe. In essence, addicts substitute a misery that is vague and confusing with a misery that is caused by a drug use.

The theory of self-medication emphasizes that addictive drugs are not equally appealing. Although a person might experiment with various drugs, they discover that they are drawn toward a certain drug (e.g., stimulants, depressants) because of what it does for them. For example, many cocaine abusers attempt to regulate inner emptiness, boredom, and fight depression. Stimulants help to overcome feelings of low energy fatigue, and low self-esteem problems associated with depression. Alcohol is frequently used as a way of coping with social anxiety. The drinking removes, at least temporarily, the stress of anxiety. Thus, the drug of choice reveals psychological problems that are painful for that person.

A study that followed over 1,200 children from birth found that individuals with depression in adolescence were at significantly greater risk of later developing nicotine dependence. Using nicotine relives the distress of major depression and less severe depressive symptoms. For an example of this on a large scale, when communism collapsed, alcohol drinking increased significantly in Russia. About 25% of Russian men die before age 55 mostly due to the alcohol use, particularly vodka. Causes of death include liver disease and alcohol poisoning, and aggressive behavior (Zaridze et al., 2014). The sense of hopelessness in concerning self and future life increased alcohol use to cope with emotional distress.

The self-medication theory of addiction provides a useful tool for the understanding and treatment of addiction. This theory explains that addictions develop in context. That is, the psychological distress and suffering increases addictive vulnerability. In the short-term, addicts can better endure their distress and cope with the realities that can otherwise feel so unbearable. This theory provides a humanistic psychological understanding for addictive behavior, one which sees people with addiction as a fundamentally vulnerable population. Effective treatment, like the self-medication theory, is based on the implied notion that the intention of drug use is not pleasure, but to find a relief from unendurable suffering and pain in the absence of alternatives.

Addiction as Rational Self-Medication

The rational addiction model assumes that individuals are fully informed and maximize preferences, and treats addiction as essentially self-medication (Becker and Murphy, 1988). Addiction is freely chosen. The model assumes that the addict is aware of the risks, but still feels that addiction is a better option than abstaining. Thus, given the opportunity, the person who becomes addicted finds the behavior rewarding and cares little about the harms the behavior is likely to cause. That is, she is a "happy" addict.

The rational model uses the terms addiction and habit as synonyms (Becker and Murphy, 1988). The key feature of the model is the presence of "addictive capital." That is, current usage increases the future marginal benefit of usage, and decreases the future baseline level of well-being. In general, the consumption of a certain good is termed to be an addiction or a habit if an increase in current consumption of the good leads to an increase in future consumption. For some activities (good habits), value can take an ever-increasing trajectory. This means that current consumption is positively related to past consumption. People who enjoy skilled activities, such as piano playing or a field of study (e.g., music or literature), find ever-increasing enjoyment as they become more skilled and more knowledgeable.

According to this account, people may recognize that addiction has negative long-term consequences, but judge that the benefits exceed the costs. The addict feels that the substance he consumes (or the behavior he chooses) makes him better off, all things considered. The drug provides immediate pleasure, relief of depression, and distraction. The attempt to self-medicate panic and anxiety leads to alcoholism is an example of rational addiction theory. An individual may drink alcohol for its tension reduction or self-escape properties. When emotional suffering is caused by intolerable conditions of life (tragedy), a quick "fix" offers immediate satisfaction, and immediate escape from misery. In short, for some addicts, to sooth irritability, anxiety, and moodiness for a small monetary price of an alcoholic drink may be a good value. That is, the drug is chosen for the need to escape from a harsh reality, and from the user's perspective, there is nothing irrational about her behavior. The rational model is also consistent with the fact that substance abuse is highly comorbid with affective disorders (depression and anxiety), although some mental problems (e.g., anxiety) may be the effects of drug use (Thombs and Osborn, 2013).

There is also evidence that aggregate drug use responds both to prices and to information about the effects of addictive substances (Chaloupka and Warner, 2001). That is, significant increases in the monetary prices of cigarettes and other tobacco products will lead to significant reductions in the use of these substances. For example, research indicates that each 10% price increase reduces youth smoking rates by 6.5%, adult smoking rates by 2% and total consumption of tobacco by 4% (Chaloupka and Warner, 2001). The price elasticity[3] of demand for alcohol (1.8) shows that the overall consumption of alcohol is price-sensitive; this shows that governments can and do encourage or discourage consumption by taxation policy.[4] There is also evidence that users are willing to reduce current consumption in response to anticipated price increases.[5]

For an anecdotal observation, Dalrymple (2006) writes about his experience as a doctor to the workers on a road-building project in Africa. Alcohol was virtually free of charge and given *ad libitum* to the contingent of British workers on the project. He observed that in these circumstances, about a fifth of British construction workers would regularly go to bed so drunk that they urinated in their sleep. Most of them had never drunk so heavily before. In 1949, China had more opiate addicts than the rest of the world put together, the exact figures were estimated around 20 million. In short order, Mao gave addicts a strong incentive to give up and the rest of the population a strong motive not to start. The motive was death for dealers or addicts. It is reported that within three years, Mao produced more cures than all the drug clinics in the world. The point is not to advocate such a draconian method, but to point out that when an incentive is sufficiently strong, addicts can abandon their addiction.

In sum, the model of rational addiction suggests that the consumption patterns for addictive substances are no different than for other goods, and the demands for addictive substances are subject to the law of a downward-sloping demand curve. That is, addiction involves a choice to engage in a behavior based on a weighing of the cost and benefits. In the Becker and Murphy model, a person for whom a good is highly addictive might voluntarily become an addict, even though he perfectly estimates the consequences of his actions, simply because he enjoys greater pleasure by being an addict than by abstaining. In reality, most of us at times behave this way despite negative consequences (e.g., continue overeating or stay in bad relationships and ignore the negative results).

The Primrose Path

This model explains that addiction results from people's lack of awareness of the impacts of current drug use on future preference (i.e., habit formation). The individuals make decisions in the moment from the strict perspective of temporary happiness, and are oblivious to the long-term consequences. This model is rooted in Herrnstein's theory that human behavior is better explained by assuming that people meliorate (improve) than by assuming that they maximize (Herrnstein and Prelec, 1992). It assumes that the addicts are completely myopic in the cognitive sense. In this model, individuals are acting against their own better judgment of what is in their long-term interest.

This account focuses on the initial stage of addiction through a series of incremental decisions with consequences that are not perceived by the individual until it is too late. For example, when a person decides whether to have a drink, she typically does not take into account that she can get addicted, or the "internality" (harm to oneself) that arises from the fact that a drink now devalues drinks in the future. Rather, she simply compares the value of a drink now with the value of abstaining now.

Addiction as a choice doesn't mean someone chooses to be an addict. No one would choose to be an addict. One day of drug use does not mean addiction. As the days accumulate, the characteristics of addiction emerge. Consequently, a person who never chose to be an addict ends up an addict (Rachlin, 2000; Hyman, 2005). Similarly, someone who has a second helping of dessert every night ends up 20 pounds heavier than he had planned. In short, choices that create an undesirable way of life are made one day at a time; they are not made at the level of a long-term lifestyle.

The Lonely Addict

Addicts commonly lack enough positive human contacts to sustain happiness, and they resort to drug intake partly as self-medication (Panksepp, 2012). Several reasons explain the role of loneliness in addictive behaviors. The social control hypothesis suggests that the absence of caring friends and family lead people to neglect themselves and indulge in health-damaging behaviors, such as eating unhealthily and not exercising. The feeling of isolation is a major source of unhappiness. The subjective experience of loneliness is painful. That is why we turn to ice cream or other fatty foods when we are sitting at home feeling all alone in the world. Problems in self-regulation specifically attributed to loneliness have manifested in alcohol abuse, drug abuse, eating disorders, and even suicide.[6] Evidence shows that loneliness affects the ability to focus and maintain attention. In one study, those students identified as lonely were less successful at imposing self-control. Loneliness, in effect, gives these individuals an attentional deficit.

Social bonding is a naturally addictive process. As noted before, social attachment produces oxytocin that powerfully promotes feelings of confidence and comfort. Positive social interactions result in the release of endogenous opioids in the brain, which may be a natural way to reduce addictive behaviors and other psychological problems. In contrast, loneliness leads to sadness, grief, and ultimately chronic feelings of emotional emptiness. Loneliness tends to lower self-esteem. If you perceive that others see you as worthless, you are more likely to engage in self-destructive behaviors and are less likely to take good care of yourself. Cacioppo (2008) shows that loneliness is a risk factor for illness and early death, right alongside smoking, obesity, and lack of exercise. From this perspective, it will be worthwhile to allocate resources to build social structures that support human connection.

Like addiction, social bonding includes an initial stage of intense positive feeling, followed by a tolerance stage, which leads to a powerful separation distress (withdrawal stage). Since we get habituated to having our companions around, the feelings of dependency may recede into the background of consciousness. Only when there is a loss of an attachment of a loved one does the separation anxiety comes to surface. As the saying goes, one never stops to wonder, until a person's gone (Frijda, 2007). This explains why lonely individuals are powerfully attracted to opiate drugs (Mate, 2010). These individuals may be self-medicating because they have chronic feelings of psychic pain that arise.[7] Mate (2010) suggests that addictive behaviors ultimately driven by our unwillingness to allow ourselves to really feel and experience pain, frustration, fear, and all the negative emotions that are part of being human. Instead, we choose the chemical shortcut to avoid those emotions, and become trapped there.

Lack of Alternative Rewards

The lack of alternative, nondrug rewards partly explains the demand for drug consumption. The idea is that our actions are governed largely by what we are rewarded for in our environment. There is now extensive research showing that providing alternative rewards to those who formerly lacked them improve addiction treatment outcomes (e.g., see Hart, 2013; Solinas et al., 2008). That is, environmental conditions play a major role in treating drug addiction and in preventing relapses. Hart (2013) notes that if you are living in a poor neighborhood deprived of options, there's a certain rationality to keep taking a drug that will give you some temporary pleasure.

Animal studies of addiction show that when alternative rewards are available to healthy animals, such as social and sexual contact and pleasant living conditions, they typically choose nondrug alternatives. After addicting mice to cocaine, the researchers then exposed them to an enriched environment. Exposing mice to an "enriched environment" during cocaine withdrawal removed abnormal behavior related to addiction. An enriched environment, for mice, is an environment which stimulates their curiosity and provides social and physical activity as well as exploration. The rats raised in a solitary condition with no options keep pressing the lever for cocaine. But when they live in an enriched environment, and are provided with alternatives reinforcements, such as sweets and the opportunity to play with other rats, they stop pressing the lever (Solinas et al., 2008).

The purpose of treatments is to produce outcomes by enhancing the value of activities that compete with drug use and to develop techniques for developing hope in a brighter future. If a choice process drives drug use in addiction, then it is in principle possible to arrange conditions (e.g., the living conditions of drug addicts) such that addicts will be persuaded to choose something other than intoxication. Humans and animals who are given limited options for fulfillment may rationally abuse drugs. On the other hand, marriage, having children, and jobs are strong rewards and also mean you have a lot to lose.

Social Influences

Addictive behavior does not take place in a social vacuum. Individual desires and beliefs are social products, which are shaped and reshaped through social interactions, and individual decisions are directly and indirectly influenced by other people's decisions.

Individual consumers are to some extent conformists. This implies that societies that are quite similar in most relevant aspects could nevertheless be quite different in terms of rates of drug abuse, simply because of differences in consumption history. Hence, once a high-consumption culture has become established, it may not be easily removed by policy measures (Moene, 1996). For example, consider the culturally accepted pattern of heavy drinking in Russia. Also, the American-born Chinese generally consume more alcohol than Asian-born Chinese.

Social norms play an important role in the regulation of substance abuse. One of the reasons that novel substances become a problem in indigenous populations is because they lack social norms that might control the use of substances. For example, in many Western societies, alcohol is used in specific events and regular times (e.g., Friday evening after work). Such a norm limits and controls the use. In contrast, populations that have been introduced to the substance more recently have no social norm for controlling its use, and thus they are vulnerable to develop substance use problems (Elster, 2001).

Socioeconomic class influences social acceptability of addictive behavior because people are generally more influenced by what their own group does than by the wider culture. Thus, the decline in smoking has been much greater in affluent middle-class circles than in blue-collar society, probably reflecting a difference in education levels as well as self-confidence about being able to change the circumstances of one's own life. Very likely, this class difference in smoking behavior will disappear with time, but change in societal norms is typically slow (Christakis and Fowler, 2008). Overall, individuals influence and are influenced by their families, their social networks, the organizations in which they participate, their communities, and the society in which they live. Furthermore, most behaviors are not randomly distributed, but are patterned, meaning that they tend to occur in clusters. Many people who drink heavily also smoke. Those who eat a healthful diet also tend to exercise.

Summary

Theses diverse models of addiction suggest that vulnerability to addiction can be explained by considering multilevel factors from the molecular to the societal. These factors include poverty, lack of employment, mental illness, and access to nondrug alternatives. These various views also present implications for treatment policies. If one considers that addiction is a willful misconduct (a freely chosen and morally wrong course of action), then the logical way to treat the problem is to punish the addict. In contrast, viewing addiction as diseases can serve to reduce possible guilt and shame about the behavior and help the addict focus on the treatment to achieve a healthy life. However, the major limitation of the disease model is that it gives limited emphasis to the role of learning and decision-making capacity in the development of addiction.

Stress and Addiction Vulnerability

Stress is a key risk factor in addiction initiation, maintenance, and relapse to drug-seeking behavior. Stress has been defined as the nonspecific response to any common demand upon the body or any alteration in psychological homeostatic processes. Stress is normally referred to adversity or hardship (distress) such as poverty or bereavement. Biologically, stressful events cause a rise of glucocorticoids in blood levels, which are considered major stress hormones. In response to stress, different regulatory systems of the body are activated to improve the ability of the organism to adapt to internal or external challenges ("fight or flight" response). "Fight or flight" is the normal response to stress, that is, all the blood goes to the muscles so that you're ready for action.

Homeostatic mechanisms keep systems in a steady state when forces outside the system threaten disruption, just as thermostats keep a house at the same temperature regardless of how hot it is outdoors. Homeostatic regulation reflects stability within a narrow range (e.g., body temperature and glucose levels that must be maintained within a narrow range). In contrast, an allostatic state is a state of chronic deviation of the regulatory system from its normal or homeostatic operating level. In other words, an allostatic system can operate in a relative broad range (e.g., blood pressure can be in a broad range).

The term allostasis refers to the constant reestablishment and maintenance of a dynamic equilibrium in the face of a fast-changing environment. Within this framework, an *allostatic load* is the biological "costs" of short-term adaptation to stress (the impact of lifelong experiences of "wear and tear"). Types of allostatic load include frequent exposure to stress, inability to habituate to repeated challenges, or inability to terminate a stress response, and an increased activation or inadequate (compensatory) response. Psychological factors, such as anticipating negative consequences, pessimism, anxiety, or worry, contribute to an allostatic load. In the long run, a high allostatic load might result in a number of negative health outcomes, such as diabetes, hypertension, cancer, and cardiovascular disease (McEwen, 2000).

The danger of allostatic load is well illustrated in the rivers of Nova Scotia. Every year, the salmon swim upstream to deposit eggs, battling the adverse current, leaping over rocks, and traveling up to a thousand miles to return to their breeding ground. After ensuring the birth of a new generation, the salmon die. The fish are killed by their own stress hormones. The stress hormones give them the enormous burst of energy needed for the journey, but ultimately reach toxic levels. This is what the scientists call a biphasic (having two phases) action of the stress response: though it can mobilize to accomplish incredible feats, it can also cause damage and death. In the case of salmon, death serves a useful purpose: it frees up the food supply for a new generation. There is no comparable purpose in the damaging side of stress on the human body, but there is a lot we can do to prevent allostatic load (McEwen, 2002).

It is important to distinguish between chronic and normal stress. Moderate and challenging stressors with limited duration are perceived to be pleasant. In other words, some individuals seek "stressful" situations (sensation-seekers or seeking out novel and highly stimulating experiences) that promote the release of stress hormones. However, intense, unpredictable, prolonged stressors produce learned helplessness and depressive-like symptoms in animals and humans. Stress increases the risk for developing depression, the common cold, influenza, and tension headaches, and often will induce people to start grinding their teeth or clenching their jaws and tensing their necks and shoulders.

The origin of allostatic load can be based on an individual psychological appraisal process. Stress responses to physical and psychological stimuli are primarily determined by the individual interpretation, the individual's ability to effectively "cope" with the stressor, but also the social context, social status, genetic factors, gender, developmental stage, and individual lifelong experiences (Arnsten, et al., 2012). The stressful event or circumstances itself is not what determines a person's response; what matters is how the person appraises the stressor and how she copes with it. Coping is generally defined as an effort to deal with stress. One can cope with stress by smoking, drinking, and overeating, which are harmful to health. One can also use reappraisal as a coping strategy by viewing the situation differently (e.g., it is no longer a big deal). What is important is the meaning the event or circumstance has for the individual (Lazarus and Lazarus, 2006).

Social status is a potent force in health and longevity in the United States. The more education and income people have, the less likely they are to have and die of heart disease, strokes, diabetes, and many types of cancer. Upper-middle-class Americans live longer and in better health than middle-class Americans, who live longer and better than those at the bottom. For example, lawyers, doctors, and scientists have fewer diseases and die at a later age than bank clerks, sales representatives, and secretaries. Bank clerks, sales representatives, and secretaries have fewer illnesses and die later than unskilled construction workers, janitors, and restaurant employees (Marmot and Wilkinson, 2006). People in jobs where they don't perceive themselves to have a lot of control are much more susceptible to developing clinical anxiety and depression, as well as stress-related medical conditions like ulcers and diabetes.

Research shows that if certain individuals are more sensitive to stress and/or if they find themselves in an environment where they do not feel that they have adequate control over this stress, then these individuals may be more likely to engage in substance abuse. Animal studies have long shown that stress can increase the desire and motivation for drug use (Al'Absi, 2007). In rats trained to self-administer a substance, stressors such as a new environment, an unfamiliar cage mate, or a change in daily routine push the animals to depend on the substance even more. Both animal and human research provides ample evidence that prenatal and postnatal stress increases vulnerability to the use and abuse of drugs. Social separation or isolations were found to increase self-administration of different drugs of abuse. For example, experiments using rhesus monkeys found that monkeys that were reared by their peers during the first six months of their life consumed more alcohol than monkeys reared by their mothers (Kosten and Kehoe, 2007). Research in human studies show that adverse childhood experiences such as physical and sexual abuse, neglect, domestic violence, and family dysfunction are associated with increased risk of addiction (Kosten and Kehoe, 2007). This suggests that exposure to stress during childhood leads to increased drug self-administration. In short, the greater the number of stressors an individual is exposed to, the greater vulnerability to develop addiction.

As discussed, one explanation for the strong linkage between stress-related disorders and drug addiction is the self-medication hypothesis which suggests that people may use drugs to cope with tension associated with life stressors or to relieve symptoms of anxiety and depression resulting from a traumatic event. For example, cocaine addicts often claim that they use cocaine because it produces feelings of power or control and clarity of thought (Al'Absi, 2007).

One group of individuals who appear to be at greater risk for substance abuse are combat veterans, especially those suffering from posttraumatic stress disorders (PTSD). Veterans with PSTD typically report a higher lifetime use of nicotine, alcohol, cocaine, and heroin than veterans screening negative for PTSD. The explanation for this correlation is the self-medication hypothesis to relieve or suppress symptoms of anxiety, irritability, and depression resulting from a traumatic event. People with an unhappy marriage, dissatisfaction with employment, or harassment issues, also report increased rates of addiction (Al'Absi, 2007). Thus, drug use functions as a means to regulate affect and soothe psychological distress.

Furthermore, evidence suggests that response inhibition may be impaired under conditions of high stress and withdrawal-related negative affect, leading to drug use, rapid progress from initiation to dependence, and relapse. The part of the prefrontal cortex that is involved in deliberative cognition is shut down by stress. Chronic stress decreases gray matter volume in the brain region that is associated with cognitive control and stress regulation. A less responsive prefrontal cortex sets up addicts to be more impulsive as well (Grant et al., 2011). For instance, high negative affect (e.g., loss of a relationship or the death of a close family member) increases the incentive value of drug use and reduces the influence of the reflective system, and thus the individual is less able to effectively cope with the negative affect and is more likely to engage in drug use.

In sum, stress may impact the risk of addiction initiation and maintenance through increasing impulsive behaviors. Thus, strategies such as learning to reduce and cope with stress are integrated into addiction treatments as tools to manage triggers that may promote drug use and relapse.

Addiction as Failures in Decision Making

Behavioral economics views drug addiction as impaired decision making. Addiction involves the continued use of drugs or engagement in a particular behavior despite adverse consequences. Drug addiction is an example of behavior driven by strong feelings. Once addicted, behavior is periodically driven by craving, which overwhelms rational deliberations concerning self-interest.

The dual decision model suggests three points that guide the addictive behavior. First, cravings affect cognitive activities, including attention. Second, certain environmental cues systematically trigger cravings. Third, these triggers are established through cue-conditioning. Specific environmental cues can induce visceral states that divert attention from the most preferred alternatives and compromises the ability of the brain to choose the most optimal option (Laibson, 2001). For instance, any of the circumstances and environments surrounding an ex-addict can provoke craving. The following describes the effect of craving on thought and behavior. What goes on in an addict's mind when he is craving for a drug?

Visceral Account of Addiction

Visceral states refer to a wide range of strong feelings (e.g., craving, hunger, pain, fear) that grab people's attention and motivate them to engage in a specific behavior. They tend to "crowd out" virtually all goals other than that of alleviating the visceral state (Loewenstein, 1996). Visceral states can be viewed as short-term fluctuations in preferences or tastes. They influence the relative desirability of different goods and actions (Loewenstein, 1996). For example, shoppers tend to purchase more food at the grocery store when they are hungry, even though they know that the state of hunger is temporary. When an individual is hungry, her attention focuses on tasks associated with obtaining food.

Paul Ekman (2003) notes that strong emotions are constraints on cognition. That is, certain choices available to someone who is calm become unavailable when he is subject to visceral states. For example, it appears to be impossible not to jump back from a striking snake. This state of mind is referred to as a refractory period, during which we don't have access to information that would change how we are feeling. In simplistic terms, strong feelings make people temporarily stupid, so they make bad choices. For example, before an unpleasant encounter, you may resolve to keep your cool. However, when provoked to anger, you lash out without pausing to consider the consequences. It is not that you do not know the consequences, you simply do not, when acting, have access to them.

The Craving Mind

Craving is usually conceptualized as an emotional state reflecting the activation of motivation to use a drug. Cravings narrow attention such that current feelings, thoughts, impulses, urges, and desire would be given extra weight, whereas future goals, ambitions, or plans seem less consequential. A craving is distinguished from hunger in being an intense, focused desire to consume a specific substance or food.

Craving produces a powerful, often overwhelming, urge to consume a drug (Sayette, 2004). Drug craving involves negative feelings; this increases the attractiveness of drug-taking behavior. Under intense craving, addicts make highly distorted tradeoffs between goods and behaviors that alleviate the pain of withdrawal. For example, for an addict who is craving drugs, food or sex has little appeal.

During craving, attention is easily captured by drug cues. The attention-grabbing feature of drug cues is known as "attentional bias" (Cox et al., 2006). This bias is a cognitive mechanism whereby attentional channeling is directed toward personally valued stimuli, despite an individual's efforts to ignore them. Once the distraction has started, it can set into motion mechanisms that eventually lead to drug use and the risk of subsequent relapse. For instance, when alcohol abusers are exposed to the sight or smell of an alcoholic beverage, or smokers are asked to hold a lit cigarette, they react with increased physiological arousal and subjective craving. Smokers may not notice the cigarette butts littering the sidewalk unless they are craving a cigarette (Field and Cox, 2008).

The attentional focus further increases the subjective craving as explained by the Elaborated Intrusion theory of desire (EI theory) (Kavanagh et al., 2005). The EI theory predicts that attentional biases lead to intrusive thoughts about substance use, but craving only occurs if the individual cognitively elaborates the initial thought through substance-related sensory imagery. Moreover, the processes appear to be mediated by addicts' impulsivity and impaired inhibitory control and their conscious attempts to suppress their craving and to avoid attending to substance cues.

Attentional bias develops partly as a consequence of classical conditioning, which causes drug-related cues to elicit in addicts the expectation that they will have an opportunity to use their substance of abuse. This expectation, in turn, causes them to experience subjective craving, and it increases the attention-grabbing properties of the drug-related cues that they encounter. Their attention, therefore, is selectively allocated to drug-related cues.

During the state of arousal, the world is experienced in a very different way than the way it is experienced after satisfying the craving (Sayette, 2004). How does one make decisions when one's perception of the world is distorted by craving? Craving distorts addicts' ability to process information due to cognitive dissonance. Cognitive dissonance suggests that addicts may modify their reasoning processes within limits to support the satisfaction of impulses. For example, a smoker may reason that "since I smoke, it cannot be very dangerous." The strong desire for a cigarette may bring the irrational belief that it won't actually do any harm. While craving, the decision to smoke just one cigarette may not seem so foolish. While smokers are not craving, the balance between pros and cons will motivate smokers to quit. That is, once the craving is diminished, the decision to smoke is reexamined from the perspective of a neutral (i.e., noncraving) state of mind. Now the negatives dominate the decision and the lapsed smoker wonders how such a mistake was made.[8] Without recognizing the powerful shifts in thinking while craving, the smokers may conclude that the relapse reflects lack of willpower or self-efficacy. In short, addicts view drug use in a more favorable light while in a state of craving. While they are not craving, the shift in balance between pros and cons will motivate them to quit.

It is instructive to note that Alcoholics Anonymous tells their members that the essence of relapse prevention is H.A.L.T.—never get too Hungry, Angry, Lonely, or Tired (Alcoholic Anonymous, 2001). This is consistent with visceral account of addiction in that addicts are being reminded that if they put themselves in certain situations, then they will not be able to resist the temptation to consume, and so they need to plan ahead.

Cold-to-Hot Empathy Gap

An important element of the visceral account of addiction is that people underestimate the extent to which strong emotions they will experience in the future will affect their own behavior. This is referred to as the cold-to-hot empathy gap. This concept describes the tendency for individuals when "cold" (i.e., not craving) to mispredict how they will behave when "hot" (i.e., craving).

The behavior stems in part because people cannot recall the intensity of their own past cravings. Human memory seems ill-suited to storing information about visceral sensations. Under extreme stress, the functioning of the hippocampus, which stores episodic memory (the sense of "it happened to me") is shut down by the glucocorticoids secreted during a trauma. Thus, the episodic memory is not laid down in the first place. After a trauma, there may be semantic memory (third-person facts after the event).

The failure to vividly recall or anticipate the discomfort of craving can help to explain the underappreciation of future craving, or, to overestimate their own abilities to resist craving. Experience thus doesn't seem to be sufficient to imprint a memory for the pain of craving. The challenge for an ex-addict is to keep "alive" memories of the unpleasantness and power of craving. One method is to expose addicts who have quit to the agonies of people who are still addicted or have recently quit and are battling against their craving.

For example, a study involving 13 heroin users provided support for the cold-to-hot empathy gap with respect to drug craving (Badger et al., 2007). The study found that addicts placed greater monetary value on receiving an extra dose of opiate five days later if they made the decision right before receiving their current opiate treatment (when they were likely to be in a high-craving state) than if they made the same decision minutes later, after they had received their current treatment and were in a low-craving state. In another study (Sayette et al., 2008) testing the empathy gap for cigarette craving, smokers who were not craving had trouble imagining what it was like to crave, and therefore they placed a lower value on future smoking compared to those who were actively craving.

If even individuals who are addicted to cigarettes cannot appreciate their own craving when they are not in a craving state, how likely is it that, for example, a teenager who has never experienced cigarette craving can imagine what it is like to crave a cigarette? Indeed, there is considerable research that youths tend to underestimate their risk of becoming addicted to cigarettes. For example, the University of Michigan's Monitoring the Future longitudinal study (Johnston et al., 1993) found that although only 15% of respondents who were occasional smokers (less than one cigarette per day) predicted that they might be smoking in five years, 43% of them were, in fact, smoking five years later (Slovic, 2001). Thus, failing to anticipate the motivational strength of cigarette craving, nonsmokers may not appreciate how easy it is to become addicted and how difficult it is to quit once addicted.

The underestimation of cigarette craving may also help to explain the frequency with which smokers attempt to quit, despite dismal rates of success. Initial efficacy (confidence) judgments often are made in a neutral state in the clinic, rather than the high states of craving that have to be endured to remain abstinent.

In one field study, for example, smokers who were attempting to quit were given palm-top computers, and at several randomly chosen times each day, they were prompted to report their self-efficacy to remain abstinent and their urges. Smokers tended to report unrealistically high self-efficacy ratings as long as they were not experiencing an intense urge to smoke. On occasions when they were experiencing intense cravings, however, their self-efficacy ratings dropped to more plausible levels (Gwaltney et al., 2005). Likewise, research has found that many smokers entering treatment report high confidence that they will quit successfully. Smokers who were induced to experience cigarette craving were less optimistic about their own ability to quit than were satiated smokers and, as a result, expressed lower intentions to quit smoking in the future.

Finally, the cold-to-hot empathy gap suggests that smokers are likely to make misinformed decisions about placing themselves in high-risk situations (e.g., parties where there will be a lot of smoking) if they are in a cold state (not craving) while they make these decisions.

Addicts may not realize that their craving may be short-lived. This suggests that while craving, an addict may overestimate the duration and intensity of future cravings. Such exaggerated perceptions of the duration of craving may help to undermine the effort to quit. Marlatt (2005) refers to craving as ocean waves that are built up to a peak state and then subside. If we think that unpleasant feelings will soon pass, we may be better prepared to "tough it out."

Impulsivity and Addiction

Individual differences in impulsivity are consistently identified as key factors in the initiation and later problematic use of substances. Impulsivity is the inclination to seek out immediate gratification at the cost of long-term gains. Sensation seeking is generally defined as a strong need for novelty, a low tolerance to boredom, and willingness to take risks for the sake of having a varied experience.

Drug addicts are often described as being impulsive, risk-taking, sensation-seeking, and as being poor decision makers (Gullo and Dawe, 2008). Addicts are insensitive to future consequences, and instead they are guided by immediate prospects. That is, they tend to choose in a manner that maximizes immediate gains without given consideration to future gains. Addicts tend to exhibit a higher temporal discounting rate (impulsivity) than normal people. That is, they prefer smaller, sooner rewards over larger, later rewards. Thus, events that are more immediate in time (such as having drugs now as opposed to the delayed consequences) have a stronger capability to influence decision making.

The initial use of illicit drugs and alcohol typically occurs during adolescence. The dominance of the affective system during adolescence increases one's vulnerability to addiction (Giedd, 2004). The uneven development of these two brain systems (cognition and affect) is thought to result in an increased risk for addictive behavior. One could also argue that some children are at high risk of developing a drug use as a result of a lack of investment in future-oriented capital during childhood in households with fewer resources to make the investment. Thus, impulsivity is an important factor in earlier stages of drug use through a general inability to inhibit behavior (Tarter et al., 2003).

For example, research suggests that attention-deficit/hyperactivity disorder (ADHD) is a significant risk factor for future drug use. Increased rates of temporal discounting among teenagers and children who were diagnosed with ADHD could be explained by the relative difficulties with cognitive functioning that arise with ADHD. In addition, individuals diagnosed with antisocial personality disorder (ADP) also tend to exhibit greater discounting of delayed rewards than controls, which could be related to relatively poor self-control (Petry, 2002).

It has been found that substance abusers exhibit greater degrees of temporal discounting than nonabusers (Bickel et al., 2007). For example, opioid-dependent patients and nondrug-using control participants chose between hypothetical money available immediately or after a delay. Opioid-dependent patients discounted significantly more than controls. Additionally, when the opioid-dependent patients chose between heroin available immediately or after a delay, delayed heroin was discounted even further than when the choice involved hypothetical money (Kirby and Barbarose, 2001). Heavy drinkers are more impulsive than light drinkers, and, consequently, use more alcohol (Reynolds et al., 2008).

Does impatience cause addiction or does addiction cause impatience? In an attempt to explore the causal direction of drug dependence and temporal discounting, Bickel and colleagues (2012) show that temporal discounting may contribute to the development of drug dependence. This suggests that steep discounting may provide a risk factor for drug use and dependence. An alternative explanation is that active drug abuse shortens the temporal horizon and actually causes increased discounting. Drug use may initially involve significant planning, but with chronic use, the behavior may evolve into more habitual actions. Thus, for an addict, the decision to continue the use may reflect the automatic system dominating deliberative process. On the other hand, drug abstinence is associated with lower levels of impulsivity. For example, after a long term of abstinence, ex-smokers displayed the same level of discounting of money as nonsmokers. Thus, chronic drug use may cause long-lasting increases in impulsivity. This suggests that addicts can return to a normal level of discounting if they cease using drug (Bickel et al., 2012).

Impulsivity has also shown to have an effect on drug treatment outcomes. The linkage of discounting to addiction points to the potential benefits of interventions for substance abuse that reduce discounting and lengthen time horizons. Persons with relatively longer time horizons and lower discount rates may be more likely to achieve successful treatment. Among alcohol and drug-dependent clients in treatment, those with a longer time perspective were more likely to finish treatment compared to those with a shorter perspective.

Impaired Insight in Addiction

Data from 2006 indicates that more than 80% of the 21.1 million addicted individuals failed to seek treatment (Goldstein et al., 2009). That is, these addicts do not recognize the need for treatment. For example, only a small fraction of heavy drinkers admit they have a drinking problem. Alcohol reduces the individual's level of self-awareness (or self-evaluation) by reducing self-control inhibition, which further contributes to alcohol consumption. However, a better self-awareness of the drinking problem improves the treatment outcome (abstinence for a year) (Goldstein et al., 2009). Individuals with enhanced awareness are likely to engage in reappraisal resulting in better emotion regulation.

What is insight? Insight or self-awareness refers to the ability to recognize and describe one's own feeling, thinking, and behaviors (Goldstein et al., 2009). The insular cortex plays a key role in interoception or subjective emotional feelings. Interoception is the collection of processes by which physiological signals in the body are transmitted back to brain, giving rise to awareness of bodily feelings (e.g. pain, touch, temperature).

Damage to specific areas of the brain (a lesion of right insula) may interrupt the ability to recognize internal signals that indicate a problem and lead to the false belief that one is okay or in control. This dysfunction leads to a lack of self-awareness and insight. For example, impaired awareness can take the form of failure to recognize an illness. Individuals with insula damage are impaired at recognizing emotion and pain in themselves and others. Indeed, the impaired insight about the severity of the addiction problem might derive these individuals' excessive drug use. For example, chronic drug abuse has been recognized to be associated with impaired self-awareness (dysfunction of the insular cortex), which manifests as compromised recognition or denial of the severity of addiction and the need for treatment (Naqvi et al., 2007).

In sum, a diminished sensitivity to internal states may explain why an addict engages in risky behavior. This poor metacognition and denial leads to poor choices and presents a challenge for addiction treatment (Verdejo-Garcia et al., 2012). As a result, low levels of self-awareness may not engage the cognitive control system to regulate behavior. Thus, tools aimed to increase an individual's self-awareness during the treatment could significantly contribute to recovery. Mindfulness is an important approach that has been shown to improve awareness and inhibitory control (Paulus and Stewart, 2014).

Summary

In sum, evidence suggests that there is linkage between poor decision making and addiction (Bechara and Damasio, 2002, 2005). Impairments in decision making are evident in addicts, regardless of the type of drug they abuse, which suggests that poor decision making may relate to addiction in general.

Addicts consistently display impaired self-control compared with nonaddicts. Addicts show a deficit in the ability to resist the intrusion of information that is unwanted or irrelevant. Difficulties inhibiting particular thoughts or memories, such as thinking about drugs, and shifting attention to something else, reflect instance of impulsivity, the tendency to make up one's mind quickly or have problems concentrating. It is extraordinarily difficult for addicts to shift their behavior when they are taking drugs, even though they know it has devastating consequences, even though they know cognitively that they should not be doing that.

People are not equally vulnerable to addiction once drugs are made available. For example, of the approximately 75% of adolescents who have tried cigarettes or used alcohol, only a minority continue to use and become dependent on these substances (Johnston et al., 2013). Some will never advance beyond experimentation. Bechara (2005) argues that prior to addiction, a degree of abnormality exists; this facilitates the progress from experimentation to addiction. For some individuals, the decision-making mechanism is relatively weak. Having poor mechanisms of decision making renders these individuals oblivious to the negative consequences, thus facilitating their escalation of drug use, and vulnerability to succumb to addiction. The source of this dysfunction can be genetic or environmentally induced. However, any subsequent excessive and chronic use of drugs can exacerbate these abnormalities.

The successful prevention programs might be developed that strengthen executive brain regions (self-control) and/or constrain activity in impulsive brain regions: policies that increase the likelihood of successful self-regulation, including the suppression of certain environmental cues (e.g., through limitations on advertising), and skills that help in emotion regulation when experiencing negative affect and stress.

Conclusion

This chapter dealt with three questions about addictive behavior: Why do they begin, why do they persist, and why do they relapse? In discussing the first question, this chapter shows that there are various pathways to addiction, such as social conditions and psychological reasons. Whether or not drug use is continued depends on individual reactions to the drug, coexisting mental illness, and alternatives to drug use that are available. For instance, individuals who lack the opportunity or ability to find other positively rewarding alternatives find that the addiction lifestyle fills a void (Vuchinich and Heather, 2003). As drug use increases, the value of the competing nondrug activities decreases.

Models of addictive behavior have different policy implications. For example, if one believes the disease model of addiction, then the effective policy is prohibition since addicts are presumed to be completely irrational when consuming. As a result, demand would be completely price inelastic (insensitive), so taxing the substance would have little or no impact on quantity demanded. In contrast, the perfectly rational model of addictive behavior offers a much wider range of public policy approaches. For example, raising taxes on alcohol and cigarettes would be predicted to lower consumption. Raising penalties for drug use would likewise decrease consumption.

When using the decision failure model, the ideal policies lie somewhere in between the disease and the rational models. If individuals have self-control problems, they may seek ways to precommit to abstaining. Gruber and Mullainathan (2005) argue that if preferences are time inconsistent, then the optimal sin tax should reflect not only all of the external costs to society, but also some of the internal costs to the individuals (self-damage). The logic is that time-inconsistent individuals may be grateful for the tax, because it forces them to pursue their own long-term benefit and take into account today the future consequences of their actions.

The dual model suggests that individuals are likely to make deliberative choices in the initial stage of addiction. However, over time, the "choice" of using a drug becomes more automatic and the impulsive system may dominate. For example, a person might decide to use alcohol because she is experiencing strong feelings of distress, but over time, the person might attend to cues related to alcohol when she experiences stress. Thus, repeated experiences are thought to lead to the development of biases related to the impulsive system, which, in turn, increase the likelihood of maintaining the addictive behavior.

The dual mind framework suggests that we need to develop interventions that will 1) decrease activation of impulsive brain regions and 2) increase activity in executive brain regions. As such, this may mean that successful treatment will require the development of two separate treatments, one for each brain region. Interventions could include medications or behavioral therapies or some combination of the two. In short, effective interventions need to: 1) decrease the reward value of the drug of choice, 2) diminish conditioned memories to the drug and drug-related stimuli, 3) increase the saliency value of nondrug rewards, and 4) strengthen self-control (frontal inhibitory) to prevent relapse. Thus, addiction recovery includes restoring balance in the motivational forces and reducing impulse (or increasing inhibition) forces.

An important issue discussed in this chapter is why addicts are so insensitive to the future consequences of their drug-seeking behavior (why do they persist?). The consensus among scientists is that drug addiction is associated with altered decision making that appears to overvalue pleasure, undervalue risk, and fails to learn from repeated mistakes. As discussed, addictive substances sometimes cause decision processes to malfunction (e.g., intense wanting or cravings). In other words, drugs distort a subconscious, hard-wired brain process into anticipating an exaggerated level of pleasure. An addict can try to overcome this effect by exercising cognitive control to no avail. Thus, addiction might be best viewed as a chronic disease, such as heart disease or diabetes, so that most addicts will require long-term treatment and relapse can be expected to occur sometimes during the treatment. Therefore, the occasional relapse is only a predictable setback, not a failure of the treatment. Thus, in the later stages, the individual may seem to lack all power of choice and free will. What are the policy implications? One approach is that because the addicts' brains are so compromised, it is necessary for others (families, friends, and professionals) to fill in as relentless supports for their inability to make decisions.

Although, addicts are a lot less in control than most people would like to believe. Nevertheless, some argue that addicts should still be held responsible for their actions (e.g., Heyman, 2009). The illusion that they are responsible may be what gets them to change their behavior. Evidence shows that people function better and are more able to deal with stress when they feel that they are in control. Believe that things are beyond your control and they probably will be. We are wired for personal responsibility, even if it's a bit fictional. Viewing ourselves as free and responsible agents is the groundwork for self-discipline and self-initiatives (Heyman, 2009).

Vohs and Schooler (2008) demonstrate that a belief in determinism is morally demotivating. They found that getting subjects to read some passages arguing that free will is an illusion (i.e., everything we do is determined by our prior beliefs, desires and intentions) subsequently made them more likely to cheat in a test (50% more than participants who read a neutral passage). Perhaps reading the deterministic texts tends to make people think of themselves as powerless. Determinism brings a kind of internal fatalism in the sense that there would be nothing one could do to influence any one's action. This view justifies feeling that one is a victim. The deterministic view undermines one's self-efficacy and diminishes self-control. As a result, they relax their control. If an addict believes that he is likely to succumb anyway, then he is less likely to resist. The belief that there is no such thing as free will leads people to stop exercising it. Of course, free choices require cognitive abilities to explore options, evaluate those options, imagine distanced consequences against immediate urges, and make choices. However, awareness that one can influence one's fate provides the motivation to seek opportunities to escape from despair (Frijda, 2013).

Notes

1 ALDH is also used in the treatment of alcohol addiction. Disulfiram is an ALDH inhibitor that, when mixed with alcohol, causes a buildup of toxic acetaldehyde resulting in unappealing reactions, such as flushing, nausea, vomiting, and a headache.
2 MAOA is an enzyme that metabolizes several neurotransmitters (e.g., dopamine, serotonin) involved in impulse control, attention, and other cognitive functions. Mutations in the normal MAOA gene lead to deficient production of the MAOA enzyme. A body of evidence indicates that the low-MAOA gene is to some extent related to a wide range of disorders, such as alcoholism, drug abuse, impulsivity, and antisocial and violent behavior (Raine, 2013).

3 The price elasticity of demand is defined as the percentage change in consumption caused by a 1% change in price.
4 Among 18–20 year olds, increasing the price of alcohol resulted in decreased automobile fatalities.
5 Some particularly skilled users also enter detox, not because they intend to remain sober, but rather because they want to increase the intensity of the next high (Elster, 2001).
6 According to a *New York Times* report, there is a resurgence of Ecstasy known as Molly (Aleksander, 2013). Molly is MDMA (Ecstacy), and is known for inducing feelings of euphoria, closeness, and diminished anxiety. The pill includes various ingredients, such as caffeine, speed, ephedrine, ketamine, LSD, talcum powder, and aspirin. The increased popularity of Molly is consistent with how people are feeling in this modern world. In other words, as people become more and more distanced emotionally because of the digital age, people are extremely hungry for the opposite: human interactions on a deeper level.
7 Taking a pain-relieving drug such as Tylenol (with the active ingredient of acetaminophen) might relieve the hurt feelings. For the brain, a hurt is a hurt, it doesn't differentiate among various kinds of hurt.
8 Addicts are usually selfish and self-centered. But when not experiencing craving, they may feel guilt and shame. Such a pattern of alternating extreme selfishness and remorse is characteristic of alcoholics and other drug addicts.

9

SOURCES OF SELF-CONTROL FAILURE IN RELATION TO SUSTAINED DIETING BEHAVIOR

Introduction

A common finding with regard to dieting behavior is that though initial success is quite prevalent, the long-term maintenance is generally quite rare. Dieters tend to display disinhibited eating in response to a wide variety of events. These events disrupt self-control and often trigger episodic overeating that wipes out all the dietary achievements have been made since the last overeating episode. Dieting has been a constant project with them. Ultimately, to avoid weight regain will require dieters to work their whole lives. However, 98% can't expect to attain this goal (IOM, 2003). The question is why do people fail to stick to their goal for eating a healthy diet in order to maintain weight loss? Why do dieters fail?

One possible answer is that people have a self-control problem in the form of a present-biased preference where one places extra value on more immediate rewards. For instance, in the moment, faced with a particularly appealing snack, we often can't resist saying no. This chapter highlights a number of interconnected motivational forces that can generate self-control failure. The aim is to provide an understanding of individual variation in the ability to resist temptations for rewards and vulnerability to impulsive behavior. In essence, this chapter identifies where the decision-making process has broken down in the context of diet relapse.

Self-control can be temporarily undermined by a number of factors, including present-bias preferences, dual decisions approach, temptations, cravings, negative moods, and so on. These factors together explain why there is conflict between long-term human intentions and short-term actions, which leads to myopic decisions.

The understanding of how the decision making can fail under certain conditions can explain irrationality, impulsivity, and even addiction. Self-control failures involving the use of alcohol and illegal drugs show the same pattern. The preference reversal is a unique aspect of individuals suffering from addiction as they lose control in the presence of drugs, even though they have expressed a desire to abstain (Bickel et al., 2012). The main problem with most self-destructive behaviors (e.g., addiction and overeating) is that the costs occur in the future, whereas the pleasures from them occur in the present. Valuations of immediate (and short-term) negative value (e.g., withdrawal) are likely to be weighed more heavily than valuations of long-term negative consequence (adverse health impact).

Self-Control Failure

The ability to resist immediate temptations in the service of a long-term goal is a key aspect of self-control (Baumeister et al., 2007). Self-control is the ability of the self to alter dominant responses or inner states such as impulses, urges, and emotions, and to replace them with a different response to fulfill larger goals (e.g., losing weight, quitting smoking, or staying calm). This ability to control behavior enables people to maintain healthy behavior throughout their life span.

Self-control failures result in the person acting in a way opposite to her better judgments or intentions. Self-control failures are an important cause of health problems, such as obesity and addiction. Indeed, it has been estimated that 40% of deaths are attributed to poor self-control (McGinnis and Foege, 1993). The annual expense of treating obesity-related illness (e.g., Type 2 diabetes, cardiovascular disease, and cancer), and the added cost of treating almost any medical condition when the patient is obese, is estimated to be $190 billion (Ruhm, 2012). In the context of weight loss and dieting, Americans spend in the aggregate many billions of dollars each year trying to lose weight through dieting or exercise, indicating the nation's desire for weight loss. National surveys indicate that approximately 30% of US adults are currently trying to lose weight and approximately 50% report having tried to lose weight in the past year. Obviously, these dieters are very motivated to lose weight, and yet, gradually, they regain the weight.

In short, the prevalence of overweight and obesity along with a high interest in dieting indicate the difficulty people face in maintaining long-term weight loss (Ruhm, 2012). In the language of public health, a self-control failure (a predisposition for excessive myopic behavior) could be considered as a risk factor.

Delay Discounting

A key concept in behavioral economics is that of how delayed rewards are discounted by individual, and deviation from the rational-choice paradigm. This model focuses on how consumers balance the consumption of a small amount of a commodity now compared to a large amount later. This section briefly reviews the central elements of delay discounting and provides a framework for identifying sources of impulsive behaviors.

A rational decision maker will choose her behavior to maximize the sum of her current and future rewards. This requires her to consider how her current actions may affect her future choice. For example, people with long-term preferences to lose weight will eat healthily and exercise, both of which require costly up-front commitments. In contrast, behavioral economics shows that individuals devalue (discount) too strongly future rewards and overemphasize near-term pleasures. This tendency is often referred to as present bias or time inconsistent behavior (Frederick et al., 2002). Time inconsistent behavior means that an individual's preference at time 1 differs from her preference at time 2. At time 1, the person chooses to overeat; at time 2, this person wishes that he had consumed a small portion.

The declining valuation of future reward is well described by a hyperbolic discounting function. For example, an ice cream may seem like a bad idea when considered a few days before it appears at a birthday party, but as the party approaches, the ice cream becomes ever more appealing while the dietary consequences will recede further into the future. Hyperbolic discounting suggests a motivational model that accounts for individuals' preference shift from one state to another. Mathematically, the hyperbolic discount function is

$$\textbf{Motivation = Reward} \div \textbf{(1 + Impulsiveness} \star \textbf{Delay)}$$

The basic elements of this model include Reward, Delay, and Impulsiveness. The increase in Delay reduces our motivation to act for the Reward. The more impulsive we are, the more sensitive we will be to the delay and the more we will discount the future. Impulsiveness multiplies the effects of Delay, and so impulsive people feel the effects of time far more acutely. In general, impulsive people feel that time passes slowly. The addition of 1 at the bottom prevents the equation from reaching to infinity if impulsiveness or delay reaches zero.

In sum, the hyperbolic discounting model describes conflicts between short- and long-term motives. This implies that any health investment activity is vulnerable to present bias, because it is hard to see the value from moment to moment. Consequently, people tend to avoid and/or delay investment health behaviors.

The hyperbolic model represents the dynamics of a self-control problem. Having a self-control problem is a sign that individuals fail to have a proper valuation of distant rewards, and they often end up acting against their own best interest. However, the model is not an explanation for why individuals have self-control problems. The following presents several select theories to explain the psychological mechanisms of hyperbolic discounting and why there is a warp in our attitude toward delay. These motives contribute to present-bias (impulsive) behavior by either undermining the self-control strength or a by leaning toward a greater tendency to desire seeking out opportunities for immediate reward.

The Divided Self

What is the mechanism of the preference reversal between distant and immediate rewards? Behavioral economics conceive the individual as a successive agent with conflicting preferences (dynamic inconsistency). Although we tend to view ourselves as a single and integrated self, people can be conceptualized as multiple selves with different points of view.[1] Individuals are simply collections of different selves at odds with one another. Many psychologists find it more useful to think of the mind as consisting of multiple states that may, to varying degrees, be in conflict with one another.[2] In this view, there is no central executive control in the form of decider. Rather, decision making is a function of a coalition of different self-states (Leary and Tangney, 2012). Indeed, the essence of a self-control problem is mainly about conflict between two selves (e.g., one who wants to be thin and the other who wants to eat).

The hyperbolic discounting model is an expression of a "divided self," of preferring, for example, indulgence for the immediate self, and prudence for the future one (Ainslie, 2001). Different selves can be thought of as having different discount rates, or being time inconsistent; one self is more present-oriented and the other is more future-oriented, both competing for control. A person is time inconsistent if the plan she makes today for a future period is different from the one actually chosen during that period.

Thomas Schelling was the first to note that people behave sometimes as if they had two selves, one who wants healthy lungs and long a life and another who enjoys smoking, one who yearns to improve himself by studying hard, and another would rather watch TV or socialize (Thaler and Shefrin, 1981). The two are in a continual contest for control. In this case, behavior is controlled by a series of myopic "Doers" who maximize immediate satisfaction and a farsighted "Planner" who maximizes the discounted sum of the doer's satisfaction (utilities). The person who makes plans and the person who fails to implement them are different parts of the divided self. Thus, no matter how strong the goal intentions, there is no guarantee that the goal will be achieved because of the Planner-Doer gap (or the intention-action gap). Consequently, the option chosen by the Doer (acting-self) will reduce total happiness over time.

The divided-self model indicates that the ultimate determinant of a person's choice is not her simple preference. Rather, people may have a variety of contradictory preferences that become dominant at different points because of their timing. If a person is a vulnerable person (e.g., has a sweet tooth) and close to a box of chocolates or a bottle of whisky, he will value these options differently than when he is far away from them. The intensity of the preference of each self may determine the option chosen. That is, the contexts or circumstances of ordinary life influence individuals' choices. One can be pulled in several directions and judging oneself after the decision is a bit like judging another person.

In sum, the divided-self model describes the behavior of a single "self" (our mental life) by the metaphor of two selves or characters in our mind. However, the interests of these two selves do not always coincide. Life seems to consist of a struggle between the short-sighted self and long-sighted self, and to balance these two is an art (Khaneman, 2011).

How do we help individuals with fragmented, multiple selves to act as if they were single? In order to correct people's time inconsistent behavior at the individual level, the solution is for individuals to exercise self-control. People can act as single individual through the exercise of self-control. Since actions are taken by the Doer, the Planner can restrict the set of alternatives in order to mitigate the Doer's desire to satisfy immediate gratification at the expense of long-run well-being.

The Dual Decision Model

The dual decision model distinguishes between two separate but interacting systems of deliberation and impulse or affective. They are also known as System 2 and System 1. The deliberative system (S2) operates mostly consciously, uses logical rules, and is verbal and deliberative. The deliberative system is typically effortful and depends on limited willpower (or impulse control) resources. We identify ourselves with the deliberative system, the conscious and reasoning self that has beliefs. The impulsive system (S1) is associative and acts spontaneously without consideration for the broader consequences of the action. Associations are formed as a consequence of learning experiences and are activated upon perceiving a cue (temptation). This conditioning captures the role of social environment over human behavior.[3] The automaticity associated with the impulsive system makes it the default option in most life situations.

The final decision is determined based on the relative strength of System1 and System 2. The ability to "balance" these two systems is critical for successful self-control and to sustain effortful control in pursuit of a particular delayed goal. Self-control failure implies that these two systems come into conflict with each other. That is, a person is both motivated to act in some particular way and also motivated to restrain that action.

In the context of the dual model, the Planner represents the reflective system, and the Doer is heavily influenced by the impulsive system. The Planner is trying to promote our long-term health, but must cope with the feelings of the Doer who is exposed to the temptations.

Impulsive actions refer to behaviors enacted without prior deliberation before or while performing the act (Frijda, 2007). Generally, impulsivity is defined as the tendency to think, control, and plan insufficiently, resulting in an inaccurate or maladaptive response (Solanto et al., 2001). Impulsive actions are driven by the present, here and now. For example, seeing and smelling freshly baked cookies can make one reach out before realizing one is on a diet. Impulsive actions are also automatic because they are overlearned. In the absence of self-control, impulsive behavior is the default option.

The reflective system is in charge of self-control in order to overcome impulses and habitual responses. The freedom that is represented in a choice not to eat the Death by Chocolate cake comes from the reflective system (a mental belief about health and weight), and it can overcome the urge to eat the cake. In this case, the impulsive system loses to reflective system in the battle to initiate an action. Individuals for whom such self-control competencies are highly accessible can more effectively and automatically use their attention control skills in the service of long-term goals.[4] Our impulsive system continuously generates impressions, feelings, and intentions. If endorsed by the reflective system, impulses and desires turn into voluntary actions (Baumeister, 2002). So the reflective system normally has the last word.

The dual decision model provides some insights why smart people (e.g., public figures) make dumb decisions and face questioning with answers such as "I don't know what I was thinking." The answer is that she probably was not evaluating or weighing properly all of the outcomes for her behavior. She was focused on the short term. Because so much of what goes on in our minds is inaccessible—that is, we don't know why we think what we do and we are often not able to say what's really causing our behavior (Gazzaniga, 2011). The answer to the question "Why did you do that?" could be "I have absolutely no idea." Indeed, much of our behavior is affected by unconscious goals and motivations (Dijidsterhuis et al., 2007). One of the central tenets of modern psychology, from psychoanalysis to cognitive dissonance, is that humans deceive themselves as to their own true motivations. People try to justify or make sense of what they did by finding reasons for it, and this uses the reflective system. For example, the person who has consumed the tempting good, but feels guilty about it, may try to alleviate his guilt. He would do so by coming up with additional reasons that justify his behavior.

Mercier and Sperber (2011) suggest that people reason to win arguments. Truth and accuracy are beside the point. People sometimes look for reason to justify an opinion they are eager to uphold. This view is consistent with *confirmation bias*, which explains why people persist in picking out evidence that supported their views and ignored the rest even in the face of overwhelming, contrary evidence. Thus, we know far less about ourselves than we feel we do. The emotional system constructs a story, and the deliberate system believes it (Wilson, 2011).

An important implication of the dual model is that there is not one, unified "self" in our mind, and it makes the very notion of a "self" something of a problem, and perhaps even quite a bit less useful than one might think (Loewenstein et al., 2007).

Self-Control Decision

Self-control is conceptualized as a deliberate and intentional attempt to override and gain control over impulsive responses driven by situational cues and immediate rewards (Baumeister et al., 2008). As discussed, the source of the preference for immediate gratification comes from the motivation of the emotion system (S1). The capacity to take long-term consequences of our behavior into account seems to be the product of our prefrontal cortex (S2). The mental processes that enable self-control include aspects of executive functions or the prefrontal cortex (PFC), emotion regulation, and temporal discounting. Executive function is an umbrella term for processes underlying flexible, goal-directed behavior. Like executives in a complex organization, the executive functions are responsible for initiating, planning, and coordinating the basic cognitive processes with which we navigate our daily lives. Executive functioning capacities underlie the popular notion of free will. Capacities for self-regulation, choice, and initiative are the psychological manifestations of free will.

Within the dual-system model, desires and urges are represented by the impulsive system, while self-control efforts are represented by the reflective system. Impulses and urges are desires and feelings of wanting in everyday life (Hofmann et al., 2011). The perception of problematic desires (or temptations) triggers an attempt to exercise self-control and resist the desire (e.g., when a person desires chocolate cake while on a diet). Addictive substances can be considered as a special class of tempting goods. However, not all desires conflict with the person's long-term goals. Desires vary in strength and therefore in their potential to motivate behavior. The stronger desire may make people more susceptible to its motivational power. If a desire is weak, then resisting it will be relatively easy and will not require a high level of strength.

The relation between the impulsive system and the self-control system is bidirectional and operates in an interactive feedback loop. The interactions between these two systems underlie the person's ability to sustain effortful control in pursuit of delayed goals (Metcalfe and Miscel, 1999). Sometimes the two parts of the brain can be in conflict—a kind of battle that one or the other is bound to lose. The question who will become the master of whom?

Hoch and Loewenstein (1991) suggested that the two components that influence the outcome of a self-control conflict are the strength of the impulse (desires and cravings) and the strength needed to overcome the urge. When an impulse becomes stronger, the self probably needs to muster up greater self-control powers to overcome the urge to act. However, in the absence of desire, there is no need for self-control (Friese et al., 2011).[5]

The diagram below depicts self-control decisions as struggles between desire strength and self-control/resistance. The success or failure depends on the relative strength of the desire and the resistance. In general, self-control succeeds when the impulse is relatively weak. As desire strength increases, the resistance becomes less effective at preventing enactment (e.g., irresistible desires such as addiction). People with low self-control are more vulnerable to failure.

The following sections outline several motivational factors that influence the balance of desire and self-control effort.

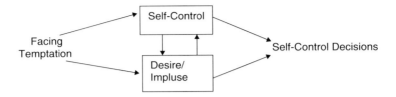

Desire

What is desire and what turns desire into temptation? Desire can be defined as a positive emotion (motivation) towards a certain object, person, or activity (Hofmann et al., 2011). Desire is the feeling of wanting to have or do something specific. Whether a given desire turns into a temptation depends on whether the desire behavior is at odds with a person's self-control goal (e.g., a healthy eating goal).

How does desire emerge? In general, desire originates in a relatively automatic manner as the brain reward systems evaluate external stimuli against the background of internal needs (e.g., hunger, craving, or feeling lonely) and an individual's learning history. As the desire gains access to working memory, the person becomes conscious. The more attention a person allocates to a rewarding stimulus (a high-caloric food), the more likely she will be to experience a subjective feeling of wanting or craving.

According to the *elaborated intrusive theory of desire*, people cognitively elaborate on the positive emotions and thoughts associated with indulgence (Kavanagh et al., 2005). The more people elaborate on their desires, the more likely it becomes that people will generate supporting cognitions that allow (license) them to indulge (e.g., I have not had a drink for a while) (DeWitt Huberts et al., 2012). This motivational reasoning may easily lead people to revise their intentions when faced with temptation. In the extreme cases, desire may overwhelm working memory and crowd out all other opposing goal representations.

How can problematic desires be regulated? The dual decision model provides a framework to moderate excessive consumption behavior via two different motivational tendencies: managing situations that trigger appetitive responses and increasing self-control capacity. Desire management can help people avoid exposure to tempting situations and stimuli in order to prevent problematic desire (Dewitte, 2012). The alternative option is a considerable investment of self-control efforts.

Willpower

Willpower is a resource that can be used to decrease or eliminate discrepancies between desire and deliberate acts of self-control (Baumeister et al., 1994).

A lack of self-control resources decreases the propensity of the self-control system to override the influence of the impulsive system on behavior and maintaining long-term behaviors. A number of situational factors can temporally impair willpower, such as ego depletion, cognitive load, stress, intoxication, and blood sugar.

Ego Depletion

Making series of choices that involve conflict (e.g., trying to impress others, or responding kindly to rude behavior) lead to ego depletion. Ego depletion leads to a loss of motivation[6] (e.g., deviating from one's diet, overspending on impulsive purchases, and reacting aggressively to provocation). For example, Tice and colleagues (2007) showed that resisting the urge to buy freshly baked cookies may later render consumers to avoid engaging in effortful processing (e.g., decrease the time spent on the subsequent choice task or postpone making any decision).

Thus, at the end of a long day, people have fewer resources to overcome the urge to consume a tempting snack than at the beginning of the day. Presumably, this is because people have exerted self-control throughout the day. Indeed, following a vacation, many people come back to work with renewed energy, saying that they feel refreshed and ready to delve back into work.

Decision making is another factor that depletes willpower, and once your willpower is depleted, you are less able to make decisions. You will look for excuses to avoid or postpone decisions. You will look for the easiest and safest option, which often is to stick with the status quo. Part of the resistance against making decisions comes from the fear of giving up options. When your willpower is low, you are less able to make trade-offs. The more you give up by deciding, the more you are afraid of cutting off something vital.

Consider, for instance, the role of poverty in self-control failures. Poverty taxes cognitive resources and causes failure. The poor are juggling rent, loans, late bills, and counting days till the next paycheck. Poverty means making painful trade-offs (sacrifices) and resisting more temptations depletes the willpower, which in turns makes them less capable of giving up, say, a smoking habit (Spears, 2011). For example, deciding whether to pay rent or buy food, to buy medicine or winter clothes, or to pay for school materials. These choices are significant, and just thinking about them seems to exact a mental cost.[7] When you can afford so little, so many things need to be resisted, and your self-control ends up being run down. The poor will end up obese. Eating well is a substantial self-control endeavor (Mullainathan and Eldar, 2013). So, why do the poor fail so badly in self-control? They lack freedom of mind. They are short not just on cash, but also short on willpower. Poverty at it very core taxes self-control capacity. This suggests that antipoverty initiatives should focus far more on relieving cognitive costs, such as altering the environment to reduce dependence on willpower. Thus, from a policy perspective, we need to treat willpower as a scarce and important resource.

Cognitive Load

Cognitive load is another factor leading to impulse reactions. The busier people are, the more likely people will behave impulsively. Notice how in the moment of stress we forget the names of people we know well. When our mind is preoccupied, our short-term mind will guide our choices. Cognitive overload (or busyness) is not the same as ego depletion. Ego depletion illustrates how acts of self-control can temporarily deplete self-control.

Evidence indicates that dieters consume more when under a cognitive load than when under no load. For example, Boon et al. (2002) found that while distracted, dieters ate more of a "forbidden" food than when not distracted. Shiv and Fedorikhin (1999) offered participants a choice between chocolate cake and carrots. Cognitive load shifted their choices heavily in favor of the cake. Under the cognitive load of rehearsing an eight-digit number, participants chose snacks based on unconscious attitudes. However, conscious attitudes prevailed under a low load (memorizing a single digit). Cognitive load interfered with dieters' monitoring of their food intake. Thus, cognitive load seems to release automatic impulses to dictate actions (Friese et al., 2008). This insight suggests that distracted shoppers with music or displays will likely increase impulse purchases.

Stress

Stress is another factor that affects one's ability to maintain one's resolution to eat well. Coping with stress involves using mental processes and willpower to control behavior (Marlatt and Witkiewitz, 2005). Self-control is quite sensitive to daily stress (Arnsten et al., 2012). As a result, we lose the ability to be reflective (regulate our behavior), and we become automatic. For example, the pressure and anxiety of a lengthy exam, even with the best preparation, often causes the test takers' reasoning abilities to slow and even shut down entirely. This experience is known as *choking under pressure* (or blanking out).

Alcohol Myopia

Alcohol loosens self-control. Alcohol myopia theory suggests that intoxication reduces self-awareness and narrows the scope of attention, limiting the ability to attend to multiple cues (Giancola, 2002). As drinkers' awareness declines, they lose self-control, so they eat more, or smoke more. Intoxication reduces resistance to desire and weakens inhibitory control. Alcohol mostly weakens the inhibition rather than foster all manners of desires (Hofmann et al., 2011). Intoxicated persons feel their desire more strongly than when sober. For example, alcohol intoxication only increases the level of aggression in response to provocation. In short, consuming alcohol hinders the prefrontal cortex's ability to perform, creating actions that "seemed like a good idea at the time," but later prompt regrets.

Licensing

Depletion may also be partly due to a generalized licensing effect. People are unaware that such unconscious processes are shaping their behavior and, therefore, they are unable to resist the influence of these unconscious processes (Khan and Dhar, 2006). The concept of self-licensing suggests that people may abandon their self-control efforts by using a justification (e.g., "I am on holiday") that allows them to indulge. That is, dieters may allow themselves to overindulge after a difficult exam. Similarly, shoppers in grocery stores are usually confronted with the fruit and vegetables section first. Grocers know that shoppers who buy the healthy items first will feel so uplifted they will buy more junk food later in their trip. When people believe they have done something virtuous, this furnishes them an excuse (or license) to behave in a more self-indulgent manner. Engaging in a difficult task allows the person to consciously or unconsciously grant himself gratifying rewards.

Blood Sugar

Glucose is a vital part of willpower. Evidence shows that exerting willpower lowers blood sugar, which reduces the capacity for further self-control (Galliot et al., 2007). The research links self-control strength to a physical resource. Brains are energy hogs. Our brains expend about 20% of the energy our bodies consume. For example, people who drink a glass of lemonade between completing tasks that required self-control performed equally well on both tasks. However, drinking sugarless diet lemonade was not as effective. The glucose itself doesn't enter the brain, but it's converted into neurotransmitters. The lack of neurotransmitters undermines cognitive function. Research has shown that serotonin depletion increases impulsivity (Bickel et al., 2012). For example, people with hypoglycemia, the tendency to have low blood sugar, are more likely than the average person to have trouble concentrating and controlling their negative emotions when provoked. Overall, they tend to be more anxious and less happy than average.[8]

Evidence also shows that bad diet could influence mood and diminished rational thought (Raine, 2013). Foods like spinach, fish, and turkey that contain tryptophan and omegha-3 have a calming effect on aggression. Serotonin is synthesized from tryptophan, which improve the brain's ability to inhibit impulsive reactions. On the other hand, the consumption of a Western diet (a high intake of total fat, refined sugars, reduced complex carbohydrate, and fiber) is associated with impaired cognitive function (Francis and Stevenson, 2013). Diets high in refined carbohydrates (e.g., white bread) can cause extreme fluctuation in blood glucose levels. This in turn triggers an inappropriately large secretion of insulin, which soaks up the available glucose out of circulation, which results in irritability and feeling on edge. Thus, dieting on junk foods can result in cognitive impairment, lack of insight (the failure to produce alternative response in conflict resolution), and overreaction to minor irritations.

Summary and Implications

In sum, the strength model of willpower provides an explanation of self-control failure. The model shows that exerting self-control draws on the same limited resource required for reflective system. Depleting resources increases the reliance on impulsive system. Thus, willpower depletion provides an alternative explanation for apparent preference reversals. The resource depletion paradigm also provides insight into strategies that can be used to improve self-control capacity.

The willpower model has several implications for how to improve self-control outcomes (Hagger et al., 2010). First, evidence suggests that you use the same stock of willpower for all manner of tasks. In other words, you use the same supply of willpower to deal with frustrating traffic, tempting food, annoying colleagues, demanding boss, and disappointed children. Thus, resisting dessert at lunch leaves you with less willpower to deal with your annoying colleagues.

Second, deliberately conserving the energy and planning its expenditures may prove helpful. A general guidance based on the ego depletion is to focus on one project at a time. Concentrating your effort on one or at most a few goals at a time increases the odds of success. For example, it makes no sense to decide that one is going to quit smoking and diet if one does not actually possess the requisite willpower to actually carry through with one's resolution. Furthermore, self-control problems are not equally costly. One's self-control can vary from domain to domain (Anreou and White, 2010). For example, a person who exhibits self-control in doing regular exercise may be an amazingly disciplined when it comes to studying. Thus, it makes sense to save one's self-control strength for certain task.

Third, the willpower model suggests that self-control capacity can be build up through practice and training. Engaging in simple, daily self-control exercises, such as avoiding unhealthy foods, leads to improved long-term maintenance of the behaviors. The state of ego depletion can be reversed through rest or relaxation. Sleep deprivation may lead to chronic state of ego depletion,[9] and insufficient sleep takes a substantial toll on performance. Research suggests that the best way to get more done in less time requires one to avoid exhaustion and skillfully manage energy by getting sufficient sleep (eight or more hours), more breaks or daytime naps, and frequent vacations (Mednick et al., 2002).

Finally, research has found that inducing positive affect is effective in overcoming the effect of self-control resource depletion. Positive affect may lead to renewed vigor toward goals such that individuals increase their efforts and motivation to expend self-control resources (Tice et al., 2007).

Working Memory Capacity (WMC)

Working memory is the most important element of the prefrontal cortex (Hofmann et al., 2012). Working memory is defined as the ability to selectively attend and remember goal-relevant information (Unsworth and Engle, 2007; Baddeley and Hitch, 1974). Due to capacity constraints, working memory can only process a limited amount of explicit information simultaneously. WMC limitations primarily reflect resource limitations rather than information storage limitations. Thus, resource limitations can interfere with self-control and goal pursuits.

WMC is important for maintaining self-control in pursuing a wide variety of goals (Broadway and Engle, 2010). Individual differences in WMC partly explain individual differences in the ability to exercise self-control.[10] WMC contributes to the successful behavior of self-control in eating, addiction, and emotion regulation (Hofmann et al., 2012). WMC helps dieters to focus their attention and resist distraction. Across diverse behaviors (viewing erotic pictures, eating, and aggression), individuals low in WMC exhibited limited capacity to inhibit impulsive responses (Hofmann et al., 2012).

Successful self-control involves the active representation of goals and goal-relevant information in working memory (Aupperle et al., 2012). Failure to remember the intention to act on the intended goal represents a common reason for failure to get started on one's goal. Working memory maintains access to relevant information and suppresses irrelevant information to shield task-relevant information from interference. For example, if our current goal is shopping for health food, when entering the grocery store, we shield our goal by preventing goal-irrelevant stimuli (high-caloric foods) to gain access to our working memory. The ability to delete quickly irrelevant information (tempting thoughts) from working memory may increase the chances to attain self-control goals (buying healthy foods).

Working memory and intelligence are associated with less discounting (Shamosh et al., 2008). Since decisions involving sooner and later rewards require individuals to manage and integrate complex information in working memory, individuals with better working memory (and higher intelligence) are more adept at shifting attention away from the tempting aspects of the immediate rewards. For example, individuals with lower intelligence are more vulnerable to save less for retirement. However, evidence shows that working memory training reduces discounting in a monetary choice task (Bickel et al., 2007).

Similar to willpower, working memory can be temporarily impaired by ego depletion, cognitive load, cravings, anxiety or stress, alcohol intoxications, and a temporary reduction in blood glucose. This means that the demands on the WMC exceed its limited resources. For example, stress and anxiety consume the available working memory resources, which might otherwise be used for self-control behaviors.[11] Many temporary states such as being drunk, lack of sleep, or just being distracted inhibit the prefrontal cortex and leave us less able to control impulses. Cravings may compromise self-control by hijacking working memory (taking up working memory resources) in the service of short-term goal fulfillment. Similarly, as people age, they experience a deficit in executive functions. The increased prevalence of obesity in late adulthood may be partially attributable to reduced capacity for self-regulation (von Hippel and Henry, 2011). In a sample of otherwise healthy adults, those who were overweight exhibited limited executive control relative to their normal-weight counterparts (Gunstad et al., 2007).

WMC can be improved by interventions, such as WMC training and mindfulness meditation. Over the course of practice, self-control that draws heavily on working memory can be replaced by well-practiced habits, reducing the need for the working memory's limited resources. The idea of the "use-it-or-lose-it" suggests that keeping cognitively active (both in social and intellectual realms) can improve brain health and function in aging.

Cue Exposure

A key lesson of behavioral economics is the power of the situation to exert on behavior in a way that overrides individuals' intentions. Temptations[12] are triggered by situational cues (stimuli) that promise immediate satisfaction at the cost of significant long-term rewards. Consumption items that are immediately available seem to exert a disproportionate pull. The temptation of inviting products or goods is more difficult to overcome when the desired product is near to the person. Relapses are frequently triggered by environmental cues (e.g., watching others drinking alcohol). In this case, a person makes a choice despite expressing a desire to avoid this very option on a prior occasion.[13]

Proximity to temptation is one of the powerful determinants of self-control. Proximity can increase the strength of desire for goods (McClure et al., 2007). Typically, temptations (a piece of a cake for a dieter, a cigarette for a "would be" quitter) are closer temporally and oftentimes spatially than overarching goals higher in one's essential goal hierarchy. The pleasure of consuming these immediate goods is both intense and immediate. In a series of classic experiments, psychologists Janet Metcalfe and Walter Mischel (1999) studied children's ability to postpone consumption of candy in order to get more candy. The findings showed that their ability to wait substantially increased if the items were not present or if they were present but covered. Similarly, research has shown that people tend to make healthier food choices when asked to choose in advance (e.g., when we decide a few months in advance about a conference dinner) than they often do in the "heat" of a grocery-shopping trip, where external cues or sensory inputs are more likely to favor energy-dense or attractively packaged foods.

Environmental cues that direct attention towards the long-term aspects of the products, such as health, may lead to healthier decisions. For example, the mandatory requirement of placement of highly emotional pictures on cigarette containers can direct attention to the long-term consequences of smoking (Fehr and Rangel, 2011). These policies are more effective than the text warnings that convey similar messages. The pictures motivate consumers to pay attention to the long-term health considerations, shifting attention from the taste to the health attributes.[14] The graphic warnings (a kind of nudge) directly target System 1, trying to make the health consequences of smoking or consuming sugar salient and to avoid or reduce consumption.

Furthermore, people adjust their behavior according to social demands. The presence of others contributes to the motivated behavior (considering the social dimensions of the choice). Being around people who are already doing what one wants to do lowers one's resistance to act. For example, a dieter who sees others eating with enjoyment may reduce resistance and thereby increase the willingness to yield to temptation.

Finally, it is known that certain foods set off a course of overeating. Sugary foods and drinks, white bread, and other processed carbohydrates tend to cause abrupt spikes and falls in blood sugar, and drive some people to overeat. After the consumption of these high-glycemic foods, blood sugar levels plummet into the hypoglycemic range, and we feel more hunger. Individuals also show greater activation in parts of the brain that regulate cravings, reward, and addictive behaviors. When blood sugar levels plummet, people have a tendency to seek out foods that can restore it quickly, and this may set up a cycle of overeating driven by high-glycemic foods. Thus, for dieters unable to control their cravings, avoiding refined carbohydrates might reduce urges and potentially help in weight loss maintenance (Ludwig, 2012). This also suggests that not all calories are created equal. That is, the type of food we are eating is quite important.

Lapse-Activated Consumption

A common pattern of self-control failure for addicts and chronic dieters occurs when they "fall off the wagon" by violating their diets or consuming the addictive substance. This is a case when minor lapses in self-control snowball into self-regulatory collapse. Marlatt and Gordon (1985) coined the term *abstinence violation effect* to refer to situations in which addicts respond to an initial indulgence by consuming even more of the forbidden substance: "just one cigarette" quickly turns into half a pack and having "just one drink" quickly turns into the whole bottle. Similarly, once the diet is broken for the day, dieters appear to give up control, perhaps anticipating starting their diets anew the next day. This kind of thinking may help the dieter to enhance her self-esteem in the present by thinking that she will improve herself in the future.

People not on diet are assumed to regulate their eating through biological signals. They eat when they are hungry and stop eating when they are full. In contrast, chronic dieters regulate their eating according to a self-imposed diet rule of permissible daily calorie intake (Herman and Polivy, 1984). These rules are used to guide food intake to achieve or maintain desirable weight. Because regulation via dieting rules and calorie limits requires cognitive resources, it is liable to break down (e.g., due to stress). Once the diet is ruined, people tend to overeat. For example, if dieters eat "forbidden" foods (e.g., a piece of brownie), their dieting is ruined. They have disinhibitory thoughts like "I've already blown my diet, I might as well continue to eat," and start overeating.[15] Also, when they expect to eat disallowed food later on, they start overeating the entire day. Urbszat et al. (2002) demonstrated that anticipation of a week-long diet, starting first thing tomorrow, leads dieters to overeat today. The anticipated deprivation may "justify" the prediet overindulgence. So, deprivation planned for tomorrow triggers (compensatory) overindulgence today. The prospect of future overeating induces feelings of hopeless about the one's ability to adhere to personal rules of dietary restraint (Herman and Polivy 2010).

In sum, the idea here suggests the danger of becoming compulsive. The desire to avoid lapses may lead one to cultivate a pathologically inflexible commitment to staying on course. For dieters who tend to think in a rigid, all-or-nothing fashion, dieting may cause overeating. Thus, failed resolutions could be harmful if they lead to depression and self-loathing. For example, when disappointment from a failure to discipline a bad habit causes us to engage in binge eating after a broken diet.

Negative Affect and the Joy of Distraction

Negative affect is among the most important triggers of self-control failure.[16] For instance, depressed people desire specific things that bring immediate gratification, and procrastinate or avoid any activity that doesn't promise immediate pleasure or involve effort.

People who are depressed tend to think of themselves as worthless (Solomon, 2001). As a result of feeling worthless, they place less value on their own well-being and are less inclined to exercise self-control when it comes to activities that harm them. These activities (e.g., drug abuse or overeating) numb their feeling and distract them from their negative affect. The desire to escape is possibly related to the persons viewing themselves as helpless and incompetent.[17] Negative emotional states are related to relapse for a number of addictive behaviors (e.g., overeating among chronic dieters and alcoholism).[18]

Individuals suffering from depression tend to ruminate, which involves fixation on their negative feelings. Their inability to inhibit or disengage from self-focused thoughts may motivate them to turn to escapist behaviors, such as binge eating or binge drinking, and to escape from aversive self-awareness (Nolen-Hoeksema et al., 2008). Rumination involves a person facing a hopeless and uncontrollable situation and rationale for avoiding taking action.[19]

Negative affect is the most cited instigator of binge-eating episodes, and binge eating appears to be associated with a decrease in negative affect. Overweight people report that feeling anxious or depressed is a major impetus causing them to eat excessively (Puhl and King, 2013). Obese people overeat to reduce negative emotions such as boredom, stress, anxiety, and loneliness. The mechanisms by which eating reduces anxiety may include increased serotonin, association of discomfort with eating, and faulty hunger awareness. They are unable to distinguish between hunger and anxiety because obese people learned to eat in response to anxiety as well as hunger (Whiteside et al., 2007). Ingestion of high fat and carbohydrate "comfort foods" dampens stress response. Indeed, sweet solutions have been shown to rapidly calm stress responses in human newborns.

Similarly, the behavior of drinking alcohol is guided by the anticipation of emotional outcomes (feeling better). The behavior makes sense from the individual's perspective. If it did not, the person would have done differently. People do not get up in the morning and say, "Today I'm going to be an alcoholic." We may feel depressed and empty. We learn that drinking eases the pain. It is undertaken to achieve a state of mind, and it most often accomplishes this. However, once the emptiness passes, we attend only to the negative consequences of excessive drinking. The negative feelings that result from the awareness of these consequences probably lead to more drinking, and the cycle continues. Thus, the impulsive behavior is like a purchase of a short-term reduction in negative affect at the price of a long-term maintenance of the negative affect-causing situation.

Individuals experiencing anhedonia (inability to experience pleasure) have a lower level of dopamine (Wise, 1980), which influences their thinking about reward-related decisions. Dopamine plays a central role in cost-benefit-analysis (Dolan and Sharot, 2011). Dopamine neurons respond to surprising rewards, and play a central role in associative learning. Thus, anhedonia is associated with an impaired ability to make reward-based decisions (to accurately represent future costs and benefits of rewards). For example, a study showed that depressed individuals exhibited a lower discount rate for future reward, possibly reflecting a diminished sensitivity to reward magnitude of the immediate option (Lempert and Pizzagalli, 2012).

Being socially rejected by others also impairs self-control. The neuroscientist Naomi Eisenberger (2004) shows that the same areas of the brain that register physical pain are active when someone feels socially rejected. Baumeister et al. (2005) show that people who experienced an instance of social rejection or exclusion showed poorer performance on a variety of tasks (e.g., drinking a healthy but bad-tasting beverage) than participants who were accepted. In contrast, positive social relationships are one of the primary motivations for exercising self-control. When your brain knows you are safe and you are with someone you can trust, it needn't waste precious resources coping with stressors.

In sum, emotional distress causes a behavioral shift toward immediate improvements in mood, and so people make poor decisions. Thus, the impulsive behavior may represent a strategic attempt to regulate affect (Tice et al., 2001). In other words, impulsive behavior may be viewed as a rational attempt to address a pressing concern.

Strong Feelings

Strong feelings (e.g., hunger or cravings) shorten the time horizon and make us impatient (Tice at al., 2001; Lempert et al., 2012) and reverse time preference.[20] These strong feelings create something like a temporary preference for a certain course of action (Loewenstein, 1996). The change in preferences, in turn, causes an individual to prefer immediate rewards, in which the benefits are delivered first and the costs come later, over options that have the opposite pattern. For example, evidence shows that hunger leads to greater caloric intake. After skipping a meal or two, people naturally consume more calories than they otherwise would when finally given the opportunity to eat (Wansink et al., 2012). Our vulnerability to hunger can arise when short-term benefits appear subjectively enormous and when long-term benefits appear subjectively small.

Addicts become so focused on immediate gratification when they are craving a drug that craving crowds out virtually all considerations. This leads to a kind of "tunnel vision" on the part of the addict. An addict may have accurate beliefs about the disastrous effects of the drug on his body or purse, and yet ignore them because of an addiction-induced myopia that leads to act against his better judgment.[21] This effect is most dramatically evident in the behavior of cocaine addicts, who report that "virtually all thoughts are focused on cocaine during binges; nourishment, sleep, money, loved ones, responsibility, and survival lose all significance" (Goldstein, 2001, p. 29). Such behaviors would seem to merit the statement "I don't know what came over me." Addicts display higher discount rates, not only for drugs, but also for money, when they are currently craving drugs (Giordano et al. 2002). Thus, addiction can be thought as a particular case of a general problem of balancing the emotional mind and self-control. Addiction impairs one's rational capacity to think clearly in order to evaluate one's behavior and consequences.

Projection Bias

Projection bias (or mispredicting future feelings) is another reason for self-control problems. Research suggests that people may not know how they will actually feel about the consequences of a decision (costs and benefits). The mental representations of future events tend to evoke less intense feelings compared to present ones. This error may explain why people prefer to enjoy rewards in the present and incur costs in the future. They may mistakenly believe that their future feelings will be less intense than their present feelings. For example, most people know how miserable they will be when it comes time to pay for their present indulgences, but they tend to underweight this knowledge (Gilbert and Wilson, 2007).

Projection bias is also known as the empathy gap (or "hot-cold empathy gap"), the inability, during a cool, rational, peaceful moment, to appreciate how we'll behave during the heat of passion and temptation (Loewenstein, 1996). The hot-cold empathy gap is one of the most common challenges to self-control. People falsely project their current preferences onto their future preferences (e.g., shopping on an empty stomach[22]). When we are in a cold state, we tend to underestimate the power of a hot state to shape our behavior. In a cold state, we cannot imagine how we will behave in a hot state. For example, people denounce junk food when they are not hungry or craving without realizing how much they want those evil cookies once they are tired and exhausted. When you plan your dieting behavior, you are often in a calm, cool state, so you make unrealistic commitments. Likewise, when in a hot state (i.e., craving) you have difficulty imagining yourself in a cold state and thus mispredict the speed with which such a state will dissipate.

For instance, depressed individuals think in terms of a future in which the present deficient condition will continue or even get worse. Their anticipation of the future is generally an extension of what they view as their present state. They seem to be unable to view their current state as having any time limits or to consider the possibility of any improvement (Beck, 2008). In other words, their bleak view of the present could lead them to expect similar negative future experiences (Kassam et al., 2008). Projection bias can also occur interpersonally. When a person projects her feeling onto another person, she may think that that person resembles herself and provide insight into the person's mind. The disturbing thoughts are attached to someone else. Projection is a defensive behavior that protects us by attributing unacceptable feelings, wishes, and impulses to someone else.

The projection bias leads people to overestimate their ability to resist temptations around them, thus undermining attempts to exercise self-control. Consistent with this idea, people will have the tendency to inaccurately report greater confidence in their ability to cope with temptation when they are in a neutral state. As a consequence of overconfidence in their actual ability to resist temptation, they overexpose themselves to tempting situations. People who think they have more self-control allow themselves to get into more tempting situations and, as a result, are more likely to give in to temptation. For example, smokers who were trying to quit and who also felt they had high self-control were less likely to have abstained four months later, on account of not being diligent enough in avoiding temptation (Nordgren et al., 2009).

Construal Level Theory (CLT) of Self-Control

The basic premise of CLT is that, from a distant perspective, one sees the forest, but from a proximal perspective, one sees trees.[23] This theory suggests that people may form abstract representations of distant, future events than near, future events (Trope and Liberman, 2010). From a distant perspective, choices are made based primarily on global concerns (why), whereas from proximal perspective, those priorities are weakened and even reversed as local concerns become more prominent (how).[24] As people get psychologically closer to the situation, their choices are increasingly influenced by more specific concerns.[25] Thus, distance impairs our ability to identify specific details of the choice. As the saying goes, "the devil is in the details." Details about options become available and clear only as one gets closer in time to the events.

Temporal distance increases the weight of high-level value and decreases the weight of low-level value. For example, a task like "maintaining good physical health" might be associated with high-level attributes like the joy of a healthy lifestyle. However, there are also low-level attributes associated with this task such as going to gym, avoiding your favorite snack, and so on. As a result, time delay shifts the overall attractiveness of an option closer to its high-level value than to its low-level value. Thus, options that are rich in high-level attributes but poor in low-level attributes (details) will appear very attractive from a great distance, but not as much from a near distance. Since we consistently frame long-term goals abstractly, the result is that we are more likely to postpone them, at least until they become short-term goals and we start thinking about them concretely.

In sum, the present places greater importance on feasibility, while the future focus on desirable attributes. Desirability refers to the value of an action's end state, whereas feasibility refers to the ease or difficulty of reaching the end state. Therefore, desirability concerns receive greater weight over feasibility concerns as psychological distance increases. Thus, from the distant future, individuals commit themselves to options with outcomes that may be infeasible but highly desirable, whereas for the near future, individuals prefer options with outcomes that are less desirable but highly feasible.

Exercising self-control requires ignoring the attraction of short-term temptations in order to pursue other long-term goals.[26] Thinking about actions in high-level terms links them to a global concern (why one performs them), and thinking in low-level terms (means) links them to a local concern (how one performs them). Thus, self-control becomes easier when people ask themselves why they are doing an activity (a high-level abstract construal) rather than how they are doing it (a low-level concrete construal).[27]

Time Perception

Hyperbolic discounting is directly related to time estimation tasks that may affect self-control problems. Time is an important dimension when individuals make decisions. Specifically, the time until a beneficial outcome can be received is viewed as a cost and is weighed against the benefits of the delayed reward. Individual differences in how they perceive the future durations may contribute to impulsive behavior (Zauberman et al., 2009). That is, individuals do not perceive time objectively (one year is not perceived to be four times as long as three months). If an individual perceives delays as subjectively longer than they actually are, this might in part account for an increased tendency to choose smaller but sooner rewards, because subjectively, the future will seem to be more distant.

Impulsive individuals experience time differently (Zauberman et al., 2009). They overestimate the duration of time intervals and, as a consequence, discount the value of delayed rewards more heavily. The altered sense of time as lasting too long is viewed as a high-cost option, which leads to the selection of alternatives with an immediate reward.

Time perception is also associated with mood states. Different mood states influence the degree to which someone attends to time or is distracted from time.

Time seems to go painfully slower when we find the class boring, and fly when we are with our lover. The adage that time flies when you are having fun has been empirically demonstrated (Droit-Volet and Meck, 2007). When we are happily engaged in an activity, especially when we are eagerly working toward a desired goal, times seem to flow freely, with no sense of boredom. Boredom can alter the perception of time.[28] Evidence shows that boredom-prone individuals may have a naturally lower level of dopamine (Toohey, 2011). This may mean that they require a heightened sense of novelty to stimulate their brains. Children with ADHD find periods of inactivity excessively boring because a lower level of dopamine affects their sense of time. For them, unoccupied minutes pass more slowly, so they feel bored much more quickly than others with normal levels of dopamine. Extroverts are more prone to boredom than introverts. Those who rely more on external than internal stimulation often perform worse on repetitive and predictable tasks.

Stimulants, including caffeine, tend to make people feel as if time is passing faster. Individuals suffering from depression or anxiety feel that time passes slowly. Individuals in the state of craving experience time differently, that is with a higher cost. For example, smokers who feel a strong urge to smoke experienced time passing more slowly (Sayette et al., 2005).

In sum, the dysfunction of the "inner clock" leads to a stronger focus on the present and an overestimation of time. Time can be distorted to appear shorter or longer than it really is. For example, the presence of shopping stores and restaurants within the airports provide distractions during the waiting period and make waiting more enjoyable.

Conclusion

This chapter reviewed several factors that influence our vulnerability for impulsive behavior, including hyperbolic brain mechanisms, salience or vividness, strong feelings, the forces of environment, and others. Self-control failure or present-biased preferences describe human behavior under hyperbolic discounting. The hyperbolic discounting model implies that people will make relatively farsighted decisions when planning in advance—when all costs and benefits will occur in the future—but will make relatively shortsighted decisions when some costs or benefits are immediate. This behavior is an expression of a "two selves" dynamic, preferring indulgence for the impulsive self and prudence for the reflective (future) one. The present-bias behavior leads to failures to maximize gains or minimize losses in the long run.

The dual model suggests that self-control failure occurs whenever the balance is tipped in favor of impulsive system, or due to a failure to appropriately engage the reflective system. Strong feelings (e.g., hunger, cravings, and stress) shorten the time horizon and make us impatient. The reflective system is impaired when cognitive resources are depleted. The dual model facilitates designing interventions aimed at breaking the impulsive behaviors with self-control competencies.

What can be done about impulsive behavior? How can we improve decisions? We are not powerless, but we are weak, and becoming self-aware of these forces actually helps to improve it. What is then needed, therefore, is protection of you from yourself. Knowing why people fail to consider future consequences is an essential ingredient in improving decision making, as well as the development of effective public policy.

Notes

1. We have all had the experience of self-talking to control our actions ("Boy, I'm getting fat," or "Just relax; it'll be just fine"), and we wish the voice in our head had a mute button. Of course, alcohol can lower self-awareness.
2. In his book *The Happiness Hypothesis*, Haidt writes: "To understand most important ideas in psychology, you need to understand how the mind is divided into parts that sometimes conflict. We assume that there is one person in each body, but in some ways we are each more like a committee whose members have been thrown together working at cross purposes" (p. 9, 2006).
3. This explains why it is easier to change our environment than to change our habits. Change the environment and then let the new cues do the work. The difficulty of changing a personal habit is like flattening a rolled-up paper that immediately rolls back into its original form.
4. Individuals with higher cognitive ability and analytic intelligence are more prone to override impulsive processing and use reflective processing to produce rational responses (Stanovich, 2010). Thus, cognitive skills allow better self-control by lowering the cost of self-control efforts.
5. William Blake, *The Marriage of Heaven and Hell* (c. 1790–1793): "Those who restrain desire do so because theirs is weak enough to be restrained." In this statement, William Blake points out that strength of such desires may not be the same for everyone.
6. It would be nice if we had a device to gauge the amount of willpower resources so we were able to regulate our behaviors.
7. For example, if a meal costs $2.00, then that $2.00 will be far more costly to someone living on $8 a day than to someone living on $30 a day.
8. Dieting essentially involves restricting one's caloric intake and produces lower glucose, which, in turn, undermines the willpower needed to refrain from eating. Foods that persistently elevate blood sugar, like those containing protein or complex carbohydrates, might enhance willpower for longer periods.
9. A sleepless night weakens self-control. According to a 2008 study by the National Sleep Foundation, American adults now get two hours less sleep per night than the average in 1960. Sleep deprivation creates impulse and attention control problems. This poor sleeping habit may be contributing to poor self-control (McGonigal, 2011).
10. Attention-deficit/hyperactivity disorder (ADHD) is associated with reduced working memory, response inhibition, and organization (Nigg, 2013). Individuals with ADHD or patients with the prefrontal cortex (PFC) damage exhibit poorer self-control behaviors. For example, speaking before one should (in ADHD).
11. For instance, according to *the next-in-line effect*, people are least likely to remember what the person who immediately preceded them said because that was when they were most self-absorbed. When people devote too much attention to themselves, they leave little cognitive room for other kinds of mental processes (Kahneman, 2011).

12 A stimulus can only represent a temptation with respect to another, long-term goal, which the individual believes is more important (e.g., overeating and being physically inactive vs the pursuit of a healthy lifestyle).
13 Marketing strategies that are focused on changing the visual saliency and attractive packages can bias choices.
14 The attempted restriction of the sale of supersized sugary drinks in New York is another example of cue management at a community level. The effort to regulate the size of soft drink containers was intended to increase salience by drawing people's attention to the seriousness of the obesity epidemic
15 This motivational explanation of overeating has been termed the "what-the-hell-effect" by Polivy and Herman (1985). The term describes the behavior of restrained eaters who overindulge when they exceed their daily calorie goal because they consider that the day is lost.
16 For example, when people engage in "retail therapy"—when the going gets tough, the tough go shopping—the so-called misery is not miserly phenomenon (Lerner et al., 2013).
17 Suicide wishes may be regarded as an extreme expression of the desire to escape.
18 The problem with stress as a risk factor is the way some people respond to stress, such as smoking or overeating. Evidence shows that men who do not openly express their anger if they are unfairly treated at work double their risk of a heart attack. Anger can produce physiological tensions if it is not released, which leads to increases in blood pressure, which eventually damages the cardiovascular system (Leineweber et al., 2011).
19 To break free from rumination, individuals are encouraged to engage in problem solving, reappraisal of the situation, and mindful practice (notice their thoughts without judging). People who simply avoid or suppress their problems through constant distraction experience their negative thoughts with greater force.
20 Similarly, sex and other strong drives produce a kind of tunnel vision. Wilson and Daly (2003) found that pretty women defeat men's ability to assess the future. The study found that male students shown the pictures of pretty women discounted the future value of the reward in an "irrational" way—they would opt for the smaller amount of money available the next day rather than wait for a much bigger reward. Female students, by the way, were more rational no matter what. For male students, an increase in sexual arousal led them to perceive future durations to be longer.
21 Alcoholics and other addicts understand what they are doing to themselves, but don't seem to be able to internalize the knowledge into a permanent life lesson. Some researchers believe they suffer from this disability because they have damaged the neural plasticity in their prefrontal cortex. They can no longer learn from mistakes. Similarly, while under the influence of intense negative emotions, getting positive advice from someone or reading self-help books may feel good temporarily, but then the knowledge evaporates immediately afterward.
22 Also, people have been advised to avoid shopping with young children, because they seem to lead to less healthy food choices (Tal and Wansink, 2013).
23 Charlie Chaplin once said, "Life is a tragedy when seen in a close-up, but a comedy when seen in a long-shot" (Neff, 2011). When we face obstacles in our life, they loom large partly because of the proximity we see them. But that narrow attitude shifts as we develop a more expansive sense of the problem and at that level, we tend to see more options. It is hard to see clearly when you are in the thick of the clouds.
24 Similarly, we tend to view the people who are close to us larger and more important than those who are distant relatives, or those who are total strangers.

25 People may have less information about distant situations. Nevertheless, people often act as if they know what someone else in the distant situation should have done.
26 There is a common saying that concerned people should "think globally, act locally: in order to do good in the world."
27 The CLT has also relevance to enhancing creativity. It is shown that creativity declines in middle age. But we are not biologically destined to get less creative. After several years of experience, people start to repeat themselves, so that it becomes more the same-old approach. They become insiders. One of the most effective ways of cultivating an outsider perspective is to feel distant from the problems. For example, try traveling and getting away from the places you spend most of your time. The travel allows one to view problems in a more imaginative way. All of a sudden, our minds are aware of those considerations that were previously suppressed. Our thoughts are constricted by the familiar experiences, and we spend a lot of energy on those facts that should be ignored.
28 The best cure for boredom is variety in experience, such as keeping as many interests as possible (e.g., books, politics, exercise, art galleries, music).

10
SELF-CONTROL
The Ability to Achieve Long-Term Goals

Introduction

This chapter provides an introduction to some basic principles of self-control in order to address a few basic questions: What is self-control? Where does it come from? Why is self-control important? What is involved in acquiring self-control?

The purpose of self-control is to protect long-term interests from the appeal of short-term desires. Self-control success is acting in line with one's long-term goals, and self-control failure is acting according with one's short-term desires. Self-control is one of the most crucial aspects of human behavior. To achieve any long-term goal, individuals need to resist the tempting, immediate, yet low-priority rewards with which the more important goals are in conflict. People who have high self-control have better outcomes in various aspects of life (e.g., academic performance, impulse control, meaningful relationships with others, and psychological adjustment). On the other hand, the majority of social and personal problems (e.g., addiction, debt, violence, academic failure, and procrastination) seem to stem from deficiencies in self-control. Thus, strategies that help people develop a sense of self-control (self-discipline) have far-reaching implications for overall human well-being.

Defining Self-Control

What is self-control? According to the *American Heritage Dictionary* (2011), self-control is defined as the "control of one's emotions, desire, or actions by one's own will." This definition of self-control refers to the exertion of control over the self by the self, which involves altering the way an individual feels, thinks, or behaves (i.e., the self is seen as an active agent). In this view, self-control can be considered as the mental control that a bored student exercises to focus (or remain awake and not to doze off during the lecture). For example, when people are experiencing negative emotions, they may distract themselves by shifting their attention to something else. The power to disengage our attention from one thing and move it to another is essential for well-being. The failure to shift one's focus from negative emotions (helplessness and hopeless) leave the mind in negative rumination. Similarly, people often attempt to up-regulate (i.e., have more of, initiate, or increase) certain emotions, either to feel good, or because they believe that certain emotions are more beneficial in specific situations.

Conceptually speaking, self-control is the capacity to override one's action tendency, desire, or impulse in order to attain another goal (Baumeister et al., 2008). This definition is consistent with the concept of free will or human freedom, which often means overcoming our short-term desires and following our long-term goals or better judgment. This definition is also consistent with the economist's principle that people behave so as to maximize total utility (happiness) within the constraints set by limited resources. Thus, failure to maximize utility is essentially a failure of self-control.

Self-control and self-regulation are often used interchangeably in the literature[1] (Baumeister et al., 2007). Self-control can be viewed as a specific case of self-regulation in which the person exerts deliberate and conscious effort to control the self.[2] In self-control, the "behavior" that needs to be overridden is often linked to basic drives or urges. Self-control refers to moderating these urges or pursuing one's well-intentioned but effortful resolution, like maintaining a diet or performing better in school. Resolution is defined as involving an intention to engage in a certain action or stand firm against future temptation (Holton, 2009).

From an evolutionary perspective, the ultimate purpose of the self-control is likely to improve the fit between the self and the environment (Gazzaniga, 2011). The inability to modify aspects of the environment required self cognitively to adjust to the surrounding environment. The best way achieve this was to have a self capable of acting according to long-term goals (i.e., delaying gratification). Evolutionary advantages (e.g., better health, cognitive capacities, and social manners) accrued for those who could set goals, move themselves toward the goal, and monitor their progress toward the goal (Adolphs, 2003).

Measures of self-control often include indices of attentional regulation (e.g., the ability to voluntarily focus or shift attention as needed) and/or the ability to delay gratification in situations of intense temptation, or stress. Delay discounting is a choice situation for studying self-control (Rachlin, 2000). A measure of the degree to which a person is impulsive (or myopic) regarding future consequences can be obtained by offering various sums at various delays and determining the individual's discounting function.

The so-called color-word Stroop task (Baumeister and Tierney, 2011) is often used to probe attention regulation mechanisms involved in suppressing distractions. In this task, subjects are required to name the ink color of words. Usually, performance is less error prone and faster if the meaning of the word is compatible with the to-be-named ink color (e.g., the word BLUE written in blue ink) than if the word is incompatible (e.g., the word GREEN written in red ink). This has been taken as evidence for word reading being automatic: a skilled reader cannot avoid reading the word despite instructions to attend only to the color in which it is printed. When the color-word stimulus is incompatible, the task (color naming) requires a great degree of self-control. The automatic habit to read the word must be overcome to report the color of the word accurately. Subjects must avoid being distracted by the word's meaning and instead focus their attention on the ink color of the word.

Self-Control Dilemma

The essence of self-control conflicts is when a goal that is higher in one's hierarchy conflicts with a lower level goal. For example, a dieter's desire to finish a meal with a sweet dessert may conflict with his desire to maintain a low calorie diet; or a student's urge to procrastinate may conflict with his desire to complete his assignments on time. Whenever these individuals contemplate the conflicting motives (i.e., goal vs temptation), they experience a self-control dilemma. In short, a self-control dilemma represents an internal conflict between the pursuits of different goals, one of which is of greater long-term importance than the other.

In general, the problem of self-control will be present to some degree in all human decisions that involve a perceived conflict between the short-term and long-term outcomes of a choice. Self-control is fundamentally a temporal conflict between behavior that maximizes value over a short time period and behavior that maximizes value over a long time period (Rachlin, 2000). Most of the major personal and social problems that afflict human beings in our society center on some failure to control or regulate ourselves. For example, addiction, obesity, debt or bankruptcy, violence, unwanted pregnancy, school failures, and anger are all colored by things like temptation, and impulsiveness. In these decisions, the individual may seek short-term gains, but incur long-term costs.

The biggest self-control challenge of all is to maintain the discipline not just for days or weeks, but for a long duration. Moreover, to maintain over time, these control efforts have to be converted from conscious and effortful to automatic control.

Self-Control a Useful Strategy in Daily Life

Self-control tools have practical applications that people can use to improve various aspects of their lives. Self-control capacity can be considered as a skill that is developed over time and the increased practice enables people to achieve future goals and outcomes.

A huge body of research has linked good self-control to a broad range of desirable outcomes, including better mental health, coping skills, healthier interpersonal relationships, superior academic performance, as well as less susceptibility to eating disorders and addiction (Offer, 2006). For example, Peterson and Seligman (2004) report that self-control is a major health asset: men with the highest self-control have a 56% reduced risk for CVD. Self-control is a vital strength and a key to success in life (Baumeister and Tierney, 2011).

Strong self-control is a very good predictor of academic performance. Self-control proved to be a better predictor of college grades than the student's IQ or SAT score, because it helped students show up more reliably for classes, start their homework earlier, and spend more time working on answers and less time watching TV (Baumeister and Tierney, 2011). Numerous studies with preschool and early school-age children have indicated that self-control is a primary influence on academic achievement (Dweck, 2011).[3] Studies of teenagers have found that self-discipline is a much better predictor of academic performance than IQ, since doing well in school requires sustained effort and postponing fun when it's time to do homework (Duckworth and Seligman, 2005).

The variety of influences of early childhood experiences, primarily those associated with early rearing experience and the conditions of the home environment, are likely to influence the development of cognitive capacity[4] and thereby the development of self-control (Blair, 2010; Heckman, 2006). For instance, poverty and stress in early childhood are associated with poor self-regulation. In contrast, an advantaged environment, in which resources and support are high and predictable, is conducive to the development of effortful self-regulation. Thus, self-control is a key to human potential and possibilities.

What makes someone very good at a given thing? Seligman (2011) writes that achievement is equal to Skill*Effort. The role of self-control or self-discipline (enters as effort) is the amount of time spent on the task. Self-control is the character trait that produces deliberate practice. Seligman recommends that if we want to maximize the achievement of children, we need to promote self-discipline. Programs that build self-control by requiring youths to sacrifice short-term pleasure for long-term gain may be the crucial element for developing academic achievement. People who succeed tend to find one goal in the distant future and then follow it forever. People who jump from one interest to another are much less likely to excel at any of them.

Skill development depends on how repetition is organized. For example, research shows that it takes approximately ten years of intense work to acquire the level of expertise to thrive in any field. It takes the brain 10,000 hours to assimilate all that it needs to achieve true mastery. The 10,000 hours rule translates into practicing three hours a day for ten years, which is indeed a common training span for young people in sports. In short, expertise in any domain (violin, math, etc.) develops as a result of around 10,000 hours of deliberate practice.

Psychologists Ericsson and associates (1993) have shown that that deliberate practice of setting specific goals and obtaining immediate feedback are key elements of expert performance in a wide range of pursuits, such as soccer, golf, surgery, piano playing, and writing. These experts have a desire to be good and they undertake the deliberate practice that would make them better. Thus, success is the result of accumulative advantages. This also implies that passion and persistence are the key ingredients of talent. If you don't love it, you will never work hard enough to be great. Thus, when it comes to choosing a life career, you should do what you love, because if you don't love it, you are unlikely to work hard enough to get very good.

Evidence shows that talent is overrated and top performers spend more hours rigorously practicing their craft. People tend to overestimate the role of talent and underestimate the role of determination and self-control among high achievers. Success in most fields is not a reflection of innate skill but rather devoted and purposeful effort. Success is a function of persistence and willingness to work hard. Many achievers regard their ability to function (attitude) in spite of pain, rejection, or adversity to be among their outstanding accomplishments. In his book *Outliers*, Gladwell (2008) demonstrates that outliers are those who have been given opportunities, and who have had the strength and presence of mind to seize them. Virtually every success story covered in the book involves someone or some group working harder than their peers.[5] In short, top performers excel not because of innate ability, but because of dedicated practice. These findings on great performers take some of the magic out of great achievement.

There is no doubt that genes place a limit on our capacities. But the brain is also plastic. We mold our brain through what we do. In *The Talent Code*, Daniel Coyle (2009) writes that every human skill is the result of electrical impulses sent along chains of nerve fibers. Basically, our brains are bundles of wires—100 billion wires called neurons, connected to each other by synapses. The rule is simple: use it or lose it. To survive, the synapse between two cells must be activated consistently. Each time you do something, practice anything, a different highly specific circuit lights up in your mind. Eventually, these skills become automatic (e.g., in sports, it is called "muscle memory"). Thus, every skill is a form of memory. From this, perspective talent is defined as the possession of repeatable skills. This body of work also suggests that older adults should be encouraged to acquire new skills, especially those considered to require "talents" they previously believed they lacked. Expert performers are always made, not born. So, practice does make perfect.

In sum, these studies conclude that while dedicated practice may not make one the best, but it does maximizes one's personal potential. Self-control is like a practical skill that can be learned by doing (Annas, 2011). Similar to the pianist, the person will need to think less and less as she becomes an expert. Excellence, then, is not an act, but a habit. Similar to going to health clubs, we can strengthen our self-control in order to become less reliant on costly external coping mechanisms (Baumeister and Tierney, 2011). People who practice small but regular acts of self-control find it easier to increase capacity to confront even bigger challenges.

Resilience

The term resilient refers to "the capacity to bend without breaking, to return to an original shape or condition" (Southwick and Charney, 2012, p. 6). It is the capacity to bounce back after adversity. It is the ability that helps people to cope positively with adversity, such as acute stress, trauma, or chronic adversity (Reich et al., 2010).

It is estimated that most people (up to 90%) will experience at least one serious traumatic event (e.g., financial distress, separation from a loved one, or medical and mental illness) during their lives (Norris and Sloane, 2007). Thus, we need to prepare ourselves to cope effectively with life adversity. Research shows that the resilient personality protects against the development of mental illness in the face of adversity.

What makes some people resilient? Southwick and Charney (2012) have identified ten critical psychological coping mechanisms that are characteristics of resilient people. They are optimism, altruism, having a moral compass or set of beliefs that cannot be shattered, faith and spirituality, humor, having a role model, social support, facing fear (or leaving one's comfort zone), having a mission or meaning in life, and practice in meeting and overcoming challenges.

Self-control is an important predictive of resilience. Resilient people have good control over impulses and have the ability to delay gratification in regards to the potential consequences of their actions. For example, training for emergencies or for military services is all about developing a sense of psychological control that becomes second nature to a soldier or emergency medical technician. Public speaking comes naturally for those who feel confident before an audience. *Self-confidence* is another prerequisite for resilience. A resilient person has a belief in her own abilities to manage life's challenges and situations effectively. A perception that a person has the necessary resources to handle a situation should reduce the perceived threat or increase the perceived efficacy of coping efforts. Human studies indicate that success in managing challenging situations can build resilience. Children grow up to be more capable in handling stress if they have had multiple, successful experiences confronting mild stress in their youth.

Self-Control and a Good Life

Self-control is something that we want for ourselves and admire in others without qualification because it leads to a good life. Self-control is a personal quality that contributes to human happiness. Research shows that people are happier, more productive, and more creative when they feel they are the origin of their behavior

(Deci and Ryan, 2002). The autonomy motive or volitional control over one's behavior is an important aspect of the development process. People are highly motivated to perceive their behavior as free and self-determined, and react to threats to their freedom in ways that restore their perceived freedom.

The Greek philosophers viewed self-control (willpower) as a major virtue, and viewed yielding to temptation as a deplorable weakness (Peterson and Seligman, 2004). To Aristotle, the purpose of life was *eudemonia* (a virtuous life), a form of happiness that is distinguished from mere pleasure. That is, happiness is not something that happens overnight, it is an activity. Happiness is a kind of virtuous activity that involves one right choice piled on another that would increase the likelihood of future right choices, resulting, eventually, in a good life. For Aristotle, "the good life" (well-being) is mostly about character strengths that involve activities that go beyond approaching pleasure and avoiding pain. Character strength involves being wise and knowledgeable, courageous, humane, and temperate. Thus, courage is not the absence of fear, but the ability to overcome that fear. In a similar vein, character is only as strong as the obstacles it overcomes. In his view, we are responsible for our dispositions, and happiness involves being effective in managing what happens (self-control) and maintaining moderation in all things. Happiness is beyond pleasure and pain; it involves success in worthwhile endeavors, friendships, and development of one's capacities. Achieving a worthwhile objective to which you haves devoted yourself makes you better off.

The Role of Self-Control in Modern Society

The self-control capacity is fundamental for success in the modern world as people now are faced with more choices and decisions on a daily basis, the "tyranny of choice" (Schwartz, 2004). The modern life places far more pressure on the ability to exercise self-control (Akst, 2011) in the face of daily temptations. Modern life is full of freedom and opportunity. For instance, technology undermines restraint by making everything happen faster. The collapse of delay between impulse and decision inevitably favor impulse over reflection and now over later. By undermining deliberation, fast times makes urges easy to gratify, and weakens the habit of deferring gratification. Self-control capacity increases the strength of goals and decreases the strength of competing temptations. The moment of reflection may provide the psychological space to make a free choice.

Technological and marketing innovation, such as TV shopping channels, and credit cards have served to alter proximity. For example, research shows that the immediacy effect explains why we spend more using credit cards versus cash (Prelec and Simester, 2001). Paying with a credit card alters the calculus of financial decisions. When you buy something with cash, the purchase involves an actual loss. Using actual cash is more painful, and leads you to spend less. That is, the purchase price is salient to the consumption (e.g., with a taxi ride, you see the meter running continuously). Credit cards, however, make the transaction abstract, so that you don't really feel the downside of spending money. Credit cards provide immediate gratification, but delayed consequences. That is, payment and consumption are decupled and in effect create the illusion that consumption is free. Salience plays an important role in people's choice.

The impact of reduced salience was demonstrated in the case of the E-Z Pass, which is used as an "electronic wallet." Finkelstein (2009) showed that in states with electronic toll collection, tolls were 20 to 40% higher than they would have been without the E-Z Pass. This study suggests that limited attention is a problem source and that once toll fees become salient, they are significantly reduced. If an important feature of a product, or an activity, lacks salience, people tend to ignore it, often to their detriment.

Technological changes have brought about a progressive shift away from physically demanding tasks to knowledge-based work requiring an enhanced mental effort. The increased cognitive demand is associated with emotional stress (such as a burnout), which is known to favor overconsumption of comfort food as a coping mechanism. As individuals turn to comfort foods to alleviate stress, the continued failure to cope with stressors may promote the development of obesity. One of the reasons why TV is so popular is because, although it is rather brain numbing, the very passivity of it is just what appeals when you feel so tired. Self-control steadily deteriorates over the course of the day. This failure is not about our innate lack of will; it is about the nature of willpower depletion.

Avner Offer (2006) argues that the capacity to exercise self-control increases with education and wealth. Prudence builds up affluence. But over time, affluence undermines prudence. What accounts for this reversal is myopic choice. Affluence is a relentless flow of new and cheaper opportunities. The self-control strategies take time and effort to develop and learn. If rewards arrive faster than the disciplines of prudence can form, then self-control will decline with affluence. Thus, the rewards of affluence produce the disorders of affluence, such as addiction and obesity.

Awareness of Self-Control Problems

An important question is this: if individuals have self-control problems, are they aware of it (sophisticated) or oblivious (naïve)? Self-awareness of how we find ourselves in vulnerable situations is the foundation of self-control. Without self-awareness, self-control becomes useless, because there is nothing to control. For example, the alcoholic who is aware of and compensates for his dispositions is a better person than the one who passively lets himself be overwhelmed by them. People overoptimistic about their capacity for self-control tend to overexpose themselves to tempting situations, leading to more frequent self-control failures in the heat of the moment (Nordgren et al., 2009).

In order to benefit from self-control strategies, we need to acknowledge that we have a problem. A naïve (a form of overconfidence) individual does not understand her self-control problem, and makes no attempt to manage it. A sophisticated decision maker perfectly understands her self-control problem, and may attempt to manage anticipated lapses of self-control by limiting future choices. The sophisticated individual will realize that her preferences will shift over time. For example, addicts must confront not only their addiction, but also their inability to quit by simply deciding to do so. As they say in Alcoholic Anonymous, recognition is the first step. The more we can understand our self-control problem, the more we can do something about it.

However, O'Donoghue and Rabin (1999) show that sophistication can sometimes backfire. Knowing that your future preferences will change can make it easier for your current self to succumb to the temptation. For example, you may consume a second serving of ice cream during lunch knowing that you will cave in during the evening and eat more of it. Thus, self-awareness can undermine our commitments and some positive illusion about oneself can be beneficial.

In many cases, when people choose to pursue short-term desires, they do not realize it will harm them in the long run. For example, the smoker may light up without considering that a single cigarette poses a health risk. A single indulgence may have negligible negative consequences. However, repeated consumption may prove serious. Thus, viewing an action in relation to future actions facilitates self-control awareness. The person who says that "one donut for breakfast won't kill me," perceives the indulgence in isolation. The dieter who is planning a new eating pattern may be more likely to perceive today's choice of a donut in relation to many future breakfast choices.

Considering a pattern of responses encourages people to consider multiple opportunities together, thus increasing self-control awareness. Thus, dieters faced with the opportunity to indulge should think about similar future consumption opportunities and avoid thinking about the current opportunity as unique or special. Becoming aware of the self-control problem will ultimately give the dieter more control and choice in terms of how he responds, and will make it more likely that his diet goals will be met.

The Key Ingredients of Self-Control

As discussed, self-control is the capacity to restrain unwanted thoughts, impulses, and desires in the pursuit of long-term goals. We humans are notoriously poor at following through with our plans. Life has a natural way of derailing even the best-laid plans. Thus, the challenge is finding ways to close the gap between good intentions and human nature. What determines self-control? Self-control depends on several factors. These factors include commitment to goals, motivation, self-efficacy, monitoring of the self and its behaviors, and willpower. These factors are necessary for effective self-control, and a breakdown or problem with any one of them is shown to undermine self-control (Vohs and Baumeister, 2011). The following sections describe a conceptual framework for motivating individuals to achieve self-control outcomes.

Goals

One has to have a goal. Goals are defined as subjectively desirable states of affairs that the individuals intend to attain through actions. A goal is a cognitive representation of a desired endpoint (Fishbach and Ferguson, 2007). A goal is a reference point around which behavior is organized (e.g., "I want to exercise in order to feel happy"). Behavior is basically guided by goals. Goals are standards that individuals use to evaluate how well they are doing now relative to where they want to end up. Self-control failure arises when the processes of goal pursuit departs from the correct course.

A goal involves a discrepancy between an actual state and a desired state, a discrepancy that creates tension that a person tries to reduce by fulfilling the goal (Lewin, 1951). By setting goals, people produce discrepancies between where they are and where they would like to be. This means that people feel good when they attain a goal (i.e., eliminate the discrepancy or need, like hunger). Thus, people's goals determine their actions as they attempt to decrease perceived discrepancies between current and desired goals. For example, when experiencing the pangs of hunger, one adopts the goal "to eat," which initiates an appropriate response. When the tension is satisfied, the goal-relevant response ends. Thus, by giving someone a goal, you can create a force within that person for movement toward the goal. They mobilize their resources and effort based on what they believe is needed to accomplish those goals (Bandura and Locke, 2003). Commitment to realizing a desired future has an energizing function and propels individuals forward on their quest toward goal attainment.

According to *the goal looms larger effect*, people's motivation to carry out the steps needed to reach a goal becomes stronger as they get closer to the goal. People can be overconfident when they begin a task and the overconfidence slowly dissolves. But, motivation increases as they get closer and closer to the goal; they naturally believe that their chance of success is getting higher and higher. Each step taken reduces the distance to completion. Each step of goal completion also produces positive affect. Thus, as we go along, each step reduces the distance to a greater extent.

It is important for people to shield their crucial goal from competing goals during goal pursuit. One way to accomplish this is by reminding themselves of its importance, in order to inhibit other goals competing with it. By keeping the overriding goal in mind and reducing the activation of counterproductive thoughts, individual are more likely to succeed (Fishbach et al., 2003).

The goal-setting process is also important. In particular, some types of goals may result in better outcomes than others because of the motivational concerns they reflect (Higgins, 1997). Poorly defined and less challenging goals are less likely to be attained. Factors such as the low perceived desirability (or feasibility) of a potential, unspecific, and distant goal may lead to the formation of weak intentions to realize the goal and to subsequent procrastination.

The more specific the goal, the better able people are to reach it. The more specific goals are more likely to be more effective. A highly abstract goal may have no obvious behavioral expression (e.g., to get healthy). Solutions tend to come when we are specific about problems. Thus, translation from more abstract to less abstract provides a means of transforming a long-term goal into a more specific and actionable short-term goal (Trope and Liberman, 2003). So rather than setting a vague goal such as "I will get healthy," set one with a specific commitment to a time and place: "I will go to the health club at 7:00 AM tomorrow." That will make you more likely to follow through. Also, it is easier to postpone vague or open-ended tasks with distant deadlines than focused and short-term projects.

Specific goals (or breaking up your goals into smaller subgoals) allow for better monitoring of progression toward the goal. Goals typically require multiple steps to be achieved. These steps can themselves be thought of as smaller, intermediate subgoals. Therefore, dividing projects into smaller and more defined parts could be helpful. Locke and Latham (2002) show that setting a specific, difficult goal (for example, writing five pages every day) is more motivating than urging people to do their best. As the old saying goes, "A journey of a thousand miles begins with a single step." Often, we adopt an intermediate goal such as obtaining a degree that motivates us to carryout sequences of actions and avoid procrastination. For instance, in order to graduate, you must complete certain courses. The prospect of the degree keeps the student on track (Millgram, 2010).

Having only one goal makes self-control more successful than when people have two or more conflicting goals. With too many goals (options), we often are afraid of making the wrong choice, so we end up doing nothing. Goal attainment may raise feelings of self-confidence, which can result in one setting more challenging goals.

Effective self-control requires disengaging from goals when progress is too slow. People who disengage from seemingly impossible goals are mentally healthier than those who stay entrapped. Dropping the frustrating goals allows one to avoid attempting the impossible, and to use one's limited effort and time more effectively. Giving up frustrating goals creates opportunities. When we are overly focused on a particular goal or outcome, we become rigid and inflexible. This narrows our options and makes us feel more constrained about our course of action.[6]

Researchers point out that striving for goals that cannot be brought to completion leads to a host of negative outcomes including negative affect, anxiety, and diminished well-being. In the same vein, those who disengage from unattainable goals experience heightened well-being. Unfulfilled and failed goals from which a person does not disengage create rumination—repeated and often intrusive thoughts about the incomplete goal. Often, they emerge in our dreams. Jostmann and Koole (2009) suggest that individuals with better coping skills (tendency toward initiative and decisiveness vs those who tend to be hesitant and indecisive) are better able to update their working memory and hence terminate the activation of unattainable goals. The updating process erases the information related to unattainable goal and focuses on information to new and potentially attainable goals.

The ancient Greek hero Sisyphus was condemned to incessantly rolling a rock to the top of a mountain, from there, it would fall back from its own weight. Some philosophers (existentialists) have regarded this tragedy as a metaphor for the futility of life itself (Camus, 1955). However, one can also ask the question why Sisyphus never disengaged from his frustrating activity even though he knew it was pointless. Like Sisyphus, many people sometimes end up on an impossible mission. Fortunately, unlike this tragic hero, people have the possibility to disengage from their unattainable goals.

Goals are often triggered or primed by one's environment. Priming refers to activating behavior through the power of unconscious suggestion. Theories of unconscious goal pursuit developed in social psychology show that goals can be activated (primed) outside of awareness by exposing individuals to situational cues that in the past were frequently associated with the pursuit of a goal (Bargh and Chartrand, 1999). There is accumulating evidence that passively priming individuals with stimuli that carry behavioral implications can influence the behavior of the individuals. Researchers have found that people who were made to think of self-discipline (by having to unscramble sentences about it) immediately made more future-oriented snack choices than those given sentences about self-indulgence. Exposing participants to words related to the elderly stereotype (e.g., senile, dementia) induces people walk more slowly[7] (Bargh et al., 1996). These individuals clearly did not have the conscious goal of walking slowly. The smell or sight of palatable food is likely to activate thoughts about eating enjoyment. Since chronic dieters are frequently thinking about dieting and eating enjoyment, they are likely to recognize cues related to palatable foods that activate eating enjoyment thoughts. In this case, the goal stored in long-term memory is retrieved and placed in short-term (or working) memory.

The idea of a unconscious goal does not diminish the role of individual volition, or free will. Instead, the idea frees goals from the grip of consciousness. That is, although consciousness may be required to deliberate a plan of action, there is no reason to assume it is required to implement the plan (Higgins, 2012). Conscious planning can create an association between a goal, a behavior, and a cue such that the presence of the cue will trigger the goal and initiate the goal-relevant response without consciousness. Repeated goal-directed actions become easier, requiring less and less effort, and in that sense, they become automatic and require only minimal monitoring. These chronic goals become associated with the individual's long-standing interests and most cherished values and motives. Thus, one way to avoid self-control failures of a particular sort is to avoid the company of those who suffer from such failures. Being around prompt, hardworking high achievers is one of the best ways of becoming prompt and hardworking, while associating with slackers is a good way of becoming a slacker.

In sum, a successful self-control response requires that one's goal be kept firmly in focus, and that one reserves the most careful decision resources for the goals that matter most. Successful self-control outcomes require individuals to be able to predict accurately and set goals that are attainable. For instance, for dieters, this means to establish realistic goals. Many look in the mirror and dream impossible goals, and it is no wonder that so many people fail to sustain their goals. You are better off using your self-control to make gradual changes that will produce lasting effects.

Motivation

One has to be motivated and committed to reach the goal. The more you want the goal, the more likely you are willing to make the efforts and sacrifices required to achieve it. Only when there's a feeling of determination to fulfill the wish is the wish transformed into a goal commitment.

Motivation is generally described as the internal drive to act toward a goal. Where does the determination, motivation, and commitment[8] to pursue a goal come from? The standard answer is that it comes from the overall benefit of a goal pursuit, to which two factors contribute: the subjective value of successful goal pursuit and the subjective or perceived likelihood of successful goal pursuit (*value*likelihood*). In other words, the strength of people's commitment to something depends on its value to them and the chance that the value will, in fact, occur.

In general, motivation is a function of expectations of future benefit (Bandura, 1977). If the goal is highly valuable, people are more motivated than when the goal is less valuable. For example, most people believe that smoking cigarettes is bad for them, and many have quit smoking in order to improve their health, but others may not value that outcome. But value alone is not enough. The meaning of commitment also includes the concept of putting your trust in something. Commitment requires a belief in the chance that something will occur as a result of this commitment. This is consistent with the beneficial effects of perceived self-efficacy on commitment because when people believe they are competent to perform the actions needed in a goal pursuit, they will also perceive that success is more likely.

Similarly, in economics, the classic expected utility model of goal pursuit proposes that commitment to a choice alternative derives from the subjective value of the outcomes of that choice and the subjective likelihood (perceived difficulty) that those outcomes will occur with the relation between these two factors being multiplicative (*value*likelihood* function). The function is multiplicative because it is assumed that there will be no commitment to the goal pursuit if the value of the goal is zero, no matter how high is the likelihood of success. It is important to note that the perceived self-efficacy (likelihood) is a motivational force in its own right. In most cases, the act is taken because a person believes it can be taken and sustained.

What makes something have positive value? Basic psychological principles hold that when people are faced with a restriction or loss of a choice, that choice or commodity becomes more attractive. Sometimes people want things precisely because they cannot have them ("the grass is always greener on the other side of the fence").[9] This is also known as *the scarcity effect*. Scarce items are low in number, and thus the likelihood of even finding them is low. It is equivalent to high difficulty. Their scarcity functions like an obstacle to goal pursuit, which intensifies the value of the goal. For an item that is attractive to begin with, its attractiveness will intensify when it is scarce. The elimination of a positive choice alternative makes it salient as an object, and increases its attractiveness. This explains why resistance to temptation creates greater positive value for the tempting objects.

People want to be efficacious in their life pursuits. Their choices of pursuing new courses of actions, how much effort to expend on them, and sustaining the effort when confronting obstacles are all influenced by their self-efficacy. Marathon runners will endure pain to challenge themselves, even with no material reward (e.g., cash prizes). These activities test our effectiveness. It is about being competent, being efficacious. But a crucial underlying factor is that the actors believe that they can do it. They perceive that the subjective likelihood of their carrying out the action is high.

Motivation to overcome obstacles is referred to as "learned industriousness" (Eisenberger, 1992). This term refers to taking pride and pleasure in exerting effort toward one's goals. People with learned industriousness are simply focused on outcomes and are less likely to categorize experience into "success" or "failure." Instead, they take pride in trying. Persistence in pursuing challenges and difficulty can actually increase resilience to deal with difficulties (Eisenberger, 1992). Resilient people are less likely to rely on smoking or substance abuse to handle their frustration.

An important way of motivating people is the use of the mental contrasting strategy (Oettingen, 2000). Mental contrasting is a problem-solving strategy for achieving goals. The strategy implies vividly imagining a desired future (e.g., overcoming a bad habit, giving a good presentation), anticipating obstacles for realizing this future, and making plans on how to overcome these barriers. For example, a study found that setting oneself the goal to stop smoking can be facilitated by mentally contrasting the feared future of negative health consequences with the current, positive reality of still having a healthy body (Gollwitzer et al., 2010). Mental contrasting is different from fantasizing, such as indulging in thoughts about the positive future that seduces a person to mentally enjoy the future in the here and now. However, mental contrasting turns free fantasies into binding goals by activating expectations.

Self-Efficacy

Self-efficacy is a crucial ingredient in self-control success. Self-efficacy refers to an individual's sense of competence or ability in general or in particular domains.

Self-efficacy is a person's perception of how capable he is to perform a specific behavior or take action and persist in that action despite obstacles or challenges. Self-efficacy is behavior specific. For example, a person may have high self-efficacy for initiating a physical activity program, but low self-efficacy for changing dietary habit.

As noted, motivation may come from perceptions of the possibility (or difficulty) that the goal can be attained. Higher self-efficacy or confidence enhances the individual's motivation and effort. A person must be confident that she has the ability to perform the actions instrumental to producing the desired outcomes. Self-efficacy is a belief that people can shape the course of their life. People who believe that they can succeed are more likely to make the effort in the first place. When a task is perceived as doable but difficult, more effort is allocated to the task. For instance, if a person loses faith in her willpower, her willpower declines, period. As she succeeds in exerting her willpower, her belief in herself grows, and her willpower grows as well.

Strong self-efficacy beliefs are important because they lead to effective self-control and persistence, which in turn lead to success. Decisions about how long to persevere are based partly on self-reflections on one's capabilities (Cervone and Pervin, 2010). In the face of difficulties, people with weak self-efficacy beliefs easily develop doubts about their ability to accomplish the task at hand, whereas those with strong efficacy beliefs are more likely to continue their efforts to master a task when difficulties arise. When low self-efficacy causes people to avoid activities, they fail to acquire knowledge and skills they might have learned had they attempted them. For example, a college student with a low sense of self-efficacy for math may avoid enrollment in upper-level math courses. The decision not to enroll then deprives him of the skills development he might have experienced.

When challenges arise, individuals with higher self-efficacy will invest more time and effort to meet the challenge. Individuals with low self-efficacy tend to see more risks and ruminate about dangers and their own inadequacies when facing stressful situations. In contrast, those with the high self-efficacy are able to transform stressful situations to make them more controllable.

Self-efficacy is similar to self-confidence, which is defined as a favorable or unfavorable attitude toward the self. Confidence in one's abilities generally enhances motivation, making it a valuable asset for individuals (Benabou and Tirole, 2002). The confident individual is more likely to persist in the face of obstacles. The idea that confidence enhances performance is illustrated as $(E \times A) \pm TD = B$, in which effort (E) times ability (A), plus or minus task difficulty (TD) equals the behavioral outcome (B). A higher self-confidence enhances the individual's motivation and effort (E). This formula explains the incentive to develop and maintain the individual's self-confidence (Benabou and Tirole, 2002). Of course, the relationship between self-confidence and achievement can be circular. You feel good about yourself, in part, because you have accomplished something well. On the other hand, it is hard to imagine people taking the first step without self-confidence.

People with higher self-efficacy are more likely to become task-diagnostic ("what do I need to do now?") when encountering self-control setbacks than self-diagnostic ("what's wrong with me?"). In the face of difficulty, people with high self-efficacy are more likely to remain task-diagnostic and to search for solution to problems. Those with low self-efficacy, however, are more likely to become self-diagnostic and reflect on their inadequacies, which distract them from their efforts to access and solve the problem (Bandura, 1997).

Self-efficacy beliefs are influenced by past performance experiences. Successful attempts at self-control attributed to one's own efforts will strengthen self-efficacy and can generalize across other domains. For efficacy to increase, people must interpret their personal experiences as evidence that they are capable of doing the task at hand. Self-efficacy beliefs can develop from our own experiences of overcoming obstacles, from observing others overcome obstacles, from social support situations that increase the likelihood of our succeeding, and from inner signals of self-efficacy such as feeling energetic. Making decisions with high confidence (decisiveness) may be less effortful than making choices and decisions with low confidence (indecisiveness).

An unrealistic belief in one's ability is the essence of overconfidence. Overconfident individuals fail to recognize their own deficiency, and are likely to overinvest in a course of actions that are likely to fail.[10] If one constantly fails in attainting a goal, then one might do well to abandon the unattainable goal,[11] and redirect one's efforts more profitably. However, we tend to be lousy at recognizing this. Thus, overconfident individuals may embark on ventures they would otherwise have avoided. Inflated self-confidence beliefs (positive illusion) can lead to complacency and diminished effort and performance over time (Maddux and Gosselin, 2011). For example, smokers with an inflated sense of self-efficacy to quit smoking are less inclined to enroll in programs to quit smoking and may have lower success rates in quitting (Duffy et al., 2010).

In the context of health behavior, high self-efficacy predicts successful weight loss, abstinence from cigarette smoking, and alcohol consumption (Rothman et al., 2008). Evidence shows that for people with eating disorders, self-efficacy predicts successful treatment outcomes (Cain et al., 2010). But, the initial success may foster overconfidence. Thus, overconfident clients completing their treatment for alcohol abuse are more likely to relapse (Goldbeck et al., 1997). People who successfully complete the initial phase of treatment tend to believe that they have proven that they can do it, but quitting may be easier than maintaining the changed behavior over the long run. As a 12-step treatment for addiction states: "every day brings you one day closer to your next relapse" (Higgins, 2012). The point of the statement is to encourage addicts to minimize the threat of overconfidence that may develop later in recovery, and remind them that addiction is a permanent condition, regardless of how long abstinence is maintained.

Self-Monitoring

The need for self-monitoring is central to self-control. One has to monitor progress toward the goal. Monitoring progress toward goal attainment creates a state of attention and concentration on goal-relevant activities. It keeps resources mobilized toward achieving the goal and minimizes the distraction of nongoal activities (Locke and Latham, 2002). Self-monitoring is a form of feedback. Immediate and frequent feedback has been shown to increase awareness of health behavior, as well as the intentions to change that behavior.

Evidence shows a consistent relationship between dietary self-monitoring and weight loss. A 24-month trial concluded that automatic daily feedback messages enhanced adherence to dietary self-monitoring and improved weight loss (Burke et al. 2012). A key success factor to weight-loss maintenance is the use of self-monitoring (Wing and Phelan, 2005). Successful dieters count calories and otherwise carefully monitor their food intake, and the cessation of that monitoring often undermines dietary efforts. Self-monitoring includes weighing frequently and recording food intake and physical activity. For example, evidence shows that people who wear pedometers get more exercise, lose weight and lower their blood pressure. For many, a pedometer provides motivation, accountability, and a sense of control.

Monitoring allows people to assess distance to the goal. This can be done by looking back at how much one has achieved, or how much more has to be done. Seeing how far one has accomplished may be more effective in promoting self-control than how much more work is ahead. Believing that one has come a long way increases commitment to the goal, thereby leading to heightened efforts to reach it.[12] For example, Koo and Fishbach (2008) show that focusing on the unaccomplished portion of a goal provides a bigger incentive for those who have a deeper commitment to the goal, while focusing on the accomplished portion better motivates people whose commitment is more uncertain.

In general, the more specific (rather than abstract) goals are, the easier it is to monitor (Liberman and Dar, 2009). For example, instead of pursuing the goal of being healthy, which is difficult to monitor, a person may adopt the goal of walking at least 30 minutes every day, which is more concrete and easier to monitor. Liberman and Dar (2009) suggest that individuals who are intrinsically motivated and pursue goals for their own sake tend to less closely monitor their progress toward goal attainment. For example, a student may enjoy reading the material rather than perceive studying only as a means to passing the exam.

Increased frequency of monitoring efforts may have unintended, negative effects. When progress is naturally slow, increased frequency of monitoring may engender frustration and disappointment. Anxiety is closely associated with increased monitoring (Gray 1982). Indeed, anxiety is a state of increased vigilance and extensive monitoring of the environment in response to potential, anticipated danger.[13]

Individuals with a low tolerance for uncertainty and ambiguity have high needs for closure and are less tolerant for situations of ambiguous feedback on their progress. For some individuals, relaxing monitoring may be seen as accepting a lack of control. Therefore, a high need for personal control is associated with increased monitoring. Patients suffering from OCD and its psychological correlates, including anxiety and compulsion, can be understood in terms of their inability to relax monitoring. Thus, OCD can be conceptualized as the consequences of intensified monitoring attempts in the face of monitoring difficulty. For example, repeated checking that doors are locked (Abramowitz, 2006).

In sum, self-monitoring failure is akin to a state of short-sightedness or myopia, in which people temporarily fail to detect discrepancies between their actual behavior and their self-control goals. Prominent examples of causes of self-monitoring failure include alcohol or other drug intoxication, drowsiness, and emotional turmoil. For example, alcohol has been argued to increase the chance of self-control failure because alcohol impairs people's ability to monitor themselves (Hull, 1981).

Willpower

Setting a desirable goal does not guarantee that one actually commits to and strives for the realization of the goal. Willpower is an important ingredient in self-control. Sticking to one's plan is hard work. Attempting to move from one's current state to a more desirable state requires a certain amount of energy. Without the willpower to bring about the changes, the best laid plans and all the monitoring in the world will not be good enough. Willpower represents vitality or psychological energy that one uses to resist other temptations in order to work toward one's goal. When in vital states, people are more active and productive, and they cope better with stress and challenges. For example, reformed alcoholics are far more likely to relapse if they are depressed, anxious, or tired. Diets are broken in evenings more than in mornings, which suggests that as the day wears on, willpower gets depleted. Also, certain states of mind are known to undermine self-control (Baumeister et al., 1998).

Regulatory Focus

There is an important distinction between motivational efforts aimed at achieving desirable outcomes (seeking rewards) from those aimed at avoiding undesirable outcomes (avoiding punishment). The regulatory focus theory proposed by Higgins (1997, 2012) describes that an individual has two motivations, namely *promotion focus* and *prevention focus*. A person with a promotion focus cares more about how to attain expected goals, while a person with a prevention focus pays more attention to how to avoid losing his possessions. For example, "it would excite me to win a contest" (seeking rewards) versus "I worry about making mistakes" (avoiding punishment). These two approaches are aspects of individual differences in the sensitivity to reward and punishment (Higgins, 2012). Promotion goals are those in which people approach ideal goals with aspiration and a sense of accomplishment, focusing on potential gains. Prevention goals are those in which people try to avoid losses by playing it safe or doing what they ought to do.

In a similar vein, according to the self-discrepancy theory, individuals are motivated by the *ideal* self and the *ought* self (Higgins, 1999). The ideal self possesses qualities that the individual personally aspires to and is intrinsically motivated to attain, whereas the ought self is comprised of qualities that people feel obligated to attain. Focusing on the ideal vs the actual self is an indication of a promotion focus. By contrast, focusing on the ought versus the actual self is an indication of a prevention focus. Discrepancies between the ideal self and the actual self produce disappointment and sadness as individuals fail to achieve their personal goals. In contrast, differences between the ought self and the actual self produce anxiety as individuals anticipate negative consequences for failing to achieve their obligation goals. Regulator focus has implications for how individuals set and pursue goals. Individuals in a promotion focus are striving toward ideals, wishes, and aspirations. They are concerned with the presence and absence of positive outcomes (gain/nongain) and are more sensitive to positive deviation from the status quo (the difference between "0" and "+1"). In contrast, individuals with prevention focus are concerned with safety and responsibility and with attending to their oughts, duties, and responsibilities. They are concerned with the absence and presence of negative outcomes and are more sensitive to the difference between "0" and "-1."

For example, consider students in the same course who are working to achieve an "A." Some students have a promotion focus orientation toward "A" as something they hope to attain (an ideal). Others have a prevention focus orientation toward an "A" as something they believe they must attain (an ought). With regard to how they pursue their goal, some students read materials beyond assigned readings as an eager way to attain an "A," whereas others are careful to fulfill all course requirements as a vigilant way to attain an "A."

The prevention focus is similar to the concept of loss aversion, which assumes that people evaluate losses more extremely than gains of a similar size (Kahneman and Tversky, 1979). Similar to prevention focus, the loss aversion predicts a general tendency for conservatism and reluctance against novelty. Thus, when individuals find themselves in a state of loss (below status quo), those with prevention focus should be willing to do whatever is necessary to get back to the status quo. In contrast, promotion-focused individuals are motivated to make progress away from the current state, since the status quo holds no special meaning to them. A measure of acceptable change is whether there is advancement away from the current state.

In the context of healthy behavior, promotion-focused individuals are more successful at initiating weight loss and smoking cessation. Prevention-focused individuals are more committed to maintaining and preserving the status quo

(Higgins, 2012). Promotion-focused individuals may rise to the initial challenge more eagerly than prevention-focused individuals.

There is mounting evidence to support the idea that all else being equal, individuals who pursue promotion goals are better off than individuals who pursue prevention or avoidance goals. Individuals who pursue promotion goals rather than avoidance goals have higher, subjective well-being and report fewer physical illness symptoms (Scholer and Higgins, 2010). Avoidance goals might be more likely to elicit anxiety or to increase feelings of threat as they remind an individual of the undesired state to be avoided, undermining effective self-control. For example, Friedman and Foster (2001) have found that individuals in a promotion focus exhibit more creative insight and creative generation than individuals in a prevention focus, in part, because being in a promotion focus encourages eager strategies and leads to a memory search for more novel responses. In contrast, people in a prevention focus are superior in analytical tasks (Friedman and Foster, 2001). Higgins (2012) argues that a promotion orientation is neither inherently good nor bad. It all depends on what end state you want. If you want to emphasize an innovative, creative product, then inducing a promotion orientation with a gain-framed incentive would be a good idea. But if you want to emphasize maintenance, then a nonloss-framed incentive is a good idea.

Regulatory focus may also moderate monitoring tendencies. A prevention focus, because of its concern with the presence and absence of negative outcomes, is likely to increase the tendency to monitor progress toward the end point. Conversely, a promotion focus, because of its concern with the presence or absence of positive outcomes, would increase the tendency to monitor progress from the starting point.

Regulatory focus can be used to make messages advocating change more effective. Messages that fit the receiver's chronic orientation appear to increase the effectiveness of self-regulation. The concept of "regulatory fit" makes people "feel right" about and engage more strongly in what they are doing. People in a prevention focus are convinced more by safety-related information (e.g., "lower risk of getting cancer"). People in a promotion focus are more strongly convinced by growth-related information (e.g., "increases energy"). Thus people assign higher value when they process information in a focus-compatible situation. For example, the goal can be to eat more fruits and vegetables for the sake of protection from harmful daily elements (safety concern), which would commonly induce a prevention orientation. The same message can be presented for the sake of increased energy and general fulfillment (accomplishment concerns), which would commonly induce a promotion orientation.

In short, persuasive messages advocating eating more fruits and vegetables can be framed such that the goal of eating more fruits and vegetables would be pursued in an eager manner or would be pursued in a vigilant manner. Using this way to create regulatory fit messages are more convincing (Cesario et al. 2013). In general, people "feel right" when they pursue life goals in a manner that fits their goal orientation and "feel wrong" when they pursue life goals in a manner that does not fit. For example, the participants in the regulatory fit conditions ate about 20% more fruits and vegetables over the following week than those in the no-fit conditions (Spiegel et al., 2004).

Conclusion

If you want to know whether someone will stick to a given resolution, you'll need to know how realistic or specific the resolution, her motivation to abide by the resolution, the strength of her desire, her level of confidence, the strength of her willpower, and so on. Thus, one's action is determined not simply by the strength of one's desire and one's determination, but also by one's willpower, and the latter component is affected by repeated exercise.

Notes

1 Other terms for self-control include *self-binding, self-discipline, willpower, commitment, self-regulation*, and *constraint theory*.
2 Self-regulation is a broad term that also includes unconscious regulation, judgments, beliefs, expectations, attitudes, and intentions.
3 For example, Montessori preschool instruction, which has been shown to lead to strong academic achievement, incorporates self-control into daily activities.
4 For example, bilingual children are better at learning abstract rules and reversing previously learned rules, even before their first birthday. People who continue to speak both languages as adults show these benefits for a lifetime. Thus, learning a second language strengthens mental flexibility, an aspect of self-control, because the languages interfere with each other and because children must determine which language the listener will understand.
5 For example, Bill Gates as a young computer programmer from Seattle attended high school that happened to have a computer club when almost no other high schools did. He then took advantage of the opportunity to use the computers at the University of Washington for hours. By the time he turned 20, he had spent well more than 10,000 hours as a programmer.
6 The goal may have become a personal rule, as people may fear that exception (goal disengagement) will undermine their ability to exert self-control when similar situations arise in the future (Ainslie, 2001).
7 The study tested whether simply priming people's stored knowledge of the "elderly" (their idea of elderly) could instigate action. Part of people's idea of the elderly is that they walk slowly.
8 Commitment means to pledge or bind oneself to some particular course of action, and for such a pledge to occur, the action must be seen as being worthwhile or accomplishing what's desired.
9 People also reject what they think is beyond their reach, like the fox who judged the unobtainable grapes to be sour (Elster, 2000). Experts say that "playing hard to get" is a most effective strategy for attracting a partner, especially in the context of long-term relationship in which a person wishes to be sure of their partner's commitment.

However, playing hard to get is less effective in men, as they are the ones who are socially expected to initiate the relationship.
10. Overconfidence is particularly prevalent when we estimate the time a task will take. It is called "the planning fallacy." Most people are not very good at predicting the length of time required for completing even commonplace tasks. If you are leaving something to the last minute, there is actually far less time than needed.
11. For example, if I were to try to break into the world of modern dance, after the first few rejections, the logical response might be practice even more. But after the 10,000th rejection, maybe I should realize that this isn't a viable career option.
12. We also experience the act as a kind of investment, which likely results in the sunk cost fallacy kicking in: people generally place too much importance to prior investment when making current decisions.
13. In authoritarian regimes, authority may be internalized, in which case it would be difficult to relax monitoring even without the physical presence of another person who monitors one's actions. For example, President Saparmurat Niyazov of Turkmenistan was a dictator famous because there were pictures or a statue of him in nearly every public space, even on wristwatches.

11
USING SELF-CONTROL STRATEGIES TO MOTIVATE BEHAVIOR CHANGE

Introduction

As discussed, at the core of self-control problems is the human tendency to overvalue immediate benefits relative to delayed benefits. This is referred to as present-biased preferences. People with present-biased preferences are willing to impose greater self-control on their future selves, but once the future becomes the present, they lack the self-control to maintain their long-term goals. The present-biased preferences result in people not behaving in their best interest (e.g., addiction and obesity). They fail to pay adequate attention to the cumulative costs of their daily small decisions. To counter this shortsighted behavior, decision makers employ self-control strategies to protect long-term goals from short-term consumption decisions. A self-control strategy helps a person to commit to behave in a certain way in the future (Elster, 2000). Self-control strategies are considered key drivers of behavior change to promote healthier behavior. These strategies change the value of the behavior by providing individuals with very immediate costs and benefits about their choices. By making immediate reward seem less salient or make the later reward more attractive, an individual can resist the immediate temptation and make choices in keeping with his best long-term goals.

This chapter describes an array of self-control strategies that are effective in helping people maintain long-term goals, using examples from addiction and obesity. These strategies are tools that enable individuals to stick to a new behavior. They are attempts to manage desire. That is, the purpose of self-control strategy is to generate an increase in the motivational strength of long-term goals and a decrease in the motivational strength of temptations. These self-control strategies are organized into external, cognitive, and internal types of commitments (or personal rules), and automatic self-control. External commitment strategies are often used for avoiding sources of temptation (e.g., not having any sweets in your house), or asking for controls. Cognitive strategies involve changing one's thoughts or beliefs about a particular behavior. Personal rules would include rules such as a resolution to smoke only after meals, jog twice a week, always finish what you started, and many similar "promises to oneself." Automatic self-control may occur in the absence of conscious intent and even without the person being aware that they are engaging in goal-directed behavior. When an action becomes automatic, the need for willpower disappears. Collectively, these strategies serve as a crutch aimed at instilling habits that become second nature, initiating actions automatically, such as the habit of brushing one's teeth before bed. They advance the transition from goals (wishes) to goal commitment.

The self-control strategies discussed in this chapter differ from "pure willpower" in that the individual is not simply forcing herself to do something, but is somehow modifying the representation of the task in such a way as to decrease the level of willpower strength that is required. People with the best self-control are those who use their willpower less often by organizing their lives to minimize temptations (Hofmann et al., 2012). In other words, they use self-control strategies to conserve their energy and outsource as much self-control as they can.

External Strategies

External strategies (incentives) are rooted in the theory of "operant conditioning" aimed for behavior modification. In the late 1930s, the late psychologist B.F. Skinner developed the theory of operant conditioning for modifying directly observable behavior. The theory suggests that all organisms tend to do what the external environment rewards them for doing. When an organism is in some way encouraged to perform a certain behavior, and that behavior is "reinforced" (rewarded by food, comfort, or money), the organism is more likely to repeat the behavior. If the behavior is repeated enough times, the behavior becomes habitual (Freedman, 2012). For example, the Weight Watcher aims are to gradually build healthy eating habits by rewarding routines in daily life. The key aspect of the Weight Watchers program is the support and encouragement they provide to help their clients gradually establish healthful eating and moderate exercise.

Cue Management

This form of self-control refers to people's attempts to choose situations that make it more (or less) likely that they will experience impulses that lead to desirable (or undesirable) behaviors. The ideal place to intervene is usually at the beginning, which involves avoiding the occasions that trigger the desire to indulge. For example, people who want to quit smoking often learn that they must stop drinking as well, because alcohol serves as a cue for cigarette craving and also causes disinhibition. It is also recommended that people who want to stop drinking or smoking avoid places where these activities go on. Society may reduce the cues that influence consumption. In the case of smoking, the government assists in removing cues to smoke, including the smoking ban and government mandate that may require packages to contain vivid and frightening images to emphasize the dangers of smoking. The sign imposes psychic costs on smoking (Sunstein, 2014).

To motivate healthy behavior, the United Kingdom Food Standards Agency (FSA) used the traffic light symbols to draw upon strong consumer associations between red and "stop" (for less healthy foods) and green and "go" (for healthier foods). In a hospital cafeteria field study, traffic light labeling was effective at increasing the sale of healthy foods labeled green and decreasing the sale of less healthy foods labeled as red (Thorndike et al. 2012). Google uses a sign in its cafeteria stating, "[p]eople who take big plates tend to eat more." The combination of this nudge and increased healthful choices has produced a real reduction in food intake. In short, these cues are used to substitute for individuals' limited willpower to avoid sources of temptation. It is better to engineer the decision context so that it is impossible to succumb to a weakness of will, rather than to rely on one's ability to resist temptation.

Eliminating Options

This strategy allows a person who foresees being tempted by a particular stimulus in the future to take measures in the present that will prevent him from giving in to the future temptation. This strategy might take the form of fully eliminating the alternative that is currently unwanted but likely to be preferred by one's future self. By doing so, the individual might limit his freedom of action. For example, addicts make efforts to keep temptation at a distance or out of sight, such as the practice of having no alcoholic beverages at home so that one has to go a store to get it. An addict may eliminate the option for drug use at least in the short run by checking into a remote treatment facility. A gambler may leave his wallet in the hotel room, carrying only a limited amount of cash into the casino. When the money is gone, the temptation to gamble more has already been eliminated. Individuals who have a gastric bypass procedure (stapling stomach) drastically reduce their capacity to overeat. A shopaholic may decide to leave her credit card at home to avoid impulse purchases of tempting goods. Parents may use this strategy to discourage youths' sedentary behaviors by making sedentary alternatives less desirable. For example, parents could locate video game systems in an unheated, unfinished basement to reduce video game playing. In short, the essence of this strategy is to lock yourself into a "virtuous" path: you make it impossible to leave the path.

Imposing Reward and Cost

These self-control strategies influence the objective value of options in the choice situation by attaching penalties to temptation and rewards to high-level goal pursuit. The purpose is to bring forward the benefits of undertaking desirable activities, or of avoiding undesirable ones. For example, some former alcoholics try to stay dry by taking disulfiram (Antabuse), a drug that has the effect of making the user violently ill if one takes a drink. Within a few minutes of ingesting alcohol, the user will experience severe nausea and vomiting. The drug helps people avoid drinking for about a week.[1] Rewards for health-related behavior are a key feature of German health insurance systems.[2] The individuals are offered bonuses for participating in check-up programs, dieting, and smoking cessation. The bonuses usually take the form of reductions in copayments (Schmidt et al., 2012).

The imposing cost strategy involves voluntary attachment of a monetary fine for failure to act according to long-term goals or preferences. For example, joining a health club is the penalty of monetary loss if one fails to show up regularly ("I paid $600, I better use it").[3] One may be required to pay a relatively large cancellation fee for missing a painful medical test.

Bryan and Hershfield (2012) argue that one reason that we ignore the future consequences is that we don't like to think about ourselves in the distant future, perhaps because we do not like to imagine ourselves as old. However, this tendency can be avoided by reminding the person that when you give in to a temptation, you are imposing a long-term cost or damage to a loved one under your care who happens to be your future self.

At a policy level, there is a large body of literature indicating that increasing prices or taxes on unhealthy activities is an effective means of changing behavior.[4] Policies to increase tobacco taxes appear to have substantial benefits in discouraging smoking activities. Similarly, evidence on the effect of alcohol prices on consumption suggests that adolescents are price responsive and some studies have found that both alcohol participation and binge drinking are responsive to alcohol prices (Saffer and Dave, 2006).

Contingency Management

Similar to imposing cost and reward, contingency management is a tool for the treatment of addiction that decreases the rewarding effect of a drug (or increase the cost of drug use). That is, the reward is contingent on abstinence and the delivery of punishment contingent on drug use. For example, an addict, upon providing a urine test that is negative for signs of drug use, receives a voucher worth of a certain monetary value. Similar to a voucher, AA meetings provide an alternative social reward (going to meetings and getting praised for staying sober) to drug use.

Contingency management interventions are among the best studied to promote abstinence by altering an addict's environment to reduce the incentive to use drugs (Higgins et al., 2002). However, it appears that making punishment contingent on giving in to temptation is more effective than making rewards contingent on goal adherence because people are more averse to prospective losses than to gains. The concept of loss aversion implies that losses loom larger than gains (about twice as large). When it comes to incentives, people hate giving up something they already own. They work twice as hard to avoid the loss than to secure a reward of equal amount. The concept of loss aversion may explain why subsidizing healthy food options tends to be less effective in promoting healthy eating compared to raising the price, such as taxing (Cawley, 2011).

Alternative Rewards

The availability and value of alternatives (e.g., social activity, employment) to drug use are an important source of treatment. For example, individuals who have a number of enjoyable alternatives to drinking may have an easier time reducing their consumption of alcohol. On the other hand, events like the loss of a friend, family members, or job, or moving to a new environment, are likely to result in the reduction of nondrug rewards.

As discussed before, chronic drug use raises the dopamine reward threshold, making nondrug alternatives (work, relationship, school, and hobbies) less enjoyable and a poor substitute for the immediate benefits of drug use. Evidence shows that study participants generally show a greater preference for drug use when the value of the alternative reward is small due to delay or high price. Studies also reveal that alternative drug-free incentives are significantly associated with increased motivation to change drug use patterns (Vuchinch and Heather, 2003). Thus, efforts to improve employment prospects, family relationships, and social interactions provide important treatment interventions.

Deciding by Default

The purpose of this strategy is to exploit automaticity. Default rules make decisions automatic and avoid using willpower. An excellent way to serve people's interests is to establish the default rule that if they do nothing at all, things will go well for them. The initial (default) position biases a preference for keeping things as they are. In short, the default rule creates a nudge that influences individuals' behavior without restricting individual choice.

Thaler and Sunstein (2008) show that "defaults" and "starting points" matter. So, for instance, if workers are automatically enrolled in a pension plan, but with the freedom to opt out if they wish, most stay in. But if they are not automatically enrolled, but have to make a conscious decision to opt in, then most stay out. The use of default in the organ donor process (one is automatically assumed to be an organ donor) has resulted an increase in organs available for transplants (Johnson and Goldstein, 2003). Thus, significantly more people are willing to be donors when the default is to be a donor than when an active choice must be made to be a donor.

The default rule can be used to encourage healthy choices without using willpower. For example, fast food restaurants that now offer soda as the default choice with a combo meal can instead make a bottle of water the default option, with soda being a substitution available only on request. The Walt Disney Company has changed the default for children's meals at their theme parks. The meals now include healthier side dishes and beverages (e.g., apples and water) as the default instead of fries and soft drinks. Thus, reframing the default option (choice context) nudges people towards good decisions, while they have the right to make bad ones. Defaults are sticky—people stay in them. If healthy foods are easily accessible, people are far more likely to choose them. People may continue with the status quo because of procrastination and inertia. The strong effects of inertia are manifested in habits, which are largely effortless and automatic (Fishbein and Ajzen, 2010). For example, many people consume more food at dinner than at lunch or breakfast, simply because they have done so in the past. Thus, to promote healthier eating, the healthiest option (smaller portion) could be set as the default option.

Social Norms

People are often influenced by the social norms. Our behavior is influenced by the people around us. Social norms are the behavioral expectations within a community (Mesquita et al., 2014). We learn from other people around us what is appropriate, and what is practical (herd behavior). Norms can be explicitly stated or implicitly observed behavior. Social norms become internalized goals, values, meanings, and thus translate into behavioral tendencies. For example, students drink more on campuses that have a strong drinking culture.

Social norms are a central part of society's choice architecture and count as a significant nudge equivalent to subsidies and taxes. Social norms motivate individuals take their cues from what others do and use their perceptions of norms as a standard against which to compare their own behavior. For example, at funerals, we know that laughing, expressing joy, or feeling glad that the person is dead is incompatible with the group's norm. In most neighborhoods, dog owners carry plastic bags when they walk their dogs. This has happened in the absence any law against not doing so. The negative emotional experience of embarrassment, shame, and guilt that arise from social misdeeds (Tangney and Dearing, 2003) is enough to guarantee these behaviors. These emotions are sufficiently unpleasant (psychic costs) that, once given a taste, people are highly motivated to regulate their behavior so as to avoid experiencing them. For example, in many communities, the social norm/attitude for smoking has changed. Consider the changing attitude toward smoking from, *Would you like a cigarette*, to *Do you mind if I smoke?* and now, *Yes, I do mind, get out of my face*. To influence behavior, youths are often provided with objective information that the use of drugs and alcohol is the exception not the norm. Thus, if you want to reduce drug use among young people, tell them how many are doing so.

Public Pledges

This strategy relies on the fact that humans care intensely about how they are perceived. When we make public pledges and then are reminded that we are not living up to those pledges, we effectively turn the people around us into our enforcers. We feel that the eyes of our friends and colleagues are on us and that they are degrading us. Self-reputation gives force to self-control. Social context matters and you are more likely to succeed if keeping your promise is a matter of honor. For example, people sometimes use the tactic of promising another person that they will make a checkup appointment by the end of the month, which creates a social pressure to carry through with their promise. This tactic creates a future social penalty to keep the promise. Making a public commitment of your intention to act puts the social spotlight on you. It boosts your egotism and pressures you to follow through in a courageous way.

Cognitive Strategies

Cognitive strategies involve changing one's thoughts or beliefs about a particular behavior. Cognitive strategies help us to find a way to make the situation work for us. We may not be able to control the external environment, but we can control how we think about it. These self-control strategies involve shifts in one's cognitive approach to an aversive task.

Mental Representation of Goal and Reward

This strategy relates to our ability to access cold cognition (e.g., focus on the negative side of the chocolate cake—calories, reappraise a donut as an efficient calorie delivery system rather than a tasty snack). A good example of this strategy is the research on delay of gratification by Metcalfe and Mischel (1999). In the study, children were better able to delay gratification when actively reinterpreting a tempting food in a manner designed to reduce its affective qualities (e.g., likening marshmallows to clouds), or distracting themselves by thinking about something else. The transformation of hot and motivating representations ("it looks yummy") into cool ones ("it looks like a cloud") facilitate willpower in the delay of gratification. When attention is not focused on the tempting reward stimuli, it makes sustained delay of gratification less effortful. The crucial skill was the way children allocated their attention. Instead of getting obsessed with the "hot stimulus," the children distracted themselves by avoiding thinking about the marshmallow. In a laboratory and one web-based laboratory, Hofmann et al. (2012) found that participants instructed to imagine a tempting food stimulus (chocolate) in unconsumable ways exhibited reduced positive automatic evaluations toward the chocolate than control participants and participants instructed to focus on consumable aspects.

In sum, the cognitive transformation of a tempting stimulus can influence the degree of automatic evaluation elicited by this stimulus. This mental transformation makes the tempting object less real. By being less real, its motivational force (its pull) is reduced, which makes it easier to delay gratification. The takeaway lesson is that attention management helps. Thinking about the things in an abstract way (the crunchy, salty pretzel might be construed as tasteless, miniature logs) reduces temptation.

Thought Suppression

Thought suppression refers to the deliberate act of trying to force the unwanted information out of your awareness.[5] Thought suppression can be considered a type of attentional deployment. However, this is not an easy task because of the paradoxical increase in unwanted thoughts that occurs subsequent to thought suppression. Like trying to sink a cork in water, the issue won't go away. In a classic experiment, when the subjects were asked not think about white bears for few minutes, they failed to suppress their thought about white bears. The white bear doesn't go away. It keeps intruding into your thought, a phenomenon the researchers referred to as a *rebound effect* (Wegner and Schneider, 2003). Similarly, trying not to think of cake makes you yearn for it more. Thus, suppression might actually produce the very thought it is intended to stifle. Research has supported this notion and confirms repeated failure by people to successfully suppress unwanted thoughts (Wenzlaff and Wegner, 2000). The research suggests that thought suppression just does not work. Persistence creates resistance; the more you try to push thoughts out, the bigger they get.

Psychologist Dan Wegner notes that whenever we try not to think about, for example, a stressful event, our mind unconsciously starts calling attention to itself to see whether or not the mind is achieving its goal. The end result, of course, is that we obsess over the one thing we're trying to avoid. To make sure you aren't thinking about white bears, you have to watch out for violations. Ironically, by actively suppressing thoughts, you help to maintain them. This mechanism forms the basis of Freudian slips; trying to repress a trauma or a temptation seems to cause the dreaded idea to surface. Thought suppression is a popular technique used to (ineffectively) combat homosexual urges or racial stereotypes. This also suggests that those who habitually use thought suppression to cope paradoxically strengthen connections with the kind of negative cognitive contents they seek to bar from their attention. What we resist persists. That is, our attempts to force the mind can rebound in exactly the opposite direction.

Addicts, such as smokers or heavy drinkers, know this confusion too well.[6] The lack of success in the ability to suppress unwanted negative thought is related to lack of success in quitting smoking. Simply trying to suppress craving-related thoughts is an ineffective coping strategy. The effort to suppress a craving for a smoke or a drink can bring to mind all the reasons to give in to the habit. At the same time, the craving seemingly gets stronger. A certain relief can come from just getting it over with, having that worst thing happen, so you don't have to worry about monitoring in anymore. As discussed before, instead of avoiding thinking about your temptation, you can mentally distance yourself from it by framing your temptation in terms of its abstract and symbolic features. For example, to delay eating cake, you should, rather than focusing on its taste and texture, focus on the snack's shape and color. By changing the focus, you tip the balance away from the stimuli-driven limbic system toward the abstraction-loving prefrontal cortex, enabling us to make a better choice. You can attribute negative qualities and consequences to every temptation to counteract its enticing features.

So, what is the solution to the problem of thought suppression? The secret is to not make an effort to suppress your thought, just move on, and your thought will naturally move to other things. If you truly wanted to stop thinking of a white bear, you would be better off allowing yourself to think of one, and then after a while, the thought would naturally go away. The attempt to actively suppress a disturbing thought, to fight it and block it, can increase the frequency of such thoughts. Accepting cravings as transient feelings may make it easier to disengage from the thought. Acceptance is defined as the process of non-judgmentally engaging with negative emotions (Kabat-Zinn, 1990).

Construal Level Theory (CLT): Seeing the Bigger Picture

As noted above, an important strategy for resisting temptation is to change how the temptation and the preferred alternative are represented or construed. The temporal construal theory suggests that people may form abstract representations of distant future events than near-future events (Trope and Liberman, 2010). From a distant perspective, choices are made based primarily on global concerns, whereas from proximal perspective, those priorities are weakened and even reversed as local concerns become more prominent. As people get psychologically closer to the situation, their choices are increasingly influenced by more specific concerns.

The basic premise of CLT is that distance is linked to the level of mental construal. A broader perspective allows us to consider multiple aspects of a situation. From a distant perspective, one sees the forest, but from a proximal perspective, one sees trees. Temporal distance increases the weight of high-level value and decreases the weight of low-level value. As a result, time delay shifts the overall attractiveness of an option closer to its high-level value than to its low-level value. Details about options become available and clear only as one gets closer in time to the events. As the saying goes, the devil is in the details. For example, a task like "maintaining good physical health" might be associated with high-level attributes like the joy of a healthy lifestyle. When we decide on a diet, we do so because the construal of its outcomes seems attractive to us. However, there are also low-level attributes associated with this task such as going to gym, avoiding your favorite snack, and so on. The present places greater importance on feasibility, while the future focuses on desirable attributes.[7] Therefore, desirability concerns receive greater weight over feasibility concerns as psychological distance increases.

Thinking about an activity in high-level (lofty thoughts or long-term goals) is related to "why," and low-level is related "how" questions. Thus, having individuals think about why they engaged in an action may remind them about the ultimate value or desirability of pursuing it. On the other hand, responding to questions related to how they engaged in an action may have prompted individuals to consider a means to pursue a goal, and be primarily concerned with the goal's attainability. "Why" questions push the mind up to higher levels of thinking and a focus on the future, and "How" questions bring the mind down to low levels of thinking and a focus on the present. Thus, self-control becomes easier when people ask themselves why they are doing an activity (a high-level abstract construal) rather than how they are doing it (a low-level concrete construal).

In sum, options that are rich in high-level attributes but poor in low-level attributes (details) will appear very attractive from a great distance, but not so from near distance. Thinking about situations in a more abstract way (consistent with long-term goals) leads to greater self-control than does thinking about the same situation in a more concrete way (emphasizing short-term temptations that conflict with the long-term self-control goal).

Creating Delays (Cooling-Off Period)

The goal of this strategy is to put more time between the person and his ability to act. By doing so, we won't fall prey to basing decisions entirely on what happens to be in our mind in the immediate moment. The mere passage of time can lower the intensity of desire. Strong emotions often dissipate with time. As the saying goes, "wait a while, if you still want it later, it may be important." If the desire passes, it probably wasn't that important. We usually get into trouble when we act impulsively without thinking things through. In general, when people contemplate any action for days (or weeks), they may choose differently. This is captured by the common advice to "sleep on" a decision.

Cooling-off laws enacted at both the state and federal level allows consumers to return certain types of purchases within a few days of the transactions. Such laws can be viewed as devices for combating the effects of projection bias[8] and the salespersons' incentives to hype. Cooling-off periods that force consumers to reflect on their decisions for several days can decrease the likelihood that they end up owning products that they should not.

Strategic Ignorance

People also attempt to reduce the intensity of temptation, the gap between their long- and short-run preferences through strategic ignorance or self-deception about the costs and benefits of perseverance or indulgence (Carrillo and Mariotti,

2000; Benabou and Tirole, 2002). One of the most difficult problems in sustaining goals is how to persist in the face of negative feedback. Strategic ignorance can help to achieve persistence. If, for instance, a person is deciding whether to embark on a specific project, she has the option to get feedback from colleagues about the likely fruitfulness of that project. The rational thinking implies having more information allows people to make better decisions. However, strategic ignorance requires not acquiring information because doing so increases the likelihood of changing one's mind. In many situations, people have the option to acquire information about the costs and benefits of their actions, but they don't. For example, individuals with inaccurately exaggerated estimates of the risk of smoking may remain strategically ignorant of the true risk in order to increase their determination to avoid smoking.

Mental Accounting

This self-control strategy can lead people to view different types of money allocations in fundamentally different ways. Mental accounting involves dividing your money into separate mental accounts that you treat differently, such as accounts for entirely discretionary or luxury spending (Thaler and Sunstein, 2008). For example, spending $100 out of $300 earmarked for fun will feel more meaningful than pulling out $100 from your entire $3,000 monthly budget. Individuals or families earmark certain sources of income to specific uses or keep in separate envelopes or "tin cans" the monies reserved for food, rent, school supplies, "fun," and the like. Spending is constrained by the amount in different accounts. When there are two parents with different preferences, envelopes and tin cans are also ways of monitoring the other (e.g., prevent "drinking the school money").

The idea that money is not fungible but is set aside for a specific purpose is engrained in consumers' vocabularies early on with terms such as "lunch money," "rainy day funds," and "mad money." People are far more likely to splurge impulsively on a big luxury purchases when they receive an unexpected windfall (e.g., tax refund) than with savings that they have accumulated over time, even if those savings are fully available to spend.

Emotion Regulation

Emotion regulation is another important self-control strategy. The ability to modify our emotional responses is a core feature of self-control. Emotion regulation generally results from emotional conflict. That is, two incompatible emotional inclinations operate at the same time. For example, one is afraid but keeps firm in the face of danger; or one avoids unsafe sex by visualizing the next morning's anxiety (Frijda, 2013). Emotion regulation serves to deal with such conflicts.

One can engage in emotion regulation in several ways (Werner and Gross, 2010). The first step is pausing and not immediately reacting to events. Pausing for a moment gives a person some breathing room, and it allows space for the emotion to begin to arise free of any interference. Second, one needs to be aware of one's emotional experience and be able to label it, since emotions differ in their manifestations. Third, one needs to determine how controllable the situation is that caused the emotion. For events that are out of one's control, adaptive regulation is to accept the situation and experience it. Fourth, one needs to act in line with one's long-term goal. This involves the ability to inhibit/control inappropriate or impulsive behaviors and act in accordance with desired goals when experiencing negative emotions. These steps are like the volume dial, rather than the on-off switch, of a radio. Implementing emotion regulation strategies that limit the intensity of negative affect could bolster an individual's ability to cope with adverse situations.

The emotion regulation literature has demonstrated that affective responses can be modulated using reappraisal, a strategy that involves deliberately controlling how one cognitively appraises the meaning of an affective stimulus (Gross, 2014). Cognitive reappraisal refers to changing how we appraise the situation we are in to alter its emotional significance, either by changing how we think about the situation or about our capacity to manage the demand it poses (e.g., the common suggestion to "imagine your audience naked when you are nervous in public speaking").

Individual explanatory style is a key appraisal that leads to negative or positive emotions. Explanatory style refers to how individuals habitually explain the causes of events and thereby influence the emotions they experience. A pessimistic explanatory style encourages individuals to believe that they are helpless, that nothing they do matters. Why bother? An optimistic explanation style encourages individuals to believe that their behaviors do affect outcomes. Those with a more optimistic style see minor hassles as sources of amusement or as challenges, whereas those with a more pessimistic style see them as catastrophes. Consider, for example, the attitude: "I must perform important tasks (e.g., losing weight) well and be approved by people I find important, or else I am an inadequate, worthless person!" This kind of self-downing is most common in depressed people. It's as if we wage a war against ourselves.

Reappraisal is the basis of cognitive behavioral therapy (CBT), which was developed by Aaron Beck. CBT is an effective way to change dysfunctional thoughts or beliefs and provide strategies for viewing future adverse events in more optimistic ways. This form of therapy is designed to enable depressed people to reevaluate the cognitive processing of information in more realistic, neutral terms. The core aspect of CBT holds that cognitions usually influence emotions and behaviors and, in the case of dysfunctional thoughts and cognitive distortions, contribute to the maintenance of negative emotions and harmful behaviors. The therapy focuses on evaluating the rationality of negative appraisals and substituting more realistic or evidence-based appraisals.[9] The role of therapists is to help patients first learn to accept themselves as they are (unconditional self-acceptance) and then to retrain themselves to avoid destructive emotions. In short, the CBT argues that people are capable of change and they can be liberated from misconceptions and learn to live their lives in a way that will leave them less prone to mental illness.[10]

In the case of addiction, CBT attempts to disrupt the learned association between drug-related cues and craving or use (Carroll, 1998). The goal of CBT is to help the addict to "unlearn" old, ineffective behaviors and "learn" new ones. The first task is to identify the high-risk situations in which the addict is likely to use drugs and thus to provide the basis for learning more effective coping strategies in those situations. For each instance of drug use experiences, the addict is required to identify the thoughts, feelings, and circumstances before the use, as well as the thoughts, feelings, and circumstances after the episode of drug use. The final component of CBT is skills training, such as reappraisal, and developing meaningful alternate rewards (relationships, work) to drug use.

Abstinence Violation Effect (AVE)

The AVE occurs when an individual views his relapse as a deviation from his commitment to absolute abstinence (Marlatt and Gordon, 1985). For example, an individual who has successfully abstained from alcohol, after having one beer, may engage in binge drinking, thinking that since she has "fallen off the wagon" she might as well drink an entire case of beer. The response often creates a feeling of self-blame and loss of perceived self-control. At a loss for why they lapsed, addicts attribute their drug use to immutable dispositional character traits (e.g., "I just stopped thinking. Obviously, I just don't have what it takes to quit smoking"). This reaction may in part be caused by a failure to recognize the changes in cognitive and decision-making processes that have occurred while in a state of craving. The AA calls this line of biased thinking as "a drink equals a drunk." But understanding and overcoming AVE is crucial to overcoming relapse. The most constructive way of perceiving relapse is to identify circumstantial factors that made it difficult to persist, and make plans for the future commitments. Successfully resisting and continued abstinence contribute to increased self-efficacy and self-confidence. Thus, the way an individual appraises the lapse is a key to sustaining long-term abstinence (Marlatt and Witkiewitz, 2005).

When an abstinence violation occurs, the attributions an individual makes play an important part in determining the trajectory of subsequent use. Attributions are explanations individuals give for the causes of events. People use different kinds of information when assigning causes to behaviors. For example, the person who gets drunk after an extended period of abstinence could make a variety of attributions about his behavior, and these attributions can affect his subsequent use. Internal attributions such as "I just don't have much self-control," or "I have a character flaw and therefore I simply can't control my actions," are likely to be associated with giving up sobriety. When abstinence is violated, individuals typically also have an emotional response consisting of guilt, shame, hopelessness, loss of control, and a sense of failure. They use drugs or alcohol in an attempt to cope with the negative feelings that resulted from their abstinence violation.

In sum, attributions often lie at the core of success and failures of self-control. An event with attributions emphasizing situational or external causes (or exceptional factors) will more likely be viewed as a mistake which can be learned from and allow one to go with new knowledge and be better prepared for similar, future situations vs a certain conclusion that one is "doomed" or "destined" to return to addiction.

Self-Immersed vs. Self-Distanced

How can individuals face negative emotions without becoming overwhelmed by them? Emotions are partial in the sense that they are focused on a narrow target. This partiality contradicts the broad perspective discussed above. Suppose that yesterday, your coworker said something that offended you deeply. You were so irritated, and all afternoon you suffered. But this morning, all of a sudden you have a different perspective. The whole matter that had caused you so much suffering suddenly seems insignificant. The passage of one day has broadened your perspective, and now you feel relief because you are seeing the bigger picture. It is remarkable how petty some issues become after the passage of just one day.

Cognitive reconstrual (interpretation) strategies are effective in reducing negative affect. Focusing on negative experiences from a self-immersed perspective is not the only vantage point people can adopt while thinking about a past event (e.g., romantic breakup). Adopting a self-distanced perspective to analyze negative feelings would reduce people's tendency to reflexively recount what happened to them. For example in a study when participants recount what happened to them in a situation (e.g., "he told me to back off," or "I was so angry"), the emotions experienced became more accessible. In contrast, participants who analyzed their feelings from a self-distanced perspective were able to reconstrue their experience in cool ways (e.g., "I understand why the argument happened"). Thus the more reconstruing and less recounting participants engaged in, the less negative affect they displayed (Kross and Ayduk, 2008). Thus, self-distancing facilitates adaptive self-reflection, whereas self-immersion would undermine it. Self-distancing facilitates the activation of relatively abstract representations of the reasons underlying the negative experience (e.g., "because we had a difference in opinion"). Such abstract construals should enable the individual to focus on her negative emotions, but without increasing negative arousal.[11]

In short, as we "stand too close" to a decision-making problem, absorbed by our own information and constraints, we may overlook how the decision-making problem affects others. When our focus is too narrow, it can lead us to miss the big picture. A wider scope would help us capture and integrate important details.

Fight Emotion with Emotion

This strategy involves the cultivation of an emotion to forestall the development of a contrary one. Francis Bacon once remarked that "reason did not have its own force, but had to get its way by playing one passion against another" (Damasio, 2003). That is, reason has to acquire the same kind of power, the same motivation that passions have, if it is sometimes to overcome them.[12]

Thus, the individual may train himself to care less about certain desires, or even to find them repulsive, by associating them with vivid, disgusting images (e.g., fatty foods with images of clogged arteries), and conversely by pairing positive images with delayed-gratification actions (receiving an award, achieving success, etc.). For example, the alcoholic struggling to maintain abstinence may direct attention away from activities that lead to drinking, or cultivate an emotional revulsion to them. Another strategy would be to think about how one would feel after breaking one's diet. Research on condom use has shown that anticipated regret about having unsafe sex increased condom use. One important way to manage fear is to become strategically angry. The emotion of fear holds us back from action. On the other hand, the emotion of anger can override our doubts about our abilities and lead us to take action (Lerner and Kelter, 2001).

Personal Rules

Personal rules (or internal commitments) are forms of personal capital that individuals create as a means of overcoming self-control problems (or present bias). The idea here is that we seek to strengthen the will rather than relying on external controls. Having personal rules as a self-control strategy helps people see current decisions as predictors of future behavior and the awareness of this linkage helps them overcome temptation. Personal rules are promises to cooperate with the individual's own subsequent motivational states (Ainslie, 2001). Ainslie attributes personal rules to coalitions of long-range and short-range interests that form around personal rules. A personal rule may take two forms: a ban on consumption of a particular kind of small rewards (e.g., cigarettes) or restriction on the circumstances under which the small rewards may be indulged (e.g., drinking is only permitted on social occasion).

The basic idea for this strategy comes from turning individual choices into a matter of principle. The strategy requires perceiving a clear link between behavior today and behavior in the future, which transforms the impulsive act from an isolated decision into a pattern of behavior. For example, smokers can reason that if they break their resolutions to give up smoking, they won't quit smoking for good.

As discussed, hyperbolic discounting is an expression of a "divided self," which predicts preference reversal or intrapersonal dilemma (multiple selves). The individual who, in the morning, prefers to avoid overeating may be aware that this preference is in danger of being defeated by her future self in the evening. Further, this reversal of preference will lead to regret afterward. This conflict between current and future selves can be illustrated in a game-theoretic context (prisoner's dilemma). In this model, a person is described as a sequence of "selves" distributed over time: you will not be (entirely) the same person tomorrow as you are today.

In the prisoner's dilemma, two accomplices are arrested and interrogated in separate rooms. The authorities give each prisoner the same choice: confess your shared guilt (in effect, betray your partner) or remain silent (and be loyal to your partner). If one betrays and the other stays silent, the defector goes free, and the silent, loyal one spends ten years in jail. If both remain loyal, both get six months. If both betray the other, both get five years. Each person has the temptation to cheat the other to gain lower punishment. When both players pursue their own self-interest, both do worse than they would have if somehow they could have jointly and credibly agreed that each would remain silent. In short, the outcomes of strategic interactions depend on the choices of others as well as on one's own choices.

	Cooperate	Cheat
Cooperate	6m, 6m	10y, 0y
Cheat	0y, 10y	5y, 5y

Payoff Matrix in the Prisoner's Dilemma

Similarly, the self-control behavior can be modeled as game theory among successive selves within an individual. If you see yourself violating your diet today, you reduce your expectation that your diet will succeed. In the "what the hell effect," once dieters lapse, they figure the day's diet is blown anyway, so they go on to finish the whole carton of ice cream, thereby doing far more damage than the original lapse. By this logic, an individual has incentives to develop a self-enforcing cooperative arrangement with his future selves. When you make an agreement and you don't keep it, you undermine your own self-trust. You can fool everybody but yourself, and you are going to pay for that, so you should be aware of the agreements you make.

Likewise, the strategic action that can be taken by the present self to forestall an anticipated reversal of preference is to find a method to precommit (cooperate) to the currently desired alternative. For instance, an alcoholic who wants to quit might be willing to avoid drinking tonight if she thinks that she will not drink in the future, but not if she thinks that she will soon start again. Knowledge that she was able to overcome the desire to drink last night might make her more confident that she will be able to overcome the desire in the future, and thus more likely to resist tonight. In short, if early selves resist temptation, future selves will be optimistic about their own ability to resist, but if early selves never overcome temptation, later selves will be more skeptical. Thus, a lapse damages self-credibility.

Bundling Choices ("If Not Now, When?")

The understanding of the intrapersonal dilemma implies making choice in a whole bundle (global approach). The decision to stop smoking is in effect a decision to begin a pattern of behavior. Not smoking tonight makes it easier not to smoke tomorrow and not smoking tomorrow makes it easier not to smoke the next day, and so on. The idea is that the individual should come to see each decisions as a possible predictor of future ones, so that giving in today raises the probability that he will do the same in the future (Ainslie, 2001). By tying together sequences of choices, the individual aligns his short-term incentives with his long-run interests. The fear of creating precedents and losing faith in oneself then creates an incentive that helps counter the bias toward instant gratification.

Howard Rachlin (2000) argues that self-control comes from choosing "patterns" of behavior over time rather than individual "acts." While the physical independence of today and tomorrow is real enough, the fact remains that actions today affect actions tomorrow. The decision to stop smoking is in effect a decision to begin a pattern of behavior. To smoke the cigarette tonight is to fail to perceive the connection between tonight's act and the pattern of acts over many nights and days. This approach emphasizes the significant cost of accumulated indulgence. The smoker who says "one cigarette won't kill me" perceives the indulgence in isolation with the negligible consequence. The patterns of choice motivate people to be less impulsive. In the context of food choice, if one's pattern of "a healthy breakfast" consists of juice, cereal, a bran muffin, and skim milk, then this person would not substitute apple pie for the bran muffin, because it would break up the pattern.[13] Viewing indulgence in isolation provides a psychological license to indulge (Khan and Dhar, 2006). Psychological licensing reflects a failure to see a single indulgence as a self-control conflict, because people assume their behavior to be different in the future.

In sum, personal rules (establishing the so-called red-line separating approved and disapproved behavior) help a person to motivate herself to resist the temptation if she believes that failing to resist this time will make futures resistance less likely. For an addict, the recovery requires a measure of integration between his different selves, and between his past and his present. Thus, it is not a good idea to make many sorts of decisions on a case-by-case basis (local choice). On a case-by-case basis, most of us would be having that second dessert or drinking that third martini at a party. Moreover, personal rules lower deliberative efforts (exerting willpower) that might otherwise be engaged by each specific instance of temptation. Thus, individuals achieve some degree of self-control relying on their internal incentives, rather than manipulation of external cues.

Automatic Self-Control

The strategies discussed so far have considered self-control to be a conscious, active process. Automatic self-control strategy may occur in the absence of conscious intent (Gollwitzer et al., 2010). This strategy can make self-control more automatic, and therefore less reliant on willpower strength. The automatic self-control strategy helps to develop habits that reduce the demands on our cognition. Automaticity refers to the absence of control. Automatic behaviors are contrasted with deliberate and attention-demanding aspects of cognition.

The repeated pursuing of a goal via a certain course of behavior builds a strong cognitive link between the goal representation and the representation of behavior. Therefore, that activation of a goal can automatically lead to the activation of the habitual means for goal pursuit. Habits refer to the unconscious execution of goal-directed behavior. For example, we do not have to consider all available supermarkets when having to do the groceries, since the goal of grocery shopping automatically activates the representation of the store we usually go to. The goal-directed habits diminish the role of conscious process in the regulation of behavior.

For larger goals to have influence on behavior, it is often beneficial to break them down into manageable, smaller goals. It is all very well to have a larger goal in mind, but without breaking it down into the necessary elements that direct behavior in specific ways, it is harder to execute. From this view, the psychologist Gollwitzer (1999) has proposed two distinct types of intention: goal intentions and implementation intentions. Goal intentions are focused on the end-point, the achievement of a particular outcome that is desired, such as losing weight. Implementation intentions, by contrast, are focused on how the task is going to be accomplished (e.g., after completing the breakfast, I am going to walk for one hour.). Implementation intentions are like subgoals in that they specify how the larger goal should be pursued, but they are also special for another reason. The specific intention is paired with an external cue, such that it is executed when the external cue is encountered in the environment. This takes the pressure off the individual to internally cue the action.

In short, this strategy makes distinction between goal intentions and implementation intentions. Typically implementation intentions work in the service of goal intentions. Having just a goal intention is not enough. One will have to deliberate about how to implement it, and one may either forget to do so or simply decide to procrastinate. For example, maintaining a diet goal may get difficult when certain internal stimuli (e.g., cravings for junk foods, ego depletion, or negative moods) or external stimuli (e.g., temptation and distraction) could potentially derail the ongoing goal. Implementation intention strategy facilitates the shielding of such goal pursuit from these interferences.

If-Then Plan

Gollwitzer (1999) shows that by transforming goals into a specific contingency plan, such as in the form "if X, then Y" (for example, "if I see a pastry, then I will avoid it"), we can markedly increase the chance of success. The furnishing of a goal intention with an implementation intention provides the person a better chance of ultimately attaining the desired goal. Whereas goal intentions in the format "I intend to achieve outcome X or to perform behavior X" describe desired end states and represent the result of the process of goal setting, implementation intentions additionally spell out in advance when, where, and how these goals should be realized. Implementation intentions automate the initiation of the action specified in the *then* component as soon as the critical situation presents itself. Forming an if-then plan automates goal striving by strategically linking critical situations (e.g., encountering a temptation) to goal-directed responses (e.g., coping with temptations). Thus, by forming an if-then plan, the rational agent (the deliberate and cool mindset) takes conscious control away from the hot, vulnerable future self. For example, an implementation intention that serves the goal intention of getting an A in a course would follow the form "*if* my roommate ask me to go out tonight, *then* I will say that I will join them next week." Such plans produce automatic behavior by intentionally delegating the control of one's goal-directed thoughts, feelings, and behaviors to specific situational cues (Gollwitzer, et al., 2010).

The implementation creates a strong link between a situational cue (if-component) and a goal-directed response (then-component). This means that the person doesn't have to exert deliberate effort when behavior is controlled by the implementation intention strategy. As a result, the self should not become depleted. Using this strategy, the individual become closed-minded (such as questioning the attractiveness of the pursued goal) and process information related to goal implementation. This automaticity would be very beneficial for individuals encountering tempting situations in which deliberate decision making is not helpful. For example, persons in a state of withdrawal from a substance to which they are addicted (who are burdened by unwanted thoughts related to the drug urge) were found to benefit from this strategy (Brandstatter et al., 2001).

Evidence shows that individuals who set implementation intentions achieve higher rates of goal attainment than individuals who do not (Gollwitzer et al., 2010). Research evidence supports that implementation intentions were associated with goal attainment in domains ranging from cancer screenings, diet, recycle, and physical exercise (Oettingen and Gollwitzer, 2010). For example, a simple goal intention to perform breast self-examination was acted upon by 50% of the subjects. However, the percentage increased to 100% by adding an implementation strategy about exactly when to do it. In another study, a motivational and informational exhortation to engage in vigorous exercise raised the rate of exercising only slightly, but an implementation intention to perform the exercise more than doubled the rate. In another study (Schweiger and Gollwitzer, 2007), participants were exposed to a series of pictures used to elicit emotional responses. The study analyzed the control of spider fear in arachnophobics. Both participants with response-focused implementation intentions ("if I see a spider, then I will stay calm and relaxed) experienced less negative affect in the face of spider pictures than a no self-regulation control group. However, the mere goal intentions to not get frightened failed to achieve this effect.

In sum, implementation intentions translate general, abstract intentions into specific behavioral plans: if X happens, then I will do Y. The strategy helps create an association between the cue and the behavior, so that when the cue is encountered, the behavior is automatically triggered. Using this strategy, a person avoids crises and uses less willpower and counteracts ego depletion.[14] By placing goal-directed behavior under the control of the situation, the execution of self-control becomes relatively automatic and less effortful.

The Counteractive-Control Strategy

This strategy suggests that in the presence of temptation cues, individuals activate the overriding goals, which remind them of their long-term priorities and help them resist the temptations. For example, when fattening food is served, dieters activate the goal of dieting, which in turn enables them to avoid the forbidden foods. The idea complements the implementation strategy that the presence of an actual temptation in the environment may lead to an activation of the higher priority (long-term) goal. Thus, automatic goal activation may dominate situational control and promote personal priorities (Fishbach et al., 2003). Consequently, the mere presentation of a temptation-related cue in the environment (e.g., a delicious chocolate cake) automatically activates the planned behavior (e.g., a slim figure). For example, the presence of donut would heighten the accessibility of the health goal to counteract the goal of comfort eating. Thus, rather than increased donut consumption occurring when donuts are present, we should see heightened healthy eating. Such a counteractive effect would only be evidenced if the health goal were important. For example, a study found that female dieters expressed greater body dissatisfaction when hungry. It seems that food deprivation served as an "alarm signal" that encouraged self-control and successful implementation of dieting intentions among restrained eaters (Myrseth et al 2009).

In summary, unlike the resource-demanding self-control mechanisms, the activation of the automatic goal tends to be relatively independent of cognitive resources. Given our limited cognitive resources for conscious self-control, delegating control to situational cues is an effective way to bridge the gap that exists between our best intentions and the successful attainment of our goals.

Conclusion

The discussions in this chapter show that people hold an array of strategies that help them secure the attainment of a more important goal in the face of temptations. The purpose of a self-control strategy is to succeed in the pursuit of long-term goals either by increasing the motivational strength of the goal or by decreasing the motivational strength of the temptation. The chapter discussed the processes that individuals use to increase the motivational strength of their high-order goals and decrease the motivational strength of their low-order temptations. It further distinguished between explicit self-control strategies that rely on conscious processing and automatic strategies that do not require conscious consideration. These families of self-control strategies are by no means mutually exclusive. Indeed, successful treatment programs often combine several interventions that correspond to a number of the strategies presented here. The selection of the specific strategies will depend on the nature of the temptation, as well as the person who will be facing it.

Notes

1 The over-the-counter Alli (Orlistat) is a popular weight-loss drug (Orlistat is available with a prescription). It partially blocks the body's ability to absorb fat. Like the Antabuse, the users who eat too much fat immediately experience the unpleasant side effects, such as gas, diarrhea, and abdominal pain.
2 Providing reward for reducing unhealthy behaviors is a practice that most parents do with their children by offering them rewards of various kinds (usually money) if they do not take up smoking before a certain age.
3 This strategy explains why individuals choose relatively more expensive annual gym memberships over "pay as you go" options, even though the latter would be less expensive for most users (DellaVigna and Malmendier, 2006).
4 When West Virginia revoked driving permits for students who were under the age of 18 and who dropped out of school, the dropout rate fell by one-third in the first year. While teens tend to be oblivious to the long-term benefits of getting a high school diploma, they do appreciate the short-term punishment of losing a license.
5 Thought suppression is also a form of cognitive avoidance (denial and minimization), which is the process of consciously trying to avoid certain thoughts.
6 Similarly, emotional material (e.g., personal emotional issues) is more difficult to suppress than is neutral information.
7 Desirability refers to the value of an action's end state, whereas feasibility refers to the ease or difficulty of reaching the end state.
8 Projection bias can cause misguided purchases of durable goods, such as home treadmills, stationary bikes, and other equipment that ends up gathering dust. Projection bias occurs when people behave as if their future preferences will be more like their current preferences.
9 Before the birth of cognitive revolution in 1960s, psychoanalysts focused on subconscious drives and defenses to understand patients. Later on, behaviorists focused on external environments such as reward and punishment to explain and modify behaviors. In contrast, cognitive therapy suggests that much of emotional pain is caused by distorted thinking and irrational thought.
10 The essence of CBT is captured by the Chinese proverb: "You cannot prevent the birds of worry from flying over your head, but you can prevent them from building a nest in your head." According to existentialism, we are free to interpret and reinterpret the meaning of our lives. For example, you can consider your first relationship (marriage), which ended in break up (divorce), to be a "failure," or you can view it as a circumstance that caused you to grow in ways that were crucial to your future happiness.

11 This approach is consistent with work on mindfulness and meditation (e.g., Kabat-Zinn, 2003) that encourages people to consider negative feelings and experiences from diverse perspectives. This also explains why counting to ten before venting our anger can help us to adopt a broader perspective, which may help reduce anger.
12 Spinoza, a seventeenth-century philosopher, recommended that we fight a negative emotion with an even stronger but positive emotion brought about by reasoning and intellectual effort. Central to his thinking was the notion that the subduing of the passions should be accomplished by reason-induced emotion and not just pure reason alone (Damasio 2003).
13 Other examples include starting monthly savings targets, jogging twice a week, writing five pages a day, always finishing what one started, conducting one's life with dignity, and many similar "promises to oneself."
14 The downside of this strategy is the difficulty (rigidity) to disengage from automatic behavior when a goal has changed, such as the difficulty adjusting to civil life for soldiers returning from war.

12
CONCLUSION

Introduction

Using the framework of behavioral economics, this book focused on ways in which decision can be impaired and the ability to pursue goals over long time spans. The chapters also illustrated how the framework of behavioral economics can be used to help individuals improve their decision-making behavior. Self-control is both difficult and expensive. The capacity for commitment is built up by education. Like a muscle, it can be trained and strengthened (and also exhausted by use). The policy implication of this method is to help individuals help themselves by making more reasoned decisions.

The behavioral economic framework predicts that we tend to pursue immediate gratification in ways that we ourselves do not appreciate in the long run. We are very committed to our long-term goal of not smoking or eating healthy food, and yet, in the moment, temptations arise that often ruin our long-term plan. In short, behavioral economics realizes that most behaviors are driven by the moment, including defective recognition of future rewards.

The self-control problems lead to the internality ("harm to self") as a within-person externality. Internality refers to cases where people make mistakes by placing too much importance on the immediate costs and benefits at the expense of the delayed consequences. We can think of internalities as occurring when we make choices that injure our future selves. Standard economics justifies policy interventions (e.g., taxation) in situations where an individual's behaviors impose externality on others (e.g., second-hand smoking). In contrast, behavioral economics recognizes the prevalence of internalities (costs that people impose on themselves), such as the long-term health consequences of obesity. The recognition of these mistakes can be used to help individuals improve their decision making and enhance their well-being.

Revealed Preferences

In economics, preference is defined in terms of choice. Economists often assume that preferences are revealed from choices individuals make (known as *revealed preference* theory). Most typically, it is revealed by what we decide to do. Revealed preference theory simply equates unobserved preferences with observed choices. That is, one can work backward from a person's choice to infer his preference. For example, the decision by smokers to have a cigarette reflects preference. Standard economic theory assumes that all observed choices are utility maximizing from the perspective of the person making decision. This implies that preference satisfaction would coincide with what they believed was good for them. The standard policy advice that stems from this way of thinking is to give people as many choices as possible. and let them choose the one they like best (with minimum government action).

But, self-control problems (or time inconsistency) raise the possibility that individual choice may not be sufficiently reliable as the source of personal well-being. For example, having recently seen the results of a cholesterol test, Joe might judge that, all things considered, that nonfat vanilla frozen yogurt is a better choice than the chocolate fudge ice cream he enjoys more. Because of habit, or mistakes, he chooses the chocolate fudge ice cream while believing that another is better. Given that what he prefers doesn't match what he judges to be best for his self-interest, there is a gap between his aspiration and action. This inconsistency in a person's preference can give rise to internal struggle, feelings of regret and deprivation, and inconsistent behavior (Schelling, 1984).

In sum, people often make choices that bear a mixed relationship to their own preference (happiness). They tend to choose the option that has the greatest immediate appeal at the cost of long-term happiness, such as taking drugs or overeating. These decisions can produce immediate pleasure, but can lead to long-term misery. In response, people develop self-control rules as antidotes to impulsivity that help them maximize happiness.

Self-control problems are ubiquitous in everyday life, such as avoiding overeating, quitting smoking, or a desire to be less impulsive or irritable person. People use all manner of strategies available to cope with these and other conflicting motivational demands of modern life. For example, they choose a course of action in a calm moment of deliberation rather than having to battle it out in the grip of powerful temptations. As discussed, these self-control strategies create habits or outsource the control of one's behavior to the environment (e.g., implementation intention). People know that they will often find themselves in conditions where they are likely to do something detrimental to their long-term goals. By the act of precommitment to their earlier choice, they avoid or resist such temptations.

We also discussed several tools that can be helpful in avoiding self-control problems. People are often unaware of their self-control problems in situations where they are most prone to lapses in control. Self-monitoring can greatly influence the nature of our self-control behavior. For example, in the context of emotional regulation, one tries to become a less aggressive person in collegial disagreements. Often, we fail to follow through on goals and plans simply because we were unable to maintain our goals active in the face of distracting stimuli. In sum, self-control strategies offer people the option to avoid temptations.

Behavioral Economic Policy

How can policy makers help individuals act according to their long-term interests? If choices don't reveal an individual's true preferences, then the restriction of personal choice becomes justifiable. Behavioral economics suggests policy interventions that could help consumers avoid making problematic choices. These policy interventions can be seen as a form of libertarian paternalism that guides consumers to be better off without necessarily restricting their choices. These policies, for instance, involve suppression of certain environmental cues (e.g., through limitation on advertising) and the dissemination of counter cues. For example, as discussed, it is well known among drug researchers that the vast majority of the huge numbers of soldiers who were addicted to heroin in Vietnam kicked the habit upon returning to the United States.

These policies augment individual willpower by "nudging" individual behavior toward self-interest without diminishing individuals' freedom to choose (Thaler and Sunstein, 2008; Sunstein, 2013). The approach is aimed to influence people's choices via choice architecture. Choice architecture is referred to organizing choices in such a way that encourages people to make the healthiest decisions. The idea is based on the assumption that the environment (or context) influences the content of our choices. For example, simply rearranging items that are currently offered within the school encourages children to buy more nutritious items[1] (e.g., placing the fruit at eye level, making choices less convenient by moving the soda machine into more distant areas, or requiring student pay cash for desserts and soft drinks). This strategy is much more effective than requiring students to eat vegetables. Moreover, when people feel as if they are freely and consciously making a choice, they take ownership of that decision and are more satisfied with the outcome.

Nudges represent soft paternalism because they are focused on altering behavior. They don't question people's choices (Sunstein, 2013). Nudges do not impose material costs or subsidize people's choices. For example, the government requires cigarettes to be sold in small packs of ten cigarettes so that people will consume less. Nudges maintain free choice. If people want to smoke or gamble, they are free to do so. Similarly, as a self-control strategy, default rules are valuable nudges. They simplify people's choices by providing automatic enrollment in programs that are usually beneficial while also allowing them to opt out.

Policies that augment individuals' willpower will improve their well-being. For example, studies from the United States and Canada conclude that those with propensity to smoke are significantly happier when excise taxes rise. The results show that price increases can serve as a self-commitment device. Thus, tobacco taxes may not only serve as a means to generate revenue, but may also help to overcome problems of self-control and prevent adolescents from starting a bad habit. That their satisfaction actually increased suggests that smoking was a choice they regretted, and that they welcomed higher taxes as an aid to self-control. When they are taxed, they smoke less and they are better off. Similarly, research evidence shows that people who watch more TV feel less safe, trust others less, are more materialistic, are less satisfied with their lives, and are more likely to be fat. A TV habit may offer short-run pleasure at the expense of long-term malaise.

In summary, the behavioral economic approach is based on changing the choice context within which individuals make decisions and respond to cues. You can provide information about the harmful effects of addiction or obesity and urge them to exercise self-control and avoid drug or certain foods. But, when they crave or become hungry, their well-intentioned self disappears, and they give in to temptations. Thus, information programs alone are not very effective in changing behavior. Behavioral economics emphasizes the power of the context to shape behavior. Context plays a powerful role in shaping individual preference and behavior. People who behave badly in some contexts often behave well in others. Thus, focusing on individuals without considering the context is like studying animal behavior by observing them in a cage rather than their natural habitat. By "nudging" individuals into a new way of behaving, behavioral economics can improve individuals' long-term well-being. The behavioral change is less intrusive, it essentially helps people to take greater personal responsibility.

Note

1 For a more information, see SmarterLunchrooms.org: http://www.smarterlunchrooms.org/research.html

REFERENCES

Abramowitz, J.S. (2006) The psychological treatment of obsessive-compulsive disorder. *Canadian Journal of Psychiatry* 51: 407–416.
Adolphs, R. (2003) Investigating the cognitive neuroscience of social behavior. *Neuropsychologia* 41: 119–126.
Agassi, A. (2009) *Open: An Autobiography*. New York: Knopf.
Ainslie, G. (2001) *Breakdown of Will*. Cambridge: Cambridge University Press.
Ainsworth, M.D.S. (1982) *Attachment: Retrospective and Prospective*. New York Basic Books.
Akerlof, G.A. (1991) Procrastination and obedience. *American Economic Review* 81(1): 1–19.
Akerlof, G.A. and Shiller, R.J. (2009) *Animal Spirits: How Human Psychology Drives the Economy, and Why it Matters for Global Capitalism*. Princeton: Princeton University Press.
Akst, Daniel (2011) *We Have Met the Enemy: Self-Control in an Age of Excess*. New York: The Penguin Press.
Al'Absi, Mustafa (2007) *Stress and Addiction: Biological and Psychological Mechanisms*. Boston: Academic Press.
Alcoholics Anonymous (2001) *Alcoholics Anonymous* (4th ed.). Torrance, CA: Alcoholics Anonymous World Services, Inc.
Aleksander, Irina (2013) "Molly: Pure, but Not So Simple." *New York Times* June 21.
Alsio, J., Olszewski, P.K., Levine, A.S., and Schioth, H.B. (2012) Feed-forward mechanisms: Addiction-like behavioral and molecular adaptations in overeating. *Frontiers in Neuroendocrinology* 33: 127–139.
American Heritage Dictionary of the English Language (5th ed.) (2011) New York: Houghton Mifflin Harcourt Trade.
American Psychiatric Association (1994) *Diagnostic and Statistical Manual of Mental Disorders* (4th ed.) Washington, D.C.: Author.
American Psychiatric Association (2013) *Diagnostic and Statistical Manual of Mental Disorders* (5th ed.) Washington, D.C.: Author.
Andreou, C. and White, M. (2010) *The Thief of Time: Philosophical Essays on Procrastination*. Oxford University Press.
Angner, E. (2012) *A Course in Behavioral Economics*. New York: Palgrave Macmillan.

Angner, E. and Loewenstein, G. (2012) Behavioral Economics. In U. Maki, D.M. Gabbay, P. Thagard, and J. Woods (Eds.), *Handbook of the Philosophy of Science. Vol 13: Philosophy of Economics*, (pp. 214–240). Oxford: Elsevier.

Annas, Julia (2011) *Intelligent Virtue*. New York: Oxford University Press

Anotony, M.M., and Stein, M.B. (2009) *Oxford Handbook of Anxiety and Related Disorders*. Oxford: Oxford University Press.

Anton, S. and Miller, P.M. (2005) Do negative emotions predict alcohol consumption, saturated fat intake and physical activity in older adults? *Behavior Modification* 29(4): 677–688.

Ariely, Dan (2008) *Predictably Irrational*. New York: HarperCollins.

Arnsten, A., Mazure, C.M., and Sinha, R. (2012) This is your brain in meltdown. *Scientific American* 306: 48–53.

Arnsten, A.F.T. (2009). Stress signaling pathways that impair prefrontal cortex structure and function. *Nature* 10: 410–422.

Ashraf, N., Camerer, C., and Loewenstein, G. (2005) Adam Smith: Behavioral economist. *Journal of Economic Perspectives* 19(3): 131–145.

Aupperle, R.L., Melrose, A.J., Stein, M.B. and Paulus, M.P. (2012) Executive function and PTSD: Disengaging from trauma. *Neuropharmacology* (62): 686–694.

Avena, N.M., Gold, J.A., Kroll, C., and Gold, M.S. (2012) Further developments in the neurobiology of food and addiction: Update on the state of the science. *Nutrition* 28: 341–343.

Baddeley, A.D. and Hitch, G. (1974) Working memory. In G.H. Bower (Ed.), *The Psychology of Learning and Motivation: Advances in Research and Theory* (Vol. 8, pp. 47–89). New York: Academic Press.

Badger, G.J., Bickel, W. K., Giordan, L. A., Jacob, E. A., Loewenstein, G., and Marsch, L. (2007) Altered states: The impact of immediate craving on the valuation of current and future opioids. *Journal of Health Economics* 26: 865–876.

Baer, J. John, Kaufmann, J., and Baumeister, R.F. (Eds.) (2008) *Are We Free?: Psychology and Free Will*. New York: Oxford University Press.

Bandura, A. (1997) *Self-Efficacy: The Exercise of Control*. New York: W.H. Freeman.

Bandura, A. and Locke, E.A. (2003) Negative self-efficacy and goal effects revisited. *Journal of Applied Psychology* 88(1): 87–99.

Bargh, J.A. (2002). Losing consciousness: Automatic influences on consumer judgment, behavior and motivation. *Journal of Consumer Research* 29: 280–285.

Bargh, J.A. and Chartrand, T.L. (1999) The unbearable automaticity of being. *American Psychologist* 54: 462–479.

Bargh, J.A., Chen, M., and Burrows, L. (1996) Automaticity of social behavior: Direct effects of trait construct and stereotype priming on action. *Journal of Personality and Social Psychology* 71: 230–244.

Bargh, J.A. and Huang, J.Y. (2009) The selfish goal. In G. B. Moskowitz and H. Grant (Eds.), *The Psychology of Goals* (pp. 127–150). New York: Guilford.

Barlow, D. H. (1988) *Anxiety and Its Disorders: The Nature and Treatment of Anxiety and Panic*. New York: Guilford Press.

Barlow, D. H. (2002) *Anxiety and Its Disorders: The Nature and Treatment of Anxiety and Panic* (2nd ed.). New York: Guilford Press.

Baumeister, R.F. (2002) Yielding to temptation: Self-control failure, impulsive purchasing, and consumer behavior. *Journal of Consumer Research* 28: 670–676.

Baumeister, R.F. (2005) *The Cultural Animal: Human Nature, Meaning, and Social Life*. New York: Oxford University Press.

Baumeister, R.F., Heatherton, T.F., and Tice, D. (1994) *Losing Control: How and Why People Fail at Self-Regulation*. San Diego: Academic Press.

Baumeister, R.F., Sparks, E.A., Stillman, T.F., and Vohs, K.D. (2008) Free will in consumer behavior: Self-control, ego depletion and choice. *Journal of Consumer Psychology* 18: 4–13.

Baumeister, R.F. and Tierney, J. (2011) *Willpower*. New York: The Penguine Press.

Baumeister, R.F., Vohs, K.D., and Tice, D.M. (2007) *The Strength Model of Self-Control. Current Directions in Psychological Science* 16: 351–355.

Baumeister, R.F., Zell, A.L., and Tice, D.M. (2007) How emotions facilitate and impair self-regulation. In J.J. Gross (Ed.), *Handbook of Emotion Regulation* (pp. 408–426). New York: Guilford Press.

Bechara, A. (2005) Decision making, impulse control and loss of willpower to resist drugs: A neurocognitive perspective. *Nature Neuroscience* 8: 1458–1463.

Bechara, A. and Damasio, A.R. (2005) The somatic marker hypothesis: A neural theory of economic decision. *Games and Economic Behavior* 52: 336–372.

Bechara, A. and Damasio, H. (2002) Decision-making and addiction (part I): impaired activation of somatic states in substance dependent individuals when pondering decisions with negative future consequences. *Neuropsychologia* 40: 1675–1689.

Beck, A.T. (2008) The evolution of the cognitive model of depression and its neurobiological correlates. *American Journal of Psychiatry* 165(8): 969–977.

Beck, A.T. and Alford, B.A. (2009) *Depression: Causes and Treatments* (2nd ed.). Philadelphia: University of Pennsylvania Press.

Beck, J.S. (1995) *Cognitive Therapy: Basics and Beyond*. New York: Guilford Press.

Becker, G.S. (1992) Habits, addictions and traditions. *Kyklos* 45(3): 327–346.

Becker, G.S. and Mulligan, Casey B. (1997) The endogenous determination of time preference. *Quarter Journal of Economics* 112(3) (August): 729–758.

Becker, G.S. and Murphy, K.M. (1988) A theory of rational addiction. *Journal of Political Economy* 96(4): 675–700.

Beevers, C.G. (2005) Cognitive vulnerability to depression: A dual process model. *Clinical Psychology Review* 25: 975–1002.

Benabou, R. and Tirole, J. (2002) Self-confidence and personal motivation. *Quarterly Journal of Economics* 117: 871–915.

Ben-Shahar, Tal. (2009). *The Pursuit of Perfect: How to Stop Chasing Perfection and Start Living a Richer, Happier Life*. New York: McGraw-Hill.

Bensi, L. and Giusberti, F. (2007) Trait anxiety and reasoning under uncertainty. *Personality and Individual Differences* 43: 827–838.

Ben-Ze'ev, A. (2000) *The Subtlety of Emotions*. Cambridge: MIT Press.

Berking, Mattias, Margraf, Matthias, Ebert, David, Wupperman, Peggilee, Hofmann, Stefan G., and Junghanns, Klaus (2011) Deficits in emotion-regulation skills predict alcohol use during and after cognitive behavioral therapy for alcohol dependence. *Journal of Consulting and Clinical Psychology*. 79(3): 307–318. doi: 10.1037/a0023421

Bernheim, B. Douglas and Rangel, Antonio (2004) Addiction and cue-conditioned cognitive processes. *American Economic Review* 94(5): 1558–1590.

Berns, Gregory (2008) *Iconoclast: A Neuroscientist Reveals How to Think Differently*. Cambridge: Harvard Business School Press.

Berridge, K.C. (2004) Motivation concepts in behavioral neuroscience. *Physiology & Behavior* 81(2): 179–209.

Berridge, K.C. and Robinson, T.E. (2003) Parsing reward. *Trends in Neurosciences* 26(9): 507–513.

Berthoz, Alain (2006) *Emotion and Reason: The Cognitive Neuroscience of Decision Making*. New York: Oxford University Press.

Bickel, W.K., Jarmolowicz, D.P., Mueller, E.T., Koffarnus, M.N., and Gatchalian, K.M. (2012) Excessive discounting of delayed reinforcers as a trans-disease process contributing to addiction and other disease-related vulnerabilities: Emerging evidence. *Pharmacology & Therapeutics* 134: 287–297.

Bickel, W. K. and Johnson, M. W. (2003) Delay discounting: A fundamental behavioral process of drug dependence. In G. Loewenstein, D. Read, and R. Baumeister (Eds.), *Time and Decision: Economic and Psychological Perspective on Intertemporal Choice* (pp. 419–440). New York: Russell Sage Foundation.

Bickel, W.K., Miller, M.L., Yi, R., Kowal, B.P., Lindquist, D.M., and Pitcock, J.A. (2007) Behavioral and neuroeconomics of drug addiction: Competing neural systems and temporal discounting processes. *Drug Alcohol Depend* 90: S85–S91.

Bickel, W.K. and Vuchinich, R.E. (2000) *Reframing Health Behavior Change with Behavioral Economics*. Mahwah: Lawrence Erlbaum Associates.

Blair, C. (2010) Stress and the development of self-regulation in context. *Child Development Perspectives* 4(3): 181–188.

Bögels, S.M., Knappe, S., and Clark, L. (2013) Adult separation anxiety disorder in the DSM-5. *Clinical Psychology Review* 33: 663–674.

Boon, B., Stroebe, W., Schut, H., and Ijntema, R. (2002) Ironic processes in the eating behaviour of restrained eaters. *British Journal of Health Psychology* 7: 1–10.

Borkovec, T. D., Alcaine, O. M., and Behar, E. (2004) Avoidance theory of worry and generalized anxiety disorder. In R. Heimberg, C. Turk, and D. Mennin (Eds.), *Generalized Anxiety Disorder: Advances in Research and Practice* (pp. 77–108). New York: Guilford Press.

Bowlby, J. (1969) *Attachment. Attachment and Loss: Vol. 1. Loss.* New York: Basic Books.

Bowlby, J. (1973) *Attachment and Loss: Vol. 2. Separation: Anxiety and Anger.* New York: Basic Books.

Brafman, Ori (2008) *Sway: The Irresistible Pull of Irrational Behavior.* New York: Doubleday.

Brandstätter, V., Lengfelder, A., and Gollwitzer, P. M. (2001) Implementation intentions and efficient action initiation. *Journal of Personality and Social Psychology* 81: 946–960.

Brocas, I. and Carrillo, J.D. (2013) Dual-process theories of decision-making: A selective survey. *Journal of Economic Psychology* 41: 45–54.

Bromberg, P.M. (2001) *Standing in the Spaces*. New York: Psychology Press.

Brook, C.A. and Schmidt, L.A. (2008) Social anxiety disorder: A review of environmental risk factors. *Neuropsychiatry Disease Treatment* 4(1): 123–143.

Bryan, C.J. and Hershfield, H.E. (2012) You owe it to yourself: Boosting retirement saving with a responsibility-based appeal. *Journal of Experimental Psychology: General* 141(3): 429–432.

Buckner, J. D. and Schmidt, N. B. (2008) Marijuana effect expectancies: Relations to social anxiety and marijuana use problems. *Addictive Behaviors* 33: 1477–1483.

Buckner, J.D., Schmidt, N.B., Lang, A.R., Small, J.W., Schlauch, R.C., and Lewinsohn, P.M. (2008) Specificity of social anxiety disorder as a risk factor for alcohol and cannabis dependence. *Journal of Psychiatric Research* 42: 230–239. http://dx.doi.org/10.1016/j.jpsychires.2007.01.002

Burke, L. E., Wang, J., and Sevick, M. A. (2012) Using mHealth technology to enhance self-monitoring for weight loss: A randomized trial. *Journal of the American Dietetic Association* 3(1): 20–26.

Cacioppo, J.T., and Patrick, W. (2008) *Loneliness: Human Nature and the Need for Social Connection*. New York: W.W. Norton.

Cain, A.S., Epler, A.J., Steinley, D., and Sher, K.J. (2010) Stability and change in patterns of concern related to eating, weight, and shape in young adult women: A latent transition analysis. *Journal of Abnormal Psychology* 119(2): 255–267.

Camerer, C., Loewenstein, G., and Rabin, M. (2003) *Advances in Behavioral Economics*. New York: Princeton University Press.

Camus, A. (1955) *The Myth of Sisyphus*. New York: Random House.

Carrillo, J. and Mariotti, T. (2000) Strategic ignorance as a self-disciplining device. *Review of Economic Studies* 67(3): 529–544.

Carroll K. M. (1998). NIH Publication 98-4308. Rockville: National Institute on Drug Abuse. A Cognitive-Behavioral Approach: Treating Cocaine Addiction.

Carson, S.H. (2011) Creativity and psychopathology: A shared vulnerability model. *Canadian Journal of Psychiatry* 56:144–153.

Carter, B.L. and Tiffany, S.T. (2001) The cue availability paradigm: The effects of cigarette availability on cue reactivity in smokers. *Experimental and Clinical Psychopharmacology* 9: 183–190.

Cawley, J.H. (2011) *The Oxford Handbook of the Social Science of Obesity*. New York: Oxford University Press.

Cervone, D. and Pervin, L.A. (2010) *Personality: Theory and Research* (11th ed.). New York: John Wiley & Sons, Inc.

Cesario, J., Corker, K.S., and Jelinek, S. (2013) A self-regulatory framework for message framing. *Journal of Experimental Social Psychology* 49: 238–249.

Chaloupka, Frank J. and Warner, Kenneth E. (2001) The economics of smoking. In A.J. Culyer and J.P. Newhouse (Eds.) *Handbook of Health Economics* (Vol. 1, pp. 1539–1628). New York: Elsevier.

Christakis, Nicholas A. and Fowler, James H. (2008) The collective dynamics of smoking in a large social network. *New England Journal of Medicine* 358: 2249–2258.

Churchland, P. (2013) *Touching a Nerve*. New York: W.W. Norton & Company.

Cisler, J.M. and Koster, E.H.W. (2010) Mechanisms of attentional biases towards threat in anxiety disorders: An integrative review. *Clinical Psychology Review* 30(2): 203–216.

Clark, D.A., Aaron, T., and Beck, A.T (2009). *Cognitive Therapy of Anxiety Disorders: Science and Practice*. New York: Guilford Press.

Clark, D.A. and Beck, A.T. (2012) *The Anxiety & Worry Workbook: The Cognitive Behavioral Solution*. New York: The Guilford Press.

Cloninger, C.R. (2012) Healthy personality development and well being. *World Psychiatry* 11(2): 103–104.

Coates, J. (2012) *The Hour between Dog and Wolf: Risk Taking, Gut Feelings, and the Biology of Boom and Bust*. Kirjastus: Blackstone Audio, Inc.

Courtwright, David (2001) *Forces of Habit: Drugs and the Making of the Modern World*. Cambridge: Harvard University Press.

Cox, W.M., Klinger, E., and Fadardi, J.S. (2006) Motivational basis of cognitive determinants of addiction. In M. Mufano and I.P. Albery (Eds.), *Cognition Addiction* (pp. 101–117). Oxford: Oxford University Press.

Coyle, Daniel (2009) The Talent Code. New York: Bantam Books.

Cramer, Phebe (2006) *Protecting the Self: Defense Mechanisms in Action*. New York: Guilford Press.

Craig, A. D. (2002) How do you feel? Interoception: The sense of the physiological condition of the body. *Nature Reviews Neuroscience* 3(8): 655–666.

Cutler, David M. and Lleras-Muney, Adriana (2010) The education gradient in old age disability. In David Wise (Ed.), *Research Findings in the Economics of Aging* (pp. 101–120). Chicago: University of Chicago.

Dalrymple, Theodore (2006) *Romancing Opiates*. New York: Encounter.
Damasio, A.R. (1994) *Descartes' Error: Emotion, Reason, and the Human Brain*. New York: G. P. Putnam.
Damasio, A. R. (1999) *The Feeling of What Happens: Body and Emotion in the Making of Consciousness*. New York: Harvest edition.
Damasio, A.R. (2003) *Looking for Spinoza: Joy, Sorrow, and the Feeling Brain*. London: Mariner Books.
Davey, G.C.L. and Levy, S. (1998) Catastrophic worrying: Personal inadequacy and a perseverative iterative style as features of the catastrophising process. *Journal of Abnormal Psychology* 107: 576–586.
Davidson, R.J. and Irwin, W. (1999) The functional neuroanatomy of emotion and affective style. *Trends in Cognitive Sciences* 3: 11–21.
Davis, C. and Carter, J. C. (2009) Compulsive overeating as an addiction disorder: A review of theory and evidence. Appetite 53: 1–8.
Dawkins, Richard (1976) *The Selfish Gene*. Oxford: Oxford University Press.
Deci, E. and Ryan, R. (Eds.) (2002) *Handbook of Self-Determination Research*. Rochester: University of Rochester Press.
DellaVigna, S. and Malmendier, U. (2006) Paying not to go to the gym. *American Economic Review* 96: 694–719.
De Witt Huberts, J.C., Evers, C., and de Ridder, D.T.D. (2012) License to sin: Self-licensing as a mechanism underlying hedonic consumption. *European Journal of Social Psychology* 42: 490–496.
Dewitte, S (2012) From will power breakdown to the breakdown of the will power model. The symmetry of self-control and impulsive behavior. *Journal of Economic Psychology* 38: 16–25.
Diamond, P. and Vartianen, H. (2007) *Behavioral Economics and Its Applications*. Princeton: Princeton University Press.
Dias-Ferreira, E., Sousa, J. C., Melo, I., Morgado, P., Mesquita, A. R., Cerqueira, J. J., Costa, R. M., and Sousa, N. (2009). Chronic stress causes frontostriatal reorganization and affects decision-making. *Science* 325: 621–625.
Dijksterhuis, A., Chartrand, T.L., and Aarts, H. (2007) Effects of priming and perception on social behavior and goal pursuit. In J.A. Bargh (Ed.), *Social Psychology and the Unconscious: The Automaticity of Higher Mental Processes* (pp. 51–132). Philadelphia: Psychology Press.
Dikotter, F., Lasmann, L., and Zhou, X. (2004). *Narcotic Culture: A History of Drugs in China*. Chicago: The University of Chicago Press.
Doctorow, E.L. (2014) *Andrew's Brain*. New York: Random House.
Dolan, R. and Sharot, T. (2011) *Neuroscience of Preference and Choice: Cognitive and Neural Mechanisms*. New York: Academic Press.
Dozois, D.J.A. and Beck, A. T. (2008) Cognitive schemas, beliefs and assumptions. In K. S. Dobson and D.J.A. Dozois (Eds.), *Risk Factors in Depression* (pp. 121–143). Oxford, England: Elsevier/Academic Press.
Droit-Volet, S., Meck, W. H. (2007) How emotions colour our time perception. *Trends in Cognitive Sciences* 11: 504–513.
Droit-Volet, S. and Gil, S. (2009) The time–emotion paradox. *Philosophical Transations of the Royal Society* (364):1943–1953.
Duckworth, A. and Seligman, M. (2005) Self-Discipline outdoes IQ in predicting academic performance of adolescents. *Psychological Science* 16(12): 939–944.
Duffy, S.A., Scheumann, A.L., Fowler, K.E., Darling-Fisher, C.S., and Terrell, J.E. (2010) Perceived difficulty in quitting predicts enrollment in a smoking cessation program for head and neck cancer patients. *Oncology Nursing Forum* 37(3):1–8.

Duffy, S.A., Missel, A.L., Waltje, A.H., Ronis, D.L., Fowler, K.E., and Hong, O. (2011). Health behaviors of operating engineers. *American Association of Occupational Health Nurses Journal* 59(7): 293–301.

Dugas, M. J., Francis, K., and Bouchard, S. (2009) Cognitive behavioral therapy and applied relaxation for generalized anxiety disorder: A time series analysis of change in worry and somatic anxiety. *Cognitive Behaviour Therapy* 38: 29–41.

Duhigg, Charles (2012) *The Power of Habit: Why We Do What We Do in Life and Business*. New York: Random House.

Dumont, Frank (2010) *A History of Personality Psychology: Theory, Science, and Research from Hellenism to the Twenty-First Century*. Cambridge: Cambridge University Press.

Dweck, Carol S. (2011) *Mindset: The New Psychology of Success*. New York: Ballantine Books.

Eisenberger, Naomi I. and Lieberman, Matthew D. (2004) Why rejection hurts: A common neural alarm system for physical and social pain. *TRENDS in Cognitive Sciences* 8(7): 294–300.

Eisenberger, R. (1992) Learned industriousness. *Psychological Review* 99: 248–267.

Ekman, P. (2003) Emotions Revealed: Recognizing Faces and Feelings to Improve Communication and Emotional Life. New York: Henry Holt.

Ekman, P. (2004) *Emotions Revealed*. London: Orion Books.

Elster, J. (1999a) *Alchemies of the Mind*. New York: Oxford University Press.

Elster, J. (1999b) *Strong Feelings: Emotion, Addiction, and Human Behavior*. Boston: The MIT Press.

Elster, J. (2001) Introduction. In J. Elster (Ed.), *Addiction: Entries and Exits* (pp. 1–40). New York: Russell Sage Foundation.

Elster, J. (2006) Weakness of will and preference reversal. In J. Elster et al. (Eds.), *Understanding Choice, Explaining Behavior: Essays in Honour of Ole-Jørgen Skog* (pp. 34–49). Oslo Academic Press.

Elster, J. (2009) *Reason and Rationality*. Princeton, NJ: Princeton University Press.

Elster J. (2010) Self-poisoning of the mind. *Philosophical Transactions of the Royal Society B* 365: 221–226.

Elster, J. and Skog, O.-J. (2000) *Getting Hooked: Rationality and Addiction*. Cambridge: Cambridge University Press.

Epstein, Mark (2013) *The Trauma of Everyday Life*. New York: The Penguin Press.

Epstein, S. (1994) Integration of the cognitive and psychodynamic unconscious. *American Psychologist* 49: 709–724.

Erickson, C.K. (2007) *The Science of Addiction: From Neurobiology to Treatment*. New York: W.W. Norton & Company.

Ericsson, K.A., Krampe, R. Th., and Tesch-Romer, C. (1993) The role of deliberate practice in the acquisition of expert performance. *Psychological Review* 100: 393–394.

Evans, G. W. (1994) Working on the hot seat: Urban bus operators. *Accident Analysis and Prevention* 26: 181–193.

Evans, J. St. B.T. (2008) Dual-processing accounts of reasoning, judgment, and social cognition. *Annual Review of Psychology* 59: 6.1–6.24.

Eysenck, M.W. (2012) *Fundamental of Cognition* (2nd ed.). New York: Psychology Press.

Fava, L. and Morton, J. (2009) Causal modeling of panic disorder theories. *Clinical Psychology Review* 29: 623–637.

Fehr, Ernest. and Rangel, Antonio. (2011) Neuroeconomic foundations of economic choice—recent advances. *Journal of Economic Perspective* 25:3–30.

Festinger, L. (1957) *A Theory of Cognitive Dissonance*. Stanford: Stanford University Press.

Field, M. and Cox, W.M. (2008) Attentional bias in addictive behaviors: A review of its development, causes, and consequences. *Drug and Alcohol Dependence* 97: 1–20.

Finkelstein, Amy (2009) E-ZTax: Tax salience and tax rates. *Quarterly Journal of Economics* 124(3) (August): 969–1010.

Fishbach, A. and Ferguson, M. F. (2007) The goal construct in social psychology. In A. W. Kruglanski and T. E. Higgins (Eds.), *Social Psychology: Handbook of Basic Principles* (pp. 490–515). New York: Guilford Press.

Fishbach, A., Friedman, R.S., and Kruglanski, A.W. (2003) Leading us not unto temptation: Momentary allurements elicit overriding goal activation. *Journal of Personality and Social Psychology* 84: 296–309.

Fishbein, M. and Ajzen, I. (2010) *Predicting and Changing Behavior: The Reasoned Action Approach*. New York: Psychology Press.

Flores, P.J. (2004) *Addiction as an Attachment Disorder*. New York: Jason Aronson.

Francis, H. and Stevenson, R. (2013) The longer-term impacts of western diet on human cognition and the brain. *Appetite* 63(0): 119–128. doi:10.1016/j.appet.2012.12.018.

Frank, R.H. (1999) *Luxury Fever: Why Money Fails to Satisfy in an Era of Excess*. New York: Free Press.

Frank, R.H. (2002) *Microeconomics and Behavior* (5th ed.). New York: McGraw-Hill/Irwin.

Frank, Robert H. (2005) Positional externalities cause large and preventable welfare losses. *American Economic Review* 95(2): 137–141.

Frankl, V. E. (2006) *Man's Search for Meaning*. New York: Beacon Press.

Frederick, Shane, Loewenstein, George, and O'Donoghue, Ted (2002) Time discounting and time preference: A critical review. *Journal of Economic Literature* 40(2): 351–401.

Fredrickson, B.L. (2009) *Positivity: Groundbreaking Research Reveals How to Embrace the Hidden Strength of Positive Emotions, Overcome Negativity, and Thrive*. New York: Crown.

Fredrickson, B.L. and Joiner, T. (2002) Positive emotions trigger upward spirals toward emotional well-being. *Psychological Science* 13: 172–175.

Freedman, David H. (June 2012) The perfected self. *The Atlantic Magazine*. 309: 41–50. http://www.theatlantic.com/magazine/archive/2012/06/the-perfected-self/308970/

Friedman, R. and Foster, J. (2001) The effects of promotion and prevention cues on creativity. *Journal of Personality and Social Psychology* 81: 1001–1013.

Friese, M., Hofmann, W., and Wänke, M. (2008) When impulses take over: Moderated predictive validity of implicit and explicit attitude measures in predicting food choice and consumption behaviour. British Journal of Social Psychology 47: 397–419.

Friese, M., Hofmann, W., and Wiers, R.W. (2011) On taming horses and strengthening riders: Recent developments in research on interventions to improve self-control in health behaviors. *Self and Identity* 10(3): 336–351.

Frijda, N. H. (1986) The Emotions. London: Cambridge University Press.

Frijda, N.H. (2007) *The Laws of Emotion*. Mahwah: Erlbaum.

Frijda, N.H. (2013) Emotion regulation and free will. In T. Vierkant, A. Clark, and J. Kiverstein (Eds.), *Decomposing the Will* (pp. 486–504). Oxford: Oxford University Press.

Fuchs, Victor R. (1982) Time preference and health: An exploratory study. In V. R. Fuchs (Ed.) *Economic Aspects of Health* (pp. 93–120). Chicago: University of Chicago Press.

Gabbard, G. O., Litowitz, B.E., and Williams, P. (2012) *Textbook of Psychoanalysis* (2nd ed.) Arlington, VA: American Psychiatric Publishing.

Gailliot, M.T., Baumeister, R.F., DeWall, C.N., Maner, J.K., Ashby Plant, E., Tice, D.M., and Brewer, L.E., (2007) Self-control relies on glucose as a limited energy source: Willpower is more than a metaphor. *Journal of Personality and Social Psychology* 92: 325–336.

Gardner, Eliot and James, David (1999) The neurobiology of chemical addiction. In Jon Elster and Ole-Jorgen Skog (Eds.), *Getting Hooked: Rationality and Addiction* (pp. 94–111). Cambridge: Cambridge University Press.

Gardner, H. (1999) *Intelligence Reframed*. New York: Basic Books.
Gawin, F.H. (1991) Cocaine addiction: Psychology and neurophysiology. *Science* 251: 1580–1586.
Gazzaniga, M. S. (2008) *Human: The Science behind What Makes Us Unique*. New York: HarperCollins.
Gazzaniga, Michael (2011) *Who Is in Charge? Free Will and the Science of the Brain*. New York: HarperCollins.
Giancola, P.R. (2002) Irritability, acute alcohol consumption, and aggressive behavior in men and women. *Drug and Alcohol Dependence* 68: 263–274.
Giedd, J.N. (2004) Structural magnetic resonance imaging of the adolescent brain. *Annals of the New York Academy of Sciences* 1021(1): 77–85.
Gigerenzer, G. (2007) *Gut Feelings: The Intelligence of the Unconscious*. New York: Viking Press.
Gilbert, D.T. and Wilson, T.D. (2007) Prospection: Experiencing the future. *Science* 317: 1351–1354.
Gladwell, Malcolm (2006) *Blink: The Power of Thinking Without Thinking*. London: Penguin Books.
Gladwell, Malcolm (2008) *Outliers: The Story of Success*. New York: Little, Brown & Company.
Goldbeck, R., Myatt, P., and Aitchison, T. (1997) End-of-treatment self-efficacy: A predictor of abstinence. *Addiction* 92: 313–324.
Goldberg, Elkhonon (2009) *The New Executive Brain: Frontal Lobes in a Complex World*. New York: Oxford University Press.
Goldman, D., Oroszi, G., and Ducci, F. (2005) The genetics of addiction: Uncovering the genes. *Nature Reviews Genetics* 6: 521–532.
Goldstein, A. (2001) *Addiction: From Biology to Drug Policy* (2nd ed.). New York: Oxford University Press.
Goldstein, R.Z. et al., (2009) The neurocircuitry of impaired insight in drug addiction. *Trends in Cognitive Science* 13(9): 372–380.
Goleman, Daniel (2004) *Destructive Emotions: A Scientific Dialogue with the Dalai Lama*. New York: Bantam Books.
Gollwitzer, P. M. (1999) Implementation intentions. Strong effects of simple plans. *American Psychologist* 54: 493–503.
Gollwitzer, P.M., Gawrilow, C., and Oettingen, G. (2010) The power of planning: Self-control by effective goal-striving. In R.R. Hassin, K.N. Ochsner, and Y. Trope (Eds.), *Self Control in Society, Mind, and Brain* (pp. 279–296). New York: Oxford University Press.
Gotlib, I.H. and Joormann, J. (2010) Cognition and depression: Current status and future directions. *Annual Review of Clinical Psychology* 6: 285–312.
Graham, J., Thomas, M. S., and Wing, R. R. (2009) Maintenance of long-term weight loss. *Medicine and Health Rhode Island* 92(2): 53–57.
Grant, J.E., Donahue, C.B., and Odlaug, B.L. (2011) *Overcoming Impulse Control Disorders: A Cognitive—Behavioral Therapy Program (Workbook)*. New York: Oxford University Press.
Gray, J.A. (1982) *The Neuropsychology of Anxiety*. New York: Oxford University Press.
Green, L., Myerson, J., and Ostaszewski, P. (1999) Discounting of delayed rewards across the life span: Age differences in individual discounting functions. *Behavioural Processes* 46: 89–96.
Greenberg, Gary (2010) *Manufactured Depression: The Secret History of a Modern Disease*. New York: Simon & Schuster.
Gross, J. J. (Ed.) (2007) *Handbook of Emotion Regulation*. New York: Guilford Press.
Gross J. J. (2014) *Handbook of Emotion Regulation* (2nd ed.). New York: Guilford Press.

Grosz, G. (2013) *The Examined Life: How We Lose and Find Ourselves*. New York: W.W. Norton & Company.

Gruber, Jonathan and Mullainathan, Sendhil (2005) Do cigarette taxes make smokers happier? *Advances in Economic Analysis and Policy* 5(1): Article 4.

Guerrieri, R. R., Nederkoorn, C. C., and Jansen, A. A. (2008) The interaction between impulsivity and a varied food environment: Its influence on food intake and overweight. *International Journal of Obesity* 32(4): 708–714.

Gullo, Mathew. J. and Dawe, Sharron. (2008) Impulsivity and adolescent substance use: Rashly dismissed as "all-bad"? *Neuroscience and Biobehavioral Reviews* 32: 1507–1518.

Gunstad, J., Paul, R.H., Cohen, R.A., Tate, D.F., Spitznagel, M.B., and Gordon, E. (2007) Elevated body mass index is associated with executive dysfunction in otherwise healthy adults. *Comprehensive Psychiatry* 48(1): 57–61.

Gwaltney, C.J., Shiffman, S., and Sayette, M.A. (2005) Situational correlates of abstinence self-efficacy. *Journal of Abnormal Psychology* 114(4): 649–660.

Hagger, M.S., Wood. C., Stiff, C., and Chatzisarantis, N.L.D. (2010) Ego depletion and the strength model of self-control: A meta-analysis. *Psychological Bulletin* 136: 495–525.

Haidt, J. (2006) *The Happiness Hypothesis: Finding Modern Truth in Ancient Wisdom*. New York: Basic Books.

Hammen, C. (2006) Stress generation in depression: Reflections on origins, research, and future directions. *Journal of Clinical Psychology* 62: 1065–1082.

Hart, Carl (2013) *High Price: A Neuroscientist's Journey of Self-Discovery That Challenges Everything You Know about Drugs and Society*. New York: HarperCollins.

Hart, D. and Matsuba, K. (2007) Pride and moral life. In J. Tracy, R. Robins, and J. Tangney (Eds.), *The Self-Conscious Emotions: Theory and Research* (pp. 114–133). New York: Guilford.

Hartley, CA. and Phelps, EA (2012) Anxiety and decision-making. *Biological Psychiatry* 72: 113–118.

Hasler, G. (2012) Can the neuroeconomics revolution revolutionize psychiatry? *Neuroscience and Biobehavioral Reviews* 36: 64–78.

Heckman, J. (2006) Skill formation and the economics of investing in disadvantaged children. *Science* 312: 1900–1902.

Heider, Fritz (1958) The Psychology of Interpersonal Relations. New York: Wiley.

Heiland, Frank and Burke, Mary (2007) Social dynamics of obesity. *Economic Inquiry* 45(3): 571–591.

Herman, C.P. and Polivy, J. (2002) Dieting as exercise in behavioral economics. In G. Loewenstein, R. Baumeister, and D. Read (Eds.), *Time and Decision* (pp. 155–178). New York: Russell Sage Foundation.

Herman, Peter C. and Janet Polivy (2010) The self regulation of eating: Theoretical practical problems. In Roy F. Baumeister and Kathleen D. Vohs (Eds.), *Handbook of Self-Regulation: Research, Theory, and Applications* (2nd ed.) (pp. 522–536). New York: Guilford.

Herrnstein, R.J. and Prelec, D. (1992) A theory of addiction. In G. Loewenstein and J. Elster (Eds.), *Choice over Time* (pp. 331–360). New York: Russell Sage Foundation.

Heyman, G.M. (2009) *Addiction: A Disorder of Choice*. Cambridge: Harvard University Press.

Higgins, E.T. (1997) Beyond pleasure and pain. *American Psychologist* 52: 1280–1300.

Higgins, E.T. (1999) Self-discrepancy: A theory relating self and affect. In R.F. Baumeister (Ed.), *The self in social psychology. Key readings in social psychology* (pp. 150–181). Philadelphia: Psychology Press/Taylor & Francis.

Higgins, E.T. (2012) *Beyond Pleasure and Pain*. New York: Oxford University Press.

Higgins, S. T., Alessi, S. M., Dantona, R. L. (2002) Voucher-based incentives: A substance abuse treatment innovation. *Addictive Behavior* 27: 887–910.

Hirsch, C.R. and Mathews, A. (2012) A cognitive model of pathological worry. *Behavioral Research Therapy* 50(10): 636–646.

Hobson, R.P. (2005) Autism and emotion. In F. Volkmar, A. Klin., and R. Paul (Eds.), *Handbook of Autism and Developmental Disorder* (pp. 406–422). New York: Wiley.

Hoch, Stephen J. and Loewenstein, George F. (1991) Time—Inconsistent preferences and consumer self-control. *Journal of Consumer Research* 17(March): 492–507.

Hofmann, W., Baumeister, R.F., Foerster, G., and Vohs, K.D. (2011) Everyday temptations: An experience sampling study of desire, conflict, and self-control. *Journal of Personality and Social Psychology* 102: 1318–1335.

Hofmann, W., Schmeichel, B.J., and Baddeley, A.D. (2012) Executive functions and self-regulation. *Trends in Cognitive Sciences* 3: 174–180.

Hogarth, R.M. (2001) *Educating Intuition*. Chicago: University of Chicago Press.

Holton, R. (2009) *Willing, Wanting, Waiting*. New York: Oxford University Press.

Horwitz, A.V. (2013) *Anxiety: A Short History*. Baltimore: Johns Hopkins University Press.

Horwitz, A.V. and Wakefield, J.C. (2007). *The Loss of Sadness: How Psychiatry Is Transforming Normal Sorrow into Depressive Disorder*. New York: Oxford University Press.

Horwitz, A.V. and Wakefield, J.C. (2012) *All We Have to Fear: Psychiatry's Transformation of Natural Anxieties into Mental Disorders*. New York: Oxford University Press.

Horwitz, A.V. and Wakefield, J.C. (2013) *Anxiety: A Short History*. Baltimore: The Johns Hopkins University Press.

Hull, J.G. (1981) A self-awareness model of the causes and effects of alcohol consumption. *Journal of Abnormal Psychology* 90: 586–600.

Hull, J. G., Young, R. D., Jouriles, E. (1986) Applications of the self-awareness model of alcohol consumption: Predicting patterns of use and abuse. *Journal of Personality and Social Psychology* 51: 790–796.

Humphreys, K.L., Eng, T., and Lee, S.S. (2013) Longitudinal association of stimulant medication treatment for ADHD and substance use and abuse/dependence: A meta analytic review. *Archives of General Psychiatry* 70: 740–749.

Huntsinger, E. T. and Luecken, L. J. (2004) Attachment relationships and health behavior: The mediational role of self-esteem. *Psychology and Health* 19: 515–526.

Hyman, S.E. (2005) Addiction: A disease of learning and memory. *American Journal of Psychiatry* 162(8): 1414–1422.

Iacoboni, M. (2008) *Mirroring People: The New Science of How We Connect with Others*. New York: Farrar, Straus, and Giroux.

Inciardi, J.A. and McElrath, K. (Eds.) (2014) *The American Drug Scene: Readings in a Global Context* (7th ed.). New York: Oxford University Press.

Ingram R.E., Atchley, R.A., and Segal, Z.V. (2011) *Vulnerability to Depression: From Cognitive Neuroscience to Prevention and Treatment*. New York: Guilford Press.

Institute of Medicine (IOM) (2003) *Weight Management: State of the Science and Opportunities for Military Programs*. Washington, D.C.: The National Academy Press.

Irvine, B. William (2006) *On Desire*. New York: Oxford University Press.

Irvine, B. William (2009) *A Guide to the Good Life*. New York: Oxford University Press.

Jackson, Mark (2013) *The Age of Stress: Science and the Search for Stability*. New York: Oxford University Press.

Johnson, E. J. and Goldstein, D. (2003) Do defaults save lives? *Science* 302: 1338–1339.

Johnson-Laird, P.N. and Oatley, K. (1992) Basic emotions, rationality, and folk theory. *Cognition and Emotion* 6: 201–223.

Johnston, L., O'Malley, P., and Bachman, J. (1993) National survey results of drug use from the Monitoring the Future study (DHHS Publication No. 93-3598). Rockville: National Institute on Drug Abuse.

Johnston, L.D., O'Malley, P.M., Bachman, J.G., and Schulenberg, J.E. (2013) *Monitoring the Future National Survey Results on Drug Use, 1975–2012. Volume II: College Students and Adults Ages 19–50*. Ann Arbor: Institute for Social Research, The University of Michigan.

Jostmann, N.B. and Koole, S.L. (2009) When persistence is futile: A functional analysis of action orientation and goal disengagement. In G.B. Moskowitz and H. Grant (Eds.), *The Psychology of Goals* (pp. 337–361). New York: Guilford.

Kabat-Zinn, J. (1990) *Full Catastrophe Living: Using the Wisdom of Your Body and Mind to Face Stress, Pain, and Illness*. New York: Dell Publishing.

Kabat-Zinn, J. (2003) Mindfulness-based interventions in context: Past, present, and future. *Clinical Psychology: Science & Practice* 10: 144–156.

Kagan, J. (2007) *What Is Emotion?: History, Measures, and Meanings*. New Haven: Yale University Press.

Kagan, J. (2008) The biological contributions to temperaments and emotions. *European Journal of Developmental Science* 2: 38–51.

Kahn, J.P. (2013) *Angst: Origins of Anxiety and Depression*. New York: Oxford University Press.

Kahneman, Daniel (2000) Experienced utility and objective happiness: A moment-based approach. In Daniel Kahneman and Amos Tversky (eds.), *Choices, Values, and Frames* (pp. 673–692). New York: Cambridge University Press.

Kahneman, Daniel (2003) Maps of bounded rationality: A perspective on intuitive judgment and choice. *American Economic Review* 93(5): 1449–1475.

Kahneman, Daniel (2011) *Thinking, Fast and Slow*. New York: Farrar, Straus and Giroux.

Kahneman, Daniel and Tversky, A. (1979) Prospect theory: An analysis of decisions under risk. *Econometrica* 47(2): 263–291.

Kandel, Eric (2012) *The Age of Insight: The Quest to Understand the Unconscious in Art, Mind, and Brain, from Vienna 1900 to the Present*. New York: Random House.

Karoly, Paul (2010) Psychopathology as dysfunctional self-regulation: When resilience resources are compromised. In J.W. Reich, A. Zautra, and J.S. Hall (Eds.), *Handbook of Adult Resilience* (pp. 146–170). New York: Guilford Press.

Kashdan, T. B., Weeks, J. W., and Savostyanova, A. A. (2011) Whether, how, and when social anxiety shapes positive experiences and events: A self-regulatory framework and treatment implications. *Clinical Psychology Review* 31(5): 786–799.

Kassam, Karim S., Gilbert, Daniel T., Boston, Andrew, and Wilson, Timothy D. (2008) Future anhedonia and time discounting. *Journal of Experimental Social Psychology* 44(6) (November): 1533–1537.

Kassel, J.D., Veilleux, J.C., Wardle, M.C., Yates, M.C., Greenstein, J.E., Evatt, D.P., et al. (2009) Negative affect and addiction. In M. al'Absi (Ed.), *Stress and Addiction*. New York: Elsevier Press.

Kavanagh, D.J., Andrade, J., and May, J. (2005) Imaginary relish and exquisite torture: The elaborated intrusion theory of desire. *Psychological Review* 112(2): 446–467.

Kawachi, I., Colditz, G.A., and Ascherio, A. (1994) Prospective study of phobic anxiety and risk of coronary heart disease in men. *Circulation* 89: 1992–1997.

Keltner, Dacher (2009) *Born to Be Good: The Science of a Meaningful Life*. New York: W.W. Norton & Company.

Kendler, K. S., Thornton, L. M., and Gardner, C. O. (2001) Genetic risk, number of previous depressive episodes, and stressful life events in predicting onset of major depression. *American Journal of Psychiatry* 158: 582–586.

Kessler, R. C. (2005) Prevalence, severity, and comorbidity of 12-month DSM-IV disorders in the National Comorbidity Survey Replication. *Archives of General Psychiatry* 62: 617–627.

Kessler, R. C., Akiskal, H. S., Ames, M. et al. (2006) Prevalence and effects of mood disorders on work performance in a nationally representative sample of US workers. *American Journal of Psychiatry* 163: 1561–1568.

Khan, U. and Dhar, R. (2006) Licensing effect in consumer choice. *Journal of Marketing Research* 43: 259–266.

Khantzian, E.J. (2003) Understanding addictive vulnerability: An evolving psychodynamic perspective. *Neuro-Psychoanalysis* 5: 5–21.

Khantzian, E.J. (2012). Reflections on treating addictive disorders: A psychodynamic perspective. *The American Journal on Addiction* 21: 274–279.

Khantzian, E.J. and Albanese, M.J. (2008) *Understanding Addiction as Self Medication: Finding Hope Behind the Pain*. New York: Rowman & Littlefield Publishers Inc.

Kirby, K .N. and Barbarose, Guastello. (2001) Making choices in anticipation of similar future choices can increase self-control. *Journal of Experimental Psychology: Applied* 7(2): 154–164.

Kirby, K.N., Petry, N. M., and Bickel, W. K. (1999) Heroin addicts have higher discount rates for delayed rewards than non-drug-using controls. *Journal of Experimental Psychology: General* 128: 78–87.

Kiverstein, J. (2012). The meaning of embodiment. *Topics in Cognitive Science* 4(4): 740–758.

Klingberg, Torkel (2013) *The Learning Brain: Memory and Brain Development in Children*. New York: Oxford University Press.

Koo, Minjung and Fishbach, A. (2008) Dynamics of self-regulation: How (un)accomplished goal actions affect motivation. *Journal of Personality and Social Psychology* 94: 183–195.

Koob, G. (2003) Drug reward and addiction. In L.R. Squire, F.E. Bloom, S.K. McConnell, et al. (Eds.), *Fundamental Neuroscience* (2nd ed.) (pp. 1127–1143). San Diego: Academic Press.

Koob, G. and Kreek, M.J. (2007) Stress, dysregulation of drug reward pathways, and the transition to drug dependence. *American Journal of Psychiatry* 164: 1149–1159.

Koob, G. and Le Moal, M. (2005) *Neurobiology of Addiction*. San Diego: Academic Press.

Koslowsky, M., Aizer, A., and Krausz, M. (1996) Stressor and personal variables in the commuting experience. *International Journal of Manpower* 17: 4–14.

Kosten, T.A. and Kehoe P. (2007) Early life stress and vulnerability to addiction: Translational studies with neonatal isolation of rat pups. In M. al'Absi (Ed.), *Stress and Addiction: Biological and Psychological Mechanisms* (pp. 105–126). San Diego: Elsevier.

Kringelbach, I. Morten and Berridge, C. Kent (2010) *Pleasures of the Brain*. New York: Oxford University Press.

Kross, E. and Ayduk, O. (2008) Facilitating adaptive emotional analysis: Distinguishing distanced-analysis of depressive experiences from immersed-analysis and distraction. *Personality and Social Psychology Bulletin* 34: 924–938.

Kurzban, Robert (2011) *Why Everyone (Else) Is a Hypocrite: Evolution and the Modular Mind*. Princeton: Princeton University Press.

Kushner, M.G., Abrams, K., and Borchardt, C. (2000) The relationship between anxiety disorders and alcohol use disorders: a review of major perspectives and findings. *Clinical Psychology Review* 20: 149–171.

Laibson, D. (2001) A cue-theory of consumption. *Quarterly Journal of Economics* 116: 81–119.

Layard, R. (2005) *Happiness: Lessons from a New Science*. London: Penguin Press.

Lazarus, R. (1991) *Emotion and Adaptation*. New York: Oxford University Press.

Lazarus, R. (1994) Psychological stress in the workplace. In R. Crandall and P. L. Perrewe (Eds.), *Occupational Stress: A Handbook* (pp. 3–14). New York: Taylor and Francis.

Lazarus, R. and Lazarus, B. (2006) *Coping with Aging*. New York: Oxford Press.

Leahy, R. (2006) *The Worry Cure: Seven Steps to Stop Worry from Stopping You*. New York: Three Rivers Press.

Leander, N.P., Moore, S.G., and Chartrand, T.L. (2009) Mystery moods: Their origins and consequences. In G.B. Moskowitz and H. Grant (Eds.), *The Psychology of Goals* (pp. 480–504). New York: Guilford Press.

Leary, M.R. (2004) *The Curse of the Self: Self-Awareness, Egotism, and the Quality of Human Life*. New York: Oxford University Press.

Leary, M.R. and Tangney, J.P. (2012) *Handbook of Self and Identity*. New York: Guilford Press.

LeDoux, J. (1996) *The Emotional Brain: The Mysterious Underpinnings of Emotional Life*. New York: Simon & Schuster.

LeDoux, J. (2002) *Synaptic Self*. New York: Viking.

Leineweber, C., Westerlund, H., Hagberg, J., Svedberg, P., Luokkala, M. et al. (2011) Sickness presenteeism among Swedish police officers. *Journal of Occupational Rehabilitation* 21: 17–22.

Lempert, K.M., Porcelli, A.J., Delgado, M.R., and Tricomi, E. (2012) Individual differences in delay discounting under acute stress: The role of trait perceived stress. *Frontiers in Psychology* 3: 1–10.

Lenton, Alison P. and Francesconi, Marco (2011) Too much of a good thing? Variety is confusing in mate choice. *Biology Letters* 7(4): 528–531.

Lerner, J.S. and Keltner, D. (2001) Fear, anger, and risk. *Journal of Personality and Social Psychology* 81(1): 146–159.

Lerner, J.S., Ye Li, and Weber, E.U., (2013) The financial costs of sadness. *Psychological Science*. doi: 10.1177/095679761245030

Lester, David (2013) An essay on loss of self versus escape from self in suicide: Illustrative cases from diaries left by those who died. *Suicidology Online* 4: 16–20.

Levinson, C.A. and Rodebaugh, T.L. (2012) Social anxiety and eating disorder comorbidity: The role of negative social evaluation fears. *Eating Behaviors* 13: 27–35.

Levitt, S.D. and Dubner, S.J. (2013) *Think Like a Freak*. New York: HarperCollins.

Lewin, K. (1951) *Field Theory in Social Science. Selected Theoretical Papers*. New York: Harper.

Lewis, H.B. (1987) Shame the sleeper in psychopathology. In H.B. Lewis (Ed.), *The role of Shame in Symptom Formation* (pp. 1–28). New Jersey: Erlbaum.

Liberman, N. and Dar, R. (2009) Normal and pathological consequences of encountering difficulties in monitoring progress toward goals. In G. Moskowitz and H. Grant (Eds.), *The Psychology of Goals* (pp. 277–305). New York: Guilford Press.

Liu, R.T. and Klieman, E.M. (2012) Impulsivity and the generation of negative life events: The role of negative urgency. *Personality and Individual Differences* 53(5): 609–612.

Liu, W. and Aaker, J. (2007) Do you look to the future or focus on today? The impact of life experience on intertemporal decisions. *Organizational Behavior and Human Decision Processes* 102(2): 212–225.

Lobel, J. and Loewenstein, G. (2005) Emote control: The substitution of symbol for substance in foreign policy and international law. *Chicago Kent Law Review* 80(3): 1045–1090: symposium volume "Must We Choose between Rationality and Irrationality."

Locke, E.A. and Latham, G.P. (2002) Building a practically useful theory of goal setting and task motivation: A 35-year odyssey. *American Psychologist* 57: 705–717.

Loewenstein, G. (1996) Out of control: Visceral influences on behavior. *Organizational Behavior and Human Decision Processes* 65: 272–292.

Loewenstein, G., Brennan, T., and Volpp, K. (2007) Asymmetric paternalism to improve health behaviors. *Journal of American Medical Association* 298(20): 2415–2417.

Loewenstein, G. and Haisley, E. (2008) The economist as therapist: The methodological ramifications of "light" paternalism. In Andrew Caplin and Andrew Schotter (Eds.), *The Foundations of Positive and Normative Economics* (pp. 210–246). New York: Oxford University Press.

Loewenstein, G. and O'Donoghue, T. (2004) Animal spirits: Affective and deliberative influences on economic behavior. Working paper, Department of Social and Decision Sciences, Carnegie Mellon University.

Loewenstein, G. F., Weber, E. U., Hsee, C. K., and Welch, N. (2001) Risk as feelings. *Psychological Bulletin* 127(2): 267–286.

Logue, A.W. (1988) Research on self-control: An integrating framework. *Behavioral and Brain Sciences* 11: 665–709.

Lopresti, A.L., Hood, S.D., and Drummond, P.D. (2013). A review of lifestyle factors that contribute to important pathways associated with major depression: Diet, sleep and exercise. *Journal of Affective Disorders.* 148: 12–27.

Ludwig, David (2012) Effects of dietary composition of energy expenditure during weight loss maintenance. *Journal of American Medical Association* 307(24): 2627–2634.

MacKilop, J., Amlung, M.T., Murphy, C.M., Acker, J., and Ray, L.A. (2013) A behavioral economic approach to health behavior. In R. DiClemente, L.F. Salazar, and R.A. Crosby (Eds.), *Theory and Practice for a New Public Health* (pp. 131–162). Burlington: Jones and Bartlett Publishers.

MacLean, P.D. (1990) *The Triune Brain in Evolution: Role in Paleocerebral Functions*. New York: Plenum Press.

Madden, G. J. and Bickel, W. K. (2010) *Impulsivity: the Behavioral and Neurological Science of Discounting*. Washington, D.C.: American Psychological Association.

Maddux, J.E. and Gosselin, J.T. (2011) Self-efficacy. In D.S. Dunn (Ed.), *Oxford Bibliographies Online: Psychology*. New York: Oxford University Press.

Maddux, J.E. and Winstead, B.A. (2012) *Psychopathology: Foundations for a Contemporary Understanding 3rd Edition*. New York: Routledge.

Magen, E., Dweck, C.S., and Gross, J. (2008) The hidden-zero effect: Representing a single choice as an extended sequence reduces impulsive choice. *Psychological Science* 19: 648–649.

Marinkovic, K., Oscar-Berman, M., Urban, T., O'Reilly, C. E., Howard, Sawyer, K., and Harris, G. J. (2009) Alcoholism and dampened temporal limbic activation to emotional faces. *Alcoholism: Clinical and Experimental Research* 33(11): 1880–1892.

Marlatt, G. A. and Katie Witkewitz (2005) Relapse prevention for alcohol and drug Problem. In G. Alan Marlatt and Dennis M.Donovan (Eds.), *Relapse Prevention: Maintenance Strategies in the Treatment of Addictive Behaviors*. (2nd ed.). New York: The Guilford Press

Marlatt, G.A. and Donovan, D.M. (Eds.) (2005) *Relapse Prevention: Maintenance Strategies in the Treatment of Addictive Behaviors* (2nd ed.). New York: Guilford Press.

Marlatt, G.A. and Gordon, J.R. (Eds.) (1985) *Relapse Prevention*. New York: Guilford Press.

Marlatt, G.A. and Witkiewitz, K. (2005) Relapse prevention for alcohol and drug problems. In G.A. Marlatt and D.M. Donovan (Eds.), *Relapse Prevention: Maintenance Strategies in the treatment of Addictive Behaviors* (2nd ed.) (pp. 1-44). New York: Guilford Press.

Marmot, M.R. and Wilkinson, G. (2006) *Social Determinants of Health* (2nd ed.). Oxford: Oxford University Press.

Martha, C. and Nussbaum, M.C. (2011) *Creating Capabilities: The Human Development Approach*. Cambridge, MA: Belknap Press of Harvard University Press.

Maslow, A. (1966) *The Psychology of Science: A Reconnaissance*. New York: Harper & Row.
Massing, Michael (2000) *The Fix*. Los Angeles: University of California Press.
Mate, Gabor (2010) *In the Realm of Hungry Ghosts*. Berkeley, CA: North Atlantic Books.
Mathews, A. and MacLeod, C. (2005) Cognitive vulnerability to emotional disorders. *Annual Review of Clinical Psychology* 1: 167–195.
May, M. (2009) *In Pursuit of Elegance: Why the Best Ideas Have Something Missing*. New York: Crown Business.
May, R. (1981) *Man's Search for Himself*. New York: Norton.
McClure, M., Laibson, D., Loewenstein, G., and Cohen, D. (2004) Separate neural systems value immediate and delayed monetary rewards. *Science* 306(15) (October): 503–507.
McClure S.M., Ericson, K.M., Laibson, D.I., Loewenstein, G., and Cohen, J.D. (2007) Time discounting for primary rewards. *Journal of Neuroscience* 27: 5796–5804.
McEwen, B.S. (2000) The neurobiology of stress: From serendipity to clinical relevance. *Brain Research* 886: 172–189.
McEwen, B.S. (2002). *The End of Stress as We Know It*. Washington, D.C.: Dana Press.
McGaugh, J.L. (2003) *Memory and Emotion: The Making of Lasting Memories*. London: Weidenfeld and Nicolson The Orion House Group Ltd. and New York: Columbia University Press.
McGilchrist, Iain (2009) *The Master and His Emissary: The Divided Brain and the Making of the Western World*. New Haven: Yale University Press.
McGinnis, J.M. and Foege, W.H. (1993) Actual causes of death in the United States. *Journal American Medical Association* 270(18): 207–212.
McGonigal, K. (2011) *The Willpower Instinct: How Self-Control Works, Why It Matters, and What You Can Do to Get More of It*. New York: Avery.
McNally, R.J. (2002) Anxiety sensitivity and panic disorder. *Biological Psychiatry* 52: 938–946.
McWilliams, N. (2011) *Psychoanalytic Diagnosis: Understanding Personality Structure in the Clinical Process* (2nd ed.). New York: Guilford.
Mednick, S.C., Nakayama, K., Cantero, J.L., Atienza, M., Levin, A.A., Pathak, N., and Stickgold, R. (2002) The restorative benefit of naps on perceptual deterioration. *Nature Neuroscience* 5: 677–681.
Meeten, F. and Davey, G (2011) Mood-as-input hypothesis and perseverative psychopathologies. *Clinical Psychology Review* 31: 1259–1275.
Mellers, B.A. and McGraw, A.P. (2001) Anticipated emotions as guides to choice. *Current Directions in Psychological Science* 10(6): 210–214.
Mercier, H. and Sperber, D. (2011) Why do humans reason? Arguments for an argumentative theory. *Behavioral and Brain Sciences* 34: 57–111.
Merikangas, K.R., He, J.P., Burstein, M., Swanson, S.A., Avenevoli, S., Cui, L., Benjet, C., Georgiades, K., and Swendsen, J. (2010) Lifetime prevalence of mental disorders in U.S. adolescents: Results from the National Comorbidity Survey Replication-Adolescent Supplement (NCS-A). *Journal of the American Academy of Child and Adolescent Psychiatry* 49(10): 980–989.
Mesquita, B. (2007) Emotions are culturally situated. *Social Science Information* 46(3): 410–415.
Mesquita, B., De Leersnyder, J., and Albert, D. (2014) The cultural regulation of emotions. In J.J. Gross (Ed.), *The Handbook of Emotion Regulation* (2nd ed.) (pp. 284–302). New York: Guilford Press.
Metcalfe, Janet and Mischel, Walter (1999) A hot/cool-system analysis of delay of gratification: dynamics of willpower. *Psychological Review* 106(1): 3–19.
Michel-Kerjan, Erwann O. and Slovic, Paul. (2010) *The Irrational Economist: Making Decisions in a Dangerous World*. New York: Public Affairs.

Mikulincer, M. and Shaver, P. R. (2007) *Attachment in Adulthood: Structure, Dynamics, and Change*. New York: Guilford Press.

Miller, Peter M. (2013) *Principles of Addiction* (vol 1). New York: Elsevier.

Millgram, E. (2010) Virtue for procrastinators. In C. Andreou and M.D. White (Eds.), *The Thief of Time: Philosophical Essays on Procrastination* (pp. 151–164). New York: Oxford University Press.

Mischel, W. and Ayduk, O. (2004) Willpower in a cognitive-affective processing system: The dynamics of delay of gratification. In K.D. Vohs and R.F. Baumeister (Eds.), *Handbook of Self-Regulation: Research, Theory, and Applications* (pp. 99–129). New York: Guilford Press.

Miskovic, V. and Schmidt, L.A. (2012) Early information processing biases in social anxiety. *Cognition and Emotion* 26: 176–185.

Miu, A.C., Heilman, R. M., and Houser, D. (2008) Anxiety impairs decision-making: Psychophysiological evidence from an Iowa Gambling Task. *Biological Psychology* 77: 353–358.

Mlodinow, L. (2008) *The Drunkard's Walk: The Story of Randomness and Its Role in Our Lives*. New York: Vintage Books.

Mlodinow, L. (2012) *Subliminal: How your Unconscious Mind Rules Your Behavior?* New York: Vintage Books.

Moene, K.O. (1996) Addiction and social interaction. Memorandum 24/1996, Department of Economics, Oslo University.

Mullainathan, S. and Eldar, S. (2013) *Scarcity*. New York: Times Book, Henry Holt and Company.

Myrseth, K.O.R., Fishbach, A., and Trope, Y. (2009) Counteractive self-control. *Psychological Science* 20(2): 159–163.

Naqvi, Nasir H., Rudrauf, David, Damasio, Hanna, and Bechara, Antoine (2007) Damage to the insula disrupts addiction to cigarette smoking. *Science* 26 (315) (January): 531–534.

Neff, K.D. (2011) Self-compassion, self-esteem, and well-being. *Social and Personality Psychology Compass* (5)1: 1–12.

Nestler, E.J. and Malenka, R.C. (2004) The addicted brain. *Scientific American*. 290(3): 78–85.

Nigg, J. (2013) Attention-deficit/hyperactivity disorder and adverse health outcomes. *Clinical Psychology Review* 33: 215–228.

Newman, Dorland W. A. (1965) *The American Illustrated Medical Dictionary* (18th ed.). Philadelphia: Saunders Co.

Nolen-Hoeksema, S. (1991) Responses to depression and their effects on the duration of depressive episodes. *Journal of Abnormal Psychology* 100: 569–582.

Nolen-Hoeksema, S., Wisco, B.E., and Lyubomirsky, S. (2008) Rethinking rumination. *Perspectives on Psychological Science* 3: 400–424.

Nordgren, L.F., van Harreveld, F., and van der Pligt, J. (2009) The restraint bias: How the illusion of self-restraint promotes impulsive behavior. *Psychological Science* 20(12): 1523–1528.

North, A., Hargreaves, D., and McKendrick, J. (1999) The influence of in-store music on wine selections. *Journal of Applied Psychology* 84: 271–276.

Norris, F., Friedman, M., Watson, P., Byrne, C., Diaz, E., and Daniasty, K. (2002) 60,000 disaster victims speak: I. An empirical review of the empirical literature, 1981–2001. *Psychiatry* 65: 207–239.

Norris, F. H. and Sloane, L. B. (2007) The epidemiology of trauma and PTSD. In M. J. Friedman, T. M. Keane, and P. A. Resick (Eds.), *Handbook of PTSD* (pp. 78–98). New York: Guilford Press.

Nussbaum, M. (2001) *Upheavals of Thought: The Intelligence of Emotions.* New York: Routledge.
Nussbaum, M. (2004) *Hiding from Humanity Disgust, Shame and the Law.* Princeton: Princeton University Press.
O'Donoghue, T. and Rabin, M. (1999) Doing it now or later. *American Economic Review* 89: 103–124.
Oettingen, G. (2000) Expectancy effects on behavior depend on self-regulatory thought. *Social Cognition* 18: 101–129.
Oettingen, G. and Gollwitzer, P. M. (2010) Strategies of setting and implementing goals: Mental contrasting and implementation intentions. In J. E. Maddux and J. P. Tangney (Eds.), *Social Psychological Foundations of Clinical Psychology* (pp. 114–135). New York: Guilford.
Offer, Avner (2006) *The Challenge of Affluence: Self-Control and Well-Being in the United States and Britain since 1950.* New York: Oxford University Press.
Ogden, T. H. (2010) Why read Fairbairn? *International Journal of Psychoanalysis.* 91: 101–118.
Olatunji, B. O., Ciesielski, B. G., Armstrong, T., and Zald, D. H. (2011) Emotional expressions and visual search efficiency: Specificity and effects of anxiety symptoms. *Emotion* 11: 1073–1079.
Olds, James (1956) Pleasure centers in the brain. *Scientific American* 105–116.
Ouimet, A.J., Gawronski, B., and Dozois, D.J. (2009) Cognitive vulnerability to anxiety: A review and an integrative model. *Clininical Psychological Review* (29): 459–470.
Oxford American Dictionary and Language Guide. New York: Oxford University Press, 1999.
Pani, P.P., Maremmani, I., Trogu, E., Gessa, G.L., Ruiz, P., and Akiskal, H.S. (2010) Delineating the psychic structure of substance abuse and addictions: Should anxiety, mood and impulse-control dysregulation be included? *Journal of Affective Disordorder* 122: 185–197.
Panksepp, J. (2001) The long-term psychobiological consequences of infant emotions: Prescriptions for the twenty-first century. *Infant Mental Health Journal* 22: 132–173.
Panksepp, J. and Biven, L. (2012) *The Archaeology of Mind: Neuroevolutionary Origins of Human Emotions.* New York: W.W. Norton & Company.
Parylak, S.L., Koob, G.F., and Zorrilla, E.P. (2011) The dark side of food addiction. *Physiology & Behavior* 104: 149–156.
Paulus, M.P. and Stewart, J.L. (2014) Interoception and drug addiction. *Neuropharmcology* 76: 342–350.
Peters, J. and Büchel, C. (2011) The neural mechanisms of inter-temporal decision-making: Understanding variability. *Trends in Cognitive Sciences* 15: 227–239.
Peterson, C. and Seligman, M.E.P. (2004) *Character Strengths and Virtues: A Handbook and Classification.* New York: Oxford University Press and Washington, DC: American Psychological Association.
Petry, N.M. (2002) Discounting of delayed rewards in substance abusers: Relationship to antisocial personality disorder. *Psychopharmacology* 162: 425–432.
Phelps, E.A. (2004) Human emotion and memory: Interactions of the amygdala and hippocampal complex. *Current Opinion in Neurobiology* 14: 198–202.
Pignatti, R., Bertella, L., Albani, G., Mauro, A., Molinari, E., Semenza, C. (2006) Decision-making in obesity: A study using the gambling task. *Eating and Weight Disorders* 11: 126–132.
Plassmann, Hilke, O'Doherty, John, Shiv, Baba, and Rangel, Antonio (2008) Marketing actions can modulate neural representations of experienced pleasantness. *The Proceedings of the National Academy of Sciences* 105(3): 1050–1054.
Platt, J. (1973) Social Traps. *American Psychologist* 28(8): 641–651.
Plutchik, R. (2003) *Emotions and life: Perspectives from psychology, biology, and evolution.* Washington, D.C.: American Psychological Association.

Polivy, J. and Herman, C. P. (1985) Dieting and binge eating: A causal analysis. *American Psychologist* 40: 193–204.

Polivy, J. and Herman C. P. (2002) The false-hope syndrome: Unfulfilled expectations of self-change. *American Psychologist* 57(9): 677–689.

Prelec, D. and Simester, D. (2001) Always leave home without it: A further investigation of the credit-card effect on willingness to pay. *Marketing Letters* 12: 1, 5–12.

Przybylski, A.K., Murayama, K., DeHaan, C.R., and Gladwell, V. (2013) Motivational, emotional, and behavioral correlates of fear of missing out. *Computers in Human Behavior* 29: 1814–1848.

Puhl, R.M. and King, K.M. (2013) Weight discrimination and bullying. *Best Practice & Research Clinical Endocrinology & Metabolism* 27(2): 1–11.

Putler, Daniel S. (1992) Incorporating reference price effects into a theory of consumer choice. *Marketing Science* 11(3) (Summer): 287–309.

Rachlin, Howard (2000) *The Science of Self-Control*. Cambridge: Harvard University Press.

Raine, Adrian (2013) *The Anatomy of Violence*. New York: Pantheon.

Ramachandran, V.S. (2004) *A Brief Tour of Human Consciousness*. London: Pearson Education Ltd.

Rangel, A., Camerer, C., and Montague, R. (2008) A framework for studying the neurobiology of value-based decision-making. *Nature Reviews Neuroscience* 9: 545–556.

Rayo, Luis and Becker, Gary S. (2007) Evolutionary efficiency and happiness. *Journal of Political Economy* 115(2): 302–337.

Redish, A.D. (2013) *The Mind Within the Brain: How We Make Decisions and How Those Decisions Go Wrong?* New York: Oxford University Press.

Redish, A.D., Jensen, S., and Johnson, A. (2008) A unified framework for addiction: Vulnerabilities in the decision process. *Behavioral and Brain Sciences* 31(4): 415–437.

Reich, J., Zautra, A., and Hall, J. (2010) *Handbook of Adult Resilience*. New York: Gilford Press.

Reynolds, B., Penfold, R. B., and Patak, M. (2008) Dimensions of impulsive behavior in adolescents: Laboratory behavioral assessments. *Experimental and Clinical Psychopharmacology* 16: 124–131.

Robichaud, M., Dugas, M. J., and Conway, M. (2003) Gender differences in worry and associated cognitive-behavioural variables. *Journal of Anxiety Disorders* 17: 501–516.

Robins, L.N., Helzer, J.E., Hesselbrock, M., and Wish, E. (1980) Vietnam veterans three years after Vietnam: How our study changed our view of heroin. In L. Bill and C. Winick (Eds.), *The Yearbook of Substance Use and Abuse* (vol. 2 pp. 213–230). New York: Human Sciences Press.

Robinson, J., Sareen, J., Cox, B. J., and Bolton, J. M. (2011) Role of self-medication in the development of comorbid anxiety and substance use disorders: A longitudinal investigation. *Archives of General Psychiatry* 68(8): 800–807.

Rollins, B.Y., Loken, E., Savage, J.S., and Birch, L. L.(2014) Effects of restriction on children's intake differ by child temperament, food reinforcement, and parent's chronic use of restriction. *Appetite* 73(1): 31–39.

Rolls, T. E. (2000) *The Brain and Emotion*. Oxford: Oxford University Press.

Romero-Canyas, R., Downey, G., Berenson, K., Ayduk, Ö., and Kang, N.J. (2010) Rejection sensitivity and the rejection-hostility link in romantic relationships. *Journal of Personality* 78: 119–148.

Rose, R.J. and Dick, D.M. (2007) Gene-Environment Interplay in Adolescent Drinking Behavior. *National Institute on Alcohol Abuse and Alcoholism* 25: 637–643.

Rothman, A.J., Hertel, A.W., Baldwin, A.S., and Bartels, R. (2008) Integrating theory and practice: Understanding the determinants of health behavior change. In J. Shah and W. Gardner (Eds.), *Handbook of motivation science* (pp. 494–507). New York: Guilford.

Ruhm, C.J. (2012) Understanding overeating and obesity. *Journal of Health Economics*. 31(6): 781–796.
Saffer, H. and Dhaval, Dave (2006) Alcohol advertising and alcohol consumption by adolescents. *Health Economics* 15(6): 617–637.
Safran, J.D. (2012) Psychoanalysis and psychoanalytic therapies. Washington, D.C.: American Psychological Association Publications.
Salsberg, S. and Thurman, T. (2013) *Love your Enemy*. New York: Hay House.
Sayette, M. (2004) Self-regulatory failure and addiction. In R. F. Baumeister and K. D. Vohs (Eds.), *Handbook of Self-regulation* (pp. 447–465). Guilford Press: New York.
Sayette, M.A., Loewenstein, G., Griffin, K. M., and Black, J. J. (2008) Exploring the cold-to-hot empathy gap in smokers. *Psychological Science* 9(19): 926–932.
Sayette, M.A., Loewenstein, G., Kirchner, T.R., and Travis, T. (2005) Effects of smoking urge on temporal cognition. *Psychology of Addictive Behaviors* 19: 88–93.
Schelling, T. (1984) Self-command in practice, in policy, and in a theory of rational choice. *American Economic Review* 74: 1–11.
Scherer, K. (2005) What are emotions? And how can they be measured? *Social Science Information* 44(4): 695–729.
Schmidt, H., Stock, S., and Doran, T. (2012) *Moving Forward with Wellness Incentives Under the Affordable Care Act: Lessons from Germany*. New York: Issues in International Health Policy.
Scholer, A.E. and Higgins, T. (2010) Conflict and control at different levels of self-regulation In R. Hassin and K. Ochsner (Eds.), *Self Control in Society, Mind, and Brain* (pp. 312–334). Oxford: Oxford University Press.
Schore, Allan A. (2012) *The Science of the Art of Psychotherapy*. New York: W.W. Norton & Company.
Schultz, H. (2012) *Onward: How Starbucks Fought for Its Life without Losing Its Soul*. New York: Rodale Books.
Schultz, W. (2006) Behavioral theories and the neurophysiology of reward. *Annual Review Psychology* 57: 87–115.
Schwartz, B. (2004) *The Paradox of Choice: Why More Is Less*. New York: HarperCollins.
Schwartz, B., Ward, A., Monterosso, J., Lyubomirsky, S., White, K., and Lehman, D. R. (2002) Maximizing versus satisficing: Happiness is a matter of choice. *Journal of Personality and Social Psychology* 83: 1178–1197.
Schwartz, Jeffrey M. and Begley, Sharon (2003) *The Mind and the Brain: Neuroplasticity and the Power of Mental Force*. New York: HarperCollins.
Schweiger Gallo, I. and Gollwitzer, P. M. (2007) Implementation intentions: Control of fear despite cognitive load. *Psicothema* 19: 280–285.
Segal, Z.V., Williams, J.M.G., and Teasdale, J. D. (2012) *Mindfulness-Based Cognitive Therapy for Depression* (2nd ed.). New York: Guilford Press.
Seligman, Martin E.P. (2011) *Flourish: A Visionary New Understanding of Happiness and Well-being*. New York: Free Press.
Selye, H. (1976) *The Stress of Life*. New York: McGraw-Hill.
Shamosh, N.A., Deyoung, C.G., Green, A.E., Reis, D.L., Johnson, M.R., Conway, A.R., . . . Gray, J.R. (2008) Individual differences in delay discounting: Relation to intelligence, working memory, and anterior prefrontal cortex. *Psychological Science* 19(9): 904–911.
Shapiro, D. (1965) *Neurotic Styles*. New York: Basic Books.
Shenhav, A. and Buckner, R.L. (2014) Neural correlates of dueling affective reactions to win–win choices. *Proceedings of the National Academy of Sciences* 111(30): 10978–10983.
Shepard, R. N. (1990) *Mind Sights: Original Visual Illusions, Ambiguities, and other Anomalies*. New York: WH Freeman and Company.

Shiv, B. and Fedorikhin, A. (1999) Heart and mind in conflict: Interplay of affect and cognition in consumer decision making. *Journal of Consumer Research* 26(December): 278–282.

Siegel, R. K. (1982) Cocaine free base abuse: A new smoking disorder. *Journal of Psychoactive Drugs* 14 (1982): 321–337.

Siegel, S. (1989) Pharmacological conditioning and drug effects. In A. J. Goudie and M. W. Emmett-Oglesby (Eds.), *Psychoactive Drugs: Tolerance and Sensitization* (pp. 115–180). Clifton, NJ: Humana Press.

Silvia, Paul J. (2006) *Exploring the Psychology of Interest*. New York: Oxford University Press.

Simon, Herbert A. (1955) A behavioral model of rational choice. *Quarterly Journal of Economics* 69(1): 99–118.

Sirois, F.M. (2004) Procrastination and intentions to perform health behaviors: The role of self-efficacy and the consideration of future consequences. *Personality and Individual Differences* 37: 115–128.

Skinner, B.F. (1953) *Science and Human Behavior*. New York: Free Press.

Skog, O.-J. (2003) Addiction: Definitions and mechanisms. In R. Vuchinich and N. Heather (Eds.), *Choice, Behavioral Economics and Addiction* (pp. 157–175). Amsterdam: Pergamon/Elsevier.

Slors, M. (2013) Conscious intending as self-programming. *Philosophical Psychology* (33): 1–20.

Slovic, P. (Ed.) (2001) *Smoking: Risk, perception, and Policy*. Thousand Oaks: Sage.

Solanto, M. V., Abikoff, H., Sonuga-Barke, E., Schachar, R., Logan, G. D., Wigal, T., . . . Turkel, E. (2001) The ecological validity of delay aversion and response inhibition as measures of impulsivity in ADHD: A supplement to the NIMH multimodal treatment study of ADHD. *Journal of Abnormal Child Psychology* 29: 215–228.

Solinas, M., Chauvet, C., Thiriet, N., El Rawas, R., and Jaber, M. (2008) Reversal of cocaine addiction by environmental enrichment. *Proceedings of the National Academy of Sciences* 105(44): 17145–17150.

Solley, C. M. and Haigh, G. (1957) A note to Santa Claus. *Topeka Research Papers. The Menninger Foundation* 18: 4–5.

Solomon, Andrew (2001) *The Noonday Demon: An Atlas of Depression*. New York: Scribner.

Solomon, R.L. (1980) The opponent-process theory of acquired motivation: The costs of pleasure and the benefits of pain. *American Psychologist* 35: 691–712.

Solomon, Robert C. (2007) *True to Our Feelings: What Our Emotions Are Really Telling Us*. New York: Oxford University Press.

Southwick, S.M. and Charney, D.S. (2012) *Resilience: The Science of Mastering Life's Greatest Challenges*. New York: Cambridge University Press.

Spears, D. (2011) Economic decision-making in poverty depletes behavioral control. *Journal of Economic Analysis & Policy* 11(1): Article 72.

Spencer, S. J., Fein, S., Wolfe, C. T., Fong, C., and Dunn, M. A. (1998) Automatic activation of stereotypes: The role of self-image threat. *Personality and Social Psychology Bulletin* 24: 1139–1152.

Spiegel, S., Grant-Pillow, H., and Higgins, E.T. (2004) How regulatory fit enhances motivational strength during goal pursuit. *European Journal of Social Psychology* 34: 39–54.

Stanovich, K.E. (2010) *Rationality and the Reflective Mind*. New York: Oxford University Press.

Steele, P. (2007) The nature of procrastination: A meta-analytic and theoretical review of quintessential self-regulatory failure. *Psychological Bulletin* 133(1) (January): 65–94.

Stern, D.B. (2011) *Partner in Thought: Working with Unfortunate Experience, Dissociation, and Enactment*. New York: Routledge.

Stossel, S. (2013) *My Age of Anxiety*. New York: Alfred A. Knopf.
Stutz, P. and Michels, B. (2012) *The Tools*. New York: Spiegel & Grau.
Subramaniam, K., Kounios, J., Parrish, T.B., and Jung-Beeman, M. (2009) A brain mechanism for facilitation of insight by positive affect. *Journal of Cognitive Neuroscience* 21: 415–432.
Sunstein, C.R. (2013) *Simpler*. New York: Simom & Scuster.
Takuya, Hayashi, Ji Hyun, Ko, Antonio, P. Strafella, and Alain, Dagher (2013) Dorsolateral prefrontal and orbitofrontal cortex interactions during self-control of cigarette craving. *PNAS* 10(11): 4422–4427.
Tal, Aner and Wansink, Brian (2013) Fattening fasting: Hungry grocery shoppers buy more calories, not more food. *Journal of American Medical Association Internal Medicine*. 173(12): 1146–1148.
Taleb, N. (2007) *The Black Swan: The Impact of the Highly Improbable*. New York: Random House, Penguin.
Taleb, N.M. (2012) *Antifragile*. New York: Random House.
Tangney, J.P. and Dearing, R.L. (2003) *Shame and Guilt*. New York: The Guilford Press.
Tarter, R.E., Kirisci, L., Mezzich, A., Cornelius, J.R., Pajer, K., Vanyukov, M. et al. (2003) Neurobehavioral disinhibition in childhood predicts early age of onset of substance use disorder. *The American Journal of Psychiatry* 160(6): 1078–1085.
Tasca, G.A., Demidenko, N., Krysanski, V., Bissada, H., Illing, V., Gick, M. et al. (2009) Personality dimensions among women with an eating disorder: Towards reconceptualizing DSM. *European Eating Disorders Review* 17: 281–289.
Tedeschi, R.G. and Calhoun, L.G. (2004) Posttraumatic growth: Conceptual foundations and empirical evidence. *Psychological Inquiry* 15: 1–18.
Thaler, R.H. and Shefrin, H.M. (1981) An economic theory of self-control. *Journal of Political Economy* 89: 392–406.
Thaler, Richard H. and Sunstein, Cass R. (2008). *Nudge: Improving Decisions about Health, Wealth, and Happiness*. New Haven: Yale University Press.
Thombs, D.L. and Osborn, C.J. (2013) *Introduction to Addictive Behaviors* (4th ed.). New York: The Guildford Press.
Thorndike, A.N., Sonnenberg, L., Riss, J., (2012) A 2-phase labeling and choice architecture intervention to improve healthy food and beverage choices. *American Journal of Public Health* 102(3): 527–533.
Thorndike, E.L. (1911) *Animal Intelligence: Experimental Studies*. New York: Macmillan.
Tice, D. and Baumeister, R.F. (1997) Longitudinal study of procrastination, performance, stress, and health: The costs and benefits of dawdling. *Psychological Science* 8: 454–458.
Tice, D., Baumeister, R.F., Shmueli, D., and Muraven, M. (2007) Replenishing the self: Effects of positive affect on performance and persistence following ego depletion. *Journal of Experimental Social Psychology* 43(3): 379–384.
Tice, D., Braslasvky, E. and Baumeister, R. (2001) Emotional distress regulation takes precedence over impulse control. *Journal of Personality and Social Psychology* 80: 53–67.
Tiffany, S.T. (1999) Cognitive concepts of craving. *Alcohol Research & Health* 23(3): 215–224.
Tillich, Paul (1944) Existential philosophy. *Journal of the History of Ideas* 5(1): 44–70.
Tononi, Giulio (2012) *Phi: A Voyage from the Brain to the Soul*. New York: Pantheon.
Toohey, P. (2011) *Boredom: A Lively History*. New Haven: Yale University Press.
Trope, Y. and Liberman, N. (2003) Temporal construal. *Psychological Review* 110: 403–421.
Trope, Y. and Liberman, N. (2010) Construal-level theory of psychological distance. *Psychological Review* 117(2): 440–463.
Tversky, A. and Kahneman, D. (1974). Judgment under uncertainty: Heuristics and biases. *Science* 185: 1124–1130.

Ulman, R. B. and Paul, Harry (2006) *The Self Psychology of Addiction and Its Treatment*. London: Routledge.
Unsworth, N. and Engle, R.W. (2007) The nature of individual differences in working memory capacity: Active maintenance in primary memory and controlled search from secondary memory. *Psychological Review* (114): 104–113.
Urbszat, D., Herman, C.P., and Polivy, J. (2002) Eat, drink, and be merry, for tomorrow we diet: Effects of anticipated deprivation on food intake in restrained and unrestrained eaters. *Journal of Abnormal Psychology* 111: 396–401.
Vaillant, G. E (1995) *The Natural History of Alcoholism Revisited*. Cambridge: Harvard University Press.
Verdejo-Garcia, A., Clark, L., and Dunn, B.D. (2012) The role of interoception in addiction: A critical review. *Neuroscience & Biobehavioral Reviews* 36(8):1857–1869.
Vohs, K.D. and Baumeister, R.F. (Eds.) (2011) *Handbook of Self-Regulation: Research, Theory, and Applications* (2nd ed.). New York: Guilford.
Vohs, K.D. and Schooler, J.W. (2008) The value of believing in free will: Encouraging a belief in determinism increases cheating. *Psychological Science* 19: 49–54.
Volkow, N.D. and Baler, R.D. (2013) Addiction science: Uncovering neurobiological complexity. *Neuropharmacology* 76: 235–249.
Volkow, N.D., Wang, G. J, Begleiter, H., Porjesz, B., Fowler, J. S., Telang, F., . . . Thanos, P. K. (2006) High levels of dopamine D2 receptors in unaffected members of alcoholic families: Possible protective factors. *Archives of General Psychiatry* 63(9): 999–1008.
von Hippel, W. and Henry, J.D. (2011). Aging and self-regulation. In K.D. Vohs and R.F. Baumeister (Eds.), *Handbook of Self-Regulation: Research, Theory, and Applications* (2nd ed.) (pp. 321–335). New York: Guilford Press.
Vuchinich, R. E. and Heather, N. (2003) *Choice, Behavioral Economics, and Addiction*. Oxford: Pergamon Press.
Wansink, B., Aner, T., Mitsuru, S. (2012) First foods most: After 18-hour fast, people drawn to starches first and vegetables last. *Archives of Internal Medicine* 172(12): 961–963.
Webster's New World College Dictionary (4th ed. Updated). New York: MacMillan, 2002.
Wedig, M. M. and Nock, M. K. (2010) Functional assessment of maladaptive behaviors: A preliminary evaluation of binge eating and purging among women. *Psychiatry Research* 178: 518–524.
Weeks, J. W. (2014) *The Wiley Blackwell Handbook of Social Anxiety Disorder*. Malden, MA: Wiley Blackwell.
Wegner, D.M. and Schneider, D.J. (2003) The white bear story. *Psychological Inquiry* 14: 326–329.
Wegner, D. M. (2002) *The Illusion of Conscious Will*. Cambridge: MIT Press.
Weller, R., Cook III, E., Avsar, K., Cox, J. (2008) Obese women show greater delay discounting than healthy-weight women. *Appetite* 51: 563–569.
Wells, A. (2009) *Metacognitive Therapy for Anxiety and Depression*. New York: Guilford.
Wenzlaff, R. and Wegner, D. (2000) Thought suppression. *Annual Review of Psychology* 51: 59–91.
Werner, K. and Gross, J.J. (2010) Emotion regulation and psychopathology: A conceptual framework. In A. Kring and D. Sloan (Eds.), *Emotion Regulation and Psychopathology: A Transdiagnostic Approach to Etiology and Treatment* (pp. 13–37). New York: Guilford Press.
Werrij, M.Q., Jansen, A., Mulkens, S., Elgersma, H., Ament, A.J.H.A., and Hospers, H.J. (2009) Adding cognitive therapy to dietetic treatment is associated with less relapse in obesity. *Journal of Psychosomatic Research* 67: 315–324.

Whiteside, U., Chen, E., Neighbors, C., Hunter, D., Lo, T., and Larimer, M. (2007) Difficulties regulating emotions: Do binge eaters have fewer strategies to modulate and tolerate negative affect? *Eating Behaviors* 8: 162–169.

Wiley, J. and Jarosz, A.F. (2012) How working memory capacity affects problem solving. *Psychology of Learning and Motivation* (56): 185–227.

Wilkinson, N. and Klaes, M. (2011) *An Introduction to Behavioral Economics: A Guide for Students*. New York: Palgrave Macmillan.

Williams, J.M.G., Barnhofer, T., Crane, C., Hermans, D., Raes, F., Watkins, E., et al. (2007) Autobiographical memory specificity and emotional disorder. *Psychological Bulletin* 133(1): 122–148.

Wilson, M. and Daly, M. (2003) Do pretty women inspire men to discount the future. *Biology Letters* (Proceedings, Royal Society of London) 270: 189–191.

Wilson, T.D. (2002) *Strangers to Ourselves: Discovering the Adaptive Unconscious*. Cambridge: Harvard University Press.

Wilson, T.D. (2011) *Redirect: The Surprising New Science of Psychological Change*. New York: Little, Brown and Company.

Wing, R.R. and Phelan, S. (2005) Long-term weight loss maintenance. *American Journal of Clinical Nutrition* 82: 222S–225S.

Wirtz, J., Kimes, S, Theng, J.H.P., and Patterson, P. (2003) Revenue management: Resolving potential customer conflicts. *Journal of Revenue and Pricing Management* 2(3): 216–226.

Wise, R.A. (1980) The dopamine synapse and the notion of 'pleasure centers' in the brain. *Trends Neurosci* 3: 91–95.

Wise, R.A. (1988) The neurobiology of craving: Implications for understanding and treatment of addiction. *Journal of Abnormal Psychology* 97: 118–132.

Wise, R.A. (1989) The brain and reward. In J.M. Liebmanand and S.J.Cooper (Eds.), *The Neuropharmacological Basis of Reward* (pp. 377–424). Oxford: Oxford University Press.

Wise, R. A. (2004) Dopamine, learning and motivation. Nature Reviews Neuroscience 5: 483–494.

Wood, W. and Neal, D.T. (2007) A new look at habits and the habit-goal interface. *Psychological Review* 14: 843–863.

Wright, R. (1994) *The Moral Animal*. New York: Random House/Pantheon.

Yang, Haiyang, Ziv Carmon, Barbara Kahn, Anup Malani, Janet Schwartz, Kevin Volpp, and Brian Wansink (2012) "The Hot-Cold Decision Triangle: A Framework for Healthier Choices," *Marketing Letters* 23 (2) (June): 457–472

Yoon, J. H., Higgins, S. T., Heil, S. H., Sugarbaker, R. J., Thomas, C. S., Badger, G. J. (2007) Delay discounting predicts postpartum relapse to cigarette smoking among pregnant women. *Experimental & Clinical Psychopharmacology* 15: 176–186.

Zaider, T., Heimberg, R., and Iida, M. (2010) Anxiety disorders and intimate relationships: A study of daily processes in couples. *Journal of Abnormal Psychology* 119(1): 163–173.

Zajonc, R.B. (1980) Feeling and thinking: Preferences need no inferences. *American Psychologist* 35(2): 151–175.

Zajonc, R. B. (1984) On the primacy of affect. *American Psychologist* 39(2): 117–123.

Zajonc, R.B. and Markus, H. (1982) Affective and cognitive factors in preferences. *Journal of Consumer Research* 9: 123–131.

Zaridze, D., Lewington, S., Boroda, A., Scélo, G., Karpov, R., Lazarev, A., . . . Peto, R. (2014) Alcohol and mortality in Russia: Prospective observational study of 151,000 adults. *Lancet* 383(9927): 1465–1473.

Zauberman, G., Kim, B.K., Malkoc, S., and Bettman, J. (2009) Time discounting and discounting time. *Journal of Marketing Research* 46: 543–556.

INDEX

Page numbers for figures and tables are in italics.

AA (Alcoholics Anonymous) 51–2, 57, 148, 184, 225, 252
ABC model of emotional distress 145–6
abstinence 55, 62, 187, 242–3
abstinence violation effect (AVE) 207, 251–2
acetaldehyde 47, 172, 191n1
action-outcome associations 10–11
action tendencies 77–8, 81, 84, 91n8, 96
adaptation 85–8, 147
adaptive brain 61–3
addiction: attachment anxiety and 136–9; as bad habits 55; biology of 57–63; causes of 20–1; characteristics of 46, 52–3; choice and 167–92; cognitive behavioral therapy (CBT) and 251; conditioning and 53–4; craving and 50–1; decision making failure and 9–13, 182–9; defined 48–9; disease theory of 48, 171–3; dissociation and 141; extinction and 55; as hijacking of brain 60; impaired insight in 188; impulsivity and 186–7; loneliness and 176–7; neural basis of 170; primrose path model of 176; reinforcement and 54–5; relapse and 51–2; reward and 48–9, 105, 177–8; as self-medication 173–6; social influences and 178–9; stages of 170–1; stress, and vulnerability to 179–82; tolerance and 49; visceral states of 183; withdrawal and 49–50
addictive behavior 2; defined 15, 46; delay discounting and 6; models of 171–9
addictive capital 174–5
ADHD (attention-deficit/hyperactivity disorder) 12, 168n4, 168n6, 187, 213, 214n10
adjustment 30
ADP (antisocial personality disorder) 187
adrenaline 83
adult separation anxiety disorder (ASAD) 130–1, 150n12
adversity 133–4, 145
affect: cognition and 99–100; defined 80, 96; depression and 114, 208; emotion and 80–2; negative 160, 173, 182, 208–9, 252; positive 204; primacy of 100
affect-as-information theory 100, 118n4
affective system 19–20, 93–102, 123–5, 186–7
Agassi, A. 45n17
agency 21n7
age, time preference and 156–7
agoraphobia 130
Ainslie, G. 55
Alcoholics Anonymous (AA) 51–2, 57, 148, 184, 225, 252

alcohol myopia 202
alcohol withdrawal symptoms 50
aldehyde dehydrogenase (ALDH) 172, 191n1
Alli 259n1
allostasis 180–1
alternative rewards 243
Ambady, N. 44n2
American Heritage Dictionary 217
American Psychological Association: *Diagnostic and Statistical Manual of Mental Disorders* (DSM 5) 53
amphetamines 47
amygdala 122–5, 132, 139
analytic learning 23–8
analytic system 95
anchoring 30, 44n10
Angner, E. 22n14
anhedonia 63, 209
Antabuse 242, 259n1
anticipation 51, 61, 129, 160–1
antidepressant drugs 112–13, 116, 147
Antifragile (Taleb) 148
anti-reward system 62
antisocial personality disorder (ADP) 187
anxiety: attachment 136–9; attention control and 125–6; decision making and 120–51; depression and 112; disorders 127–32; fear and 121–3, 130; fear of missing out (FOMO) 87–8; influence on thinking of 141–4; monitoring and 233; posttraumatic growth and 147–8; procrastination and 167; psychoanalysis and 139–41; self-medication and 126–7; taming of 145–7; theories of 132–6
anxiety sensitivity (AS) 131
Anxiety Sensitivity Index (ASI) 131, 150n13
appearance-equals-reality rule 43
appraisal 77–9, 84–5, 99–100, 250–1
a-process 62
Aristotle 90n2, 118n10, 223
arousal 142–3, 184
ASAD (adult separation anxiety disorder) 130–1, 150n12
AS (anxiety sensitivity) 131
ASI (Anxiety Sensitivity Index) 131, 150n13
associative learning 53, 197
attachment anxiety 136–9
attentional bias 183–4
attention control 125–6

attention-deficit/hyperactivity disorder (ADHD) 12, 168n4, 168n6, 187, 213, 214n10
attribution 35–7, 82
Augustine: *Confessions* 163
automatic (intuitive) learning 23–8, 37–8, 95, 96, 197, 243–4
automatic nervous system 149n1
automatic priming 100
automatic self-control 256–8
AVE (abstinence violation effect) 207, 251–2
Avicenna 150n8
avoidance 56, 123, 130, 137–8, 143

Bacon, F. 253
basic emotions 79–80
Baumeister, R. 209
Beck, A. 113–14, 146, 250
Becker and Murphy model 176
Becker, E.: *The Denial of Death* 126–7
Becker, G. 48, 88, 157, 176
behavior: addictive 1–2, 6, 46, 171–9; control of 13–16; defensive 143; impulsive 6, 14, 166; instinctive 24; learned 133; novelty-seeking 67; over time 161–3, 195–6; risk-taking 42–3; role of emotion in 93; self-control failure and 193–216; strategies for changing 239–60
behavioral economics 3–6, 263–4
behaviorism 259n9
belief 39–42
Benabou, R. 249
Bentham, J. 82
Bernheim, B. 94
Berridge, K. 64
Berthoz, A. 72
Bickel, W. 22n14, 154, 187
binge eating and drinking 116, 208–9
Bing Nursery School 158
Biven, L. 5–6
Blake, W.: *The Marriage of Heaven and Hell* 214n5
Blink: The Power of Thinking without Thinking (Gladwell) 24
blood sugar 203, 207
Boon, B. 202
boredom 47, 213, 216n28
Borkovec, T. 146
bounded rationality 34, 45n15
Bowlby, J. 130

b-process 62
brain: adaptive 61–3; executive 158; left- and right-brain model 118n7; pleasure center of 47–8, 59–61; regions of 58, 67, 93–4
broaden-and-build theory 83, 138
Bryan, C. 242
Büchel, C. 157
Buddha 88
Buddhism 73
bundling choices 255

Cacioppo, J. 177
caffeine withdrawal symptoms 50
causality, illusion of 37–8
CBT (cognitive behavior therapy) 116, 146–7, 250–1, 259n9–10
Chaplin, C. 215n23
Charney, D. 222
childhood experience, adverse 133–4
choice 97; addiction and 167–92; anxiety and 144; architecture 263; bundling 255; consistent behavior over time and 161–3; delay and 154–5; ego depletion and 201; emotion and 3; intertemporal 6, 152; local *vs.* global approach to decision making and 163–5; over time 152–69; preferences and 105, 262; procrastination and 165–7; rational 3–6, 11, 78, 164–5, 194–5; scarcity and 31; self-control and 223–4
choking under pressure 142–3, 202
chronic stress 180–2
chunking 56–7, 69n8
Clark, D. 146
classical conditioning 53–4, 184
CLT (construal level theory) 211–12, 216n27, 247–8
coca 46–7
cocaine 47–9
cognition 72, 186–7; affect and 99–100; biases in 23–45, 113; capacity 31, 157–8; decision making and 2; deficit 158–9; distortions in 113; emotion and 77–9, 82–3, 183; mood and 81; self-control strategies and 245–9, 252; stress and 182
cognitive behavior therapy (CBT) 116, 146–7, 250–1, 259n9–10
cognitive dissonance 39–40, 43, 184
cognitive load 158–9, 202
cognitive psychology 5, 44n1

cold reasoning 8, 14, 94, 245
cold-to-hot empathy gap 184–6, 210–11
cold turkey 62–3
color-word Stroop task 218–19
commitment 3, 14, 229
comorbidity 112, 126, 130, 150n11, 172, 175
complex emotions 79–80
compulsions. *see* obsessive-compulsive disorder (OCD)
conditioned stimulus (CS) 52–5
conditioning 52–5, 133, 184, 240
confabulation 103
Confessions (Augustine) 163
confirmation bias 40–1, 198
conscious decision making 7–9
construal level theory (CLT) 211–12, 216n27, 247–8
context 4, 28–9, 264
contingency management 242–3
cooling-off period 248
cool reasoning 158
coping 181, 222
correlation, causation and 37
cortex 58, 94
cost-benefit analysis 3, 13, 114, 209–10
cost strategies 241–2
counteractive-control strategy 258
Coyle, D.: *The Talent Code* 221
craving 1, 49, 168, 182–4; cold-to-hot empathy gap and 185–6; defined 50–2, 183; extinction and 55; habit and 57; thought suppression and 246–7; as toxic 69n3
creativity 216n27
cross-sensitization 63
crystallized intelligence 27, 44n7
CS (conditioned stimulus) 52–5
cues: dopamine and 61; environmental 50–2, 55, 97, 182, 206–7; habit and 57; management of 215n14, 240–1; situational 198–9, 258; temptation 258; wanting *vs.* liking and 64–5
curiosity 67

Dalrymple, T. 175–6
Daly, M. 215n20
Damasio, A. 81, 110, 122, 159, 167
Dar, R. 233
Darwin, C. 76, 149n2; *The Expression of the Emotions in Man and Animals* 91n6
Darwinian approach 106

Dawkins, R.: *The Selfish Gene* 107–8
decision biases 23–45
decision making 1, 9–11; anxiety and 120–51; cognition and 2; by default 243–4; delay discounting and 6–8; ego depletion and 201; emotion and 1–3, 93–119; failure in 9–13, 23, 170, 182–9; five steps to 9–10; hot-cold decision triangle framework 8; impairments 109–11; local vs. global approach to 163–5, 255
decision utility 32–3
defense mechanisms 140–1
defensive behavior 143
delay discounting 6–8, 14, 152–60, 194–5
deliberation 13–15, 26, 56, 98, 197
Denial of Death, The (Becker) 126–7
dependence *see* addiction
depressants 173
depression: affect and 114, 208; anxiety and 112; defective reward systems and 172; dopamine and 59–60; nicotine dependence and 174; projection bias and 211; vulnerability to 111–16
Descartes, R. 74
desensitization 144
desensitiziation 55
desirability 259n7
desire 167–8, 199–200; belief and 39–42; Elaborated Intrusion (EI) theory of 184, 200; intoxication and 202; sources of 107–8; unconscious 139–40; wanting vs. liking and 63–5
despair 148
determinism 191
Diagnostic and Statistical Manual of Mental Disorders (DSM 5; American Psychological Association) 53
Diamond, P. 22n14
Dick, D. 173
dieting behavior, self-control failure and 193–216
different self 7
dimensionality 80
disconfirmation 41
discounting: age and 156–7; cognitive capacity and 157–8; deep 154; delay 6–8, 14, 152–60, 194–5; exponential 161; hyperbolic 7, 162–5, 195–7, 212, 253–4; success and 158; temporal 14, 186–7
discount rate 6–7, 152–4, 196
disease theory 48, 171–3

disengagement 227–8
dissociation 140–1
distraction 27, 158–9, 208–9
disulfiram 191n1, 242
divided self 7, 196–7, 253–4
Doctorow, E. 21n6
dopamine 12, 46, 59–61, 68, 150n10, 171–3; boredom and 213; cost-benefit analysis and 209; deficiency 114; depletion of 63; reward prediction error and 65–6; sensitization and 63
dopaminergic neurons 59
doubt 132
dread 121. *see also* anxiety
drugs: availability of 29; dangers of 1–2; delivery of 60; injecting of 47
DSM 5 (*Diagnostic and Statistical Manual of Mental Disorders*; American Psychological Association) 53
dual decision model 7–9, 12, 15, 182, 190, 197–9
dual mind 93–102, 115–6, 117n1, 123–5
dysphoria 59–60, 114

economics, defined 3
Ecstasy (MDMA) 192n6
"Education for Life" (course) 16
ego 94, 139, 141
ego depletion 125, 150n7, 201–4
Eisenberger, N. 209
Ekman, P. 75–6, 183
Elaborated Intrusion theory of desire (EI) 184, 200
Eldar, S. 30–1
Elster, J. 168n8
emotion: adaptation and 85–8; affect and 80–2; appraisal and 84–5; choice and 3; cognition and 77–9, 82–3, 183; decision making and 1–3, 93–119; definition and functions of 71–92; desire and 107–8; expression of 76–7; fighting emotion with 253; intellect and 107; lack of, procrastination and 167; pacing reward and 89; regulation of 160, 173, 249–51
emotional distress, ABC model of 145–6
enactment 140–1
endorphins 61
endowment effect 35–6
enriched environments 178
environmental cues 50–2, 55, 97, 182, 206–7
Epstein, S. 95

Ericsson, K. 221
erroneous sense-making 103–4
estrangement 140–1
ethanol 126
eudemonia 223
euphoria 48–9
evolutionary perspectives 135–6, 156
executive brain 158
existentialism 259n10
expectation effects 34–5
expected utility model 229
experienced utility 32–3
explanatory style 250
exponential discounting 161, *162*
exposure therapy 124, 144
Expression of the Emotions in Man and Animals, The (Darwin) 91n6
external strategies 240
extinction 55
extroverts 213

facial expressions 76–9
failure 148; decision making 9–13, 23, 170, 182–9; fear of 167; of self-control 193–216
false logic 113–14
fear 121–3, 130
fear of missing out (FOMO) anxiety 87–8
feasibility 259n7
Fedorikhin, A. 202
"Feeling and Thinking: Preferences Need No Inference" (Zajonc) 108
fight or flight 121, 179
Finkelstein, A. 224
Fishbach, A. 233
fluid intelligence 27, 44n7
focusing illusion 86–7
FOMO (fear of missing out) anxiety 87–8
food addiction theory 115–16
forethought 15
Foster, J. 235
Francesconi, M. 117–18n3
Frankl, V. 51, 90
Frank, R. 88
Fredrickson, B. 83; *Positivity* 91n10
free will 11, 101–2, 118n5, 218
Freudian slips 246
Freud, S. 94, 112, 139–40
Friedman, R. 235
frontal cortex 65–6, 124–5
frontal lobe disease 158–9

FSA (United Kingdom Food Standards Agency) 241
fundamental attribution error 37

GAD (generalized anxiety disorder) 126–8
Gage, P. 159
Galvin, P. 45n20
gambler's fallacy 38
gambling 70n17
Gardner, H. 43
gateway effect 63
Gazzaniga, M. 103
generalized anxiety disorder (GAD) 126–8
genes 11, 107–8, 171–3
Gladwell, M. 44n2; *Blink: The Power of Thinking without Thinking* 24; *Outliers* 221
glucocorticoids 179, 185
glucose 203
goal-directed system 10–11, 256
goal intentions 256–8
goal looms larger effect 226
goals: defined 226; desire and 107; habit and 56; long-term 3, 14, 217–38, 239; mental representation of 245–6; short-term 239
Goldberg, E. 67
Goldstein, A. 65
Gollwitzer, P. 256–7
Google 241
Gordon, J. 207
graduation 80
Green, L. 156
Gruber, J. 190

habit 2, 5, 198, 244; addiction as 55; decision making and 10–11; defined 56, 256; deliberative system and 26; formation of 48, 56–7; goal-directed 256; negative and positive 48; rational self-medication and 174–6; stress and 11
habituation 63, 85–9
Haidt, J. 103–4, 117n1, 148; *The Happiness Hypothesis* 214n2
halo effect 25
H.A.L.T. (Hungry, Angry, Lonely, or Tired) 184
happiness 45n14, 222–3
Happiness Hypothesis, The (Haidt) 214n2
Harreveld, F. van 42–3
Hart, C. 178
Hasler, G. 114
health halos 44n5

Hebb, D. 104
hedonic adaptation 86–7
hereditary anxiety 132–3
Herman, C. 215n15
heroin 49
Herrnstein, R. 176
Hershfield, H. 242
Higgins, E. 234–5
high-glycemic foods 207
hippocampus 125, 185
Hoch, S. 199
Hofmann, W. 245
homeostasis 62, 69n11, 180
hopelessness theory 114
hot-cold decision triangle framework *8*
hot reasoning 14–15, 94, 158, 210–11
hubris 73, 90n4
Hume, D. 145
Hungry, Angry, Lonely, or Tired (H.A.L.T.) 184
hyperbolic discounting 7, 162–5, 195–7, 212, 253–4
hypocrisy 39

id 94, 139–40
ideal and ought self 235
if-then plan 256–8
IGT (Iowa Gambling Task) 110–11
illusion of causality 37–8
immediate rewards 6–7, 14, 152, 198–9, 210
impartial spectator 73
impatience 155, 187
implementation intentions 256–8
implicit learning 26
impulse *200*; control 166; reactions 202; strength of 199
impulsive: actions 197–8; behavior 6, 14, 166; decision making 7–9, 12; desires 2; processes 8, 21n11; system 13, 197–201
impulsivity 154, 157, 170, 195, 212; addiction and 186–7; defined 168n5; genetic factors for 172; serotonin depletion and 203
incidence 44n8
inertia 244
inhibitory control 125–6
In Pursuit of Elegance (May) 89
insight 188
instinctive behavior 24
instrumental desires 106–7
insular cortex 13, 68. 131, 188
insulin 203

intelligence 27, 44n7
Intelligence and How to Get It (Nisbett) 158
intention-action gap 196–7
intentional objects, emotion and 77
intentions 256–8
interest 89
internality 261
interoception 13
interpretation 143, 252
interpreter system 103
intertemporal decisions 6, 152
intoxication 202
introspection 79
introverts 213
intuitive (automatic) learning 23–8, 37–8, *95*, 96, 197, 243–4
Iowa Gambling Task (IGT) 110–11
ironic effects of mental control 142
irrational behavior 16
irrational preferences 162
isolation 176–7

James, W.: *The Principles of Psychology* 17
jealousy 130–1
Johnson, M. 187
Jostmann, N. 227–8
joy 148
judgements 30
jumping to conclusions 142; anxiety and 120
Jung-Beeman, M. 83

Kagan, J. 104, 132
Kahneman, D. 4
Kandel, E. 5
Kierkegaard, S. 128
Klaes, M. 22n14
Koole, S. 227–8
Koo, M. 233

lapse-activated consumption 207–8
larger/later (LL) reward *155*, 161
Latham, G. 227
law of diminishing returns 32
Layard, R. 16
learned behavior 133
learned helplessness 114, 133
learned industriousness 230
learned self-perception 42
learning: associative 53, 197; intuitive (automatic) and analytic 23–8, 37–8, *95*, 96, 197, 243–4; mistakes and 66; traps 26–43

Index **295**

LeDoux, J. 82, 100, 123
left- and right-brain model 118n7
left-handedness 70n19
left hemisphere 67, 70n19
Lenton, A. 117–18n3
Lewis, H. 90n3
Liberman, N. 233
libertarian paternalism 263
Libet, B. 102
libido 94
licensing effect 203, 255
liking *vs.* wanting 12, 63–5
limbic brain 58
Lincoln, A. 45n22
LL (larger/later) reward *155*, 161
Lobel, J. 72
local approach to decision making 163–5, 255
Locke, E. 227
Loewenstein, G. 72, 199
loneliness 176–7
long-term goals 3, 14, 217–39
long-term memory 27–8
loss aversion 36, 235, 242–3
low and high road 123

Madoff, B. 45n24
magical thinking 38
MAOA 191n2
marginal utility 32, 48
marijuana 47
Marlatt, G. 186, 207
Marriage of Heaven and Hell, The (Blake) 214n5
Maslow, A. 43
Mate, G. 177
maximizing 33–4
May, M.: *In Pursuit of Elegance* 89
May, R. 101, 122
McGaugh, J. 27
McGaugh 28
MDMA (Ecstacy) 192n6
melancholia 112
memory: craving as 50; emotion and 83–4; short- and long-term 27–8; working 26–8, 204–6; working memory capacity (WMC) 204–6
mental accounting 249
mental contrasting strategy 230
mental illness 15
mental representation 245–6
Mercier, H. 198
metacognitive strategies 51, 73

Metcalfe, J. 206, 245
Milner, P. 60
mimicry 81, 91n9
mind: design of 4; as dual 93–102, 115–16, 117n1, 123–5
mindfulness 13, 73, 146–7, 188
mirror neurons 81, 91n9
misattributions 82
Mischel, W. 158, 206, 245
miscommunication 77
misery is not miserly phenomenon 215n16
mistakes 66
miswanting 33
mixed emotions 79–80
Mlodinow, L. 38
modularity 21n4
Molly (MDMA; Ecstacy) 192n6
Monitoring the Future study 185
mood 24–5, 80–3, 203, 212–13
mood-congruent bias 114
mood-congruent recall 84
morphine 47
motivation 104–8; defined 32, 229; dopamine and 59; ego depletion and 201; erroneous sense-making and 103; psychoanalysis and 139; role of emotion in 93; self-control and 229–30; unconscious 5–6; utility and 32
Mullainathan, S. 30–1, 190
Mulligan, C. 157
multitasking 69n13
Murphy, K. 176
muscle memory 221
myopia 31–2, 161–2, 202, 224
mystery moods 81

narrative bias 38–9
National Institute of Mental Health 127
National Sleep Foundation 214n9
negative affect 160, 173, 182, 208–9, 252
negative habits 48
negative reinforcement 66
negative visualization 88
neocortex 58, 69n10, 90, 93–4
nerd effect 43
neural basis of addiction 170
neural plasticity 26, 58–9, 215n21
neural sensitization 63
neuroadaptations 12
neurons 58
neuropeptide Y (NPY) 132–3
neuroticism 167

neurotransmitters 46–7, 59–61, 171–2, 191n2, 203; depression and 112–13; sensitization and 63
neutral stimulus 53–4
next-in-line effect 214n11
nicotine withdrawal symptoms 49–50
Nietzsche, F. 148
Nisbett, R.: *Intelligence and How to Get It* 158
Nordgren, L. 42–3
normative statements 154
not-me state 140
novelty 89
novelty-seeking behavior 67
NPY (neuropeptide Y) 132–3
nudging 5, 241–4, 263–4

obesity 1–2, 115–16, 194
objects, emotion and 77
obsessive-compulsive disorder (OCD) 10, 131–2, 234
O'Donoghue, T. 225
Odyssey, The 14–15
Offer, A. 224
Olds, J. 60
omegha-3 203
onset of emotions 75
"On the Primacy of Affect" (Zajonc) 108
operant conditioning 54–5, 240
opiate withdrawal symptoms 49
opium 47
opponent process 62–3
opportunity cost 31, 155, 168n1
optimism 42–3
optimistic explanatory style 250
options, eliminating 241
orbital prefrontal cortex 159
orbitofrontal syndrome 158–9
Orlistat 259n1
ought self 235
outcome valence 124
Outliers (Gladwell) 221
overconfidence 42–3, 232, 238n10
overeating 2, 6
ownership 35–6
Oxford American Dictionary and Language Guide 74
Oxford English Dictionary online 87

pacing reward 89
pain 33–6, 49, 59–61, 78
palatability 115–16
panic 121

panic disorder (PD) 130–1
Panksepp, J. 5–6, 69–70n15
parasympathetic nervous system 149n1
parenting 130, 135, 160
Parkinson's disease 150n10
passion 72–4, 94
paternalism 263
pathology, defined 21n8
pattern-seeking bias 37–8
Pavlov, I. 53, 69n6
Pavlovian system 10, 53–4
payoff matrix 254–5
PD (panic disorder) 130–1
Pennebaker, J. 39
perceptual judgment 24
Percy, W. 127
perfectionism 167
persistence 67
personal rules 253–5
pessimistic explanatory style 133, 250
Peter, J. 157
Peterson, C. 220
PFC. *see* prefrontal cortex (PFC)
Phelps, E. 124
phobias 123, 126, 135
physiological expression 76–7
Pignatti, R. 118n15
placebos 99
Planner-Doer gap 196–7
planning fallacy 238n10
Plato 73
Platt, J. 154
pleasure 12, 16, 48–9, 78; centers 60; drug use and 47–8; gap 63–5; immediate 6; principle 139; pursuit of 33–4, 59–61; wanting *vs.* liking and 63–5
pledges, public 245
Pligt, J. van der 42–3
Plutchik, R. 79–80
policy interventions 1, 6
Polivy, J. 215n15
positive affect 204
positive habits 48
positive time preference 153
Positivity (Fredrickson) 91n10
post hoc fallacy 103
posttraumatic growth 147–8, 151n18
posttraumatic stress disorders (PTSD) 182
poverty 159–60, 201
practice 220–2
predicted utility 32–3
prediction error 65–6

preference 59, 105; choice and 105, 262; conflicting 196–7; emotion and 77–8, 81–2, 210; irrational 162; revealed 262–3; reversal 7, 50, 196–7
prefrontal cortex (PFC) 139; affective system and 19–20; alcohol and 202; cognitive capacity and 158–9, 182; damage to 214n10; neural plasticity of 215n21; self-control and 199; stress and 51, 125; willpower and 101; working memory and 204–5
prefrontal lobe 100
present bias 7, 14, 163, 166, 193–5, 239
pressure 142–3
prevalence 44n8
prevention focus 234–6
pride 73
primary emotions 79–80
primary withdrawal 50
priming effect 21n5, 51, 100, 228
primrose path model 176
Principles of Psychology, The (James) 17
prisoner's dilemma 254–5
probabilities 124
problem of silent evidence 43
problem-solving skills 145
procrastination 2, 165–7, 244
projection 140, 210–11, 259n8
projective identification 137
promotion focus 234–6
proximity 97–8, 206, 215n23, 223–4
psychoactive substances 46–8
psychoanalysis 94, 139–41, 259n9
psychology, defined 3
psychotherapy 90, 147
psychotropic plant substances 46–7
PTSD (posttraumatic stress disorders) 182
public health 1–3, 15, 120–1, 194
public pledges 245
punishment 47–8, 54–5, 166
Putler, D. 36

qualitative feel of emotions 78

Rabin, M. 225
Rachlin, H. 255
Ramachandran, V. 103
random processes 37–8
Rangel, A. 94
rational addiction model 174–6
rational choice 3–6, 11, 78, 164–5, 194–5
rationality 34, 45n15, 161–2
rationalization 103

rational self-medication 174–6
rational thinking 9, 203
Rayo, L. 88
reappraisal 250–1
reason 72–3, 94, 107–8, 124
reasoning 198
rebound effect 246
recovery 52
refined carbohydrates 203, 207
reflective system 21n11, 93–102, 123–5, 198–9
refractory period, defined 183
regulatory focus 234–7
rehearsing 27–8
reinforcement 54–5, 66, 240
rejection sensitivity (RS) 137
relapse 51–2, 170–1; abstinence violation effect (AVE) and 251–2; craving and 183–4; delay discounting and 6; depression and 113, 116; diet and 193; recovery and 52; sensitization and 63; special occasions and 164; triggers of 206
remembered utility 32–3
reptilian brain 58
resilience 151n18, 222, 230
response inhibition 182
revealed preference 32, 262–3
reward 12, 104–8; addiction and 48–9, 105, 177–8; alternative 243; anhedonia and 209; anticipation of 61; defined 105–7; delayed 6–8, 14, 152–60; drug addiction and 105; habit and 57; immediate 6–7, 14, 152, 198–9, 210; impulsivity and 157; lack of alternative 177–8; maximizing 195; mental representation of 245–6; operant conditioning and 54; pacing of, and emotion 89; prediction error 65–6; punishment and 47–8, 166; reinforcement and 54–5; smaller/sooner (SS) and larger/later (LL) *155*, 161; strategies 241–2; system of 59–62, 172; unpredictable 65–6; valuation process 11
reward, delay, and impulsiveness model 195
right-handedness 70n19
right hemisphere 67, 70n19
risk 42–3, *124*
Robins, L. 69n5
Rolls, T. 105–6
Roosevelt, F. 149–50n3
Rose, R. 173
routine 57
routinization 67

RS (rejection sensitivity) 137
rumination 115, 215n19, 227
Russell, B. 149

S1 (System 1 mechanisms) 7–9, 23–9, 37–40, 43–4, 123–6, 197–9, 206–7
S2 (System 2 mechanisms) 7–9, 23–9, 37, 40, 94–102, 123–6, 197–9
SAD (social anxiety disorder) 128–9, 135–6
salience 224
Sartre, J. 118n5
satisficing 33–4
scarcity effect 230
scarcity mindset 30–2
Schelling, T. 196
schemas 113, 133–4, 146
Schooler, J. 191
Schore, A. 72
Schultz, W. 65
Schwartz, B. 34, 86
SCRs (skin conductance responses) 110
secondary withdrawal 50
selective processing 27
selective serotonin reuptake inhibitors (SSRIs) 147
self 7, 196–8, 253–4
self-awareness 14–15; alcohol and 202; defined 188; drug abuse and 13; self-control and 224–5
self-confidence 41, 167, 231
self-control 2–3, 12, *200*; automatic 256–8; behavior change and 239–60; construal level theory (CLT) of 211–12; decisions 198–200; defined 194, 217–19; development of 220; dilemma 219; ego depletion and 201, 204; failure 193–216; goals and 217–38; happiness and 222–3; modern society and 223–4; motivation and 229–30; outcomes of good 220; practice and 220–2; problems 13–15, 162, 165–7, 261–4; purpose of 217; regulatory focus and 234–7; resilience and 222; self-awareness and 224–5; self-efficacy and 229–32; self-monitoring and 233–4; sleep and 214n9; strategies 219–22, 239–60; stress and 202; willpower and 234, 240; working memory capacity (WMC) and 205
self-deception 41, 198, 248–9
self-defeating behavior 2, 5, 21n1–2, 134
self-destructive behavior 1, 15–16, 21n1

self-diagnostic 232
self-discrepancy theory 235
self-distanced strategies 252
self-efficacy 143–4, 167, 229–32
self-fulfilling prophecy 41–2
self-immersed strategies 252
self-interest 1, 33–4, 262
Selfish Gene, The (Dawkins) 107–8
self-licensing 203
self-medication 1, 115, 126–7, 173–6
self-monitoring 233–4, 238n13, 262–3
self-reflective consciousness 94
self-regulation 101–2, 176–7, 218, 237n2
self-regulatory collapse 207–8
self-schema 113
self-serving biases 42
self-talking 214n1
Seligman, M. 220
Selye, H. 149
sensation seeking 186
sense-making: erroneous 103–4
sensitization 63, 69n13
separation anxiety 130
serotonin 46, 171, 203
serotonin hypothesis 112–13
SES (socioeconomic-status) 159–60
Shiv, B. 202
short-term consumption decisions 3, 14, 195, 210
short-term gains 6–7
short-term goals 239
short-term memory 27–8
shyness 128
Siegel, R. 52
silent evidence, problem of 43
Simon, H. 34
sin 73
Sisyphus 228
situational cues 198–9, 258
skin conductance responses (SCRs) 110
Skinner, B. 54, 240
Skog, O. 51
sleep, self-control and 214n9
Slors, M. 15
smaller/sooner (SS) reward *155*, 161
Smith, A.: *Theory of Moral Sentiments* 73
SOBER breathing space 51
social anxiety disorder (SAD) 128–9, 135–6
social control hypothesis 177
social emotions 79–80
social environments 11, 29, 197
social influences 178–9

social norms 84–5, 91n8, 244
social rejection 209
social traps 154
socioeconomic class 179–81
socioeconomic-status (SES) 159–60
soft paternalism 263
Solomon, A. 112–16
Solomon, R. 72, 90
somatic marker theory 109–11
Southwick, S. 222
Spencer, J. 118n11
Sperber, D. 198
Spinoza 72, 260n12
SSRIs (selective serotonin reuptake inhibitors) 147
SS (smaller/sooner) reward *155*, 161
St. Augustine 128
stimulants 213
stimulus 53–4, 84, *97*
stimulus-response principles 94
stoicism 88
strategic ignorance 248–9
strength model of willpower 204
stress 119, 202; craving and 51–2; generation hypothesis 113–14; habit formation and 11; responses to 215n18; self-control and 202; vulnerability to addiction and 179–82; working memory and 27
stress-diathesis model 133
stressors 180–2
striatum 93
strong feelings 209–10
structural theory 139
subcortical structures 93–4
subjective emotional experiences 78
success, discounting and 158
sudden onset of emotions 75
sunk cost fallacy 238n12
Sunstein, C. 243
superego 94, 139
superstition 38
surprise 66–7
sympathetic nervous system 149n1
synapses 58–9, 221
System 1 mechanisms (S1) 7–9, 23–9, 37–40, 43–4, 123–6, 197–9, 206–7
System 2 mechanisms (S2) 7–9, 23–9, 37, 40, 94–102, 123–6, 197–9
systematic errors 6

Takuya, H. 51
Taleb, N. 151n20; *Antifragile* 148

Talent Code, The (Coyle) 221
task-diagnostic 232
telescopic faculty 154–5
temporal discounting 14, 186–7
temporal distance 155–6, 211–12, 247–8
temporal proximity 97–8
temporary preference, emotion and 77–8
temptation 14, 57, *200*, 201, 206, 258
terminal desires 106–7
Thaler, R. 243
Theory of Moral Sentiments (Smith) 73
thin-slicing 24
Thorndike, E. 54
thought suppression 246–7, 259n5
threat perceptions 10
Tice, D. 201
Tillich, P. 127
time: perception 212–13; preference 152–61, 209–10; pressure 98, 117–18n3
Tirole, J. 249
tobacco 47
tolerance 49, 63, 144–5
trade-off thinking 31, 201
transaction perspective 36
transient emotions 75–6
traumas 140, 173, 185
treatment failure 6
triune brain *58*
tryptophan 203
tunnel vision 210, 215n20

UIS (University of Illinois Springfield) 16
uncertainty 142, 155–6, 234
unconditioned stimulus (US) 53–4
unconscious decision making 7–9
unconscious desire 139–40
unconscious goal pursuit 228
unconscious motivations 5–6
United Kingdom Food Standards Agency (FSA) 241
University of Illinois Springfield (UIS) 16
University of Michigan 185
Urbszat, D. 208
urges 199
US (unconditioned stimulus) 53–4
utility 3–4, 32–3, 45n14, 82, 104–5

Vaillant, G. 55
valence 78, 124
valuation processes 8–10, 13–14, 194
value, delay and 154–5
value expectation 35
Vartianen, H. 22n14

ventromedial prefrontal cortex (VMPF) 159
violation of expectations 89
visceral brain 58
visceral reactions 9
visceral states 183
vividness effect 98, 124
VMPF (ventromedial prefrontal cortex) 159
Vohs, K. 191
Volkow, N. 171–3
voluntary actions 198
Vuchinich, R. 22n14
vulnerability 14, 21n12; to addiction 136–9; to anxiety 134; to depression 111–16; stress, addiction and 179–82

Walt Disney Company 244
wanting *vs.* liking 12, 63–5
Webster New Collegiate Dictionary 74
Wegner, D. 246
Weight Watchers weigh-ins 168n10
well-being 64, 67, 223–4
Wells, A. 146–7
what-the-hell-effect 215n15, 254–5
WHO (World Health Organization) 111, 127

Wilkinson, N. 22n14
willpower 52, 57, 101–2, 200–4, 231; behavioral economic policy and 263–4; defined 200–1; glucose and 203; self-control and 234, 240; strength model of 204
Wilson, M. 215n20
Wilson, T. 108–9
Wirtz, J. 33
Wise, R. 50
wishful thinking 41
withdrawal 49–50, 62–3
withdrawal-related negative affect 182
women, anxiety disorders and 127
working memory 26–8, 204–6
working memory capacity (WMC) 204–6
World Health Organization (WHO) 111, 127
worry 125–8, 141–2
Wright, R. 103

Yoon, J. 154

Zajonc, R. 82, 124; "Feeling and Thinking: Preferences Need No Inference" 108; "On the Primacy of Affect" 108